THE ITALIAN LEGACY
IN PHILADELPHIA

EDITED BY

ANDREA CANEPARI AND JUDITH GOODE

THE

ITALIAN LEGACY IN

PHILADELPHIA

HISTORY, CULTURE, PEOPLE, AND IDEAS

TEMPLE UNIVERSITY PRESS

Philadelphia • *Rome* • *Tokyo*

TEMPLE UNIVERSITY PRESS
Philadelphia, Pennsylvania 19122
tupress.temple.edu

Library of Congress Cataloging-in-Publication Data

Names: Canepari, Andrea, editor. | Goode, Judith, 1939– editor.
Title: The Italian legacy in Philadelphia : history, culture, people, and
  ideas / edited by Andrea Canepari and Judith Goode.
Description: Philadelphia : Temple University Press, 2021. | Includes
  bibliographical references and index. | Summary: "The Italian Legacy in
  Philadelphia examines the impact and influence of Italian arts, culture,
  people, and ideas on the city of Philadelphia from the founding to the
  present"— Provided by publisher.
Identifiers: LCCN 2020053113 | ISBN 9781439916476 (cloth)
Subjects: LCSH: Italian Americans—Pennsylvania—Philadelphia—History |
  Philadelphia (Pa.)—Civilization—Italian influences. |
  Italy—Relations—Pennsylvania—Philadelphia. | Philadelphia
  (Pa.)—Relations—Italy.
Classification: LCC F158.9.I8 I83 2021 | DDC 974.8/110451—dc23
LC record available at https://lccn.loc.gov/2020053113

∞ The paper used in this publication meets the requirements of the American National Standard for
Information Sciences—Permanence of Paper for Printed Library Materials, ANSI Z39.48-1992

Printed in the United States of America

9 8 7 6 5 4 3 2 1

To our families for their support

and to the many Philadelphians whose different engagements

with the Italian legacy in the city have provided us with

new insights and perspectives.

ANDREA CANEPARI

JUDITH GOODE

CONTENTS

FOREWORD • Joe Scarnati • *xi*

FOREWORD • Joseph M. Torsella • *xiii*

PREFACE • Andrea Canepari and Judith Goode • *xv*

ACKNOWLEDGMENTS • *xvii*

PROLOGUE   Linking Philadelphia to Italy: A History of the Italian
              Consulate General in Philadelphia • Andrea Canepari • *1*

INTRODUCTION • Judith Goode • *19*

I   INDEPENDENCE AND EARLY REPUBLIC

INTRODUCTION • Judith Goode • *27*

1   Palladians in Philadelphia • Jeffrey A. Cohen • *31*

2   Cesare Beccaria's Influence on the Philadelphia Constitutional
     Convention • William B. Ewald • *41*

3   Thomas Jefferson and Joseph Mussi: Enjoying Milanese Life
     in Philadelphia • Maurizio Valsania • *44*

     SIDEBAR 1 • Garibaldi's "American Brother" and Piedmontese Consul:
     The Philadelphia Story of Angelo Garibaldi • Salvatore Mangione • *50*

4   Rome, Italian Émigrés, and Jesuit Education in Nineteenth-Century
     Philadelphia • Carmen R. Croce • *52*

5   Artists of the Capitol in Philadelphia • Barbara A. Wolanin • *62*

II THE EXPANDING INDUSTRIAL METROPOLIS

New Wealth, New Elites, and New Institutions of Knowledge, Arts, and Culture

INTRODUCTION • Judith Goode • 75

6 Henry Charles Lea's Italy: A Philadelphia Businessman and Scholar's "Grand Tour from Home" • Cam Grey • 80

7 Philadelphia Society and the Grand Tour • Lisa Colletta • 87

8 The Union League of Philadelphia: The Italian Legacy • Barbara J. Mitnick • 99

9 *David* at the Pennsylvania Academy of the Fine Arts: Italian Influences on Curriculum and Art Making • Albert Gury • 110

10 "Pompeii Comes to Philadelphia": The Wanamaker Bronzes in the University of Pennsylvania Museum • Ann Blair Brownlee • 116

11 "A Dazzling Array": Italian Art and the Philadelphia Museum of Art • Jennifer A. Thompson • 122

12 The Italian Legacy in the Gardens of Early Twentieth-Century Philadelphia • Raffaella Fabiani Giannetto • 135

13 The Neapolitan *Presepio* at the Glencairn Museum • Joseph F. Chorpenning • 144

14 The Italian Legacy in Philadelphia: Opera and Instrumental Music • Stephen A. Willier • 149

15 The Curtis Institute of Music and Italy • David Serkin Ludwig • 163

16 Italy on Display: Representing Italy in the 1876 Centennial and the 1926 Sesquicentennial • Steven Conn • 167

III MADE IN AMERICA

Immigration, Community Formation, and Varieties of Creative Italian American Experience

INTRODUCTION • Judith Goode • 179

17 Marking Place: Brief Notes on Building Patterns in Italian American South Philadelphia • Jeffrey A. Cohen • 184

18 How South Philadelphia Became Known as Italian • Judith Goode • 189

SIDEBAR 2 • From Southern Italy to Southern New Jersey: Italian Success in the Garden State • Cav. Dr. Gilda Battaglia Rorro Baldassari • 207

19 Italian American Leaders in Business and Politics • Scott Gabriel Knowles, Maegan Madrigal, and Isabella Sangaline • 208

20 Drawn from the Boot: The Italian Artists of Philadelphia • William R. Valerio • 221

SIDEBAR 3 • The D'Ascenzo Studio • Jean M. Farnsworth • 232

21 A Family of Italian American Artists • Jody Pinto • 234

22 Jazz in the Neighborhood and the World • Chris William Sanchirico • 239

    SIDEBAR 4 • South Philly Musicians Remix Mural • Jeremy Goode • 244

    SIDEBAR 5 • Two Iconic Sports Figures • Jeremy Goode • 247

23 Romaldo Giurgola, Architect: "The Reluctant Master" • Alan Greenberger • 249

    CHRISTOPER COLUMBUS MONUMENT • 257

24 An "Extremely Emotional Love Affair": Robert Venturi, Rome, and Italy
    • Luca Molinari • 258

IV CONTEMPORARY PHILADELPHIA

Experiencing the Italian Legacy in the Branded Global City

INTRODUCTION • Judith Goode • 267

25 Italy, Philadelphia, and the University of Pennsylvania
    • Chris William Sanchirico • 271

    SIDEBAR 6 • Vittorini's *Threads of Life* Lives On • Pietro Frassica • 286

26 Dr. Gonnella's Journey from the Mountains of Basilicata
    to the Medical Wards of Philadelphia • Salvatore Mangione • 288

27 Temple University and Its Italian Connection • Judith Goode • 296

    SIDEBAR 7 • NIAF and Its Links to Philadelphia • Joseph V. Del Raso • 306

28 The Simeone Foundation Automotive Museum • Fred Simeone • 308

29 Italian Gastronomy and Its Many Roles in a Cosmopolitan City
    • Judith Goode • 315

30 Recalling Italy in Bricks and Mortar • Inga Saffron • 327

31 From Rocky to Botticelli, Italian Philadelphia: Concerts, Shows, Exhibits,
    and Conferences in a City in Pennsylvania Where the "American Dream"
    Speaks Our Language • Paolo Valentino • 349

    SIDEBAR 8 • Rocky Balboa: Icon of the City • Judith Goode • 354

AFTERWORD Ciao Philadelphia: Creation of an Italian Cultural Initiative
               and Volume • Andrea Canepari • 357

List of Contributors • 387

Index • 393

Joseph B. Scarnati III, President Pro Tempore of the Pennsylvania Senate, during an event of the cultural month Ciao Philadelphia at the Union League, October 2016.

(Photo: Richard Barnes)

FOREWORD

I AM HONORED AND PRIVILEGED TO KNOW Andrea Canepari, former consul general of Italy in Philadelphia, current Italian ambassador to the Dominican Republic, and one of the editors of this book jointly with Temple Professor Emerita Judith Goode. Since meeting Andrea several years ago, I have been inspired by his dedication to expanding the relationship between the Commonwealth of Pennsylvania and Italy.

From art and culture to economics and politics, this book provides a thoughtful and expansive overview of the long-established ties between Italy and one of the most important cities in the United States—Philadelphia. Philadelphia is the largest city in Pennsylvania and has long been referred to as the birthplace of America. Philadelphia is where colonists came together centuries ago to move forward and create a new nation of opportunity and promise. Protecting Italian American ties was important then and is just as important today.

I am very proud of my Italian heritage and have long believed it is vital that we work together to preserve and share Italian American culture, history, and traditions. In 1901, my great-grandparents immigrated to America from the Calabria region of Italy. My family later operated the Rocky Grill restaurant in Brockway, Pennsylvania, for many years.

When my great-grandparents came to America in the beginning of the twentieth century, they came in search of the American dream. They, like so many immigrants in our commonwealth, were ambitious and hardworking individuals. They sought a land full of possibilities, where their heritage was welcomed and people learned from one another.

We undoubtedly have an obligation to those who sacrificed so much for us, a compelling duty to work together to keep the American dream alive. In order to ensure that dream exists for future generations, we must work to strengthen our ties to our heritage and the countries from which our ancestry hailed.

In every city that I have visited in Italy, I have met benevolent, warm, and wonderful people who embrace culture and heritage. My hope is that Italians visiting Philadelphia will be embraced by those same sentiments. By sharing our stories and our journeys, we will protect and build on Italian American ties both now and in the future.

Joe Scarnati
Pennsylvania Senate President Pro Tempore

Joseph M. Torsella, State Treasurer for the Commonwealth of Pennsylvania, speaking at a Ciao Philadelphia event in June 2017. (Photo: Giò Martorana)

FOREWORD

I SPENT A FEW YEARS OF MY LIFE as a diplomat. Too little time (and probably too little talent) to become a good diplomat myself, but long enough to learn what makes a great one.

Great diplomats are born connectors. They see links, or even better, *potential* links, between people, interests, and places that are invisible to others, and they build bridges the rest of us then cross. It's a talent that is becoming even more important in a world that increasingly plays to our sense of differences rather than strengthening our sense of commonalities.

Andrea Canepari, current Italian ambassador to the Dominican Republic and the editor of this book along with Dr. Judith Goode, is one of those world-class diplomats and connectors. I saw it daily when he was Italy's consul general in Philadelphia, where his affection for his two homes was palpable and his enthusiasm for building new connections between them contagious.

So this delightful book, a labor of love, is really a continuation of his diplomacy by other means. It unearths and highlights centuries of connections—in the arts, commerce, science, the built environment, politics, and so on. Though some are well known, many are surprising, and collectively they are staggering in their breadth and impact.

As a Pennsylvanian, I benefit daily from this rich and deep relationship. As the treasurer of Pennsylvania, I see firsthand the enormous economic value it has created. And as the first Italian American treasurer in the history of our commonwealth, I take a special pride in seeing this legacy get the book it deserves.

I hope seeing the extraordinary harvest that the relationship between Italy and Philadelphia has yielded over the centuries will inspire all readers, as it has me, not just to appreciation but to action. To becoming, in other words, better "diplomats" ourselves—cultivating, nurturing, and expanding those connections that have so enriched our region and can enrich it so much more in the future.

Joseph M. Torsella
State Treasurer for the Commonwealth of Pennsylvania and U.S. Representative to the United Nations for Management and Reform (Ret.) 2011 to 2014

PREFACE

THIS VOLUME WAS CONCEIVED by Andrea Canepari, current Italian ambassador to the Dominican Republic and former Italian consul general in Philadelphia, after many years of living in Philadelphia while studying for an LL.M. at the University of Pennsylvania Law School and later representing Italy as the Italian consul general. His experiences revealed a rich and complex Italian legacy woven into the fabric of the city that was not always immediately evident. In order to promote public awareness of this legacy, Canepari developed a public diplomacy program called Ciao Philadelphia (see the Prologue and Afterword). During this program, he came to know a wide variety of Philadelphians with deep knowledge about Italy and Italian culture. The next step was to further document this Italian legacy by involving the major cultural institutions and universities of the region. The inspiration for the Philadelphia project was the book *The Italian Legacy in Washington, D.C.: Architecture, Design, Art and Culture*, coedited by Canepari and published in 2008. Canepari continued to build on that framework as editor in 2021 of *The Italian Legacy in the Dominican Republic: History, Architecture, Economics, and Society*, the third of an ongoing multivolume series that aims to enhance our understanding of the Italian presence in other societies.

Using his broad network of contacts in the city developed through Ciao Philadelphia, Canepari set out to tell the stories of the many Italians and Italian Americans who helped shape Philadelphia. He brought together experts from many relevant cultural institutions in the region to contribute what became forty essays in a way that would mirror the enthusiasm offered by the city of Philadelphia and its institutions to Ciao Philadelphia. Thanks to the wonderful group of essays assembled in the book, it is possible to explore almost all the dimensions of the centuries-long cultural dialogue between Italy and Philadelphia.

Judith Goode became a partner in the project when Canepari began to work with Temple University Press. As a professor of anthropology and urban studies, Goode had been teaching, researching, and writing about postwar Philadelphia's peoples, communities, and urban development policies for four decades; one of her largest projects was about South Philadelphia. Throughout her career, she focused on how history and political economy shaped both institutions and everyday life. She was the complementary counterpart for the project: with her expertise in urban anthropology and in research, she could create a unifying framework for essays coming from very different academic disciplines, find unexpected connections, add her own scholarly contributions from her knowledge of urban ethnography, and finally, blend these elements in a harmonic symphony.

Goode shaped the book around four turning points in Philadelphia's history. In each of them, connections between Philadelphia and Italy are examined through the movement of people, objects, and ideas between the two places and the incorporation of Italian elements into the built environment, social relations, and institutions of the city.

At the same time, the centrality of the visual permeates this volume. Canepari paid great attention to the iconographic structure of the book, teaming up with the authors in order to visually add to the written words another dimension able to appeal to every reader, not only academic ones. Extensively illustrated with archival photos, drawings, and sketches, the book is also enriched by new photographs by Philadelphian photographers and the Italian photographer Giò Martorana, who portrayed the city through Italian eyes.

While the volume begins and ends with two Italian contributors, Andrea Canepari and Paolo Valentino, the core of the volume comes from a wide range of voices representing different fields of interest and backgrounds but all sharing an appreciation for the variety and spirit of the Italian legacy.

Authors Andrea Canepari and Judith Goode

ACKNOWLEDGMENTS

THIS BOOK HAS BEEN MADE POSSIBLE by the efforts of Pennsylvania Senate president pro tempore Joe Scarnati.

This work was supported by a grant from the Commonwealth of Pennsylvania, Pennsylvania Department of Community and Economic Development, Marketing to Attract Tourists.

visitpa.com

INSTITUTIONS AND COLLECTIONS COLLABORATING ON THIS PUBLICATION

Bryn Mawr College; City of Philadelphia; Commonwealth of Pennsylvania; Consulate General of Italy in Philadelphia; Curtis Institute of Music; Drexel University; Independence National Historical Park; Pennsylvania Academy of the Fine Arts (PAFA); Philadelphia Museum of Art (PMA); Princeton University; Rothman Orthopaedic Institute; Rowan University; Saint Joseph's University; Temple University; The American University of Rome; The Union League of Philadelphia; Thomas Jefferson University; University of Pennsylvania; University of Pennsylvania Law School; University of Pennsylvania Museum of Archaeology and Anthropology (Penn Museum); Woodmere Art Museum.

ORGANIZATIONS AND INSTITUTIONS PARTICIPATING IN CIAO PHILADELPHIA, THE ITALIAN CULTURAL INITIATIVE

Associazione Regionale Abruzzese; American Jewish Committee; Anti-Defamation League; Center for Italian Studies at the University of Pennsylvania; Christopher Columbus Association–Delaware County; City of Philadelphia; Delaware Commission on Italian Heritage; Delaware County (DELCO); Drexel University; Duquesne University School of Law; EFASCE of Philadelphia; Filitalia International–History of Italian Immigration Museum; Hood College; Il Circolo Italiano of the Main Line; Independence National Historical Park–National Park Service; Independence Seaport Museum; International Opera Theater; Kimmel Center for the Performing Arts of Philadelphia; National Italian American Foundation (NIAF); National Museum of American Jewish History, a Smithsonian Institute Affiliate; New Jersey Italian and Italian American Heritage Commission (NJIHC); New Jersey Legislature; Opera Delaware; Opera Philadelphia; Order of Sons of Italy in America (OSIA); Passyunk—East Passyunk Avenue Business Improvement District; Pennsylvania Department of Community and Economic Development; Pennsylvania House of Representatives; Pennsylvania State Senate; Philadelphia Classical Guitar Society; Philadelphia Museum of Art; Professionisti Italiani a Philadelphia (Pi-Philly); Reading Public Museum; Rosemont College; Rowan University; Sbarro Health Research Organization (SHRO); Simeone Foundation–Automotive Museum; Sons and Daughters of Italy (OSIA); St. Joseph's University; Studio Incamminati—School for Contemporary Realist Art; Temple University; The American University of Rome; The Children's Hospital of Philadelphia; The Church of the Advocate in Philadelphia; The College of Physicians of Philadelphia; The Commonwealth of Pennsylvania; The Franklin Institute; The Mütter Museum at The Pennsylvania Academy of the Fine Arts (PAFA); The Philadelphia Convention & Visitors Bureau (PHLCVB); The South 9th Street Business Association; Thomas Jefferson University; The Philly Pops; The Union League of Philadelphia; The 1492 Society; UNICO Rehoboth Area Chapter; University of Pittsburgh–PittLaw; University of Pennsylvania; University of Pennsylvania Museum of Archaeology and Anthropology (Penn Museum); Villanova University; Widener University; Woodmere Art Museum.

WITH SPECIAL THANKS TO

American Airlines; CGI; Dilworth Paxson LLP; Duane Morris LLP; Fedegari Technologies; KPMG; Parke Bank; PECO Energy Company; Pennoni; PES; PREIT; Rothman Institute; Southeastern Pennsylvania Transportation Authority (SEPTA); The Philadelphia Convention & Visitors Bureau (PHLCVB); Today Media INC.

THE ITALIAN LEGACY
IN PHILADELPHIA

Linking Philadelphia to Italy

A History of the Italian Consulate General in Philadelphia

ANDREA CANEPARI

EVEN BEFORE THE UNIFICATION OF ITALY IN 1861,[1] various Italian states, including the Republic of Genoa, the Kingdom of Piedmont-Sardinia, the Papal State, the Kingdom of the Two Sicilies, and the Grand Duchy of Tuscany, entertained diplomatic or consular relations with the United States.[2] In Philadelphia, Count Joseph Ravara was accredited by U.S. president George Washington on October 25, 1791, as Consul General to the United States of the doge and governors of the Republic of Genoa.[3] Giuseppe Ravara was born around 1760 from a family of merchants. He had a high formal education and knew Latin, English, French, and Spanish. He was sent to Philadelphia as a representative of the house Pedemonte e Ardizzone and then worked for Willing, Morris and Company.[4] The annexation of the territory of the Republic of Genoa by the Kingdom of Sardinia (sanctioned in 1815 by the Congress of Vienna) made the Savoy monarchy pursue an active trade policy that was driven by the hope of succeeding in the role previously held by the Ligurian Navy. This context makes it easier to understand the reason behind the dense consular network in the United States, which includes one Consulate General in Philadelphia and eleven other Consulates of lower rank in the cities of the East Coast.[5] In 1840, the Piedmont's consular network was reformed, and the leading role was transferred from Philadelphia to the Consulate General in New York.

EVOLVING ROLES OF THE CONSULATE IN NINETEENTH AND TWENTIETH CENTURIES

Starting from Giuseppe Ravara, the first Italian Consul in the United States (1791), all the way to today, Italian diplomatic and consular representations have changed

Casa dello Stato di Pensilvania in Filadelfia

Bernardoni incise

Early nineteenth-century Italian print of the Pennsylvania State House, now called Independence Hall—drawn by Paolo Fumagalli. The Italian print reads, "Casa dello Stato di Pensilvania." It was published in a multivolume work by Giulio Ferrario entitled *Ancient and Modern Costumes*. Issued in 1821, the book describes the State House (or Independence Hall) as a "must see" site in North America. (From the collection of Andrea Canepari)

in order to answer to evolving needs coming from both motherland Italy and the Italian and Italian American communities residing in the diplomatic and consular jurisdictions. For example, to understand the tasks, priorities, characteristics, and "mental attitude" of the diplomatic agents of different Italian states in the United States during the nineteenth century, it is important to read the instructions sent by the Piedmont's Secretary of State for Foreign Affairs, Clemente Solaro della Margherita, to the Sardinian Chargé d'Affaires in Washington, Augusto Avogadro di Collobiano, on December 7, 1838.[6] In that letter, he argues,

Our relations with North America would seem at first glance to be purely commercial relations, given the distance that separates us, but the distances that are now attenuating through the multiplication of communication channels and the endless relationships that have been established between the old and the new world have created between them such a complication of interest that any political commotion that is being prepared or that arises in one of the two continents must necessarily have a great impact on the other.[7]

Later in the letter, Solaro continues, "Your concern will also extend to political investigations and the study of commercial interests."[8] Besides the relevance that these instructions have even today, it is important to note that, at the time, the Piedmontese diplomats were mainly observers of American politics, both domestic and foreign, in light of the most relevant European events. Whenever possible, the same diplomats would also become promoters of their own country and of its commercial possibilities.[9] This modus operandi continued until the turn of the century, when the migratory phenomenon from Italy substantially changed the activities, functions, and roles of the Italian diplomatic and consular representations in the United States.[10]

As recalled by Richard N. Juliani,[11] the Consulate General in Philadelphia, from its early origins, influenced the continued identity and cohesion of Italians and Italian Americans as a community. According to Juliani, after the success of the Risorgimento and the Unification of Italy in 1861, the Consuls were very influential in the early immigrant colony, particularly through their efforts to eliminate the exploitation of "slave children" as street musicians by padrone masters. In the era of mass immigration (1881–1921), the Consulate assumed the responsibility to provide a haven of hope for new arrivals in a strange land.[12] While controversy swirled over the so-called padrone system and opposition to immigration began mounting, Consul Nicola Squitti was appointed in 1884 and led the Italian community in observing the Unification of Italy at its annual celebration on September 20, thus enabling Italians to retain their identity, even while they were evolving toward a newer sense of becoming Italian Americans. In 1905, Consul Squitti also turned attention toward facilitating relief efforts for the earthquake victims of Calabria, an undertaking that would be repeated with similar tragedies in Sicily, as elsewhere—including San Francisco—in later years. When Consul Giacomo Fara Forni arrived in 1906, Juliani recalls that Philadelphia's Italians turned out in massive numbers to greet their new Consul, as they would on other occasions to celebrate Italy's emergence as a modern nation—as well as to renew their ties with their homeland.[13]

However, it should be noted that while Little Italy in South Philadelphia had by then emerged as a strong and enduring local entity,[14] the Consulate still had to exercise much effort against hostility directed toward Italians as well as internal disputes initiated by community leaders. With an increasing emphasis on naturalization as a precondition for employment, the role of the

Letter from Secretary of State Thomas Jefferson to Consul General Joseph Ravara, May 25, 1793. (Library of Congress, Manuscript Division, Thomas Jefferson to Joseph Ravara—05-25, 1793. Manuscript/Mixed Material. Retrieved from the Library of Congress, www.loc.gov/item /mtjbib007459/)

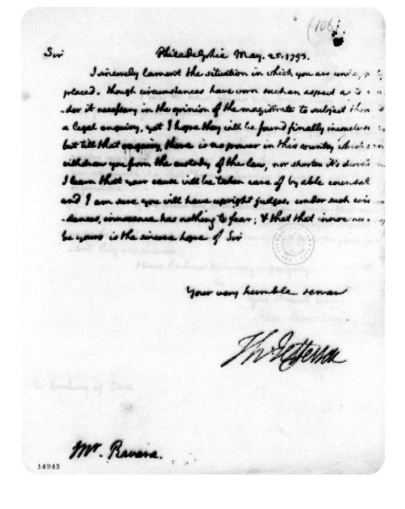

Consulate evolved further as it addressed the challenge of assimilation—how Italians could remain Italian while also becoming Americans. In 1909, Count Luigi Aldrovandi, serving as Royal Consul, joined Philadelphia's mayor and other officials in celebrating Columbus Day as an official holiday, also extolling the contributions of Italians to their adopted nation.[15] Count Luigi Provana del Sabbione arrived in 1909 as the next Royal Vice Consul on the eve of the First Italian Congress on Immigration, organized by the Ministry of Foreign Affairs in Rome, and he represented the importance of Philadelphia. By the time of the succession of Giulio Cesare Majoni as Consul two years later, however, according to Juliani, the Italian government had shifted its priorities in response to international politics, which would soon become manifested by Italy's war with Turkey in 1911 and the entry into the Great War in 1915. According to Luconi, war-related nationalism helped Italian Americans reestablish their ethnic identity between the turn of the twentieth century and the end of World War II. Although most Italian immigrants and their offspring lacked some sense of national consciousness upon arrival to the United States, they developed it following Italy's 1912 conquest of Libya.[16] Juliani mentions in his history of the Italian Consulate that Gaetano Emilio Poccardi would oversee the interests of Italy as Consul, especially during the difficult mobilization of reservists from among the immigrant population in Philadelphia. The enormous citywide celebration of the visit of General Armando Diaz, the leader of Italy's armed forces at the end of war, probably provided the apex of the period in November 1919. In 1921, the Consulate faced an estimated two hundred thousand in the "Italian" population.

Recognized as one of the major destinations for Italian immigrants to the United States, Philadelphia was chosen for official visits by Italian dignitaries interested in meeting the representatives of the Italian American community. On November 20, 1931, the Order Sons of Italy hosted a dinner in Philadelphia at the Bellevue-Stradford Hotel in honor of the Italian Foreign Minister, Dino Grandi. During his welcome speech to the Italian Minister, the Assistant Secretary of State, James Grafton Rogers, highlighted the successful history of assimilation of Italian Americans, describing them as "adopted children": "You are the Sons of Italy, but you are joining in a welcome which is of, for, and by America."[17]

With the strengthening of fascism, Juliani notes that a long era of amicable relations between the U.S. and Italian Consuls started fading away, which was quickly succeeded by increasing estrangement. This is also reflected in the restrictive immigration policy imposed by new legislation in the 1920s by which the United States effectively turned its back on its former ally in the recent war.[18] With the outbreak of World War II and old friends finding themselves as enemies, the U.S. government froze Italian assets, forbade Italians from leaving American shores, required them to come under State Department surveillance as enemy aliens, and closed their consulates. Although the state of belligerence between Italy and the United States lasted only two years, the Italian consulate in Philadelphia remained closed for six years before finally being reopened in 1947, with Corrado Orlandi

Picture of the old Italian Consulate General on 717 Spruce Street in an article about Italian reservists' rush to register for the army, as printed in the *Evening Public Ledger*, August 18, 1915. (*Evening Public Ledger.* [Philadelphia (Pa.)], 18 Aug. 1915. Chronicling America: Historic American Newspapers. Lib. of Congress. https://chroniclingamerica.loc.gov/lccn /sn83045211/1915-08-18/ed-1/seq-2/)

Dinner offered in Philadelphia by the Order Sons of Italy (OSIA) on November 20, 1931, at the Bellevue-Stratford Hotel in honor of the Italian Foreign Minister, Dino Grandi, and his wife, Antonietta Brizzi (*center*), in the presence of the Archbishop of Philadelphia, Cardinal Dennis Joseph Dougherty (*left*), and Mayor Harry A. Mackey (*right*). Also in the photo are Italian Ambassador to the United States Giacomo de Martino, John M. Silvestro (supreme venerable OSIA), Eugene V. Alessandroni (Judge of the Court of Common Pleas), Consul General Agostino Ferrante dei Marchesi di Ruffiano, and the Governor of Pennsylvania, Gifford Pinchot. (Catholic Historical Research Center of the Archdiocese of Philadelphia)

Office of the Consulate General of Italy in the Public Ledger Building across from Independence Hall, Philadelphia.
(Photo: Gary Horn)

Contucci being named as Consul in Philadelphia. With the return of peace, there was a surge of Italian immigration in the two decades before the next reform of American immigration policy.

While today the relationship of Italy and the United States has become stronger than ever before, and while the descendants of the thousands of Italian immigrants who chose to make their lives in the United States have become even more Americanized, the Consulate General of Italy in Philadelphia (located until 1991 at the 2128 Locust Street historical site and from 1993 to the present located at 150 South Independence Mall West) remains an important resource for preserving the link of all Italians with their ancestral homeland, as well as maintaining the solidarity of their communal life in an increasingly globalized world. According to Juliani, the Consulate, through its programs of services and cultural exchanges, further strengthens the ties of cooperation between Italy and the United States while also facilitating the retention and revitalization of transnational identity.

CONSULATE GENERAL PROGRAMS IN RECENT TIMES

This framework of strengthened cultural and economic cooperation provides the backdrop for the work done by the Consulate General of Philadelphia during the years when I had the privilege to serve as Consul General in Philadelphia (2013–2017).[19] The Consulate worked not only to provide efficient consular services throughout its jurisdiction but also to propose a new image of Italy by creating living bridges between Italy and the Philadelphia region through scientific, economic, and cultural initiatives of cooperation.

Proposing a new, more modern and accurate image of Italy was key to the work of the Consulate as authoritatively indicated by His Excellency the Ambassador of Italy to the United States Armando Varricchio in his visit to Philadelphia in October 2016. On that occasion, after a lecture at the prestigious Wharton Business School of the University of Pennsylvania on "Speaking on Italy, the EU and the Transatlantic Relationship," Ambassador Varricchio met the establishment of the Commonwealth of Pennsylvania and important businessmen in a reception at The Union League of Philadelphia. In his speech at the reception, Ambassador Varricchio highlighted the importance of creating "a direct connection to what is lively now in Italy, a country with a great past but looking ahead to the future."[20] His words were immediately echoed by the President of the Pennsylvania Senate, Joseph Scarnati, who linked the Italian cultural initiatives presented that evening with the future, while continuing being "proud of our past, our contribution as Italian Americans."[21]

In the years 2013–2017, several research institutions, icons of Philadelphia's cultural environment, deepened their relations with the Italian Consulate General, forging mutually beneficial partnerships. For instance, as highlighted by Julie Mostov in her contribution in the book on the history of Drexel in 2016,

> Drexel also established a close relationship with the Italian Consulate, highlighting the enormous assets of Philadelphia as an innovation and research hub, home to world-class cultural institutions, and site of Italian-American heritage. At the same time, this partnership highlights Italy as an important leader in innovation, design, entrepreneurship, and sustainability. Recent joint efforts include a program highlighting climate-proof cities and Italy's cutting-edge approaches to urban sustainability.[22]

In October 2014, to create awareness about the wealth of opportunities existing between the Philadelphia area and Italy, I envisioned the first edition of the Italian cultural month, Ciao Philadelphia (in 2021 in its eight edition; see Afterword), in partnership with area civic, academic, cultural, and business leaders.[23] Ciao Philadelphia developed as a series of more than seventy events at its peak, initially during the month of October (chosen as Italian cultural month since in October Italian Americans celebrate Columbus Day) and later throughout the year, meant to highlight the contributions of Italians and Italian Americans to Greater Philadelphia. In a region greatly influenced by Italian culture, Ciao Philadelphia aimed to highlight the area's cosmopolitan, sophisticated, and international character

The Consulate General of Italy in Philadelphia helps in raising civic engagement, as well. The Philadelphia All City Orchestra, on its seventieth anniversary, raised substantial funds when they sent their 120 members from Philadelphia High School to Music Festivals in Italy. As a sign of the partnership, CG Andrea Canepari was the narrator of Copland's *Lincoln Portrait* during the Italy Tour Send-Off Concert at Verizon Hall—Kimmel Center for the Performing Arts, June 18, 2015. The event was part of Ciao Philadelphia. (Photo: Richard Barnes)

while also recognizing the vital contribution of its Italian and Italian American communities. "What Ciao Philadelphia does is showcase the talent and culture of some people who trace some of their bloodlines back to Italy. . . . By showcasing culture and talent, hopefully new relationships will develop that lead to trade and commerce," pointed out Joe Jacovini, Chairman of the Executive Committee of the law firm Dilworth Paxson, in the article in the *Philadelphia Inquirer* announcing the first edition of Ciao Philadelphia.[24]

As Consul General of Italy in Philadelphia, I felt that Ciao Philadelphia represented an articulation of my mission to strengthen the bridges between Italy and Philadelphia and foster understanding of our shared cultural heritage, as I had the opportunity to express in my op-ed in the *Philadelphia Inquirer* in October 2014, on the eve of the first Ciao Philadelphia edition.[25] By 2016, Ciao Philadelphia was extended beyond Philadelphia, South Jersey, and Delaware to include Pittsburgh and Maryland, all part of the same consular jurisdiction.

The extensive media coverage[26] that the Consulate General and Ciao Philadelphia received in Philadelphia and Italy helped raise interest and awareness. An editorial to support the initiatives of the Italian Consulate General in the *Philadelphia Inquirer* on October 2, 2015, stated, "The connections between Philadelphia and Italy run deeper than great cuisine, including influences on colonial architecture and politics. Andrea Canepari, Italy's Consul General, rightly wants to strengthen them with Ciao Philadelphia, the second annual month-long celebration of

Italo-Philadelphian links."[27] This endorsement is in line with the enthusiastic reception of Ciao Philadelphia by every landmark institution of the region with an Italian influence, as well as all major universities,[28] bringing together Italians, Italian Americans, and "friends of Italy." Events included operas, concerts, film screenings, food celebrations, exhibits, Italian race cars, performances, lectures, and tours uniquely created for Ciao Philadelphia at Independence Hall National Park, the Philadelphia Museum of Art, the Pennsylvania Academy of the Fine Arts, the University of Pennsylvania Museum, and the Union League. Through these different collaborations, Ciao Philadelphia helped promote awareness about new opportunities with Italy in the Greater Philadelphia region. Ciao Philadelphia was designed not only as a way to appreciate the Italian cultural heritage but also as a way to connect the region with contemporary Italy, opening doors for growing economic and academic exchanges, as written by Jeff Blumenthal in his article "Italy Says Ciao, Philadelphia," published in the *Philadelphia Business Journal* on October 17, 2014.

One of the concrete examples of the opportunities created by this growing awareness was the dual international medical degree program hailed as the first of its kind in the world. This program allows doctors to practice in both the United States and the European Union, thanks to an agreement between Rome's Università Cattolica del Sacro Cuore (UCSC) and Thomas Jefferson University in Philadelphia. Under the terms of the agreement, medical students at UCSC could earn a bachelor of science degree from Thomas Jefferson University and a doctor of

Mayoral news conference presenting the first edition of Ciao Philadelphia on October 1, 2014, City Hall Mayor Reception Room, Philadelphia. At the podium are Mayor Michael Nutter, Councilman Mark Squilla, and CG Andrea Canepari. (Photo: Gary Horn)

Dr. Steve Klasko, President of Thomas Jefferson University, accompanied by Dr. Mark Tykocinski (Provost) and Ignazio Marino (Senior Vice President, Professor of Surgery, and former Mayor of Rome) with Franco Anelli (President of Università Cattolica) and Rocco Bellantone (Dean) at the signing of the Partnership Agreement between Jefferson and Cattolica. Rome, November 11, 2018. (Courtesy Thomas Jefferson University)

medicine degree from the Sidney Kimmel Medical College at Thomas Jefferson University or from the School of Medicine and Surgery at UCSC, all within just six years. The arrangement is groundbreaking because of the difference in medical education requirements between the United States and Europe. The President of Thomas Jefferson, Steve Klasko, highlighted the role played by the Consul General in Philadelphia in the signing of the agreement in an article that appeared in the *Philadelphia Inquirer* in May 2017.[29]

Another concrete example of the opportunities created by increased awareness was the creation of Italian courses for English-speaking children in the public schools of the city of Philadelphia, leading to the creation of English-Italian bilingual schools. The idea behind this initiative, supported by the Consulate General and shared by the school authorities of the city of Philadelphia, was that through the study of the Italian language students could not only broaden their learning abilities but also acquire the tools to better understand the international and global world of today and tomorrow.[30]

Ciao Philadelphia was never intended as an exclusively Italian American initiative but rather meant as an inclusive effort open to all dimensions of the rich Philadelphian social fabric. Ciao Philadelphia was home to initiatives realized by non-Italians, such as the ones resulting from a successful partnership between the Italian Consulate General and the American Jewish Committee of Philadelphia and Southern New Jersey. In 2016, building on the common desire to create living bridges between Italy and the Philadelphia region, the National Museum of American Jewish History in Philadelphia, a Smithsonian Affiliate Institution, also joined the Ciao Philadelphia celebrations and organized special Ciao Philadelphia tours.

The attention raised by Ciao Philadelphia and its outward-looking nature helped the Consulate General in carrying out some of its other missions, including tackling global issues. In fact, the Consulate General of Italy is the only consulate general remaining in the city of Philadelphia and one of the few truly international platforms in the region. It is in this context that several initiatives were organized, such as the commemoration of International Holocaust Remembrance Day, including ceremonies and public discussions at the Congregation Mikveh Israel and lectures at Thomas Jefferson University as highlighted by the *Jewish Exponent*[31] and an op-ed entitled "Holding Fast to Values of Human Dignity, Freedom" in the *Philadelphia Inquirer*.[32]

Today, the Italian Consulate General in Philadelphia still fulfills the three tasks it has had since its inception: promoting commercial cooperation, providing services to Italian citizens, and maintaining the cultural link to Italy of its community

Italy is the only country with an operating Consulate General in Pennsylvania. Italian CG Andrea Canepari was invited to address—as a sign of special recognition to Italy from the Speaker's podium—the Pennsylvania House of Representatives in Harrisburg on June 6, 2016. (House of Representatives, Commonwealth of Pennsylvania) while it undergoes the natural Americanization process. However, a new task has emerged, and new stakeholders have approached the Consulate General, as the experience of Ciao Philadelphia has shown. The Consulate General is now developing a new form of cooperation with Italy in the economic and scientific fields by including the "friends of Italy" and encouraging them to interact with Italy to create new opportunities and living bridges between the two sides without being limited to a focus on Italian ethnicity.[33] Ciao Philadelphia created awareness among Italians, Italian Americans, and friends of Italy about the Italian influence in the Philadelphia region and connected all three groups to Italy by creating a platform useful for both the Philadelphia region and Italy together.

ITALIAN CONSULS IN PHILADELPHIA

The following is a list of Italian Consuls and Vice Consuls in Philadelphia (1870 through 2019) as compiled by Richard Juliani:[34]

- Alonzo M. Viti, unofficial, honorary consul (1864–1876)
- Count Goffredo Galli (1876–1884)
- Count Nicola Squitti di Palermiti e Guarna (1884–1889)
- Count Annabile Raybaudi Massiglia (1889–1895)
- Guglielmo Slaviz, acting consul (1894–1897)
- Carlos Filippo Serra (1895–1896)
- Giulio M. Lecca (1896–1899)
- Angelo Dall'Aste Brandolini (1899–1902)
- Count Girolamo Naselli (1902–1906)
- Angelo Dall'Aste Brandolini, Vice Consul (1902–1906)
- Giacomo Fara Forni (1906–1909)
- Luigi Villari Vice Consul (1907–1909)
- Count Luigi Aldrovandi Marescotti (1909–1911)
- Count Luigi Provana del Sabbione, Vice Consul (1909–1911)
- Giuseppe Gentile, Vice Consul (1910–1912)
- Meriggio Serrati, Vice Consul (1910–1911)
- Giulio Cesare Majoni (1911–1914)
- Nobile Carlo dei Marchesi de Constantin di Chateauneuf, Vice Consul (1912–1913)
- Gaetano Emilio Poccardi (1914–1921)
- Guido deVincenzo, Vice Consul (1915–1923)
- Giuseppe Gentile, in charge of the Consulate (1917)
- Guglielmo Silenzi (1920–1921)
- Luigi Sillitti (1921–1926)
- Vittorio Siciliani (1926–1928)
- Mario Orsini Ratto (1928–1929)

- Agostino Ferrante dei Marchesi di Ruffano (1929–1932)
- Giovanni Maria Pio Margotti (1932–1936)
- Edoardo Pervan (1937–1939)
- Ludovico Censi (1939–1942)
- Suspension of consular services (1942–1947)
- Corrado Orlandi Contucci (1947)
- Silvio E. Daneo (1949–1951)
- Ludovico Barattieri di San Pietro (1951–1956)
- Giovanni Luciolli (1956–1959)
- Edgardo Sogno Rata del Vallino (1959–1961)
- Gian Piero Nuti (1961–1967)
- Antonio Carloni (1967–1972)
- Letterio Carlo, acting consul (1972–1973)
- Filippo Anfuso (1973–1975)
- Onofrio Solari Bozzi (1975–1978)
- Giancarlo Riccio (1980–1982)
- Giuseppe Cassini (1982–1987)
- Luca del Balzo di Presenzano (1987–1990)
- Franco Giordano (1990–1993)
- Valentino Simonetti (1993–1997)
- Anna Della Croce di Dojola Brigante Colonna (1997–2000)
- Lorenzo Mott (2000–2004)
- Stefano Mistretta (2004–2008)
- Luigi Scotto (2009–2013)
- Andrea Canepari (2013–2017)
- Pier Attinio Forlano (incumbent)

NOTES

1. The formation of the modern Italian state culminated in 1861 with the unification of most of the Italian peninsula under the Piedmont-Sardinia, ruled by the Savoy into the Kingdom of Italy. Italy incorporated Venetia (1866) and the former Papal States (including Rome) by 1870. Before the Italian unification (also known as the Risorgimento), the Italian peninsula was fragmented into different kingdoms, city-states, duchies, and republics.

2. Office of the Historian, United States Department of State, "History of Recognition, Diplomatic, and Consular Relations, by Country, since 1776: Italy," https://history.state.gov/countries/Italy.

3. P. Castagneto, "Old and New Republics: The Diplomatic Relations between the Republic of Genoa and the United States of America," in *Rough Waters: American Involvement with the Mediterranean in the Eighteenth and Nineteenth Centuries*, ed. S. Marzagalli, J. R. Sofka, and J. J. McCusker (Liverpool: Liverpool University Press, 2010), 103.

4. S. Rotta, "La corrispondenza di Giuseppe Ravara, Console Generale della Repubblica di Genova presso gli Stati Uniti," in *Italia e America dal settecento all'età dell'imperialismo*, ed. G. Spini, A. M. Martellone, R. Luraghi, T. Bonazzi, and R. Ruffilli (Venice: Marsilio, 1976), 169–217.

5. Cinzia Maria Aicardi and Alessandra Cavaterra, eds., *I Fondi Archivistici Della Legazione Sarda E Delle Rappresentanze Diplomatiche Italia~ Negli U.S.A. (1848–1901)* (Rome: Istituto Poligrafico e Zecca dello Stato, 1988), 10.

6. Ibid., 12.

7. Seg. S. registro 292, copialettere: Legazione negli Stati Uniti d'America, Solaro a Collobiano (my translation).

8. Ibid.

9. Today nations are expanding commercial diplomacy to promote trade and investments. See H. Ruel, *Commercial Diplomacy and International Business: A Conceptual and Empirical Exploration* (Bingley: Emerald Group, 2012).

10. "Diaspora diplomacy" is recognized as an increasingly important activity for diplomats now and in the years ahead. K. Rana, *21st Century Diplomacy, a Practitioner's Guide* (London: Continuum International, 2011).

11. Richard N. Juliani, "The Consulate General of Italy in Philadelphia: A Bridge between Two Cultures" (unpublished manuscript).

12. Ibid.

13. Ibid.

14. Richard N. Juliani, *Building Little Italy: Philadelphia's Italians before Mass Migration* (University Park: Pennsylvania State University Press, 1998).

15. See Chapter 16, by Steven Conn, Chapter 31, by Paolo Valentino, and my Afterword.

16. Stefano Luconi, "The Impact of Italy's Twentieth-Century Wars on Italian Americans' Ethnic Identity," *Nationalism and Ethnic Politics* 13, no. 3 (2007): 465–491.

17. "Address by Assistant Secretary Rogers at a Dinner Given by the Sons of Italy," in Press Releases, Publications of The Department of State, November 21, 1931, no. 258, p. 478.

18. Richard N. Juliani, "The Consulate General of Italy in Philadelphia: A Bridge between Two Cultures" (unpublished manuscript).

19. The overall mission of the consulate was established in accordance with the instructions set by the Italian Ministry for Foreign Affairs and by the Italian embassy in Washington, DC.

20. From the video "Fedegari Presents 'APPASSIONATI' Ciao Philadelphia 2016 Inaugural Reception," October 25, 2016. https://www.youtube.com/watch?v=91Sym_Ue8Y8.

21. Ibid.

22. J. Mostov, "Drexel's Global Reach," in *Building Drexel: The University and Its City, 1891–2016* (Philadelphia: Temple University Press, 2017), 353.

23. As a sign of interest from the business sector, Ciao Philadelphia was sponsored by several U.S. companies such as KPMG, PREIT, Rothman Institute, SEPTA, CGI, PECO, Pennoni, Parke Bank, American Airlines, Dilworth Paxson, Duane Morris, Philadelphia Energy Solutions, Today Media, and Fedegari Technologies INC. The Commonwealth of Pennsylvania and PHL CVB Philadelphia Visitor and Convention Bureau also supported Ciao Philadelphia, an initiative aimed at creating new international opportunities.

24. E. Edinger-Turoff, "Celebrating Philadelphia's Italian Craftmanship in Phila," *Philadelphia Inquirer*, September 30, 2014.

25. "Linking to Italy: Ciao Philadelphia," op-ed, *Philadelphia Inquirer*, October 5, 2014.

26. See the following articles in the press:

U.S. ARTICLES
- E. Edinger-Turoff, "Celebrating Philadelphia's Italian Craftmanship in Phila," *Philadelphia Inquirer*, September 30, 2014.

- K. Dougherty, "Linking to Italia—Ciao Philadelphia," *Philadelphia Inquirer*, October 5, 2014.
- J. McDevitt, "Italian Culture the Focus of Series of Events in Philadelphia," CBS Philly, October 5, 2014, https://philadelphia.cbslocal.com/2014/10/05/italian-culture-the-focus-of-series-of-events-in-philadelphia/.
- "Ciao, Italia," *Philadelphia Inquirer*, October 2, 2015.
- J. N. DiStefano, "Philly Friends of Italy, on a Big Boat," *Philadelphia Inquirer*, October 5, 2015, https://www.inquirer.com/philly/blogs/inq-phillydeals/Prominenti-on-a-big-boat.html.
- "Four Days of Columbus Day," *Philadelphia's The Public Record*, October 8, 2015.
- T. Jimenez, "Month Long Celebration of Italian Culture Wraps Up This Week," CBSPhilly.com, October 26, 2015, https://philadelphia.cbslocal.com/2015/10/26/month-long-celebration-of-italian-culture-wraps-up-this-week/.
- "Finding Italy in Philadelphia," *National Italian American Foundation* 27, no. 1 (Fall 2015): 13.
- B. A. Zippi, "Canepari's Ciao Philadelphia Event: A Month Long Celebration," *Delaware Valley Italian-American Herald*, September 7, 2016, http://www.italianamericanherald.com/caneparis-ciao-philadelphia-event-a-month-long-celebration/.
- E. Moran, "Philly and Environs Pay Tribute to Italy," *Philadelphia Inquirer*, October 6, 2016.
- M. Newall, "From Italy to Phila, Con Amore," *Philadelphia Inquirer*, February 21, 2016.
- S. Krotzer, "Temple Honors 2016 Global Philadelphia Award Recipient," *Temple Now*, January 25, 2017, https://news.temple.edu/news/2017-01-25/andrea-canepari-2016-global-philadelphia-award.
- J. Meyer and A. Canepari, "Holding Fast to Values of Human Dignity, Freedom," *Philadelphia Inquirer*, January 27, 2017.
- L. Spikol, "International Holocaust Remembrance Day, Commemorated with Mortality Discussion," *Jewish Exponent*, February 2, 2017.
- J. N. DiStefano, "Buon Viaggio: Italian Envoy Leaving Phila with Portfolio of Achievements," *Philadelphia Inquirer*, May 28, 2017.
- J. N. DiStefano, "Italy's Man in Philly Promoted to Caribbean," *Philadelphia Inquirer*, May 28, 2017, https://www.inquirer.com/philly/business/italys-man-in-philly-was-match-com-for-deals-20170525.html.

TV AND RADIO
- "Talk Philly: Ciao Philadelphia," CBS Philly, October 8, 2014, https://www.youtube.com/watch?v=GWt9GUypj0Y.
- L. Rosalsky, "Ciarrocchi Receives Highest Badge of Honor in Italy," CW Philly, October 8, 2014, https://cwphilly.cbslocal.com/ciarrocchi-receives-highest-badge-of-honor-in-italy/.
- A. Vitarelli, "Ciao Philadelphia: Celebration of Italian Culture," 6ABC Philadelphia, October 9, 2014, https://6abc.com/343336/.
- "Bringing Together Philadelphia and Italian Culture with Ciao Philadelphia," CBS Philly, https://philadelphia.cbslocal.com/video/3303799-bringing-together-philadelphia-and-italian-culture-with-ciao-philadelphia/.
- "Ciao Philadelphia 2016 Celebrates Italian Heritage All Month Long," NBC10, October 7, 2016, https://www.nbcphiladelphia.com/entertainment/the-scene/CIAO

-Philadelphia-2016-Celebrates-Italian-Heritage-All-Month-Long_Philadelphia
-396309181.html.
- "06/13/17 The Honorable Andrea Canepari, Musician Brendan Evans and Mermaid Rescue Week's Jim Stephens," *In the Know with David Oh*, WWDB, June 15, 2017, https://wwdbam.com/episodes/in-the-know-061317/.

ITALIAN ARTICLES
- F. Cerisano, "La Riscossa Di Filadelfia—Philadelphia's Comeback," *Italia Oggi*, April 16, 2015.
- P. Valentino, "From Rocky to Botticelli," *Corriere Della Sera*, October 24, 2015.
- "Andrea Canepari, Console Generale Di Filadelfia," *Corriere TV*, October 26, 2016, https://video.corriere.it/andrea-canepari-console-generale-filadelfia/d20d60de-9acc -11e6-97ec-60bd8f16d4a5.
- G. Sarcina, "Not Just Renzi and Obama: America's Passion for Italy," *Corriere Della Sera Online*, October 27, 2016, https://www.corriere.it/extra-per-voi/2016/10/26/non-solo -renzi-obama-passione-usa-l-italia-451ccd5a-9b57-11e6-92af-45665cb81731.shtml.
- F. Cerisano, "Diplomazia Che Spinge L'Italia," *Italia Oggi*, August 30, 2017, https:// www.italiaoggi.it/news/diplomazia-che-spinge-l-italia-2205542.
- D. Ripamonti, "Andrea Canepari, L'ambasciatore Che Sa Ripartire Sempre Da Zero," *Via Sarfatti 25—Rivista della Bocconi*, September 28, 2017, https://www.viasarfatti25 .unibocconi.it/notizia.php?idArt=18580.
- D. Ripamonti, "Andrea Canepari, the Ambassador Who Knows How to Start from Scratch," *Via Sarfatti 25—Bocconi Magazine*, September 28, 2017, https://www.viasar fatti25.unibocconi.eu/notizia.php?idArt=18681.

27. "Ciao, Italia," *Philadelphia Inquirer*, October 2, 2015, A18.

28. The following organizations were partners of Ciao Philadelphia from 2014 to 2017: American Jewish Committee; Associazione Regionale Abruzzese DELCO; Christopher Columbus Association—Delaware County; College of Physicians of Philadelphia; Delaware Commission on Italian Heritage; Drexel University; Duquesne University—School of Law; EFASCE of Philadelphia; Filitalia International—History of Italian Immigration Museum; Hood College; Il Circolo Italiano della Main Line; Independence National Historical Park—National Park Service; Independence Seaport Museum; International Opera Theater; Kimmel Center for the Performing Arts of Philadelphia; National Museum of American Jewish History—a Smithsonian Institute Affiliate; Opera Philadelphia; Opera Delaware; Order of Sons of Italy in America; Passyunk—East Passyunk Avenue Business Improvement District; University of Pennsylvania Museum; Pennsylvania Academy of the Fine Arts; Philadelphia Classical Guitar Society; Philadelphia Museum of Art; Philly Pops; Reading Public Museum; Rosemont College; Rowan University; Simeone Foundation—Automotive Museum; Studio Incamminati—School for Contemporary Realist Art; Sons and Daughters of Italy; St. Joseph's University; Temple University; the American University of Rome; the Children's Hospital of Philadelphia; the Church of the Advocate in Philadelphia; the College of Physicians of Philadelphia; the Franklin Institute; the Union League of Philadelphia; the 1492 Society; the South 9th Street Business Association; Thomas Jefferson University; UNICO Rehoboth Area Chapter; University of Pittsburgh—PittLaw; University of Pennsylvania; Villanova University; Widener University; Woodmere Art Museum.

29. Joseph N. Distefano, "Buon Viaggio: Italian Envoy Leaving Phila with a Portfolio of Achievements," *Philadelphia Inquirer*, May 28, 2017. "It was Canepari, alongside scholars such as Ignazio Marino, a Jefferson transplant surgeon and former mayor of Rome—who assisted in putting together the Italy-USA exchange of scientists and scholars that led us to Cattolica—Klasko added."

30. Matteo Greco, " Insegnare Italiano a Giovani Studenti Americani: Resoconto Di Un Progetto Oltreoceano," *Babylonia Finestra* 2 (2020): 114–117, http://babylonia.ch/fileadmin /user_upload/documents/2020-2/20_Finestra_Greco.pdf. Matteo Greco, "A Brief Practical Guide for L2-Teachers: K-2 American Children Learn Italian," *Humanising Language Teaching* (forthcoming).

31. Liz Spikol, "International Holocaust Remembrance Day Commemorated with Morality Discussion," *Jewish Exponent*, February 1, 2017.

32. Written by Andrea Canepari, Consul General, and Judith Myer, Board Chair of the Pennsylvania/Southern New Jersey/Delaware Region of the Anti-Defamation League, January 27, 2017.

33. Regarding academic views on the transnational spirit of Italy, see P. Janni and G. McLean, *The Essence of Italian Culture and the Challenge of a Global Age*, Cultural Heritage and Contemporary Change, ser. 4, West Europe, vol. 5 (Washington: Council for Research in Values and Philosophy, 2003). Piero Bassetti promoted research on the concept of "Italicity" as freeing up a rich Italian cultural content that is communicable across borders, lived and developed by not only the Italian diaspora but also many who would engage and be engaged by it. See N. D'Aquino, *La rete italica, Idee per un Commonwealth: Ragionamenti con e su Piero Bassetti* (Rome: Italic digital Editions, 2014).

34. Richard N. Juliani, "The Consulate General of Italy in Philadelphia: A Bridge between Two Cultures" (unpublished manuscript).

INTRODUCTION

JUDITH GOODE

CONTEMPORARY IMAGES of the relationships between Italy and Philadelphia are popularly associated with Italian Americans who settled in the city during the mass European immigration between 1880 and 1920 in response to expanding industrialization. This volume demonstrates that there has been a much longer and deeper relationship between Italy and Philadelphia from colonial times, that the Italian American experience is much more complex than commonly imagined, and that cultural ties continue to develop today in new ways.

We look at Philadelphia's Italian legacy through the flow of ideas, people, objects, and cultural practices between Italy and the United States and follow particular examples of how Italian styles and motifs become inscribed in material forms, such as architectural designs and structures in the civic center and in local neighborhood landscapes, and in nonmaterial forms, such as major civic institutions as well as social relationships and patterns of everyday activities that shape life and identity in the city. We aim to bring together lesser-known examples of the presence of Italy in this city, as well as the more recognized Italian markings of space, icons, and institutions. Our goal is to highlight gems heretofore overlooked in the built environment and the arts institutions of the city while also exploring the legacy through neighborhood landscapes and "made in America" art and cultural practices that have been infused in everyday experiences and popular enjoyments throughout the city. Understanding Philadelphia's unique and ever-changing urban context is central to this task.

In Philadelphia, this legacy begins with the aesthetic and social ideals brought to the United States by Italian elites and adopted by those creating the political philosophies and built environment of the new republic. In this era, the ideas and aesthetics of classical civilization, revitalized during the Renaissance and Enlightenment, used aesthetic forms to convey and connect beauty and morality. Moral values such as democracy, justice, patriotism, and productivity were linked to certain symbols and styles. Acquiring the "civilizing" knowledge and values of classical and Enlightenment societies was important in and of itself.

Wealthy Philadelphians traveled frequently to Italy during the expanding industrial period of the nineteenth century and brought back vast numbers of art and artifacts that focused on the significance of neoclassical and Renaissance aesthetic and moral values. As wealth inequality grew, collecting such cultural forms also helped demonstrate family status and create social hierarchy and exclusivity among industrial and financial elites. Italian artifacts with their associations with early civilization were especially significant.

As more Italians settled and formed communities in the city from the 1850s onward, another piece of the Italian legacy originated in the contributions of immigrants who established permanent communities in the late nineteenth and early twentieth centuries. Italian craftsmen and merchants began arriving in Philadelphia first in the 1850s–60s and then as part of the massive 1880–1920 immigrant waves from southern and eastern Europe. We explore the formation of localized Italian American communities during this time and the stories of families and individuals as they are absorbed into the social fabric of the city, thereby creating new forms of art and culture from their Italian and U.S. experiences.

Some forms and skills of this "made in America" culture were brought from Italy, while others were developed through education and training as the descendants of immigrants became Italian Americans and were educated in U.S. institutions. Early Italian American art was often used to decorate elite homes and institutions. Other forms were produced locally during everyday life in relatively bounded ethnic communities in the decades of urban change through the depression, World War II, and its aftermath. After the war, many of these forms became part of mainstream culture.

Finally, we explore the impact of Italian forms on the contemporary development of a cosmopolitan, multicultural city eager to become an important node in the global economy, as cheaper travel and new forms of communication create new possibilities for links between Philadelphia and Italy. This all takes place in an era of frequent shifts and reactions in arts movements as well as the increased valuation of and respect for popular and folk art forms aided by new electronic technologies and the advent of broadcast and social media.

The essays come from a variety of disciplines and methods. They vary in style and substance. Some of the essays take a long historical view of change within institutions. Others examine in-depth interpretations of lives and careers, as well as particular spaces, projects, and objects in architecture, art, music, and cuisine.

There is no attempt to find an "essential" Italian-ness; rather, this volume attempts to find encounters and relationships between Italy and the United States in terms of a perceived spirit of Italy or aesthetic style (Italianate), homages to particular Italian gardens and buildings, and specific contributions made in America by those of Italian heritage. Being "Italian" is not fixed in meaning but varies in time, in place, and in the life experience and social networks of people, institutions, and groups. Some essays look at the very processes through which core ideas, motifs, and symbols get reworked in different epochs of city history and aesthetic movements.

To understand the legacy, impact, and influence of Italian arts and culture on the city of Philadelphia since independence requires an understanding of how cities are dynamic, especially in terms of their built environments and diverse populations. We look at Philadelphia during four periods in which the city changed its position in the nation and the world. Such turning points reshaped the spatial contours of the city and its social composition. Central to the framework of the volume are the ways in which political and economic shifts shaped structures of power, social class, and ethnic division and how this related to new forms and values in arts and culture.

The Italian nation was equally dynamic, experiencing major changes during the mid-nineteenth-century period of national unification and twentieth-century conflicts and political movements. The encounters between both peoples and institutions, as well as the relationships between both states, shape the contacts and processes of Italian influence as illuminated in the Prologue to this volume.

The colonial city of Philadelphia was the largest in the North American colony and the site of the founding of the republic and the capital in the early federal period. As it lost its political and economic centrality, it became a major industrial metropolis, a center of manufacturing and wealth accumulation with an enlarged territory. The mass eastern and southern European immigration wave that flowed to new industry (1880–1920) was met by growing anti-immigrant reaction, and a legal cessation of immigration in the early 1920s. By that time, multigenerational ethnic groups were crafting their new hyphenated cultural practices in a depression context. Participation in the war effort played a major role in the acceptance of white ethnic communities as Americans and expanded ties between the ethnic groups themselves and the native born.

After the war, from 1945 to the 1970s, there was a period of postwar optimism and affluence. Through GI Bill–supported higher education and FHA mortgage loans, many children of immigrants moved into the middle classes and left the city for the suburbs as U.S. policies underwrote suburbanization and urban blight. Soon after, in the 1960s, deindustrialization further impoverished the city's residents and infrastructure. By the 1970s, urban policies in Philadelphia, as in other rust-belt cities, undertook a new kind of restructuring of the city hoping to make it more competitive as a node in the global economy.

Philadelphia's economy is today dependent on "eds and meds," a nickname for higher education in general and academic medical training and health care. New "creative knowledge workers" who work in these and related industries have generated consumption styles and markets favoring cosmopolitanism. Exploding new forms of popular arts and entertainment have emerged in the modern consumerist era. What effects have these changes had on the Italian legacy?

To answer this question, we look at Philadelphia's Italian legacy in four sections, each framed by a key transformation in the city's political, economic, and social structures. The introduction to each section provides more specific context for the essays that follow. The four sections are briefly described below in terms of the structure of the city and the mode of Italian influence.

Independence and Early Republic. The city was key in the British colonial economy and as a center for debate, for the drafting of documents declaring independence, and for governing the new democratic republic. Philadelphia was the largest city in the new nation. Italian ideas and architectural designs were brought in through key Renaissance and Enlightenment texts and the presence of largely transient highly educated elites such as diplomats, artists, large-scale traders, and members of religious orders.

The Expanding Industrial Metropolis: New Wealth, New Elites, and New Institutions of Knowledge, Arts, and Culture. As the nineteenth century progressed, Philadelphia lost its central political and economic roles to New York and Washington, DC, but it developed as an industrial powerhouse and railroad transportation center for the nation as it expanded in territory. During this period, the scions of the new wealthy class traveled to Italy to experience a grand tour of European high culture and brought back Italian ideas, designs, and objects such as antiquities and aesthetic wonders, which formed the core of a burgeoning new City Beautiful—a landscape of arts and culture institutions that expressed the city's importance. Italian motifs and objects contributed heavily to this project.

Made in America: Immigration, Community Formation, and Varieties of Creative Italian American Experience. The decades from 1880 to 1920 saw massive immigration from eastern and southern Europe to the industrial cities and regions of the United States. A most direct Italian legacy and continuous engagement between Italy and the United States occurred through these decades and continues in new forms today. Many in this immigrant wave were drawn to South Philadelphia by an incipient structure of Italian institutions—parishes, boardinghouses, and provisioning enterprises that catered to food and other specific needs and also served the needs of dispersed Italian American settlements. Contacts with Italy diminished after immigration was restricted legislatively and by the Depression and Second World War. Over time, generations of Italian Americans contributed to a made-in-America array of Italian-derived arts and cultural practices based on multiple aesthetic movements and played a significant role in leadership in the city.

Contemporary Philadelphia: Experiencing the Italian Legacy in the Branded Global City. A new set of relationships between Philadelphia and Italy developed through the restructuring of global economic and political systems. Independence from colonial rule, new global financial and trade institutions, widely accessible and cheaper transportation, and mass and new social media enabled increased flows of capital, people, ideas, and goods across national borders. By the 1970s, the concept of globalization was widely used to describe these changes. In Philadelphia this was first experienced as deindustrialization as plants relocated to find cheaper labor. New immigrants also arrived as a result of new laws. Urban planning responses involved public and private partnerships investing in restructuring the economy from industry to one based on highly educated workers, referred to as creative, professional, or knowledge workers, by building on the large base of institutions of "eds and meds." Strategies for attracting knowledge workers and university students as residents as well as national and global tourists included branding the city as diverse and cosmopolitan. These processes increased the flow of people and ideas across the Atlantic and set a new value on Italian design, styles, food, and people who could easily travel back and forth.

These sections refer to processual changes that cannot be clearly bracketed by dates. They consider the world relationships that restructure specific local political economies and produce new social structures and cultural ideas. For example, the formation of a wealthy consuming class and the era of mass immigration overlap in time and are interrelated, since new workers were needed for the expanding U.S. economy with labor actively recruited in southern and eastern Europe. But the ways in which this affected the Italian legacy in Philadelphia were very different. In one case, U.S. elites traveled to bring the cultural capital of elite European arts and culture back to burnish and refine the city's standing; in the other, new populations with specific artisan skills arrived to reproduce traditional arts and ultimately to create new cultural forms.

I

INDEPENDENCE AND
EARLY REPUBLIC

INTRODUCTION

JUDITH GOODE

COLONIAL PHILADELPHIA PLAYED A MAJOR ROLE in the British colonial regime. It was the North American control center for the linked British trade circuit including New Orleans, the Caribbean, and Britain. During the colonial period, contacts between the city and other places were constrained by British control. With the notable exceptions of some residents with large trading fortunes and the presence of slave labor, the socioeconomic order resembled the republic of equal citizens drawing livelihoods from small farms and business enterprises that Jefferson and his colleagues envisioned in their founding documents opposing the idea of monarchic rule and hereditary aristocracy. Production systems were organized around owners, journeymen, and apprentices in small workshops, which offered mobility. Society was materially more equal than it would become as industry expanded.

The early city was small in footprint and walkable. Residences and economic activities were clustered in high-density low-rise buildings around the Delaware River port. The city from north to south was only nine blocks. The east-west boundaries went from river to river (Delaware and Schuylkill) with dense clustering along the Delaware and some industry along the Schuylkill but very little settlement between. The density of economic activities and the fact that residences were attached to artisan workshops or trading warehouses meant that there was little class segregation in space. Alleyways that subdivided blocks were used for housing servants, apprentices, and other workers.

Leading up to the war for independence and the early republic, as settlers chafed under British control, diplomatic and trade engagements were formed with other European nations. The site of the drafting of all formal founding documents, the city became the political center and first capital. The political philosophies of the seventeenth- and eighteenth-century European Enlightenment increasingly traveled to this cosmopolitan colonial city along with the material arts and architectural forms symbolically linked to them. They had emerged from Greco-Roman civilization, especially as reinterpreted during the Italian Renaissance.

The essays in this section illustrate Italian connections through which key ideas were transmitted through texts or through individual elite Italians and how they were received by the individuals and institutions of the city connected to the founding and development of the new nation. We know about some Italians residing in the city at this time who were elites with a cosmopolitan view acquired through experience in aristocratic court life or through education by private tutors or at Italian universities. Many of them moved back and forth between the hemispheres.

Some European Enlightenment ideas came to Philadelphia indirectly through books, such as Andrea Palladio's designs (Chapter 1) and Cesare Beccaria's legal theories (Chapter 2). Often these ideas were discussed between the activists involved in the independence movement and educated Italian elites who resided in the city, as in the relationship between Joseph Mussi and Thomas Jefferson (Chapter 3) or between Italian Jesuits and the city's Catholic community (Chapter 4). Before the unification of Italy, Joseph Ravara was the first Consul General from an Italian state, the Republic of Genoa (see Prologue). Angelo Garibaldi was a Piedmontese Consul and brother of the Italian unification hero Giuseppe Garibaldi (see Sidebar 1). Other examples include the Da Pontes, senior and junior, affiliated with the early decades of the University of Pennsylvania (language and literature). They later became major sponsors of Italian opera (Chapters 14 and 25).

For the most part, the small number of elite Italians were closely and personally linked to English-speaking Philadelphians as well as to networks of other educated Italians residing in cities up and down the eastern seaboard. The establishment of a significant Italian community with residential clustering and institutions did not develop until the second half of the nineteenth century.

Chapter 1. In "Palladians in Philadelphia," Jeffrey A. Cohen tells us about the work of Andrea Palladio (1508–1580), who closely studied the details of ancient Roman architecture and codified them in his famous Renaissance treatise on the principles of balance and proportion. These principles were used first for public structures such as churches and monumental public sites, and they were copied by the richest nobility. Cohen's chapter traces how this classical text traveled to England, where it had a broad effect in enabling moderately wealthy households to acquire a pedigree. Brought to the United States from England, Palladian design had a great influence on the founding fathers in constructing Philadelphia's early republic civic spaces, but it also was wildly popular among the new expanding wealthy class both within the city and in country estates.

Chapter 2. William B. Ewald's essay, "Cesare Beccaria's Influence on the Philadelphia Constitutional Convention," tells us about the important influence of Italian Enlightenment political thought on the ideas of the founders of the republic by focusing on the influence of Cesare Beccaria on human rights and criminal law. This interest in Italian legal theorizing has been carried into the present by the Justinian Society, a group of jurists of Italian descent who maintain an interest in these issues and present an award in Beccaria's name.

Chapter 3. In "Thomas Jefferson and Joseph Mussi: Enjoying Milanese Life in Philadelphia," Maurizio Valsania examines the interesting case of the friendship between Thomas Jefferson and Joseph Mussi, a well-read Italian merchant in the city. Jefferson, who had steeped himself in ancient civilizations and built Monticello using Palladian designs, also spoke and read Italian. While he had acquired most of his knowledge through books, he later experienced Italy firsthand when he traveled through northern Italy while serving the United States as a diplomat in Paris. Valsania demonstrates Jefferson's continuing interest in Italy through this little-known story of his later, personal one-on-one relationship with Mussi. Jefferson resided with Mussi during the summer of the drafting of the Constitution, and from then on they conducted a long correspondence focusing on their mutual interest in Italian agricultural culture.

Chapter 4. In "Rome, Italian Émigrés, and Jesuit Education in Nineteenth-Century Philadelphia," Carmen R. Croce tells the story of Jesuit influence on Philadelphia in spite of an earlier distrust of the order by the founders of the republic and the tension between Jesuits and the Vatican. He traces the specific influences of Italians in the development of Jesuit institutions of learning as they promoted the sciences and the humanities in the city through the nineteenth century as well as their significance today.

Chapter 5. Barbara A. Wolanin's essay, "Artists of the Capitol in Philadelphia," tells us a little-known story about two major Italian artists, Constantino Brumidi and Filippo Costaggini, who created splendid painted altarpieces and murals in the Catholic churches of Philadelphia. After first being commissioned to decorate the U.S. Capitol in DC, these two artists and the successors they mentored came to Philadelphia to produce their creations for an expanding Catholic church building program.

CARPENTER'S HALL PHIL.ᵃ

1

Palladians in Philadelphia

Jeffrey A. Cohen

Over three centuries of building in Philadelphia, architectural reflections of Italy appeared again and again, both on urban streets and in houses dotting the city's peripheries. For American architects, builders, and clients of nearly every generation, drawing upon Italian models offered the benediction of a distant cosmopolitanism. It also served as a recurring source of well-known buildings that came to provoke and embody the next critique of design practice. The favor for these Italian forms from afar was national, and before American independence it reigned widely across British Atlantic colonial landscapes. As designers and clients, Philadelphians were often key actors in a continuing conversation with Italian buildings.

To a perhaps surprisingly degree, this trans-Atlantic conversation was extremely episodic, turning successively to distinct, often diametrically contrasting languages of form. Sources of visual influence oscillated from classical to medieval, intensely enriched to restrained, heavy to light, vividly colorful to monochromatic, and from highly ordered and formal to rustic, picturesque, and rambling. Each generation looked to its own chapter in Italy's long and varied history of architecture, as Americans were drawn to different moments, types, regions, and formal values. But enthusiasms for specific Italian models generally walked in step chronologically as products of shared international architectural dialogues. They looked intently, for instance, to Palladian villas from about the 1740s to the 1780s, to Tuscan villas in the 1840s and 1850s, to Venetian palaces in the 1860s and 1870s, to Lombard churches at various moments between the 1850s and the 1930s, to medieval hill towns in the 1950s and 1960s, and later to the sleek and vivacious Italian modernism of the 1960s. Different aspects of classical antiquity were recurrent referents, from ethereal Pompeiian decorative schemes (1780s to 1810s) to the imposing marble monumentality of Roman temples and the massive red-brown ruins of the Roman baths (1790s–1810s and 1890s–1930s). And some categories of emulation were less matters of time than of type, so that baroque grandeur was called on at multiple points between the 1840s and 1930s for imposing churches and government buildings.

The recurrent turn to Italy probably owes something at its start to the "grand tour," initially for patrons more than architects, many of whom depended on the circulation of books and prints rather than on actual visits. One could argue that in Western design dialogues, most chapters in Italy's built history already enjoyed a validating cultural familiarity. Italian buildings, new and old, also embodied successive modern critiques—often through the mediation of British, French, and German architects and writers—positing potent challenges to reigning architectural orthodoxies. Issuing from a center of what the West saw as its shared heritage, historic Italian buildings sometimes lay patiently in wait, reminding designers of venerated places whose appeal had been overlooked in contemporary work.

THERE ARE MANY CHAPTERS and subchapters in this fickle American romance with Italian architecture, but one might start here with the earliest of those described above, the hearty embrace by eighteenth-century Americans for house forms rooted in the sixteenth-century work of Andrea Palladio in the Veneto. This was something evident from New England to Georgia in eighteenth-century hous-

Andrea Palladio, architect, Villa Badoer, 1557–1563, Fratta Polesine, Italy. (Photo: Stefano Maruzzo)

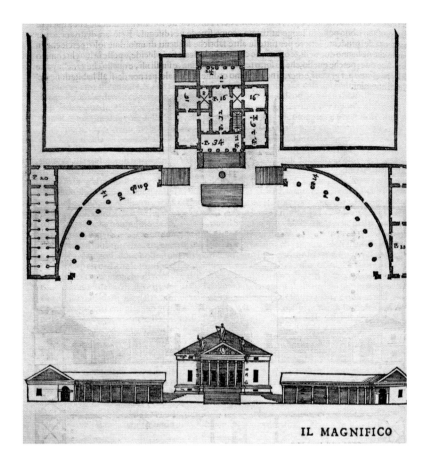

es of large plantation owners, smaller family farmers, and urban merchants alike. In this long design episode, the attraction to Italy came though Britain. By adopting a characteristic set of Palladian forms, culturally and socially ambitious Americans of many stripes projected identities in the same architectural language as a British aristocracy. Philadelphians of means were among those most avidly drawn to this image of adherence to a gentlemanly ideal and image.

For them, Palladio was less a known persona than a book, or rather a series of books that descended from his *Quattro Libri dell'Architettura* (1570). The images and text in his book described ideally defined classical orders, from columns to individual moldings, each profile with a name but, more pointedly, an emphasis on a beauty in proportions even of room sizes and unornamented walls, as one sees in inscribed pairs of dimensions in *piedi* on his plates. His designs addressed two types of homes in the country. One kind was the centerpiece of a working agricultural estate, where utilitarian outbuildings symmetrically framed a house that was a demonstration of purposeful classical self-identification, its central volume capped by a pediment that recalled the forms of ancient roman temples. In the other type, a version of that house at the center, usually rendered at a smaller scale, would be constructed as a villa, standing alone in a natural setting as a retreat, typically near but apart from the city's density.

This book and these house forms engendered a remarkable enthusiasm in Britain from the 1710s into the 1760s, a century and a half after Palladio's conception

ABOVE LEFT: Villa Badoer, plan from Palladio, *Quattro Libri dell'Architettura* (Venice, 1570). (Courtesy of Library of Congress, https://www .loc.gov/item/47044047/)

ABOVE RIGHT: Palladio, *Quattro Libri*, 1570, title page. (Typ 525 70.671, Houghton Library, Harvard University)

of them. There they were embraced by the landed gentry for their country houses and sometimes their suburban villas—most famously that of the champion of this neo-Palladian movement, Richard Boyle, Lord Burlington, who built his villa at Chiswick (1727–1729) on the Thames outside London. The grandest of the English Palladian houses were published in plan and elevation in the first three volumes of a great folio compendium titled *Vitruvius Britannicus* (3 vols., 1715–1725), which adopted the name of the ancient Roman author of the best-known early treatise on architecture. These British houses likewise cultivated this image of high classical culture in the countryside. And despite their great size, in an eighteenth-century context they stood as fundamentally antibaroque, as British visual arguments for a taste based in proportion, restraint, and ultimately an aristocratic class's reasoned claim to social and political authority. They also embodied Enlightenment values that ultimately framed American arguments for independence and democracy.

In what was to become the United States, a land without Britain's long-ordained social order of inherited noble titles tied to massive land holdings, this language was largely adopted as a signal of ambition, translating wealth and classical knowledge into a bid for respectability, social standing, political citizenship, and even leadership. American iterations were found among an aspiring class up and down the Atlantic colonies, shaping country homes such as George Washington's Mount Vernon and Thomas Jefferson's Monticello, those of appointed royal governors such as William Tryon in North Carolina, and the houses of an assembled elite in cities such as Annapolis. These Palladian mansions and villas appeared here at a range of scales, materials, and locations, if always far more modest than the grand stone country house complexes in Britain such as Wanstead House, Stourhead, and Holkham Hall, which dwarfed all American examples. And design models were offered in a flurry of British books, such as *A Book of Architecture* (London, 1728), by James Gibbs, several of which found their way into genteel Philadelphians' early libraries.

In Philadelphia the material for such Palladian houses was typically brick, but nearer the city's periphery that was often the local schist, whose stubborn roughness, tamed with some pains by chisel or applied stucco, could make the emulation of this distant ideal all the more compelling—as in the 1760s riverside expansion of John Bartram's house in present-day southwest Philadelphia, with its grand portico, a strikingly ambitious yet visibly homespun effort to project an imagery of classical conversance and British identity devised out of the local stone, an evocation echoing far from roots in Lord Burlington's London and Palladio's Veneto.

The location of Philadelphia's more literally Palladian houses was generally one of two places: in the verdant suburban periphery, set into the landscape, the proper place for a villa within easy reach of the city; or, more surprisingly, positioned along the elite corridors of the city proper. An early instance of the former was Belmont, built about 1745 by Richard Peters on a hill a few miles northwest of the city and now part of Fairmount Park. Peters had a large city residence near Third Street,

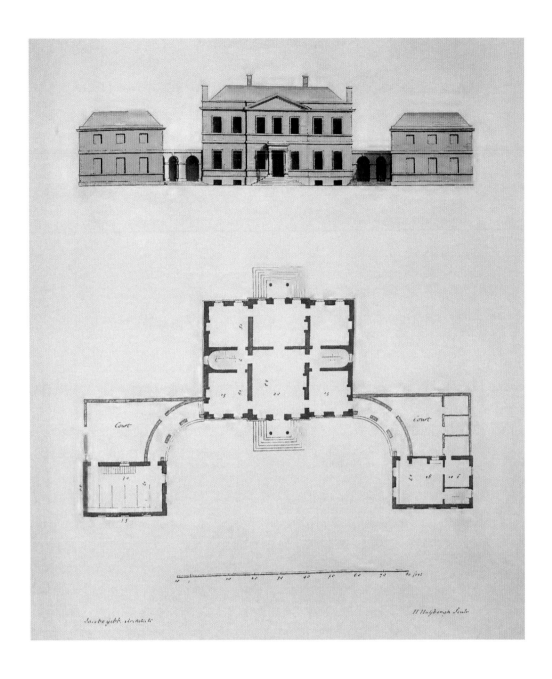

A house for a gentleman in Yorkshire. (From James Gibbs, Book of Architecture [London, 1728], pl. 63)

but Belmont was his place to entertain and retreat in the nearby picturesque countryside, enjoying an enviable prospect over the then-distant city. Several similarly conceived houses also looked over the Schuylkill River, including Mt. Pleasant (1762–1765), built for the wealthy Scottish privateer John McPherson as his visible bid for social standing, while the local champion of the species was Lansdowne (dem.), built in 1773–1777 for Pennsylvania's last colonial governor, John Penn. All unmistakably displayed characteristic elements of their Palladian models.

The other setting, locating such a house in the heart of the city, brought such genteel, cosmopolitan self-projection into far more public corridors of visibility. One who dreamed intently of this was Charles Norris, probably aided by his brother Isaac. Their family papers include plans of a set of related designs, apparently from the early 1750s, that envisioned such a pedimented house flanked by quadrant wings in a frontal perspective. A plan for a larger version of the house

echoed Palladio's concern with symmetry and room proportion within and presented a grand portico at its entrance. Both designs were probably meant for a site set back on a deep lot on Chestnut Street one block east of the Pennsylvania State House (now Independence Hall). As ultimately built there, the Norris house was indeed impressive in its size, symmetry, and situation, but it had not taken the winged, pedimented, distinctly marked Palladian form that Norris had entertained on paper.

A couple of decades later and just two blocks west, though, there was a more richly realized villa design presenting itself on Chestnut Street, in the new front from 1774 added to the older Carpenter-Dickinson house. Here the imprint was striking, and the debt to Palladio and to the British neo-Palladians unmistakable.

More common on city streets than such a five-bay house front was an urban contraction of residential form suited to more typical city lots that were narrow and deep rather than broad. Among the grandest surviving examples is the 1765–1766 house on South Third Street of Charles Stedman (later known as the Samuel Powel house), representing a townhouse version commonly referenced by historians as "two-thirds Georgian." The frontispiece, sometimes with half columns or pilasters supporting an entablature and cornice, marks the

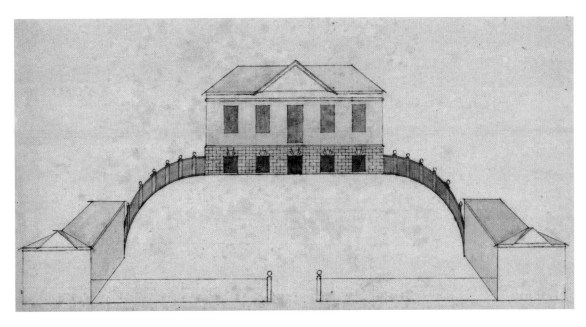

location of an entrance hall along one side of the house that led to parlors on the other. At three or two bays across, these abbreviated the full Georgian five-bay house but could be presented at a range of scales and degrees of interior finish that sometimes matched the larger examples, with room cornices, baseboards, chair rails, mantels, door enframements, and balustrades all ennobled by approved classical profiles.

ABOVE: Palladian perspective, ca. 1750, Norris family papers (Coll. 454). (Image courtesy the Historical Society of Pennsylvania)

Some institutional designs, such as the 1761 vision for the Pennsylvania Hospital and that carried out for Carpenters' Hall (1770–1774), also clearly embraced such models. The latter, the city's most idealized realization of a Palladian vision, was effectively the guildhall and showpiece of the capacities of the city's most sophisticated builders. There one sees the volumetric point symmetry of a Greek cross in a design that descended, ultimately, from Palladio's Villa Rotunda.

The main arteries of Philadelphia's satellite towns offered more scope for fuller domestic embodiments of the Palladian ideal. Some houses, such as Cliveden (1765–1767) and much later Vernon (1803), both set back on large lots along Germantown Road, visibly distinguished themselves by siting and form from the smaller houses and older mansions nearby that fronted immediately on the turnpike.

Dotting a discontinuous arc around the city's periphery were several other pedimented, symmetrical houses that drew from Palladian models, these set off by themselves as small domains among nature and sometimes agriculture, navigating the performative range between the large country seat and the villa. Just northwest of the central part of the city lay one of the earlier and largest examples, Bush Hill (1749–1751), seven bays across and three stories tall, home to the Hamilton family, while to the city's south lay the Wharton family's seven-bay house, Walnut Grove (1747–1750), site of the Meschianza, a notorious 1777 masked ball during the British occupation of the city.

To the northeast of the city were Port Royal (1765–1767), Chalkley Hall (ca. 1770), and Walnut Grove (1777). Further west lay Bellevue in Francisville,

Port Royal, 1765–1767, Frankford, Philadelphia. Northwest view of exterior. (Photograph: Stanley Jones, 1937, Historic American Buildings Survey, HABS PA, 51-PHILA, 5, Library of Congress)

with a similar front, and more Schuylkill villas, including Laurel Hill (1766) and the Thomas Mifflin house (ca. 1778). To the west was the initial, temple-fronted form of the Woodlands from the mid-to-late 1760s (the house was greatly expanded and transformed in Late Georgian/Federal taste in the 1780s). And ambitious farmers also participated; further west stood the Twaddell house, located in a once-rural district since swallowed up in a sea of late nineteenth-century rowhouse development.

One might name a dozen or two more houses that intently adopted this very legible set of forms, inserting classical pediments amid the long entry front of simple side-gabled volumes, taming ad hoc parts into an orchestrated composition, and often marking an axis with a Palladian triple window—almost a badge of membership in a group defined by such self-casting. Houses like these struck notes of consonance that asserted a social kinship, creating disconnected points in a legible landscape of gentility with deep roots in cinquecento Italy, though the antecedents known by most of their owners were probably those in Britain.

This architectural chapter started to draw toward a close beginning in the last decades of the eighteenth century, transformed incrementally by the attenuated proportions, the decorative weightlessness, and the volumetric animation of Adamesque/Federal taste, and it was soon supplanted by other new tides in design. Palladian form became old-fashioned in the eyes of many, especially those of a new generation of neoclassicists led by the first professional architects to practice in the city, including Benjamin Latrobe and his students Robert Mills and William Strickland, who looked to larger geometries in design and associative allusions to a wide range of eclectic forms.

A half century later, another Italian chapter would open, again domestic and again referencing the villa but in other ways completely contrary to Palladian models. The new Italianate villas often proffered intent asymmetries and three-dimensional freedom in place of the frontal, symmetrical address of the Palladian villa, and they often garbed the suburban residential escape of downtown merchants and factory owners in allusions to rambling farmhouses that grew incrementally over generations in the rolling landscape of Tuscany. A new set of models found favor among a new set of architectural consumers.

FURTHER READING

Ackerman, James A. *The Villa: Form and Ideology of Country Houses*. Princeton: Princeton University Press, 1995.

Hague, Stephen. *The Gentleman's House in the British Atlantic World 1680–1780*. New York: Palgrave Macmillan, 2015.

Kornwolf, James D. *Architecture and Town Planning in Colonial North America*. 3 vols. Baltimore: Johns Hopkins University Press, 2002.

O'Gorman, James F., et al. *Drawing toward Building: Philadelphia Architectural Graphics, 1732–1986*. Philadelphia: Pennsylvania Academy of the Fine Arts, 1986.

Peterson, Charles E. "Philadelphia Carpentry According to Palladio." In *Building by the Book*, vol. 3, edited by Mario Di Valmarana, 1–52. Charlottesville: Center for Palladian Studies in America, 1984.

Reinberger, Mark E., and Elizabeth McLean. *The Philadelphia Country House: Architecture and Landscape in Colonial America*. Baltimore: Johns Hopkins University Press, 2015.

Wise, Herbert C., and H. Ferdinand Beidleman. *Colonial Architecture for Those about to Build*. Philadelphia: J. B. Lippincott, 1913. https://archive.org/details/cu31924089418986.

Wittkower, Rudolf. *Palladio and English Palladianism*. London: Thames & Hudson, 1985.

2

Cesare Beccaria's Influence on the Philadelphia Constitutional Convention

WILLIAM B. EWALD

THE INFLUENCE ON THE AMERICAN FOUNDERS of English and Scottish thinkers—John Locke, David Hume, William Blackstone, Algernon Sydney, Sir Edward Coke, Adam Smith, and many others—is well known. So is the influence of such French Enlightenment thinkers as Montesquieu and Jean-Jacques Rousseau. But the Enlightenment was an international phenomenon, and there were also significant (and frequently overlooked) influences on the American founding from the Netherlands, Germany, Switzerland, and especially Italy.

The Italian influences are widespread. Many of the founders had received a solid grounding in Latin and in classical Roman history, and several of them had expanded this linguistic knowledge so that they were able to read Italian as well. Thomas Jefferson, Benjamin Franklin, John Adams, and James Madison all fall into this category, and it is no accident that Jefferson called his home "Monticello."

One of Jefferson's close friends was the Italian physician Philip Mazzei, who settled close to him at Monticello. Mazzei was remarkably well connected and carried out correspondences with George Washington, Franklin, Adams, and Madison. The Neapolitan philosopher and jurist Gaetano Filangieri was admired by Franklin, and they carried out an intellectual correspondence that lasted until Filangieri's death.

The influences are not limited to intellectual matters. The admiration for Italian art and architecture was pervasive, and just outside of Philadelphia, the town of Paoli was named for the Corsican patriot Pasquale Paoli.

But of all the Italian intellectual influences, the most significant by far is that of the criminologist and legal reformer Cesare Beccaria. Beccaria was born in Milan in 1738. Northern Italy was then a part of the Austro-Hungarian Empire, and Beccaria, as a young man, served for a while as an inspector of prisons. He was horrified by what he saw. The criminal law across the Western world in the eighteenth century can only be described as savage. Even petty crimes were treated as capital offenses, there was no proportion between crime and punishment, prisons were a scene of filth and degradation, executions were a common public spectacle, torture was routinely used to extract confessions, and trials were conducted in haste, often in secrecy, and with minimal procedural safeguards. The great historian of the common law, Toby Milson, famously began his chapter on criminal law with the words, "The miserable history of crime in England can be shortly told. Nothing worth-while was created." The same thing was true across Europe.

Beccaria's great project was the reform of the law of crime and punishment. His book, *Dei delitti e delle pene*, appeared in 1764. He was twenty-six years old. It is arguably the greatest single work on criminal law in the history of Western civilization. It made him an international celebrity.

Beccaria sought to put the entire criminal law on a rational foundation. He argued against torture on the ground that it coerced false confessions. He argued that the purpose of the criminal law was not revenge but the deterrence of harm to society and that punishment should be no greater than what was needed to achieve deterrence. This entailed a drastic reduction in the severity of most criminal punishments.

Beccaria was one of the first to argue that laws must be made clear, public, and intelligible to the common people. This led him to endorse the principle of *nulla poena sine lege*—no punishment without a written law—and to argue for an explicit codification of the laws.

Marble statue of Cesare Beccaria by Pompeo Marchesi on the staircase of the Palace of Brera, Milan. Beccaria's contribution to the modern penal system is recognized each year in Philadelphia by the Cesare Beccaria Award, cosponsored by the Criminal Justice Section of the Philadelphia Bar Association and the Justinian Society, a Philadelphian legal organization founded in 1935 and comprising attorneys, judges, and law students of Italian ancestry. (Accademia di Belle Arti di Brera)

Above all, Beccaria argued for a total abolition of the death penalty. In the context of the eighteenth century, this was a drastic proposal, and he was the first major criminal theorist to call for complete abolition. In his view, the goal of deterrence could be adequately satisfied by life in prison. There was no need to take the additional step to capital punishment.

Beccaria's book was an immediate and worldwide success. It was translated into all the major European languages. He was hailed in extravagant terms by the English philosopher Jeremy Bentham and inspired his own lifelong project of reforming the common law of England. Catherine the Great invited him to Russia to reform its system of criminal law. He was celebrated by the philosophes in Paris: Voltaire wrote a preface that appeared in subsequent editions of his work.

It is not surprising, therefore, that Beccaria also had a profound influence on the founders of the American republic. Franklin, Adams, and Madison all studied his work, as did the Philadelphian James Wilson. At the time of the Constitutional Convention, the writings of Beccaria were widely available from Philadelphia booksellers.

His greatest influence, however, was on Jefferson. In 1776, immediately after writing the Declaration of Independence, Jefferson returned to Virginia to undertake the project of revising the state's laws. The aim was to place them on a rational, enlightened, and republican foundation. Jefferson seems at the time to have regarded this project as even more important than the Declaration itself. His chief guide throughout was the writings of Beccaria, whom he cites frequently and in depth—and in Italian.

Beccaria today is little remembered in the United States. But his influence on the formation of the new American legal system was immense, especially in the field of criminal law, where he has no real competitor. We owe to him, and to other thinkers of the Italian Enlightenment, an enormous debt.

Independence Hall, Philadelphia.
(Photo: Giò Martorana)

FURTHER READING

Bessler, John D. *The Birth of American Law: An Italian Philosopher and the American Revolution*. Durham, NC: Carolina Academic, 2014.

Hostettler, John. *Cesare Beccaria: The Genius of 'On Crimes and Punishments'*. Hampshire, UK: Waterside, 2011.

Milsom, S. F. C. *Historical Foundations of the Common Law*. London: Butterworth, 1981.

3

Thomas Jefferson and Joseph Mussi

Enjoying Milanese Life in Philadelphia

Maurizio Valsania

THOMAS JEFFERSON HAD FOND MEMORIES of Paris. He spent five years there, from August 1784 to September 1789, and perfected his personal style. He enhanced his manners and deepened his firsthand experience of the beau monde. On this score, painter Mather Brown gives us a dandy, a young fastidious man conscious of his social status and ready to capitalize on his seductive power.[1]

It was a tad too much, some would say. When William Maclay, a senator from rural Pennsylvania, met Jefferson in May 1790, he was flabbergasted. Jefferson had just returned from Paris, and Maclay was fearful that the years in Europe had mollified the sinews of Jefferson's republicanism: he "sits in a lounging Manner on one hip, commonly, and with one of his shoulders elevated much above the other." Maclay could not make sense of the spectacle of refinement and good manners he was seeing, and the only conclusion he reached was that this dandy Jefferson "had been long enough abroad to catch the tone of European folly."[2]

But Jefferson had not lost his mind. Far from having turned into a fop, a molly, or a skulking aristocrat, Jefferson entered public service right after his return to the American shores—the best part of his political career was yet to come. Appointed Secretary of State on March 22, 1790, Jefferson got into what was perhaps one of the most demanding, roughest, toughest, least satisfying periods of his life. The continuous spats with Alexander Hamilton, then Secretary of the Treasury, put Jefferson in real distress.

Jefferson did not find his position as Secretary of State rewarding, let alone amusing. In early 1792, he tried to quit, but President George Washington convinced him to bear up and to postpone his resolution. In October of that same year, he again met with Washington and voiced openly the frustration that Hamilton kept triggering in him: "I had heard him say that this constitution was a shilly shally thing of mere milk and water, which could not last, and was only good as a step to something better."[3]

Hamilton was no monarchist, but this man put Jefferson on edge like no one else. Washington had to pour into the boiling pot of Jefferson-Hamilton controversy all his patience and sound judgment in order to pacify the two. But the quarrel was not over. In March 1793, Jefferson again announced his intention to resign, and on December 31, 1793, he proclaimed himself out of this political game once and for good: "I now take the liberty of resigning the office into your hands," he wrote to the president.[4]

THE READERS OF THIS ESSAY are about to discover that the last five weeks spent by Thomas Jefferson in Philadelphia, while he did his chore in the Washington administration, were not only frustration and unhappiness. On December 1, 1793, Jefferson again took quarters in the famous Graff House—where he had penned the Declaration of Independence—at the corner of Seventh and Market Streets. The house was now in the hands of an Italian merchant, who had refurbished it. His name was Giuseppe (or Joseph) Mussi. This man was in the unique position to soothe the grieving Jefferson.

A few words about Mussi are now called for. Giuseppe Mussi, from Milan, arrived in Philadelphia sometime around 1784. A smart young man, he emigrated to Pennsylvania both to find better opportunities and to escape the Austro-Hungarian yoke. In 1786, he took the oath of allegiance to the State of Pennsylvania and became citizen.

In Philadelphia, Mussi thrived into a prominent merchant and an important asset for the local community. He imported dry goods, olive oil, and wine from Europe and sold a large assortment of fine and coarse cloths by the package or piece, mostly from Amsterdam. Over the years, he ran shops and managed warehouses in more than one place in the city. He had a business in Chestnut Street near Third Street; by 1795, he relocated to 37 North Water Street in the Upper Delaware Ward—which made Mussi a neighbor of one of the wealthiest men in the nation, the grocer Steven Girard; and by 1825, he moved his activities to 180 Spruce Street. That Mussi was an active member of the community is demonstrated by his generous donation, five pounds and ten shillings, to Old St. Joseph's Church in Willings Alley.[5]

Although not from a noble dynasty, Mussi was not the typical early twentieth-century uprooted, downtrodden migrant either. During the eighteenth century, Italians who migrated to America were few, and most of them decided to cross the Atlantic for reasons other than sheer economic necessity. A distinguished

Mather Brown, 1761–1831. Portrait of Thomas Jefferson, 1786. (Courtesy of the National Portrait Gallery, Smithsonian Institution, Washington. Bequest of Charles Francis Adams; Frame conserved with funds from the Smithsonian Women's Committee. [Public domain] https://commons .wikimedia.org/wiki/File:Mather _Brown_-_Thomas_Jefferson _-_Google_Art_Project.jpg)

cohort of notable Italian migrants can be remembered. Florentine Philipp Mazzei, for example, was an aristocrat and a visionary enthused by the new independent nation, and Giuseppe Ceracchi was already an accomplished, renowned artist. These men kept their association with Italy and Europe alive—they were citizens of the two worlds. Joseph Mussi was this type of citizen as well, and when Jefferson arrived at Seventh and Market he found a cultured and civilized man, much more than what he was bargaining for.[6]

Jefferson's expectations were not very high. Hamilton was a pain in the neck, but, even worse, an epidemic of yellow fever had struck Philadelphia during the previous months. People had died by the thousands, possibly five thousand residents. Jefferson himself had escaped the city and got used to roaming about, going from Germantown to Philadelphia and back, in a general lack of comforts: "Tho becoming less mortal," he had written to his friend James Madison on September 1, the disease "is still spreading, and the heat of the weather is very unpropitious. I have withdrawn my daughter from the city, but am obliged to go to it every day myself."[7]

From September to November, Jefferson had relocated to Germantown. But he had not liked the experience. Cramped with evacuees from Philadelphia, in Germantown there was not a single cot left: "As a great favor," Jefferson wrote to Madison at the beginning of November, "I have got a bed in the corner of the public room of a tavern: and must so continue till some of the Philadelphians make a vacancy by removing into the city." Jefferson resented leasing modest rooms and dining in cheap taverns—Monticello was incomparably fancier. Lacking better options, however, Jefferson's circle could not afford to be picky: "I have got good lodgings for Monroe and yourself," Jefferson wrote again to Madison in mid-November; "that is to say, a good room with a fire place and two beds, in a pleasant and convenient position, with a quiet family. They will breakfast you, but you must mess in a tavern; there is a good one across the street. This is the way in which all must do, and all I think will not be able to get even half beds."[8]

When Jefferson arrived at Mussi's on December 1, he found his dream come true. Mussi had lured him into his "mansion" at the end of November, and Jefferson soon discovered that the Italian was true to his words: "Mr. Crosby having Communicated to me your desire to be accommodated in my house, give me leave to assure you sir that your Coming will afford me great deal of pleasure. My appartements are furnished in the Italian Stile [sic], as you have seen; I have an excellent Cook from Milan, and you Shall have accommodations to your own wishes, both for appartements, and table. I am preparing a good bed for you, and Shall be glad to know when you intend to be here."[9]

Italian furniture, an Italian cook, a good bed, and the prospect of amiable conversation? Jefferson was suddenly reenergized. Hamilton and national politics could have sapped his vigor, but Jefferson took an unexpected plunge into a little Italian world. Unfortunately, Adrien Petit, his trusted French cook, had to board at a nearby tavern and could not exert his culinary virtues. Jefferson was also accompanied by James Hemings, a cook himself and an enslaved man. At Mussi's, Hemings could not do much. He simply beheld the differences and similarities between Italian and French preparations.[10]

Jefferson had long been an Italian, so to speak, intellectually and emotionally. Many aspects of his home, work, and personal tastes had been influenced by Italian culture. He had read into Italian art scholarship and architecture—Palladio being the most striking example and the very template on which he built Monticello. He had taught himself Italian while a student at the College of William and Mary. He had played Italian music with instruments built by Italians.

During his Paris years, Jefferson had had an earlier actual encounter with Italian life, including Milanese life. On February 28, 1787, a forty-four-year-old Jefferson, traveling alone and anonymously, left Paris for a three-month journey to southern France and northern Italy. On April 10, he entered Nice, then in the dominion of Savoy. By April 15, he passed the Col de Tende, went through Limone Piemonte, and slept in Cuneo. On April 16, he was in Centallo, Savigliano, Poirino, and eventually Turin. By April 20, after a short visit to Vercelli, the world capital of rice, he arrived in Milan. Pavia was in his itinerary on April 23, and on May 2 he again crossed the border and returned to France.[11]

Of all the places he visited, Milan seems to have struck Jefferson deeply, for better and for worse. He did not quite get the beauty of the Duomo, for instance—given his neoclassical taste, Gothic architecture was for him tantamount to barbarism. The Duomo was "a worthy object of philosophical contemplation, to be placed among the rarest instances of the misuse of money." But Jefferson appreciated the "houses painted al fresco," Villa Roma, Villa Candiani, and Villa Belgioiosa: "The salon of the casa Belgioiosa is superior to any thing I have seen."[12]

In Milan, he was greeted and shown around by Count Francesco dal Verme, the descendant of one of the most notable families in Italy. This aristocrat had everything that could please Jefferson: he was classy and civilized and yet skilled and interested in science, philosophy, and travels—modern and traditional at once.

Joseph Mussi was not a patrician by any European standard, but he must have reminded Jefferson of Count Dal Verme. Just like Dal Verme, Mussi had connections and belonged to the civilized world. When immediately after the American Revolution Count Luigi Castiglioni—another Milanese aristocrat, chevalier of the Order of St. Stephen, and a member of the Philosophical Society of Philadelphia—undertook his voyage within the United States, he picked Mussi as a travel companion. Mussi was with him during his foray into Bethlehem, some fifty miles north of Philadelphia. Castiglioni eventually proclaimed Mussi an amiable youth, "*un giovane di amabili maniere*."[13]

We cannot know for sure what passed between Jefferson and Mussi during the five weeks spent on Seventh and Market. The Milanese cook must have pampered Jefferson. Jefferson and Mussi must have struck up conversations about Milan, Italy, art, and the beau monde. We do not need any leap of imagination to surmise that Jefferson at some point must have told Mussi about his own Italian trip. Jefferson must have emphasized his *italianità*—his being an Italian. The two must have shared some nightcaps while seating in a "lounging manner on one hip." We can also be certain that going back every night to his temporary Italian home provided Jefferson with a respite from "uncivilized" politics. For a few weeks, he could play the dandy again.

Jefferson left on January 5 and returned to his Italian villa, Monticello. The journey was rather painful and took him almost two weeks to complete. As soon as he was in a position to resume his letter writing, Jefferson assured his friends that this time he was done with politics. Before leaving Philadelphia, Jefferson had paid Mussi "5. weeks board 75 D[ollars]." He also paid him for vinegar, fifty slabs of marble, and, of course, wine.[14]

Joseph Mussi to James Madison, June 9, 1794.
(Library of Congress, Manuscript Division, James Madison Papers. Retrieved from the Library of Congress, https://www.loc.gov /item/mjm013089/)

The two remained on friendly terms. Writing to James Madison in June 1794, for example, Mussi pressed him to give "my best Compliments to Mr. Jefferson." Jefferson, in turn, kept relying on him: "It will not be long," he wrote Mussi in September, "before I may trouble you with a request of a supply of groceries similar to the last. . . . Your repeated offers of your kind services, I receive with many thanks, and with the continuance of your permission I will avail myself of them from time to time."[15]

Jefferson did actually avail himself of Mussi. Tea, clover seeds, olive oil, and groceries in general ran unhampered from Philadelphia to Monticello during the three peaceful years Jefferson stayed at Monticello, from January 1794 to the end of 1796.

NOTES

1. See William Howard Adams, *The Paris Years of Thomas Jefferson* (New Haven, CT: Yale University Press, 2000).

2. William Maclay, *Journal of William Maclay, United States Senator from Pennsylvania, 1789–1791*, ed. Edgar S. Maclay (New York, 1890), 272.

3. Thomas Jefferson, "Notes of a Conversation with George Washington, 1 October 1792," *The Papers of Thomas Jefferson Digital Edition*, ed. James P. McClure and J. Jefferson Looney (Charlottesville: University of Virginia Press, 2008–2018), http://rotunda.upress.virginia .edu/founders/TSJN-01-24-02-0393, accessed January 29, 2018.

4. Thomas Jefferson to George Washington, December 31, 1793, *The Papers of Thomas Jefferson Digital Edition*, http://rotunda.upress.virginia.edu/founders/TSJN-01-27-02-0584, accessed January 29, 2018.

5. For further information, see Richard Juliani, *Building Little Italy: Philadelphia Italians before Mass Migration* (University Park: Pennsylvania State University Press, 1998), 29–30. Mussi died in 1832 without immediate heirs.

6. In the 1790s, New York and Philadelphia, the two largest cities in America, with populations of 33,000 and 28,500 inhabitants, hosted a handful of Italian immigrants—about twenty in New York and fewer than ten in Philadelphia. See Howard R. Marraro, "Italo-Americans in Pennsylvania in the Eighteenth Century," *Pennsylvania History: A Journal of Mid-Atlantic Studies* 7 (1940): 159–166.

7. Thomas Jefferson to James Madison, September 1, 1793, *The Papers of Thomas Jefferson Digital Edition*, http://rotunda.upress.virginia.edu/founders/TSJN-01-27-02-0005, accessed January 29, 2018. On the yellow fever, see Jim Murphy, *An American Plague: The True and Terrifying Story of the Yellow Fever Epidemic of 1793* (New York: Clarion Books, 2003); Michael Oldstone, *Viruses, Plagues and History* (New York: Oxford University Press, 1998).

8. Thomas Jefferson to James Madison, November 2, 1793, and Thomas Jefferson to James Madison, November 17, 1793, *The Papers of Thomas Jefferson Digital Edition*, http://rotunda.upress.virginia.edu/founders/TSJN-01-27-02-0263, accessed January 29, 2018.

9. Joseph Mussi to Thomas Jefferson, November 28, 1793, *The Papers of Thomas Jefferson Digital Edition*, http://rotunda.upress.virginia.edu/founders/TSJN-01-27-02-0420, accessed January 29, 2018.

10. On Jefferson, Hemings, and Petit at Mussi's, see Annette Gordon-Reed, *The Hemingses of Monticello: An American Family* (New York: W. W. Norton, 2008), 496.

11. For Jefferson's unabridged itinerary, see "Journey through France and Italy (1787)," *Thomas Jefferson Encyclopedia*, https://www.monticello.org/site/research-and-collections/journey-through-france-and-italy-1787, accessed December 4, 2020. See also Thomas Jefferson, "Notes of a Tour into the Southern Parts of France, &c., 3 March–10 June 1787," *The Papers of Thomas Jefferson Digital Edition*, http://rotunda.upress.virginia.edu/founders/TSJN-01-11-02-0389, accessed January 29, 2018; George Green Shackelford, *Thomas Jefferson's Travels in Europe, 1784–1789* (Baltimore: Johns Hopkins University Press, 1995).

12. On the Duomo, see Thomas Jefferson, "Memorandum Books, 1787," *The Papers of Thomas Jefferson Digital Edition*, http://rotunda.upress.virginia.edu/founders/TSJN-02-01-02-0021, accessed December 4, 2020. On the Casa Belgioioso, see Thomas Jefferson, "Notes of a Tour into the Southern Parts of France, &c., 3 March–10 June 1787, 21–22 April, Milan," *The Papers of Thomas Jefferson Digital Edition*, http://rotunda.upress.virginia.edu/founders/TSJN-01-11-02-0389, accessed January 30, 2018.

13. Luigi Castiglioni, *Viaggio negli Stati Uniti dell'America settentrionale* (Milan, 1790), 2:4.

14. Thomas Jefferson, "Memorandum Books, 1794," *The Papers of Thomas Jefferson Digital Edition*, http://rotunda.upress.virginia.edu/founders/TSJN-02-02-02-0004, accessed January 30, 2018.

15. Joseph Mussi to James Madison, June 9, 1794, *The Papers of James Madison Digital Edition*, ed. J. C. A. Stagg (Charlottesville: University of Virginia Press, 2010), http://rotunda.upress.virginia.edu/founders/JSMN-01-15-02-0253, accessed January 30, 2018; Thomas Jefferson to Joseph Mussi, September 17, 1794, *The Papers of Thomas Jefferson Digital Edition*, http://rotunda.upress.virginia.edu/founders/TSJN-01-28-02-0113, accessed January 30, 2018.

Second page of a note written by Mr. Burke, the Philadelphia stonemason who in 1907 (twenty-five years after Giuseppe Garibaldi's death) was trying to figure out what to do with the tombstone of Giuseppe Garibaldi's older brother, Angelo Garibaldi, which he had removed from St. John the Evangelist Church after the disastrous fire of 1899. As advised by Father O'Reilly (the church rector), Mr. Burke had not returned the tombstone, since Angelo Garibaldi's remains had already been repatriated. The rector had also informed Mr. Burke that Angelo Garibaldi was indeed the brother of "the revolutionary Joseph Garibaldi." In the second page of the note, Mr. Burke describes the tombstone, which had on its front the profile of Angelo Garibaldi with the following Latin inscription:

**ANGELO GARIBALDI
HIC JACET OSA [SIC] S/B OSSA
AMICI LUGETTI**

Eventually the tombstone was sent to the Museum of the Archdiocese of Philadelphia, where in the late 1930s it was lost. (Image used with permission of the Catholic Historical Research Center of the Archdiocese of Philadelphia, MC 8: Martin I.J. Griffin Papers)

GARIBALDI'S "AMERICAN BROTHER" AND PIEDMONTESE CONSUL

The Philadelphia Story of Angelo Garibaldi

SALVATORE MANGIONE

BORN ON THE FOURTH OF JULY, Giuseppe Garibaldi quite aptly dedicated his life to fighting for freedom on two continents. In the process, he became a sort of pop star even before *pop* became a word. When he visited London in 1864, for example, half a million enthusiastic people filled the squares just for the pleasure of welcoming him. "Garibaldi is like no one else," wrote Georges Sand in 1859. A century later, A. J. P. Taylor called him "the only wholly admirable figure in modern history." Yet what is less known about Garibaldi is his connection with the United States. This encompassed a stint as an immigrant in the early 1850s (living in Staten Island with Antonio Meucci, the true inventor of the telephone[1]); a commission by Lincoln at the height of the American Civil War (Garibaldi declined since he first wanted Lincoln to emancipate the slaves); and the tragic story of Angelo, his "American brother." According to Giuseppe's *Memoirs*, this brother was the inspiration behind Garibaldi's love for Italian literature and history. Angelo may even have been the inspiration behind some of Garibaldi's idealism, since he was an outspoken critic of the slavery he had encountered in the United States.

Three years older than Giuseppe, Angelo had moved to America in 1825, when at the age of twenty-one he came to work as an assistant to the Consul of the Kingdom of Sardinia. Within seven years, he settled in Philadelphia and became Consul himself. Then a bout of cholera in 1834, malaria in early 1835, and a serious shortage of funds caused by delayed payments of his salary forced him to request repatriation. Unfortunately, funds arrived too late, and Angelo passed away. The events surrounding his death actually present us with the touching story of one Italian expatriate lovingly trying to help another. In fact, the Neapolitan Domenico Morelli de Curtis, Consul of the Kingdom of the Two Sicilies, not only tried to nurse his sickly northern compatriot back to health but also provided Garibaldi with the Philadelphia home where Angelo eventually died of an "apoplesia [*sic*] di sangue" in November 1835. He was only thirty-one years old.

They buried him in center city Philadelphia, in the Catholic Church of Saint John Evangelist on Thirteenth and Chestnut. Yet it is likely that his 1835 death might have had even wider repercussions. Angelo and Giuseppe (twenty-eight years old at the time) were very close. When the younger Garibaldi fled Italy in 1835 under a death warrant, his brother's illness may have prompted him to choose South America rather than the United States. It was indeed in Rio where Giuseppe began his ascent as "Hero of the Two Worlds," and the rest, as they say, is history.

NOTE

1. Antonio Meucci's contributions to the invention of the telephone were recognized by the U.S. Congress with Resolution 269 of June 11, 2002. Still, the issue remains controversial. For more information on this fascinating piece of Americana, see Suzanne Deffree, "Meucci Acknowledged as Telephone Inventor, June 11, 2002," *EDN*, June 11, 2019, https://www.edn .com/meucci-acknowledged-as-telephone-inventor-june-11-2002/.

The Church of St. John the Evangelist as it appeared when Angelo Garibaldi was still buried there. The church had been consecrated as the Catholic Cathedral of Philadelphia just three years before Angelo Garibaldi's death. Over the span of almost two centuries, St. John would see the first American performance of Mozart's *Requiem Mass* (1834), provide first communion and confirmation for St. Katharine Drexel, and be the home for St. John Neumann as the fourth Bishop of Philadelphia. In February 1899, the old church of St. John was completely destroyed by a fire; it was subsequently rebuilt over a period of several years. (Image used with permission of the Catholic Historical Research Center of the Archdiocese of Philadelphia, MC 8: Martin I.J. Griffin Papers)

4

Rome, Italian Émigrés, and Jesuit Education in Nineteenth-Century Philadelphia

Carmen R. Croce

> I do not like the late resurrection of the Jesuits. . . . Shall we not have swarms of them here, in as many shapes and disguises as ever a king of the gypsies . . . himself assumed?
>
> In the shape of printers, editors, writers, schoolmasters, etc.? . . . If ever any congregation of men could merit eternal perdition on earth and in hell, . . . it is this company of Loyola.
>
> Our system, however, of religious liberty must afford them an asylum.
>
> —John Adams to Thomas Jefferson,
> from Quincy to Monticello, May 6, 1816

ADAPTING ALL THINGS TO "THE CIRCUMSTANCES OF PERSONS, TIMES, AND PLACES"

THAT WISE ADVICE FROM St. Ignatius Loyola (founder of the Society of Jesus) served Jesuit missionaries well wherever their ministries took them. It must have been particularly helpful to those Europeans, reluctant missionaries, exiled from their homelands in the wave of revolutions that swept the continent in the nineteenth century. What passed for religious liberty in eighteenth-century America was, at best, toleration, but even that was a godsend compared to the virulent anticlericalism experienced by the clergy in Europe. Adapting to "the circumstances of persons, times, and places" required mediating between cultures, embracing secular culture, and engaging the non-European other—all standard features of the Jesuit worldview and particularly useful with the indigenous peoples of the American West. This dual engagement with Roman and secular culture at every level was unique to the Jesuit Order and supplied a welcome corrective to American provincialism.

In 1733, Jesuit pioneers from the Maryland Mission of the Society of Jesus's English Province established St. Joseph's, Philadelphia's first Catholic church, just two blocks from Independence Hall. This "Popish" or "Roman chapel," as it was called, was built in the shadow of a Quaker Almshouse for protection. Disguised as a private residence and surmounted by a chimney instead of a cross, the chapel was carefully hidden from the street. Its third iteration, built on the same site in 1839, was "a church as carefully hidden away as a martyr's tomb in the catacombs," according to Agnes Repplier, grande dame of Philadelphia letters; this church continues to this day to bear witness to less tolerant times in America and to justify Repplier's apt simile. It was on this site that Saint Joseph's College undertook to adapt the plan of studies common to Jesuit colleges throughout the world to the culture and circumstances of the colonial city of Philadelphia.

ROME AND THE NEW REPUBLIC IN 1789

Given John Adams's hyperbolic fear of Jesuits and his assertion that Catholics were "rare as earthquakes in America," irony delights in events of the year 1789, for at that moment in history when the Constitution of the United States was effected and George Washington was elected president of the nation, the institutional Catholic Church was formed in America with the erection of the diocese of Baltimore and the appointment of John Carroll as the nation's first bishop.

That same year, Carroll established Georgetown Academy, which became the first Catholic university in America. John (Giovanni Antonio) Grassi, S.J., among the first Italian Jesuits to emigrate to America, was appointed ninth president of Georgetown and superior of all Jesuits in the United States within two years of his arrival here in 1810. Thus, Grassi became America's first Italian-born college president. The cosmopolitan Grassi provided an ideal link between town and gown in President James Madison's Washington.[1] Upon his return to Italy a few years later, Grassi was assigned to the Propaganda Fide, enabling him to mold events in America from the Vatican and to foster mutual understanding.

A LINKED NETWORK OF JESUIT COLLEGES IN THE EASTERN UNITED STATES

By 1852, the Jesuits of the Maryland Province (in 1833 the Maryland Mission was elevated to a province) had established a network of six colleges on the East Coast in what Emmett Curran has called "a highly centripetal intellectual endeavor." Among these were Holy Cross (1843), Saint Joseph's (1851), and Loyola in Baltimore (1852), with Georgetown (1789), the oldest and most prestigious at the center, an aggregate that elevated these institutions beyond local enterprises.[2] Jesuit leadership and faculty were shared among the colleges and parishes of the province. An educational tradition and curriculum common to all Jesuit universities at the time allowed Georgetown to award degrees to students at Holy Cross in 1849 and Saint Joseph's in 1860 in response to difficulties at those institutions. But corporate strength was no antidote to the vexing shortage of qualified Jesuit faculty, for there were fewer than forty Jesuits in America in 1848.

ITALIAN INFLUENCE ON JESUIT INSTITUTIONS

Successful integration of Italian Jesuits such as John Grassi in the period preceding the Risorgimento emboldened others to seek asylum in America when Italy began expelling priests of the religious orders. Indeed, the revolutions that erupted throughout the continent and so traumatized the European Church in 1848 were a godsend to the Jesuit educational enterprise in America.

The arrival of Jesuit exiles from Rome was especially propitious for Georgetown, for its faculty was immediately strengthened by the arrival of so many eminent scholars. The famous astronomer Francesco De Vico, S.J., arrived that year armed with letters of introduction from the U.S. ambassador to England. De Vico, along with other priests and seminarians who had taken asylum in England, were warmly greeted upon their arrival in Washington by President James K. Polk and Georgetown president James Ryder, S.J. De Vico was offered the directorship of the college observatory.[3]

El modo de Roma reflected to some extent the ancient ideal, classical and Christian, of Rome as exemplary center. In this context, the center was Jesuit Rome, not the Rome of classical antiquity or of the papal curia. As early as 1548, "Ignatius Loyola urged that young Jesuits be sent to Rome that they might better learn the Institute of the Society and its style of life, and when he founded the Collegio Romano in 1551, he wanted it to be the 'form and exemplar' for other colleges of the Society."[4]

In a nod to Ignatius, the Maryland Province sent five of its most promising American seminarians to study in Rome in 1820. James Ryder, the most brilliant of this cohort, returned to Georgetown as an ordained priest nine years later inspired to shape American Jesuit institutions in the image of their European forebears. By 1839, Ryder had rebuilt St. Joseph's Church in Philadelphia in advance of the eponymous college, a necessary link in the network of eastern Jesuit colleges centered on Georgetown. Six years later, as provincial, Ryder set off for Italy in search of Italian Jesuits to staff his colleges and parishes in the East.

Angelo Paresce, S.J., and the four hundred other Jesuits who fled to America from Italy during the Risorgimento accepted the normative stature of Rome and were determined to imprint its traditions wherever they went. And so, serving as "Brokers of Culture," in historian Gerald McKevitt's expression, the emigres consistently advanced a "supranational form of Catholicism among the populations they served.... Wherever they went, the Church was more Roman when they left."[5]

While the architectural splendors of the style known as "Jesuit baroque" were neither transferable nor appropriate to the new American republic, the Jesuit churches of Rome were often quoted in the style and program of decoration of Jesuit churches and early collegiate structures here, especially after the arrival of the Europeans. Rome's Church of the Gesù and the Roman College (now the Pontifical Gregorian University), founded by Ignatius Loyola in 1551, "that great and blessed Roman nursery," were *sine qua non* in this regard.

Not merely quoted but sacrosanct was the *Ratio Studiorum*, the Jesuit educational plan of studies common to all Jesuit schools since the founding of their first college at Messina in 1548 and further developed for the Roman College. A seven-year course rooted in Renaissance humanism that regulated Jesuit colleges worldwide, the *Ratio* provided uniformity of cultural context and norms with emphasis on Latin and Greek and the works of classical authors, especially Cicero and Virgil. The *Ratio* continued to structure Jesuit education in America until the early years of the twentieth century, when conformity to national norms mandated more varied and vocational programs of study.

All religious orders of men and women celebrated saints of their particular orders and devotions associated with them. While the Jesuits are perhaps best known for advancing the cults of the saints of the Society of Jesus, St. Ignatius Loyola, St. Francis Xavier, and St. Aloysius Gonzaga, among others, their contribution to Catholic culture was far more strategic. Indeed, ultramontane pieties advanced by Italian Jesuits sought to integrate Americans into a single Catholic culture that transcended national boundaries. In the process of standardizing devotional life, they promoted Italian pieties, which one scholar has compared to other forms as "more indulgent, occasionally more superficial but also more human and popular."[6]

The Italian Jesuits' efforts were ably reinforced by Francis Kenrick, third bishop of Philadelphia (1842–1851). Kenrick was a strict liturgist who required priests to wear the Roman frock coat, began the insistence on the title *father* for the clergy, replaced the popular "English ritual" with the "Roman ritual," and standardized devotions on the Roman model.[7] By 1851, Bishop Kenrick had gone far toward providing Philadelphia the "Church of Laws, not of men." It was, however, a Roman church, not an American, Irish, or German one.

"God alone can repay the province of Naples for all it has done for Maryland"— this effusive statement was made by Joseph Keller, S.J., provincial of the Maryland Province, in 1872 and refers to the contribution of the Neapolitan Jesuit émigrés to elevate Georgetown College and to found Woodstock College, Maryland, a national seminary for the cultivation of Jesuit priests. Of all the reforms introduced by the Italians, the restructuring of clerical education at Woodstock was their crowning achievement. Americans were able to pursue the same course of studies that was standard in Europe, thus pulling them into the intellectual orbit of the Catholic Church and the Society of Jesus worldwide.[8] By the 1890s, Woodstock emerged as the intellectual center of American Catholic ultramontanism that privileged papal authority over all other religious and temporal authorities.[9]

Having outgrown the site of its founding in Willing's Alley just a few blocks from Independence Hall, Saint Joseph's suffered the vicissitudes of twenty years of construction on its imposing new campus just north of Philadelphia's City Hall. All the Italian émigrés who came to Philadelphia served at Saint Joseph's in those transitional decades: by 1889, only Charles Cicaterri, S.J., remained to celebrate the reemergence of Saint Joseph's College from its long sleep.

"Jesuit colleges must always have a church attached to them . . . we have the Roman College with a church; professed houses like the Gesù in Rome with a church, and so elsewhere," wrote Burchard Villiger, S.J., rector of Saint Joseph's in 1871.[10] Villiger's determination to build a Jesuit church in Philadelphia equal in scale to the Roman Gesù delayed the reopening of the college by a full decade or more, so extravagant were the costs. His journal compares both edifices in various dimensions of length, width, and height and finds that his Philadelphia prototype excelled in volume if not in richness of decoration. Reputed to be the tallest structure in Philadelphia before the construction of City Hall tower, the exterior of the Philadelphia Gesù was said to be "Roman" in style, but it is not an exact replica of the Roman Gesù.

The interior is magnificent with its cavernous unobstructed nave, said at the time to be the largest in the United States. The program of decoration is unmistakably Italian, a style that mandated multiple named altars and the importing from Italy of numerous relics of saints. In the early Christian era, reverence was shown

Interior of the Church of the Gesù, Philadelphia, ca. 1900. (Saint Joseph's University Archives)

to martyrs to the faith by constructing altars over their graves. Thus, altar and tomb were joined based on faith in the resurrection of the body and the intercessory power of martyred saints.

Villiger's projects were always marked by triumphalist zeal, and it follows that his Church of the Gesù would be richly endowed with altars, relics, and sacred art. These were the attributes that conferred status on European churches, and he was determined to mold his Jesuit church and college in Philadelphia according to its European antecedents. From 1876 to 1891, Villiger amassed hundreds of relics with the help of Benedict Sestini, S.J., director of Georgetown's observatory, and Carlo Piccirillo, S.J., of Woodstock College. The acquisition is described by Villiger in his notebook: "Received from Rome where they had been venerated for more than 120 years in a chapel of a noble family, who being reduced to poverty, were obliged to sell their palace and chapel treasurers." The pride of this collection was the wax effigies of bodies of three early Christian martyrs encased and exposed under three of the Gesù's thirteen altars, the relics of these saints being either embedded in the waxen bodies or enclosed in adjacent reliquaries.

Pietro Folci, S.J., 1822–1890. (Saint Joseph's University Archives)

Saint Joseph's Church, Prep, and College benefited pastorally and academically from the ten Italian émigrés who served there between 1852 and 1895, especially Peter M. Folchi, S.J.; Charles Cicaterri, S.J.; Francis Xavier Di Maria, S.J.; and Joseph M. Ardia, S.J. The accomplishments of six of the Saint Joseph's Ten have been lost in the churn of history because they ministered in the shadow of these four extraordinary émigrés to the Maryland Province.

First among these was Fr. Peter Folchi, born in Rome and assigned to Saint Joseph's as dean of studies in 1852. In Folchi's first year, he turned a section of the college building into a museum of science and natural history, founded the college Literary Circle, held the first religious services for the city's Italian Catholic community, and advertised and organized, with Cosimo Antonio Della Nave, S.J., a meeting with the Italians to plan a new church, founded that year as the Church of St. Mary Magdalen de Pazzi, the first Italian national parish in America. Folchi's advertisement in the parish bulletin that "two Italian ladies are available for singing lessons two nights a week" indicates his abiding interest and outreach to the Italian community in matters large and small.

A typical Jesuit college was beginning to take shape in Philadelphia: "Jesuit schools in Europe were often at the center of the culture of the towns and cities where they were located: typically, they would produce several plays or even ballets per year, and some maintained important astronomical observatories."[11] And so it

Interior of Old Saint Joseph's Church, Philadelphia. (Saint Joseph's University Archives)

was with Saint Joseph's through Folchi's Literary Circle and Philomelian Society. Both societies took their first bows to the public in 1853 with a concert and exhibition at Philadelphia's Sansom Street Hall. That evening saw the performance of the first song composed by the students and set to music by Pasquale Rondinella, the well-known vocal teacher and composer hired by Folchi as the college's first professor of music. Folchi's enthusiasm for Italian culture extended to the new college chapel: "While the Jesuits furnished the sacred oratory, Folchi provided the music, and Sunday after Sunday, the choir echoed with the voices of Madame Marietta Gazzaniga, Signor Pasquale Brignoli, and Signor Alessandro Amodio and other distinguished singers of the Italian opera then fulfilling engagements in the inaugural season of the [Philadelphia] Academy of Music."[12]

Charles Cicaterri, educated at the Roman College, served for nearly twenty years in various roles at Old St. Joseph's, the college, and the Church of the Gesù, including spiritual director and admonitor to successive Jesuit rectors. Bishop Wood's confidence in Cicaterri was apparent in 1868 when he named him temporary rector of the Church of St. Mary Magdalen de Pazzi in response to a conflict between the bishop and that Italian national parish. Cicaterri spent the rest of his life at Saint Joseph's, where his last assignment was chaplain of St. Joseph's Hospital, founded within steps of the college and the Church of the Gesù.

Fr. Di Maria was the other Italian émigré to minister at Saint Joseph's until the end of his life. Born in Caserta and educated at the Jesuit college at Naples, Di Maria emigrated to America in 1841 and taught at other Jesuit colleges before arriving in Philadelphia in 1861. He spent his last decade in pastoral ministry at Old St. Joseph's Church and the college. He continued the ministry to the African American community begun by Thomas Lilly, S.J. Parish sacramental records provide details of many conversions and baptisms among that community before the founding, in 1886, of the Church of St. Peter Claver, the first Roman Catholic parish for the black community in Philadelphia.

A Neapolitan of noble birth, Fr. Ardia was educated at the Roman College before emigrating to America in 1848. Ardia served at Saint Joseph's for twenty-six years. As rector for half of those years, Ardia became close friends with investment banker, Francis A. Drexel, who had been baptized in 1824 and married in 1860 at Old St. Joseph's. From his office nearby, Drexel often stopped by St. Joseph's to play the church organ in the afternoon. Later, his daughter, Katherine, canonized St. Katherine Drexel in 2000, taught catechism to African American youngsters in the parish hall, a ministry that also animated the activities of Frs. Ardia and Romano.

Upon Drexel's death in 1885, Saint Joseph's College received $72,000 from his estate; Old St. Joseph's Church received an equal amount. Ardia's name was

Filippo Costaggini, 1839–1904, *The Exaltation of St. Joseph into Heaven*, oil on canvas, 1886, Old St. Joseph's Church. (Saint Joseph's University Archives)

Joseph M. Ardia, S.J., 1816–1907, oil on canvas, Old St. Joseph's Church.
(Saint Joseph's University Archives)

mentioned in Drexel's will in connection with both these bequests. Ardia passed the college's bequest on to Villiger, who used it to complete construction of the new campus and Church of the Gesù. Part of the bequest to Old St. Joseph's was used to enhance the church interior, including the commission to Filippo Costaggini for his painting *The Exaltation of St. Joseph into Heaven*. But the bulk of the money, perhaps as much as $50,000, was used as a revolving loan fund for colleges of the New York–Maryland Province over a fifty-year period when the expansion of American Catholic higher education was a major preoccupation of the Society of Jesus.[13]

The end of the Ardia pastorate in 1886 marked the beginning of the end of a difficult and uncertain era at Saint Joseph's. The completion of the expansive new campus and the Church of the Gesù was assured, as was the reopening of the college. All of the Italian émigrés, except Fr. Cicaterri, had either returned to Italy or moved on to other ministries. They were replaced throughout the East by Jesuits of Irish descent. After Ardia, more than one hundred years would pass before another Italian Jesuit would succeed to the pastorate at Old St. Joseph's.

CONCLUSION

And so, the Italian Jesuits came to America, four hundred strong, most with a profound appreciation for the American ideals of liberty but with concerns about reconciling that liberty with the interests of the Roman Catholic Church. English, French, and German clergy had been here before them, and the Irish would come after, but the contributions of the Italian émigrés to the church in America and to American secondary and higher education were totally disproportionate to their numbers and time in this country. "Within a decade of their arrival in 1848, Europeans had already transformed American Jesuit life."[14]

They came as if in fulfillment of John Adams's dire prediction to Thomas Jefferson that "swarms" of Jesuits would arrive "in the shape of printers, editors, writers, and schoolmasters." But the Jesuits didn't undermine American liberty; they strengthened it by testing its limits, nudging it forward, and educating its immigrant classes, for with the Jesuits came libraries, scientific instruments, and an appreciation of art, science, music, theater, and culture—the very treasures that distinguished Philadelphia in the colonial era. Thus, the city's three Jesuit institutions—Old St. Joseph's Church, St. Joseph's Prep, and Saint Joseph's University—reflect their Roman Catholic and Jesuit heritage as well as the ethos and culture of the city of Philadelphia.

Lessons learned in Philadelphia, Washington, Maryland, and Boston served the Italian Jesuits well as they moved on to the American West, where a significant network of schools supported by the Piedmontese and Neapolitan Provinces was established throughout the California, New Mexico, and Rocky Mountain Missions. The Italians codified Native American languages and published grammars. Jesuits who had learned the craft of printing at Woodstock College established mission presses that printed the first Spanish-language books in America and used them in classroom instruction. Most notably, the Italians founded numerous prep schools and five colleges in the West—Santa Clara and San Francisco in California, Gonzaga and Seattle in Washington, and Regis in Denver. Eventually, twenty-one of the Italians became presidents of American colleges, most of them in the West.

But the benefits were to flow in both directions, for in John O'Malley's phrasing, "We cannot presume that the ship sails through the sea of history without being touched by it. Just as Jesuits sought to transform the identity of others through their missionary work, Jesuit identities were themselves sometimes deeply affected by those encounters." The Italian Jesuits' sojourn in America shaped Vatican opinion about the American church and the challenge of American exceptionalism, in ways it could not otherwise have done.

NOTES

1. Robert Emmett Curran, S.J., *The Bicentennial History of Georgetown University: From Academy to University, 1789–1889*, vol. 1 (Washington, DC: Georgetown University Press, 1993), 70.

2. Ibid., 130.

3. Gerald McKevitt, S.J., *Brokers of Culture: Italian Jesuits in the American West, 1848–1919* (Stanford: Stanford University Press, 2007), 44.

4. John W. O'Malley, S.J., *The First Jesuits* (Cambridge, MA: Harvard University Press, 1993), 340–341.

5. McKevitt, *Brokers of Culture*, 259.

6. Ibid., 192.

7. Dale B. Light, *Rome and the New Republic* (Notre Dame, IN: University of Notre Dame Press, 1996), 270.

8. McKevitt, *Brokers of Culture*, 75.

9. Gerald L. McKevitt, "Italian Jesuits in Maryland: A Clash of Theological Cultures," *Studies in the Spirituality of Jesuits* 39, no. 1 (2007): 45.

10. Francis X. Talbot, S.J., *Jesuit Education in Philadelphia: Saint Joseph's College, 1851–1926* (Philadelphia: Saint Joseph's College, 1927), 78.

11. John W. O'Malley, S.J., "Introduction," in *Ratio Studiorum: Jesuit Education, 1540–1773*, ed. John Atteberry and John Russell, exh. cat. (Chestnut Hill, MA: John J. Burns Library, Boston College, 1999), 10.

12. "Saint Joseph's College: Souvenir of Golden Jubilee," November 1901, Philadelphia, unpaginated booklet.

13. Financial records of Old St. Joseph's Church in the Archives of Saint Joseph's University.

14. Gerald L. McKevitt, "Italian Jesuits in Maryland," 23.

5

Artists of the Capitol in Philadelphia

Barbara A. Wolanin

MANY PHILADELPHIANS do not know that their city contains murals by artists who also painted in the United States Capitol. Constantino Brumidi (1805–1880), who had worked for Popes and decorated palaces and a theater with murals, was considered one of the best painters in Rome. He was enticed to come to America to paint altarpieces and murals in the churches and cathedrals being constructed to serve the growing number of Catholics. He emigrated in 1852 after being released from prison for his role in the Republican Revolution, and he immediately applied for American citizenship. In 1855 he painted his first fresco in the new House wing of the Capitol, gaining a place on the payroll and the charge to embellish rooms and corridors with murals in the classical and Renaissance traditions he had mastered in Rome. His monumental Capitol frescoes are the almost five-thousand-square foot *The Apotheosis of Washington*, 180 feet above the floor in the eye of the dome, painted in 1865; and the *Frieze of American History*, painted to resemble carved stone, encircling the base of the new cast-iron dome. The frieze was carried on from his designs after Brumidi's death by a younger Roman artist he recommended, Filippo Costaggini (1837–1904). Brumidi also created paintings and murals for churches on the East Coast in Washington, Baltimore, New York, and Philadelphia.[1]

In Philadelphia, he was commissioned by Bishop James Frederic Wood, in charge of construction from 1857, to create murals for the enormous Cathedral Basilica of Saints Peter and Paul. The cathedral was designed by Napoleon LeBrun in 1846 and finally dedicated in 1864 despite disruptions caused by the Civil War.[2] Wood had studied in Rome for seven years and could have met Brumidi there and fully understood the technique and value of true fresco.

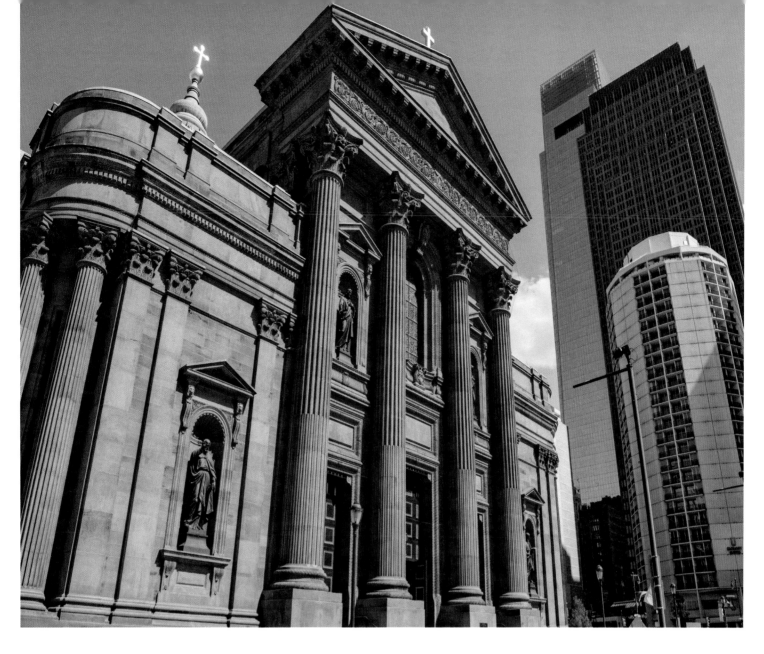

Cathedral Basilica of Saints Peter and Paul (1864), designed by Napoleon LeBrun in 1846. The facade is inspired by Italian models such as the church Santi Ambrogio e Carlo Borromeo dei Lombardi al Corso at Rome, the Madonna di Carignano at Genoa, and San Andrea at Mantua. (Photo: Giò Martorana)

Interior of the Cathedral Basilica of Saints Peter and Paul. Behind the altar, Constantino Brumidi painted the Crucifixion under a lunette of God the Father and the dove of the Holy Spirit, flanked by illusionistic statues of saints. The frescoes were destroyed when the church was enlarged. (Catholic Historical Research Center of the Archdiocese of Philadelphia)

The dome of the Cathedral Basilica of Saints Peter and Paul in Philadelphia has five circular oil-on-canvas paintings: the Assumption of the Blessed Virgin into Heaven and the four Evangelists, by Constantino Brumidi. (Photo: Giò Martorana)

Brumidi worked on murals for the new cathedral for three years, completing them in 1863 and 1864, while he was waiting for the Capitol dome to be ready for his fresco. Behind the altar in fresco, Brumidi painted a monumental *Crucifixion*, with the figure of Christ set against a dark sky with rays of light falling on him and his mother and followers grieving below. It was flanked with illusionistic stone statues of saints Peter, Paul, John, and James. Above it was the lunette depicting God the Father and the dove of the Holy Spirit. On the transept walls, he painted images of statues of the twelve apostles in darks and lights to resemble carved stone as in his design for the frieze in the Capitol Rotunda. His apostles were described as "more life-like than statues could

be—more rounded and solid than one could think a painting could be."[3] These frescoes are known only from photographs, as they were destroyed when the church was expanded in 1956–1957, as were a Transfiguration and an Annunciation he painted in the chapels.[4]

Still visible today in the dome above the transept 156 feet from the floor is his central *Assumption of the Virgin* and rondels of the Four Evangelists writing in their books in the pendentives, all painted in oil on canvas in Washington and adhered in place. Painted in the vivid hues made possible by the oil medium, the Virgin rises to the heavens with her tight hand raised, her head bursting with light, surrounded by cherubs, shown as if seen from below. His Philadelphia dome composition may have built on his final design for the Capitol's *Apotheosis of Washington*, where the figures are painted as if seen from below as in Italian domes seen in Rome such as S. Andrea della Valle (he had exhibited an Assumption in Mexico in 1855, the year after the event was made doctrine by the Pope).

The next year Brumidi added two large sixteen-by-twenty-five-foot frescoes on either side of the transept, *Adoration of the Magi* and *The Nativity (Adoration of the Shepherds)*. Only his composition for the two scenes survives, as after being damaged by water they were covered with canvas and recreated by Filippo Costaggini in

Copies in oil on canvas of Constantino Brumidi's *The Nativity (Adoration of the Shepherds)* and *Adoration of the Magi* were painted on opposite sides of the transept in fresco in 1864, which reflect his dramatic compositions. (Photo: Giò Martorana)

St. Augustine Catholic Church, Philadelphia, Pennsylvania, 1848. Two large oil-on-canvas paintings flanking the altars were painted by Filippo Costaggini. (Photo: Giò Martorana)

Top: Detail of Filippo Costaggini's painting of St. Joseph Patron of the Augustinians on the west wall of St. Augustine Roman Catholic Church. Signed and dated 1882. (Photo: Giò Martorana)

Bottom: Fresco over the center aisle of St. Augustine Church, *Translation of St. Augustine to Heaven,* by Nicola Monachesi. Monachesi worked for well-known local residents such as Stephen Girard, Joseph Bonaparte, and George Cadwalader, and he was employed by the city's foremost architect, William Strickland, as reported by Richard N. Juliani, *Building Little Italy.* (Photo: Giò Martorana)

1889, "restored" by his son Louis Costaggini by early 1909, and then repainted again more than once.[5]

Before Filippo Costaggini (1837–1904), who had come to America in 1870, was adding scenes designed by Brumidi to the Capitol frieze (1880–1889), he had painted an altarpiece in St. Augustine Roman Catholic Church on North Lawrence Street near Fourth and Vine Streets in Philadelphia. He followed Nicola Monachesi (1795–1851), another Roman trained in the neoclassical tradition at the Academy of Saint Luke in Rome, as were Brumidi and Costaggini. Monachesi had painted the fresco *St. Augustine in Glory* on the ceiling of St. Augustine in 1848, preceding Brumidi's first fresco in America.[6] Costaggini's contributions to the church include twelve-foot-high oil paintings, *St. Joseph Patron of the Augustinians* and *Our Mother of Consolation,* with both central figures holding the Christ Child. Costaggini created paintings for many churches in Philadelphia in the 1870s and 1880s, including St. Joseph's, St. Agatha, St. Charles Borromeo, St. Philip Neri, and the cathedral, as well as for churches in many other cities.[7]

Brumidi was so appreciated by Thomas Ustick Walter, the architect of the new wings and dome of the Capitol, that the architect asked him to decorate the ceilings of his new house at Morton and High Streets in Germantown, unfortunately no longer extant. Brumidi gave Walter his first oil study for the *Apotheosis of Washington,* which Walter placed under the canopy of his bed. That painting is now in the Athenaeum of Philadelphia, along with Walter's personal letters and many of his architectural drawings, another link between Philadelphia and the U.S. Capitol.

Rotunda of the U.S. Capitol, Washington, DC, with frescoes *The Apotheosis of George Washington*, 1865, by Constantino Brumidi, and the *Frieze of American History*, begun by Brumidi around the base of the dome in 1878 and continued by Filippo Costaggini. (Architect of the Capitol)

Study for *The Apotheosis of Washington*, Constantino Brumidi (1805–1880). Oil on canvas, ca. 1863. The study served to paint *The Apotheosis of Washington* in the Rotunda of the U.S. Capitol, Washington, DC. (Walter Collection, The Athenaeum of Philadelphia)

NOTES

1. For more on Brumidi's life and work, see Barbara A. Wolanin, *Constantino Brumidi: Artist of the Capitol* (Washington, DC: U.S. Government Printing Office, 1998). Dr. Wolanin is now curator emerita after serving for thirty years as curator for the architect of the Capitol.

2. James F. Connelly, ed., *The History of the Archdiocese of Philadelphia* (Philadelphia: Archdiocese of Philadelphia, 1976), 252–254.

3. "The Great Roman Catholic Cathedral in Philadelphia," *Constitutional Union* (Washington), November 17, 1864, 1, includes detailed descriptions of the murals and their impact.

4. "Local Catholic News," an unidentified clipping, describes the paintings in progress with Brumidi's "constant care and attention."

5. Letter from Louis Costaggini to the Joint Committee on the Library, January 27, 1909, Records of the Architect of the Capitol. When visiting the cathedral in the 1990s, the author was told by a priest that the scenes had recently been repainted.

6. Monachesi's importance has been highlighted by Celeste A. Morella, who prepared detailed and convincing nominations for Philadelphia's Registry of Historic Places for both Brumidi's murals in Saints Peter and Paul and Costaggini's in St. Augustine.

7. "Old St. Augustine Catholic Church in Philadelphia," booklet by Reverend Arthur Ennison, OSA, preserved by the Philadelphia Historical Commission; E. De Merolla, Vice Consul of Italy, Baltimore (in support of Costaggni's bid to complete the frieze), February 20, 1880, Records of the Architect of the Capitol.

II

THE EXPANDING INDUSTRIAL METROPOLIS

New Wealth, New Elites, and New Institutions

of Knowledge, Arts, and Culture

INTRODUCTION

Judith Goode

PHILADELPHIA GRADUALLY LOST ITS POLITICAL and financial centrality to Washington, DC, and New York after the early federal period. However, as production shifted from small skilled artisan-apprentice workshops to factory-based, capital-intensive mass production and mass distribution using new power sources and transportation systems, the city became by many measures the dominant manufacturing city in the nation.

In 1854, the footprint of the city was greatly enlarged as the city annexed Philadelphia County, which was filled with small mill towns and farms. As industrial power moved up the scale from water powered to engine driven, factories and industrial zones became noisy, crowded, and odorous.

While textiles, clothing, and other consumer goods continued to be important products, the city began to produce the very machines enabling mass production and distribution—including railroad and tram cars themselves. The new metropole filled in space between the former mill towns along the Delaware and Schuylkill with enlarged industrial factory zones and surrounding worker row homes. New forms of transportation enabled the elite to relocate away from the unpleasantness of heavy industry to more bucolic, wealthy enclaves along rail lines in areas such as the Main Line, Chestnut Hill, and Elkins Park, creating opportunities to use Italian architecture and landscape designs.

By the middle of the nineteenth century, private fortunes grew based on expanding industry and capital investment in production, transportation, commerce, and publishing as well as the financial institutions and professional services that underwrote them. This new production and accumulation of wealth produced a new upper class who emulated the British in their participation in the European grand tour circuit. Italy contained many of the classical and Renaissance sites that had become an important part of the education and refinement of taste for families aspiring to maintain their upper-class rank.

Earlier Italian influences on the emerging republic came mostly through indirect inspiration of neoclassical Renaissance and Enlightenment political and moral philosophy. Now, as we can see in Chapter 7, the families with new fortunes promoted widespread travel and direct experience of Italy as a means of cultivating the cultural taste and refinement appropriate to the emerging upper-crust Philadelphia society. As the century progressed and family fortunes consolidated through marriage, the consumption of valued forms of art and culture enhanced status within the exclusive group of families.

A vast amount of Italian material culture was brought back to Philadelphia through this engagement. The role that the grand tour played was built on more than aesthetics; it included classical and neoclassical moral and political philosophies as well. To achieve status as an educated person included aesthetically experiencing and appreciating aspects of Italian architecture and landscape design and collecting paintings and art objects.

Italy was also a source of new findings and interpretations about the past as the empirical turn of the Enlightenment promoted knowledge production through archival and archeological studies of history. The essays offer examples of Italian engagements leading to individual contributions to academic knowledge in this period of restructuring academic disciplines within universities and learned societies.

Earlier practices of private social exclusivity (such as private museums, landscapes, and social clubs) developed in conjunction with a culture of civic virtue through philanthropy and public service. As elite power grew, so did an ideology of obligation to public service to soften the effects of growing inequality by opening access to learning institutions. Collecting could now be a way to bring important objects and experiences for the benefit of a larger society.

When Philadelphia was selected to host the centennial celebration of the United States in 1876, this signaled its importance. Many of the specific exhibits and buildings became the foundation of new privately funded but publicly accessible institutions for promoting and teaching arts and culture. At the turn of the twentieth century, these efforts culminated in the formation of an array of new institutions in the city that collected, interpreted, and displayed knowledge: new university disciplines, libraries, learned societies, expeditions, world's fairs, and museums. The interest in the arts, architecture, and urban design was used in the creation of the buildings for this end.

Again, the renowned artists and archeological discoveries of Italy played a major role in this thread linking Italy to Philadelphia, where aesthetic objects and designs were collected for teaching and display. These institutions not only educated and edified local Philadelphians; they also helped boost the reputation of the city as a manufacturing powerhouse and cultural beacon.

Italian culture is well represented in the construction of the two zones of key civic institutions created at the turn of the twentieth century: the Broad and Market area of finance, commerce, and government (banks, department stores, the massive City Hall, and musical venues) and Philadelphia's early twentieth-century response to the European City Beautiful movement (see Chapter 20), which included the Benjamin Franklin Parkway, a splendid boulevard extending northwest of the city and rimmed by learned societies, libraries, academies, and museums. Both sites became locations for parades and celebrations of the city as a whole.

The first three essays in this section look at immersion in things Italian from the perspective of elite individuals and families. Each explores a different interplay between the themes of work and leisure, civic virtue, scholarly interests, and status through consumption.

Chapter 6. Cam Grey's essay, "Henry Charles Lea's Italy: A Philadelphia Businessman and Scholar's 'Grand Tour from Home,'" tells us about Lea's decades-long exchange of letters with an Italian aristocrat. Lea demonstrates the ways in which one could combine a role in family business with a serious scholarly interest. He also shows how an intense and dedicated interest in early civilization in Italy could be accomplished without ever experiencing Italy directly.

Chapter 7. Lisa Colletta, in her essay, "Philadelphia Society and the Grand Tour," looks at the changing work and leisure experiences of several wealthy families over several generations. She especially explores later generations who no longer had careers but were leisure-class expatriates and who continued to make contributions to Philadelphia while emulating Italian nobility through political association and conspicuous consumption.

Chapter 8. Barbara J. Mitnick's essay, "The Union League of Philadelphia: The Italian Legacy," demonstrates how Italian culture influenced one exclusive social club in the city through prominently displayed paintings and sculpture produced by American artists inspired by training in Italy. An Italian chef trained in court styles of European cuisine has also left his mark on current club menus. It is interesting to note that besides the material discussed in the essay, the Union League art collection contains many paintings on the walls and sculptures in the hallways by Italian artists that were acquired in Italy and represent some of the artists who were frequently visited on the grand tour circuit. Mitnick concludes with a more recent case of influence. Echoing the post–World War II opening of opportunities to the children of turn-of-the-century immigrants, there has been a recent assumption of club leadership by three Italian Americans who are additional examples of Italian American leaders to those discussed later in Part III.

The next seven essays in this section deal with the Italian legacy in the city's major cultural institutions that developed after the Civil War through the first two decades of the twentieth century. Together these essays demonstrate the value of Italian objects and artifacts, their perceived value to education and the interactions between wealthy civic benefactors, and the Italian and American middlemen through which collections were acquired. Many individuals and families had art experts who served as agents. Academy-trained artists in Rome, Florence, and Naples built galleries to exhibit paintings and sculpture to visitors. Many of those who brought back treasures sought to run private galleries in their homes but soon increasingly served a less exclusive public, especially as a means of teaching future artists.

VISUAL ARTS AND DESIGN

Chapter 9. Albert Gury in his essay "*David* at the Pennsylvania Academy of the Fine Arts: Italian Influences on Curriculum and Art Making" illustrates the long-term centrality and national prominence of the classical and Renaissance casts in PAFA's training program. PAFA, established in 1805, the early federal period, is the most venerable Philadelphia arts institution, and from the beginning, plaster casts from Italy were central to training.

Chapter 10. Ann Blair Brownlee's essay, "'Pompeii Comes to Philadelphia': The Wanamaker Bronzes in the University of Pennsylvania Museum," tells us the story of John Wanamaker and his roles as a board member of the University of Pennsylvania Museum and as a donor of funds for Italian excavations focused on Etruscan (see also Chapter 25) and Roman cultures. In this chapter, we learn about the transactions involved in acquiring spectacular bronze castings from a Naples foundry specializing in facsimiles of archeological artifacts for the early development of the Penn Museum. We get a clear picture of the system of brokers and agents that grew to promote this commerce and the role that the grand U.S. world's fairs played in cultural engagements with Italy and other nations.

Chapter 11. Jennifer A. Thompson's essay, "'A Dazzling Array': Italian Art and the Philadelphia Museum of Art," shows how the PMA was generated by the Philadelphia Centennial Exhibition and benefited from grand tour collections. We see the breadth of engagements with Italy through time and the ways in which the museum increasingly extended more inclusive access. As the museum adapts to a changing world, it has broadened the art movements it represents and cultivates a diverse audience. Throughout, it has continued to relate closely to Italy.

Chapter 12. Raffaella Fabiani Giannetto's essay, "The Italian Legacy in the Gardens of Early Twentieth-Century Philadelphia," looks at the inspiration of Roman gardens based on classical Roman values in early twentieth-century gardens in the Delaware Valley, especially under the influence of William Eyer. She explores the virtues associated with features of Italianate gardens and shows the shift away from the Roman notion of morally virtuous productive work (the "gentleman farmer").

Chapter 13. Joseph F. Chorpenning's essay, "The Neapolitan *Presepio* at the Glencairn Museum," demonstrates how a collection of an early popular artisan tradition of *presepios* (Italian crèches), rather than the fine art of the academies, was brought back from Italy in the early decades of the twentieth century when a Philadelphia woman, attracted to this highly skilled artisanship in this popular religious display, collected it over a decade, piece by piece.

VOCAL AND INSTRUMENTAL MUSIC

The Italian musical legacy in Philadelphia begins with the arrival of Italian opera troupes bringing Italian opera, stagecraft, and performers to the city. In turn, new public venues, such as the Academy of Music and the newly renovated Met, developed to house impresario-sponsored events. Institutions for musical education and training developed. In the early twentieth century, Italian influence on instrumental music performances became prominent, such as those of the world-famous Philadelphia Orchestra and many other ensembles.

Chapter 14. Stephen A. Willier's essay on "The Italian Legacy in Philadelphia: Opera and Instrumental Music" tells us about the first impresarios and visiting stars and their popularity. Opera in the city was institutionalized through the construction of venues such as the Academy of Music and the training of Philadelphia-born singers by well-known teachers who entered the international world of opera. The second part of Willier's essay focuses on the significant role played by Italian performers in the major instrumental ensembles in the early twentieth century.

Chapter 15. David Serkin Ludwig's essay, "The Curtis Institute of Music and Italy," focuses on the importance of major Italian-heritage faculty and students in training students as composers, soloists, and major contributors to Philadelphia's significant ensembles. Many were prominent in the global music world.

TRANSITION TO PART III

Chapter 16. Steven Conn's essay, "Italy on Display: Representing Italy in the 1876 Centennial and 1926 Sesquicentennial," contrasts the 1876 U.S. centennial celebration to the 1926 sesquicentennial celebration in order to provide key insights into the relationships between the concerns of the two nations, as well as the nature of the Italian American presence in the city, thus providing a transition from Part II to Part III. We can see how the presence of an Italian American community made a difference in how Italy was represented in 1926. We also see how the respective circumstances of the newly unified Italian state and the boosterish city of Philadelphia gave different degrees of significance to the two entities. The bicentennial was presented at a time when city elites were promoting the local and national economic strength. Many Philadelphians were already familiar with the masterpieces of classical and Renaissance art. Italy, in the midst of forming a nation, decided to participate late, and the hurried selections, and their random display, disappointed. In contrast, by 1926, the growing Italian American community and the city were actively trying to work against anti-immigrant nativism. The community developed its own display to represent itself on its own terms. However, the event was generally a failure in terms of promoting the event to the region and nation, since the audience was small.

6

Henry Charles Lea's Italy

A Philadelphia Businessman and Scholar's
"Grand Tour from Home"

Cam Grey

I T IS NOWHERE RECORDED THAT HENRY CHARLES LEA (1825–1909) ever visited Italy. While this is not in and of itself especially noteworthy, his lack of personal familiarity with the country whose influence on Philadelphia is the focus of the present volume may seem to disqualify him as an appropriate subject of study. Lea has been described by Edward Peters, formerly the Lea Professor in the Department of History at the University of Pennsylvania, as "a successful Philadelphia publisher, real-estate magnate, civic leader and reformer, philanthropist, the nation's first Mugwump, and its greatest scholarly historian of the nineteenth century."[1] He was active in both the municipal politics of Philadelphia and affairs on the national stage.[2] His international reputation as a scholar of medieval legal, political, and religious history—especially his still-seminal study of the Inquisition—garnered him a slew of honorary degrees and memberships of many of the most prestigious learned societies of Europe, including several, indeed, in Italy.[3]

Over the course of his life, Lea also amassed a personal scholarly library comparable to any contemporary institutional library in the United States.[4] This library—now located in the Kislak Center for Special Collections, Rare Books and Manuscripts, on the sixth floor of the University of Pennsylvania's Van Pelt Library—and the means by which Lea acquired it provide the impetus for the present contribution. On the strength of the library's bibliographical holdings, it is clear that Lea's relationship with Italy was, in fact, intimate and sustained, mediated as it was through intricate webs of scholarly collaboration, mutual obligation, and friendship. These webs, revealed by his voluminous and variegated correspondence with an impressively broad array of scholars, diplomats, and politicians, functioned analogously to the personal experiences and face-to-face contacts that a contemporary such as John Wanamaker developed during his frequent Italian sojourns. As a consequence, we should view Lea as both significantly influenced by Italian scholarly traditions and heavily influential on them. We should, moreover, acknowledge that his interest in and knowledge of Italian politics, society, and culture were extensive and that he developed and maintained deeply personal relationships with Italian correspondents throughout his adult life. In what follows, I illustrate these propositions with reference to Lea's correspondence with the Italian count and medieval historian Ugo Balzani (1847–1916). First, however, I offer a brief biography of Lea, situating him within the social, cultural, political, and intellectual world of late nineteenth-century Philadelphia.

Lea's parents were Isaac Lea, a naturalist of some note and scion of a Philadelphia Quaker family, and Francis Anne Carey, daughter of prominent Philadelphia publisher Matthew Carey. They engaged the Irish American theoretical mathematician Eugenius Nulty as tutor to Henry and his older brother, Matthew Carey Lea, and the two gained all the elements of a classical education. Henry, in particular, displayed a precocious facility for languages and analytical thought, as well as interests in chemistry, conchology, and poetry. The family is known to have taken one trip to Britain and France, in 1832—during which time Henry attended a French school in Paris.[5]

However, unlike many of his contemporaries, for Lea this early experience of Europe was not a precursor to the repeated, self-conscious travel on the Continent that is often grouped under the descriptive rubric of the grand tour. In 1843, Lea entered into the publishing business of his grandfather, Matthew Carey. Initially, he also continued to pursue his eclectic interests in poetry, natural science, and chemistry, but in 1847, the combined toll of these disparate professional and intellectual demands precipitated the first of several

ABOVE RIGHT: Henry Charles Lea. (Henry Charles Lea Papers, Kislak Center for Special Collections, Rare Books and Manuscripts, University of Pennsylvania)

RIGHT: Count Ugo Balzani. (Henry Charles Lea Papers, Kislak Center for Special Collections, Rare Books and Manuscripts, University of Pennsylvania)

breakdowns in his physical and mental health. On the advice of his doctor, he put aside all scientific research and poetic pursuits for the next ten years. Instead, he turned to reading history—an undertaking regarded as rather less taxing on his strength—and began a journey through eighteenth- and seventeenth-century French courtly politics, which ultimately led to Jean Froissart, the fourteenth-century court historian, and Villehardouin, the thirteenth-century chronicler of the Crusades. In seeking to evaluate the reliability of these texts, Lea found himself stymied by a dearth of resources in Philadelphia; he therefore turned to booksellers and libraries in Europe, first for works of reference and then increasingly for scholarly accounts and contemporary sources.

So began a career, or perhaps better, a resolutely pursued hobby—undertaken in the interstices between running his publishing business, participating in the civic life of Philadelphia, and contributing both in print and monetarily to a variety of philanthropic and social causes—as a "scientific" historian, focused not simply on engagement with modern writers but much more heavily and unusually on the marshalling and evaluation of original evidence. This method, revolutionary at the time, was intimately linked to his practices of acquiring books, and those practices, in turn, relied on increasingly elaborate networks of personal interaction. These interactions were, almost exclusively, transacted through letters. Lea traveled to England in 1873 but was forced to return home immediately upon his arrival to attend to the death of his mother. A second trip, in 1879, was an attempt to remedy yet another breakdown in his health, and as a consequence he scrupulously avoided intellectual pursuits. Indeed, it appears that on this occasion he even eschewed the opportunity to meet, face-to-face, the Irish intellectual historian Arthur Lecky, with whom he had by this time developed a long-standing and intimate friendship.[6]

Lea's epistolary friendship with Lecky may be tracked from an initial, more formal and scholarly phase through signs of increasing familiarity to intimate, frank exchanges between close friends.[7] But it is by no means the only example of the multiple dimensions and complex arcs that such friendships took through Lea's life of deep, intimate, yet physically vicarious engagement with the culture, politics, and history—both contemporary and medieval—of Europe. Indeed, his correspondence with Count Ugo Balzani—a familiar also of Lecky's—eloquently demonstrates both the intimacy that such friendships clearly achieved and their pivotal role in anchoring and diffusing Lea's networks of contacts across Europe. Balzani was himself a historian of considerable skill and distinction, who would later be elected president of the Reale Società romana di storia patria. Preserved among the Henry Charles Lea papers in Penn's Kislak Center for Special Collections, Rare Books and Manuscripts, this correspondence comprises a sizable collection of letters written by Balzani, in English and in a fine and legible hand, which date from February 1889 until shortly after Lea's death in 1909.

Lea's initial contact with Balzani was mediated through the agency of Pasquale Villani, with whom Lea corresponded and developed a friendship from 1875.[8]

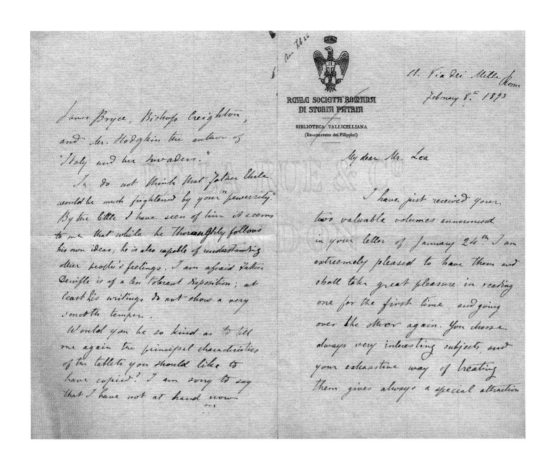

Letter from Balzani to Lea, dated February 8, 1893, and written on the note paper of the Reale Societa romana di storia patria. (Henry Charles Lea Papers, Kislak Center for Special Collections, Rare Books and Manuscripts, University of Pennsylvania)

Initially, Lea's principle interest appears to have been to obtain access to the library of the Vatican, a task on which he had by this time been engaged since at least the early 1870s. Nonetheless, it is clear from Balzani's courteous and eloquent responses that, from the start, Lea intended this relationship to be mutually implicated, multidimensional, and ongoing. The first preserved letter in the archive, written from London where Balzani was at that time residing and addressed (as were all the letters in this correspondence) "Dear Mr Lea," opens with what is clearly a response to a request by Lea for assistance in accessing libraries and archives in Rome (February 24, 1889):[9]

> I have written at once to a friend in Rome asking him if he would undertake
> to make researches and copies for you in the roman libraries and archives.
> If he accepts, you may rely upon his work as he himself is a scholar and is
> familiar with all our libraries and archives including the Vatican.

Balzani goes on to acknowledge the veracity of a small correction of historical fact offered by Lea, before graciously acknowledging Lea's own contribution to the subject. While it is not clear whether the work of Lea's to which Balzani refers was offered as a gift by his correspondent or acquired by other means, it is certainly the case that, later in their relationship and in correspondence with others, Lea regularly both gave and received scholarly books and articles as expressions of shared intellectual interests, not to mention tokens of esteem and—ultimately—friendship.[10]

The initial focus of this correspondence on access to bibliographical resources in Rome was relatively quickly complemented by other subjects, both scholarly and personal. Indeed, in a letter dated September 15, 1889, Balzani responds a touch defensively to exhortations by Lea to see to his own health, observing, "I am afraid I do not deserve just now the kind and wise advice you are giving me about the sparing of my strength." This was, of course, a topic with which Lea was himself intimately and painfully familiar, and one that was to infuse their later letters as the two traded sympathetic stories of lumbago and grippe.[11] In any event, it would certainly seem that Lea's epistolary forwardness bore fruit rather quickly, for in a letter of January 26, 1890, Balzani offers Lea belated New Year's wishes, "wishes warmly felt though they come from a new friend."

This mix of scholarly respect and burgeoning friendship appears to be the foundation for Balzani's suggestion, just under a year later (Balzani, January 11, 1891), that Lea send a copy of his *History of the Inquisition* to another Italian historian, Ernesto Masi—whom Balzani describes as "one of our most charming writers of essays"—with the explicit intention of ensuring a wider dissemination of Lea's work and ideas through the Italian scholarly community. Lea appears to have followed his new friend's advice, for a brief note by Masi on Lea and his work duly appeared in *Nuova Antologia* the following year.[12] A further indication of the intimate interweaving of professional respect and personal affection in the relationship between the two may be found in Balzani's letter of February 8, 1893, in which he reports on the decision of the Reale Società romana di storia patria to elect Lea to its ranks, declaring warmly, "It is an honour and a pleasure for me that this recognition of your great historical merits should have come while I am presiding this Society."

Still greater intimacy between the two is evident from Balzani's expressions of grief at the death of his wife, first in response to Lea's words of sympathy and then later in several moving soliloquies on his sense of loss and dislocation.[13] Interspersed, however—and alongside an ongoing and enduringly robust intellectual and scholarly strand in their correspondence—we witness also a keen and detailed knowledge of the political events unfolding in both countries. Balzani's opening sentences in a letter of November 10, 1896, refer explicitly to the fiercely contested U.S. presidential election of that year, in which the conservative Republican William McKinley prevailed over William Jennings Bryan—whose platform Lea clearly opposed, although rather uncharacteristically he did not involve himself particularly heavily in campaigning or electioneering that year.[14] Greater political turmoil was soon to envelop Italy in the form of the assassination of its king, Umberto I, a man known personally to Balzani. Indeed, in a letter dated September 28, 1900, Balzani observed pessimistically, "The world is entering into a phase for which strong governments are required whatever their form may be."

It appears that these two great figures of nineteenth-century medieval history and contemporary politics, separated by the Atlantic Ocean and never actually meeting face-to-face, nonetheless turned to each other in facing troubled personal and political times and constructed a multidimensional, mutually supportive, ongoing friendship out of an initial request by one for the scholarly assistance of the other. The latter years of their correspondence, punctuated as always by their shared interest in matters scholarly and textual, are also peppered with detailed references to their own and each other's children, personal invitations to visit, and regrets at their continuing separation.[15] Indeed, the final letter in the collection is a response from Balzani to the executors of Lea's estate, in which the Italian medievalist reflects on their twenty-year relationship (September 26, 1912):

> I reckon among the privileges of my life to have been for many years in correspondence with him, and though I never had the pleasure of meeting him, I have long been honoured by his friendship.

Henry Charles Lea, Philadelphia printer, historian, and civic leader, appears never to have visited Italy. Nonetheless, he was intimately enmeshed in its politics, culture, and scholarship.

NOTES

1. Peters, 34.
2. Bradley, 175–236, offers full and detailed accounts.
3. A complete list of Lea's honors may be found in Bradley, 361–362.
4. For statistics, see Peters, 38–39.
5. Bradley, 15–16, 40–45.
6. Bradley, 158–162; Peters, 52.
7. Auchmuty.
8. Bradley, 155. For the ongoing friendship of Balzani and Villani, see, e.g., Balzani's letter of January 1, 1892.
9. The individual in question is a certain Guido Levi, whom Balzani confirms as Lea's agent and direct correspondent in a letter of March 19, 1889.
10. In the correspondence between Balzani and Lea alone, see, e.g., Balzani, April 29, 1889; Balzani, December 2,1889; Balzani, August 31, 1890; Balzani, January 11, 1891; Balzani, April 4, 1896; Balzani, May 13, 1896; Balzani, August 29, 1896; Balzani, May 26, 1900.
11. For mentions of grippe and lumbago, e.g., Balzani, January 11, 1893; Balzani, March 15, 1895.
12. Masi; noted also in Balzani, September 11, 1892. See Balzani's thanks to Lea for a flattering notice in *The Nation*, Balzani, September 28, 1900.
13. For examples of sympathy, loss, and grief, see Balzani, April 4, 1896; Balzani, August 29, 1896; Balzani, May 26, 1900. Note also Balzani's acquisition of a portrait of Lea to hang in his study in Rome and his sending of a photograph of himself to Lea (Balzani, July 5, 1896).
14. Bradley, 236.
15. For example, regrets at Lea's inability to accept an invitation to visit Italy (Balzani, March 9, 1903); Balzani's daughter's dashed hopes of meeting Lea (Balzani, December 27, 1907); Lea's daughter and son-in-law's traveling to meet Balzani and his daughter (Balzani, March 3, 1909).

BIBLIOGRAPHY

Auchmuty, J. J. "The Lecky-Lea correspondence in the Henry Charles Lea Library of the University of Pennsylvania, Philadelphia, U.S.A." *Hermathena*, no. 92 (1958): 45–61.

Balzani, U. Letters from Ugo Balzani to Henry Charles Lea, February 24, 1889–September 26, 1912. Series I, Box 2. Henry Charles Lea Papers, Kislak Center for Special Collections, Rare Books and Manuscripts, University of Pennsylvania.

Bradley, E. S. *Henry Charles Lea: A Biography*. Philadelphia: University of Pennsylvania Press, 1931.

Masi, E. "Uno storico americano dell'Inquisizione. [E. C. Lea]." *Nuova Antologia*, no. 123 (1892): 653.

Peters, E. M. "Henry Charles Lea and the Libraries within a Library." In *The Penn Library Collections at 250: From Franklin to the Web*, 33–59. Philadelphia: University of Pennsylvania Library, 2000.

7

Philadelphia Society and the Grand Tour

Lisa Colletta

HOUGH THE TRADITION OF THE GRAND TOUR ORIGINATED with the English aristocracy, who sent their sons off the Continent to finish their education before embarking on careers, Americans took to it with relish during the nineteenth century. The building of a nation required more than just mercantile energy, and as soon as industrious Americans grew rich enough, they followed in their British cousins' footsteps, beating a path to culture in the great capitals of Europe. The ultimate aim of the grand tour was always Italy, the center of classical learning and Renaissance art, but the first families of Philadelphia had a different relationship with Italy than did those of New York and Boston. The city's Quaker roots made anything overtly showy suspicious, and foreign travel, especially to Catholic Italy, had to be approached with caution lest it ruin one's morals. However, throughout the nineteenth and into the twentieth century, wealthy and well-heeled Philadelphians made the tour and returned to the city to foster cultural institutions, such as the Athenaeum, the Museum of Art, and the Philadelphia Orchestra. The art and culture of Italy not only influenced the architecture of the city; it also nurtured a cultural coming of age that connected the city with Italy in interesting and often surprising ways.

Unlike New York or Boston, Philadelphia doesn't have a ready list of notable, eccentric Italophiles. There is no one who really compares to the Carnegies, the Rockefellers, or Isabella Stewart Gardner in terms of connoisseurship or flamboyance, but this lack of colorful ostentation is precisely what Philadelphia's first families prided themselves in. During the nineteenth and early twentieth centuries—the heyday of the American grand tour—the puritan heritage of the city's Quaker roots continued to influence the cultural identity of Philadelphia's upper classes. In *The Perennial Philadelphians: The Anatomy of an American Aristocracy*, Nathaniel Burt claims that the twin myths of Philadelphia are that the city is both "utterly lacking in gaiety," characterized by "Quaker slowness and sobriety," and that it is the "citadel of an extremely frosty upper class almost wholly devoted to snobbishness and horses" (9). Perversely, Burt goes on to add, "Like many myths, both of these are based in solid fact" (9). These two "solid facts" are important when thinking about the effects of the grand tour on the city, because unlike Boston and New York, Philadelphia's more conspicuous rivals, the city's first families seemed to go out of their way not to advertise their travels to the decadent Old World.

The Protestant character of the city, including that of one of its most famous citizens, Benjamin Franklin, has a lot to do with the ways Philadelphians confronted European culture. Franklin, who may have been one of the most intellectual and cultured men of the Enlightenment—but who affected otherwise—founded what is now the University of Pennsylvania, one of the eight Ivy League institutions in the United States. In founding Penn, Franklin essentially established the model for American higher education, which combines "the finer arts and sciences" with the professions and substitutes moral philosophy for denominational divinity. This pragmatic and very American approach to education also influenced the way many Americans embarked on the grand tour. For America's upper classes, travel to Europe was almost a national duty. The aim was to acquire classical learning, but one was obliged to retain a healthy skepticism toward the Old World because European culture was educational but morally perilous. With a Protestant sense of practicality and an American sense of superiority, they sent their sons (mainly) to Europe to get a little culture, but the point was to return better able to manage and build a nation.

The first families of Philadelphia were primarily doctors, lawyers, and businessmen, or what the *Dictionary of American Biography*, *Who's Who*, and the *Social Registry* refer to as "capitalists," and from the eighteenth to the early twentieth century many of them remained fixtures in Philadelphia society: Biddle, Cadwalader, Kuhn, Wharton, Pepper, Drexel, and Merrick. In *Philadelphia Gentlemen: The Making of a National Upper Class*, Digby Baltzell explains that inclusion in this American elite depended on many factors, but primary among them were distinguished past achievement (i.e., making a lot of money) and family continuity. The majority of Old Philadelphia families that predate the Civil War made their fortunes in trade: Samuel Wharton was a merchant and land speculator, Anthony Morris was a brewer, and Clement Biddle was a merchant. However, by the second generation many of them had become statesmen, bankers, lawyers, doctors, or clergymen. In the late nineteenth and early twentieth centuries, they are also listed as philanthropists, sitting on governing boards of the Philadelphia Academy of the Fine Arts, the Philadelphia Museum of Art, the Athenaeum, the University of Pennsylvania, and the Philadelphia Orchestra.[1]

Histories and biographies mention in passing that scions of elite families made their grand tours to finish their education, and upon their return they dutifully married well, nurtured children and fortunes, and became pillars of the establishment, without making too much show of their travels. However, the offspring of a few famous Philadelphia families were some of the most eccentric grand tourists, and to the suspicion of their families and to Old Philadelphians, they took to the European ideal of gentlemanly idleness. In the nineteenth century, Philadelphia's gentry class might not have had to worry about making money, but "a man was expected to do something" (Burt 99). When the progeny of a wealthy family didn't "work," they were seen as triflers in the eyes of Old Philly, even if their prestige emanated from inherited wealth and leisure activities and interests. Being a successful and industrious businessman might be respectable, but it was not enough to make you a leader, and among the successful American capitalist "aristocracy" there was tension between family wealth, social class, and worldly sophistication. In the late nineteenth and early twentieth centuries, Philadelphia was full of people of proper standing who were by wealth and heredity presidents and directors of banks and businesses, members of law firms and medical practices, but who were really busy at other things such as traveling, collecting art, or dabbling in politics.

The life of Dr. William Camac is a brilliant example of the nineteenth-century gentleman not practicing his profession. He came from a wealthy and distinguished family, and his turn of mind tended toward the study of flora and fauna, which he engaged in with full Victorian learned amateurism. He fell in love with a girl from a strict Quaker background who would never marry a "do-nothing," so he enrolled in Jefferson Medical College and became a doctor. Once married, he never did a day of medical work, though he was always known by his title of Dr. Camac. He traveled throughout Europe and devoted himself to botany and the natural world. Upon his return, he founded America's first zoo, the Philadelphia Zoo, in 1874 and supported numerous institutions in the city such as the Union League, the Academy of the Fine Arts, the Horticultural Society, as well as numerous musical societies. His country house was a magnet for cultured Philadelphians and included a conservatory full of exotic plants and was famous for its palms. In an incomprehensible act of eccentricity (at least among Philadelphia circles), he spontaneously decided to pack up the whole family, servants and all, for a journey to the Mediterranean, ending with a houseboat sail up the Nile. The friend to whom Dr. Camac entrusted all his affairs absconded with everything, and when he returned to Philadelphia he was ruined.

John Marshall Paul and John Rodman Paul, cousins and doctors, traveled together for their grand tour from 1823 to 1825, visiting the major capitals of Europe and calling on hospitals throughout the continent. John Marshall Paul's older brother, Comegys Paul, had graduated from Princeton in 1802 with a degree in law. Despite his law degree, he had keen literary interests that he indulged during his European travels, which fostered a particular love of classical literature nurtured in Italy. Never very interested in his father's dry-goods business, Comegys was a gentleman lawyer who spent most of his time at the Philadelphia Athenaeum and helped sponsor the Library Company of Philadelphia. John Rodman Paul was not as literary as his cousin, but he was extremely invested in the governing of Philadelphia civic life. After his retirement at the age of forty, he became the president of the Board of Managers of the Wills Eye Hospital, treasurer of the College of Physicians, and a trustee of the University of Pennsylvania, among other things.

The illustrious Paul family, with its history of cultured gentleman doctors, spawned James Paul, better known as "James the Marquis" (Burt 101). Sent down from Princeton for "idleness, too much smoking, and the reading of French novels," he was allowed to return only upon renouncing those pleasures (Burt 101). Surprisingly, he graduated from Princeton and went on to pursue a medical degree. The reward for his diligence was a grand tour, paid for by his father, during which he not only tasted the pleasures of Paris and Rome but returned with what Burt calls the "largest consignment of French novels ever to enter the country" (101). He spent the rest of his life smoking cigars, reading French novels, and lunching at the Philadelphia Club, but never practicing medicine.

Whether doctors, lawyers, or financiers from Princeton, Harvard, Yale, or the University of Pennsylvania, nearly all wealthy Philadelphian families went on some kind of grand tour. England was a natural destination, despite the Revolutionary War, but the Continent was the site of real refinement and polish: Paris was for good manners and the latest fashions, but Rome was the home of culture. Those Philadelphia grand tourists who returned did—for the most part—what was expected of them and took their place among the financial, political, and cultural leaders of the city. However, some of the most interesting stories are of those who never made it back, and that is where the connections between Italy and Philadelphia become dramatic and rather more interesting.

The Kuhn family was one of Philadelphia's oldest, "solid Germantown," according to Burt, and among the four influential families that founded institutional medicine in America: Shippen, Morgan, Rush, and Kuhn (105). The families predate the American Revolution, and all married well early on. They all studied abroad and "took the grand tour, meeting famous people, acquiring manners, and when they came home fought the British as patriots, fought each other as competitors" (Burt 105). Every generation of the Kuhn family seems to have had its adventurers, though, despite being stalwarts of Philadelphia society. The lure of Europe seemed too compelling for some. The Kuhn family papers reveal that Peter Kuhn, a nephew of the upright Philadelphia doctor Adam Kuhn, lived most of his life in Gibraltar, along with one of his sisters. He was appointed United States Consul at Genoa in 1804 and served for several years. In 1807, he was arrested as an enemy agent by Napoleon's Minister of Police for wearing the Cross of Malta, which had been awarded him by the British. Napoleon himself wrote, ordering the arrest:

> To M. Fouch E. Minister of Police, Rambouillet, 7th September 1807, Give orders to have Mr. Kuhn, the American Consul, at Genoa, put under arrest for wearing a Cross of Malta, given him by the English, and as being an English agent. His papers will be seized, and an abstract of them made, and he will be kept in secret confinement until you have made your report to me. This man having received a foreign decoration ceases to be an American. I am sorry, by the way, you should have communicated with the Ambassador of the United States. My police knows no Ambassadors. I am master of my own house. If I suspect a man I have him arrested. I would even have the Ambassador of Austria arrested, if he was hatching anything against the State. (*Kuhn Family Papers*, 12)

When the U.S. government firmly requested his release, it nearly caused an international incident.

The next generation of the Kuhn family had one side that dutifully returned from their grand tours to the Quaker City and became "well-known in the social and financial world" (*Peter Kuhn Family Papers*, 12). That side became patrons of the arts, and to this day, the C. Hartman Kuhn prize is awarded annually by the Philadelphia Orchestra to a member of the orchestra "who has shown ability and enterprise of such character as to enhance the standard and the reputation of The Philadelphia Orchestra" (*The Philadelphia Orchestra Newsletter*). Perhaps influenced by their intrepid great-uncle, the other side of the family, represented by sons Charles and Hartman, spent much of their lives abroad and never returned to the stolid life of business or medicine. Charles married Louisa Catherine Adams, the great-granddaughter of President John Quincy Adams, the granddaughter of President John Adams, and the sister of Henry Adams. Charles and Louisa both died abroad, he in France in 1899 of "unspecified causes" and she in 1870 at Bagni di Lucca from a tetanus infection as a result of a foot injury she received in a carriage accident. Her brother Henry Adams described her as "quick, sensitive, willful—or full of will—energetic, sympathetic, and intelligent . . . and like all good Americans [she] was hotly Italian" (Adams, *Education* 85). For the Kuhns, Italy was "the land of poetry & art & beauty" (Robertson 130), and she and Charles Kuhn were at the center of Anglo-American life in Florence, hosting dinner parties and commenting on both Italian and American politics. They promenaded in Cascine Park, attended the opera, and danced all night at parties during Carneval. Charles idled away hours at the Jockey Club and read newspapers at the Gabinetto Vieusseux library. Hardly the life of a "proper" Philadelphia gentleman, but the lives of Charles and Louisa Kuhn in Florence embodied a certain kind of expatriate life in

Italy that many Americans emulated, an experience that greatly affected American art and letters as well as Italian intellectual life during the decades surrounding the Risorgimento and the founding of modern Italy.

Just months before Louisa's own death in 1870, Charles Kuhn's older brother Hartman died from an equally tragic accident. The Kuhn family papers say he died in his sleep while visiting Rome, and his headstone in the Non-Catholic Cemetery in Rome states simply:

HARTMAN KUHN

BORN PHILADELPHIA FEB 22D 1832

DIED ROME JAN 21T 1870

AS FOR GOD HIS WAY IS PERFECT

PSALM XVIII

Henry Adams wrote to his friend Charles Milnes Gaskett in a letter dated March 7, 1870:

> *You must remember poor Hartman Kuhn in Rome! He was a good fellow, though he had too much of the Philadelphian in him, and his wife was a very attractive little woman, I suppose you must have heard of his death at Rome by his horse falling back on him. It was terrible affair, but I have not heard the details, and am too sorry for him to wish to hear anything so painful. My sister, however, in Florence, has been much distressed about it. (Letters 182)*

Maitland Armstrong, who was then the Consul General for Italy, further explained the mystery in his memoir *The Day before Yesterday: Reminiscences of a Varied Life*. Like his younger brother, Hartman was lured to life in Italy, but either despite Adams's comment about him being too much the Philadelphian or proving it to be true, Hartman liked to join the English in hunting and riding in the countryside outside of Rome. Armstrong describes him as being "an awfully nice fellow, handsome and dashing," and he had several fine horses. However, he had the bad habit of checking his mount just as it was rising to the jump, which threw the horse out of its stride. He was out with his groom in the countryside trying to correct this habit, when he pulled on his horse so suddenly that it fell on him. His internal injuries were very serious, and despite the emperor's own physician attending him he died a few days later (Armstrong 237–328). He left a young wife and a son, who died unmarried. Charles and Louisa Kuhn had a daughter, who died in infancy, and the last Kuhn brother in that line was killed in the Civil War, so that was the end of the adventuring side of the Kuhn family from Philadelphia.

One of the most famous Philadelphia families in Rome was that of George Washington Wurts and his wife, the heiress Henrietta Tower. Wurts was born in Philadelphia in 1843 and inherited a significant fortune from his father, who died in 1858 after having founded the Delaware and Hudson Canal Company. After George's grand tour, he clearly preferred Europe to the grim interests of his father's business and moved to Florence at the age of twenty-two to become the assistant to George Perkins Marsh, the first United States minister to the Kingdom of Italy. Young George Wurts embodied the ideals of the grand tour: the son of wealth, keen to learn the ways of the world, not overly intellectual, and destined for a diplomatic career. George Perkins March found the Philadelphian "a young gentleman of fortune" who was "cultivated, hard-working, descreet, intensely loyal" (Lowenthal 340). Wurts was taken on without pay and quickly became as indispensable to Marsh as he was famous for being "elegant and snobbish," sporting two dozen pairs of gloves and a solid gold dinner service (Lowenthal 304). Wurts became Secretary of the Legation in 1869 and was transferred to St. Petersburg, Russia, in 1882. In 1892 he was transferred back to Rome, and in 1898 he married the immensely rich heiress Henrietta Tower, also from Pennsylvania.

The grave of Hartman Kuhn in the Non-Catholic Cemetery in Rome. (Courtesy of the Cimitero Accattolico per gli stranieri, Rome)

Wurts never fulfilled his ambition to become an ambassador, though a *New York Times* gossip piece from February 9, 1909, rumored that he was about to be appointed, reporting that even King Victor Emmanuel would find Wurts *persona gratissima*. Despite his over thirty years in diplomatic service, Wurts is arguably most notable for his art collection, accumulated over years of travel and idiosyncratically added to by his wife, Henrietta. George Nelson Page, the nephew of the former ambassador to Italy Thomas Nelson Page, fascist and Minister of Popular Culture under Mussolini, and founder of *Lo Specchio* (*The Mirror*), among other notorious things, described the Wurtses in decidedly unflattering terms. Whether due to politics or to the fact that Page was a relation of Wurts's first wife, Emma Hyde, whom Henry Adams described as very pretty and cultured, Page's dislike for the Wurtses is palpable.[2] He described George Wurts in his book *L'americano di Roma* as "*un uomo di mediocre intelligenza, vano e scontroso, ma di artistiche che lo rendevano un fine intenditore di musica, di pittura e di oggetti antichi*" (Fachechi 339).[3] Henrietta from Pottsville, Pennsylvania, fared worse. She is described as socially inept, "*una vecchia zitella della famiglia Tower, anche de Philadelphia, persona che accomunava a una brutezza proverbiale una vistosa rendita, che la poneva tra le più ricche ereditiere perfino in America*" (Fachechi 339).[4]

The Wurtses lived grandly at the Plazzo Mattei in the center of Rome, which was furnished with a magnificence that stunned even the most wealthy and audacious Italophile collectors of the nineteenth century. In 1902 the couple bought the Villa Sciarra on the Janiculum Hill. It was never their main residence in Rome but was used only as a summer home, with Henrietta initiating the season with a grand party for the new fellows at the American Academy, which had moved down the road in the Villa Aurelia (Geffcken and Goldman 240–241).[5] The Villa Sciarra has a rich history that dates to the sixteenth century, but the Wurtses added to the main palazzo and cultivated the gardens in the Romantic nineteenth-century fashion, adding statues, winding paths, and an immense birdcage to house their collection of white peacocks. George Wurts died in 1922, and in 1930 Henrietta gave the Villa to Mussolini, with the proviso that it become a public park. When she died in 1933, she left her entire art collection to Mussolini, also requesting that it go a public museum. Mussolini referred to the Wurts gifts as "magnificent, the handsomest ever bestowed on Rome" (Fachechi 339), and he installed the collection in Palazzo Venezia, where it forms a substantial part of the permanent collection there. According to Grazia Maria Fachechi, the collection is unique in Italy for its breadth and eclecticism, including not only important Italian paintings and art objects but also fabrics, tapestries, porcelain, and figurines from Russia and the Middle and Far East that are unique to Italy. The Wurtses are no longer talked about in Philadelphia circles, but their influence on collecting and their role in Italian American relations during the nineteenth and twentieth centuries remains one of the most intriguing stories of the century. Not forgetting her hometown, upon her death Henrietta set up the Henrietta Tower Wurts Foundation, which continues to this day to fund Meals on Wheels and provides small grants to organizations that serve disadvantaged young people and the elderly.

The relationship between Philadelphia and Italy is complex, as this volume attests. Without that relationship, the art and architecture of the city would be very different, and the culture of both places is forever marked by the connections. The wealthy families of Philadelphia who took grand tours and returned to

The Villa Sciarra.
(Photo: Lisa Colletta)

influence the political and cultural life of the city have left their mark on nearly every cultural institution and in nearly every facet of civic life. The grand touring tradition coincided with the building of the nation, and the wealthy and educated classes returned from Europe with ideas that contributed to the foundations and values of a young country trying to forge an identity that was both indebted to and different from Europe. However, I would also argue that those who stayed in Europe, bought palaces, married European aristocrats, and hosted salons among the expatriate intelligentsia also left a lasting legacy. Their influence cut both ways, affecting America's literary and artistic sense of itself as well as influencing Europe's burgeoning democracies, as expatriate Americans led salons, entertained intellectuals, and wrote frequent tracts and books about the political causes in Italy and the rest of Europe.

Plaque at the Villa Sciarra in honor of the Bequest to Benito Mussolini, whose name has since been removed. (Photo: Lisa Colletta)

Literary America in the nineteenth century would be a very different thing if it were not for the likes of the Wurtses, Kuhns, Pauls, Morgans, and Haseltines who went to Europe, collected extravagantly, lived beautifully, and died romantically (often to be buried in the Non-Catholic Cemetery in Rome). The trope of the wealthy American abroad became so entrenched in our national literature as to almost seem cliché, and it works as both an inspiration and a cautionary tale.

The graves of George Wurts and Henrietta Tower Wurts in the Non-Catholic Cemetery in Rome. (Photo: Lisa Colletta)

Without the grand tour experience of America's founding families, we would not have Henry James, Edith Wharton, Mark Twain, or later, in a different form, Ernest Hemingway, F. Scott Fitzgerald, or even one of the most famous Philadelphians, Grace Kelly. Italy represented a historical past, but it also seduced with its Catholicism and sensuousness. In the case of grand touring, these anxieties could be sharply focused, and with good reason. In a young country, and in a city like Philadelphia with a society based on hereditary wealth, status, and position, the actions of wealthy heirs were of utmost importance, because in many ways their choices represented the future of the country to the present generation. America's experience of Italy through the grand tour helped it shape its national identity and define itself as an inheritor of historical greatness, a new and better democratic empire. Travel to Italy reaffirmed and reified American values and an American sense of exceptionalism, and those travelers who returned did so convinced that America was the best country in the world. As Jeremy Black expressed it, a good many grand tourists returned to America "as better informed xenophobes" (12). However, a good many also took from their experiences and invested in the arts and culture. The city of Philadelphia represents one of the most interesting examples of the influence of the grand tour on American culture.

NOTES

1. For a more detailed examination of Philadelphia family histories from 1682 to 1940, see E. Digby Baltzell, *Philadelphia Gentlemen: The Making of a National Upper Class* (New Brunswick: Transaction, 2009), 71.

2. Emma Hyde Wurts died in Rome on April 16, 1880. She too is buried in the Non-Catholic Cemetary in Rome.

3. "A man of medicore intelligence, frivolous and petulant, but equipped with artistic endowments that make him a refined connoisseur of music, painting, and antiques" (my translation).

4. "An old maid from the Tower family, also from Philadelphia, she combines a proverbial ugliness with an enormous income that makes her among the most wealthy heiresses even in America" (my translation).

5. The Villa Aurelia is another storied palazzo bought by a wealthy Philadelphian, Clara Jessup Heyland. Upon her death in 1909, she left it to the American Academy.

WORKS CITED

Adams, Henry. *The Education of Henry Adams*. Modern Library, 1931.

———. *The Letters of Henry Adams, 1858–91*. Edited by Worthington C. Ford. Riverside Press, 1930.

Armstrong, Maitland. *The Day before Yesterday: Reminiscences of a Varied Life*. Scribner, 1920.

Baltzell, E. Digby. *Philadelphia Gentlemen: The Making of a National Upper Class*. Transaction Press, 2009.

Black, Jeremy. *Italy and the Grand Tour*. Yale University Press, 2003.

Burt, Nathaniel. *The Perennial Philadelphians: The Anatomy of an American Aristocracy.* University of Pennsylvania Press, 1963.

Fachechi, Grazia Maria. "George Washington Wurts, Henrietta Tower, Una Collezzione 'di curiosità e opera d'arte' e una villa 'magnificent, the handsomest ever bestowed on Rome.'" In *Riflessi del Collezionismo tra Bilanci Critici e Nuovi Contributi,* edited by Giovanna Perini Albani and Anna Maria Ambrosini Massari. Leo S. Olschki, 2014.

Geffcken, Katherine, and Norma W. Goldman. *The Janus View from the American Academy in Rome: Essays on the Janiculum.* American Academy in Rome, 2007.

The Kuhn Family Papers: The History and Roster of the Peter Kuhn Family in the U.S.A. Published privately, 1932.

Lowenthal, David. *George Perkins Marsh: Prophet of Conservation.* University of Washington Press, 2000.

The Philadelphia Orchestra. https://www.philorch.org.

Robertson, Robert J. "Louisa Catherine Adams Kuhn: Florentine Adventures, 1859–1860." *Massachusetts Historical Review,* vol. 11, 2009, pp. 119–151.

The Union League of Philadelphia, 1865. Italian National Day, June 2, 2015, during Italian cultural month, Ciao Philadelphia. (Photo: Gary Horn)

8

The Union League of Philadelphia

The Italian Legacy

BARBARA J. MITNICK

THE UNION LEAGUE OF PHILADELPHIA, the first in the United States, was founded in 1862 during the Civil War by a group of men determined to support President Abraham Lincoln and the federal government in the salvation of the American Union. Although living and working in a city also populated with Southern sympathizers, they were dedicated to fostering "unqualified loyalty to the government . . . and unwavering support of its measures for the suppression of the Rebellion." In 1865, this first mission was a triumph.[1]

Today, it is clear that the ongoing success and longevity of the Union League of Philadelphia has resulted from expanded focus and goals during the more than 150 years of its existence, along with the creativity and abilities of its staff and its members. A significant legacy has been established, which includes the important presence of Italian Americans.

In 1862, while the Union League began as a local organization to provide assistance to the nation to save the American Union, the Risorgimento (resurgence) in Italy had recently originated as a national movement to unify the Italian kingdoms and city-states into a single nation-state. These events on opposite sides of the Atlantic provide an intriguing historical juxtaposition.

A significant effect of the Risorgimento, especially on southern Italians, was the negative consequence of the resulting state protectionist economy. Along with improved availability of transatlantic travel, the result was an increase in Italian immigration. As documented in the records of the American census, from 1850 to 1870, well before the era of mass migration, there was a fourfold increase in the number of Italian-born immigrants living in Philadelphia.[2]

At the Union League, it appears that only one of its founding members, American-born Anthony J. Antelo (1820–1903), was of Italian ancestry.[3] At the same

Nunzio (Annunziato) Finelli, ca. 1880. (Photograph courtesy of Madeline Riker, 5 times great grandchild of Nunzio Finelli)

time, newly arrived immigrants to Philadelphia (including Italians) could hardly aspire to membership in the Union League, an elite and expensive organization even at its inception. Although they could have found it to be a place of employment, regrettably there is no surviving documentation for that speculation, since many relevant Union League records were lost in a devastating League House fire in September 1866, barely sixteen months after the building's completion.

There is, however, important evidence of employment availability related to the early culinary history of the Union League. Its first major chef was Naples native Nunzio (Annunziato) Finelli (1835–1886), who had sailed for America in 1858 as chief cook on the U.S.S. *Constellation*, a coveted appointment likely the result of his reported training in a Naples hotel operated by his father. After arriving in Philadelphia in 1859, Finelli began his American career at the city's newly opened Girard House Hotel.[4]

In August 1861, shortly after the onset of the Civil War, Finelli enlisted in Captain Charles Collins' Zouaves d'Afrique Company. Some four months later, on January 1, 1862, his reputation soared in response to the major banquet he created for Union General Nathan Banks and his staff. In December 1862, after recovering from serious injuries sustained the previous August during the Battle of Cedar Mountain, Finelli returned to Philadelphia, where in early 1863 he became chief chef at the Union League, a position he would hold until his death.[5] By 1879, his stellar reputation during the 1860s and 1870s culminated in his assumption of complete charge of the Union League's dining operations. In that year, in the Annual Report of the Union League, Finelli was identified as "a caterer of well-known capability and established reputation . . . highly satisfactory in every way."[6]

Finelli's recipes reflected a more sophisticated perspective than would appear to result from a straightforward conversion of Italian dishes to American tastes. As identified by the current executive chef of the Union League, Martin Hamann, many of Finelli's recipes were of French origin with ingredients written in French. That would seem surprising, but as architect John Fraser (1825–1906) designed the first Broad Street League House utilizing clear French Second Empire sources, Finelli's French recipes moved securely into the mainstream of the league's most desirable culinary innovations—a sophisticated legacy coming from its Italian chef and an approach to dining still experienced there. Finelli's "Oysters Finelli" is similar to current offerings, and his sweet bread croquettes remain on the league's New Year's Day menu. Moreover, in its relatively new Mise en Place dining room, Chef Hamann notes that oysters and beer also recall Finelli's bill of fare.[7]

During his tenure at the Union League, Finelli continually paid homage to his Italian heritage when he opened various catering establishments in Philadelphia, including the fine Italian restaurant Café Finelli at Broad and Chestnut in 1876. He is also remembered for his personal imprint on menus for important Union League dinners, such as one he created for a major event held in honor of John Russell Young (1840–1899), who in 1882 was named Envoy Extraordinary and Minister Plentipotentiary to the Qing Empire.[8] In the twentieth century, the Italian American tradition was ably continued by chef Peter Grassi (ca. 1895–1970), who "made many gourmet dishes standard fare at the Union League. His artful arrangements made historic settings."[9]

ITALIAN LEGACY IN ART AND ARCHITECTURE

Along with the early and continuing influence of important international aspects of the cuisine at the Union League, commissions and acquisitions of artwork also began. James L. Claghorn (1827–1884), a founding Union League member and noted Philadelphia collector, who maintained a private art gallery in his West Logan Square residence, began the effort in 1863, along with autograph collector Ferdinand J. Dreer (1812–1902), when they acquired *Equestrian Portrait of George Washington* (1842), by Thomas Sully (1783–1872), for the Union League.[10] At the same time, American artists studying in Italy before the Civil War brought the style and substance of Italian history painting and portraiture (and therefore its legacy) to the Union League in works often containing American subject matter. A significant example in the collection is *First Reading of the Declaration of Independence* (1861), by Union League member Peter Rothermel (1812–1895), who had studied in Rome.[11] And continuing in the later nineteenth and early twentieth

Peter Rothermel. *First Reading of the Declaration of Independence*, 1861. Oil on canvas mounted on board. (Courtesy of the Abraham Lincoln Foundation of The Union League Archives)

ABOVE: James Henry Haseltine. *America Mourning Her Fallen Brave*, 1867. Marble. (Courtesy of the Abraham Lincoln Foundation of The Union League Archives)

RIGHT: Horace Trumbauer, Fifteenth Street League House, 1908–1910. Photograph: 1940. (Courtesy of the Abraham Lincoln Foundation of The Union League Archives)

centuries, Italian and Continental works featuring European iconography often were acquired by well-to-do Americans during grand tours of Europe. Major works from that period now in the Union League collection include *Declaration of Love*, by Arturo Ricci (1854–1919), and *Church of the Madonna Della Salute, Venice*, by Martin Rico y Ortega (1833–1908).[12]

The Union League's sculpture holdings also reflect strong Italian sources. A prominent example currently on view in the Broad Street League House merging Italian methods, materials, and style with an American subject is *America Mourning Her Fallen Brave* (1867), commissioned from sculptor and Union League member

James Henry Haseltine (1833–1907). Modeled in Rome, the work features an allegorical figure of "America" wearing a Phrygian (liberty) cap embellished with thirteen stars signifying the original thirteen colonies. As noted in 1867 by the American art critic Henry Tuckerman, Haseltine had expressed "the artist's fine ideal of a 'proud sorrow.' . . . With such an air a mother might come, after years had passed, to the grave of her brave dead."[13]

The artistic Italian legacy at the Union League is also evident in the architectural style of its five-story Fifteenth Street building, completed in 1910. As noted, John Fraser's first Broad Street League House of the 1860s was designed in a French Second Empire style, the most up-to-date and fashionable of the middle of the nineteenth century. Likewise, the Fifteenth Street addition, created by Horace Trumbauer (1868–1938), represents a significant stylistic approach of its own later time, the Italianate Palazzo—a major component of the then-popular Beaux Arts. Its French- and Italian-inspired motifs, including pilasters and balustrades, also can be found in several buildings designed by leading American architectural firms of this later period, such as McKim, Meade and White and Carrere and Hastings.

At the Union League, it is also referenced in the confluence of history, art, and architecture in the Lincoln Memorial Room, by Jacob Otto Schweizer (1863–1955), which was based on his studies in the 1890s of Italian Renaissance architecture in Florence.[14]

Jacob Otto Schweizer. The Lincoln Memorial Room, 1916–1917, west wall. Bronze, marble, and wood. The Union League of Philadelphia. Presented by the Art Association, 1917. (Courtesy of the Abraham Lincoln Foundation of The Union League Archives)

THE UNION LEAGUE AND ITALY

By the late nineteenth century, as the Union League continued to maintain its prominent position in Philadelphia, the Kingdom of Italy began to recognize the city's importance with regard to Italian interests. In 1876, Count Goffredo Galli was appointed to serve as the first Italian General Consul in Philadelphia. In 1897, Giulio M. Lecca (Consul from 1896 to 1899) became the first in his position to become a member of the Union League, thereby specifically underscoring the significant political and cultural association between the Italian Consul's office and the Union League. Subsequent Consuls and League members included Giulio Cesare Majoni (Consul 1911–1914, Union League member 1912), Gaetano Emilio Poccardi (Consul 1914–1921, Union League member 1914), and Andrea Canepari (Consul General 2013–2017, Union League member 2016).[15]

The recent Philadelphia tenure of Consul General Andrea Canepari (in 2017 appointed Italian Ambassador to the Dominican Republic) holds particular significance with regard to the Italian legacy in Philadelphia. After earning academic degrees in Italy in both economics and law, Consul General Canepari completed a Master of Laws degree at the University of Pennsylvania in 1999, the year he joined the Italian foreign service. After several diplomatic postings, in 2006 he was relocated to Washington, DC, where he became First Secretary for American Politics and Relationships to the United States Congress. During his years as Consul General in Philadelphia, Canepari was given the 2016 Global Philadelphia Award, a biannual award from Temple University, in recognition of his activities and

The Honorable Andrea Canepari, Consul General of Italy, receiving the 2016 Global Philadelphia Award from the President of Temple University, Richard M. Englert (*left*) and Provost JoAnne Epps (*right*).
(Photo: Shefa Ahsan)

efforts in building international bridges and making Philadelphia a more prominent international destination. He has served locally on numerous committees and boards, including the Papal Event Committee (providing support and guidance for the Papal visit to Philadelphia in 2015), the Board of Presidential Advisors to Thomas Jefferson University, and the Board of the Studio Incamminati—School of Contemporary Realist Art. In November 2015, Canepari began his service as an honorary founding member of USA250, an organization created to promote the celebrations in Philadelphia of America's 250th anniversary in 2026. In addition, Consul General Canepari's decorations at the international level include Knight of the Order of Merit of the Italian Republic and Knight of Magistral Grace of the Sovereign Military Order of Malta.

In 2007, during his years in Washington, DC, Canepari served as coeditor of *The Italian Legacy in Washington, D.C.: Architecture, Design, Art and Culture*, the publication that established the format and standard for the current Philadelphia legacy project and continues to underscore his commitment to building bridges between Italy and Philadelphia.[16]

PAST IS PROLOGUE

The Union League of Philadelphia was founded by innovative and creative risk takers who merged their business acumen, financial strength, and cultural understanding with intense patriotism. It was an extraordinary group of men, emerging primarily from the wealthiest and best-educated segments of Philadelphia society. In the early period, this first group of founding innovators also filled the club's membership, instituted successful programs, and fulfilled its first and most significant mission. To maintain this early success would be a difficult act to follow. After the Civil War, the composition of the population would change and become less exclusive. A new group would have to emerge to sustain the Union League.

In the 1980s, political and gender barriers at the Union League began to come down, while at the same time a challenge remained to find the leadership necessary to nurture and grow the organization. Those in recent and successful charge have included several outstanding Union League presidents including Thomas Pappas and Joan Carter, a member of the first class of women to be admitted to Union League membership in 1986. At the same time, and with regard to the subject of this essay, it is intriguing that in the twenty-first century, three of the past presidents of the Union League mainly responsible for its recent success are the descendants of Italian American immigrants—and thus a serious component of the Union League's important Italian legacy.

In the late twentieth century, as the organization was reaching a crossroads, the Italian American influence would become important. The twentieth century had been a period of growth and challenge for the organization. Would the Union League grow, or would it retrench into a smaller, less important organization, servicing the needs of fewer and fewer members? Would it take the risks necessary to expand its quality, its membership, and its place in the community? It is fortunate that three Italian Americans, major honorees for the many contributions they have made to their communities and their nation, were ready and willing to make a difference. Today we have the results of their efforts: membership numbers have increased, the facilities have vastly improved, the programming has expanded its audiences, and the institution thrives.

The positive qualities and the direction taken by recent Italian American presidents of the Union League, in turn, recall the attributes and financial acumen of its founders. And until this small group came on the scene in the late twentieth and early twenty-first centuries, the Union League was retrenching. It needed new direction in order to survive and prosper. This group, including Daniel L. DiLella Jr. and Frank Giordano in the first decade of the twenty-first century and Gregory Montanaro in the second, came forward to provide the necessary leadership. Once again, in Philadelphia, a few major citizens, recalling the founders of the nation in the eighteenth century and the Union League founders in the nineteenth—risk takers all—came on the scene and made a serious difference.

With this recent success in mind, I invited the three recent Italian American presidents to take part in a discussion to present and review their Union League contributions.[17] Daniel L. DiLella had recently been appointed by the president of the United States to serve as chairperson of the Semiquincentennial Commission for the United States of America (passed by Congress in 2016 to celebrate the 250th anniversary of the United States).

Dan is President, Principal, and CEO of Equus Capital Partners Ltd. a major, multifaceted real estate private equity fund. His superb management skills, dedication, and philanthropy are also reflected in his support for the Villanova University real estate business school program. In 1987, when he became a Union League member, he harbored several negative impressions of the quality of the club's interiors, cuisine, and financial support for new initiatives. As a result, Robert Wilder, president at the time, recruited Dan to join various committees, including House and Finance. After serving on the board and then as Vice President, he became the Union League's sixty-third president in 2003.

Dan's Union League contributions were and have continued to be legendary. He shepherded a master plan through in 2003 and an expansion of the Inn at the League to eighty-four rooms, among other initiatives. Indeed, Frank Giordano and Greg Montanaro identify Dan as the "progenitor," their originator or forefather— the individual who set goals for the financial health of the club and then succeeded in putting it on a sound financial footing. In fact, it has taken Dan, identified as the risk taker, to make this happen regardless of whether he would have to endure the possible slings and arrows of the Union League membership.

Frank Giordano, who supported and then built on Dan's positive goals and outcomes, became his immediate successor. Currently the highly successful Pres-

Former Union League presidents Daniel L. DiLella, Frank Giordano, and Gregory Montanaro with Consul General Andrea Canepari at the Union League during Italian National Day, June 2, 2014. (Photo: Gary Horn)

ident and CEO of the Philly POPS, America's largest stand-alone pops orchestra, Frank has recently been named by the president of the United States as Executive Director of the President's Semiquincentennial Commission. He also is the recipient of numerous honors, including the Order of the Merit of the Italian Republic by the Ambassador of Italy and Honorary Consul of Malta. Frank also is President and CEO of the Atlantic Trailer Leasing Corporation, a transportation and storage equipment company that has been in the Giordano family since 1949.

Frank's connection with the Union League reaches back to his childhood, when, at the age of twelve or thirteen, he recalls a ride on Broad Street when he queried his father about the "brown building" they were passing. "That's for the big people" was his father's response! Years later, Frank would become one of those "big people," when he was elected the sixty-fourth president of the Union League in 2005 and chose to pose for a photograph on the brown building's prominent front steps. Soon, at a meeting of members in which suggestions were made to reduce the size, scope, and quality of the Union League in an attempt to restore its financial viability, Frank protested that he did not become active in the organization in order to "preside over its demise." He has continued to maintain that positive philosophy, as he has worked to increase membership, improve the functioning of the organization in projects including the acquisition of the Union League garage, raise money for major initiatives including the President's Fund and the Sir John Templeton Heritage Center, and support the Italian cultural month, Ciao Philadelphia, and major tours including "Italian Art and Inspiration at the Union League."

"Dan was the Revolution, and Frank built the Republic," according to Gregory Montanaro, Vice President and Executive Director of the Office of the President and Executive Director of Federal Affairs for Drexel University. He has been named Honorary Consul of the Republic of Austria to Philadelphia and environs, and he has been awarded membership in the Most Venerable Order of the Hospital of St. John of Jerusalem by Queen Elizabeth II.

Greg also contributes his expertise to numerous boards, committees, and organizations. In 2015, he became the Union League's sixty-ninth president and quickly began to provide serious new initiatives as well as build on the successes of his predecessors. He has presided over a major capital campaign, continued to maintain high levels of membership, and added innovative programming. His understanding of the Union League's prior descent into fiscal challenge, now happily turned around in recent years, involves his evaluation of recent generations as the inheritors of the earlier successes of the risk takers. Indeed, it has taken a new group of innovators such as Gregory Montanaro to earn and continue the Union League's classification beginning in 2012 as the "No. 1 City Club in the Country" by the Platinum Clubs of America.

Today, the Union League of Philadelphia has come full circle. It began its role as a superb resource to assist the federal government in the salvation of the Union. Today it continues to serve the requirements and challenges of a new era, which has come to include the legacy of not only its historical and cultural heritage but also members of the twenty-first century's Italian American community of Philadelphia.

NOTES

I am grateful to Theresa Altieri Taplin and Keeley Tulio, of the Union League of Philadelphia, for their assistance.

1. For the history of the Union League of Philadelphia, see Barbara J. Mitnick, Chief Contributor and General Editor, *The Union League of Philadelphia: The First 150 Years* (Philadelphia: Abraham Lincoln Foundation of the Union League of Philadelphia, 2012).

2. For a recent study of Italians in Philadelphia during this period, see Richard N. Juliani, *Building Little Italy: Philadelphia's Italians before Mass Migration* (Philadelphia: Pennsylvania State University, 1998), p. 147, table 1 (117 Italian-born residents in 1850), and p. 232, table 15 (482 Italian-born residents in 1870).

3. Antelo's passport application dated April 11, 1868, reveals that he was not an immigrant, but "a native of Philadelphia and a citizen of the United States." See *Ancestry.com*, https://www .ancestry.com/imageviewer/collections/1174/images/USM1372_154-0436?treeid=& personid=&rc=&usePUB=true&_phsrc=Zzl2&_phstart=successSource&pId=1556375, accessed January 23, 2021. Antelo was included in the December 27, 1862, initial list of Union League members.

4. Rev. Norman R. Goos, "Nunzio Finelli: An Immigrant Ancestor's Story," *Atlantic County Historical Society: Sixty-Seventh Yearbook with Historical and Genealogical Journal* 17, no. 3 (December 2014), pp. 54–68.

5. Ibid., p. 61.

6. "Annual Report of the Board of Directors of the Union League of Philadelphia," December 8, 1879, pp. 10–11.

7. Barbara Mitnick, interview with Martin Hamann, Executive Chef of the Union League, January 16, 2018.

8. John Russell Young was a journalist, author, and diplomat. He was the eleventh president of the Union League (1893–1895) and the seventh librarian of the U.S. Congress (1897–1899).

9. Peter Grassi served as head chef at the Union League for thirty-five years and retired four years before his death; he was succeeded by his brother Ambrogio. See obituary, "Peter Grassi Dies, Chef at Union League," *Philadelphia Inquirer*, March 28, 1970, p. 14.

10. *Equestrian Portrait of George Washington*, by Thomas Sully, was the first major history painting to enter the Union League's collection. See Mitnick, *Union League of Philadelphia*, pp. 132, 137–138.

11. For Peter Rothermel, see Mark Thistlethwaite, *Painting in the Grand Manner: The Art of Peter Frederick Rothermel (1812–1895)* (Chadds Ford, PA: Brandywine River Museum, 1995); Mitnick, *Union League of Philadelphia*, pp. 139–142.

12. For a compilation of publications dealing with the art collections at the Union League of Philadelphia, see Mitnick, *Union League of Philadelphia*, p. 154n3.

13. For Haseltine, see Mitnick, *Union League of Philadelphia*, pp. 149–150. Haseltine was a student of Joseph A. Bailly in Philadelphia before continuing his studies in Italy and France. See also Henry T. Tuckerman, *Book of the Artists* (New York: James F. Carr, 1967), p. 598 (reprint of first edition published by G.P. Putnam and Sons, 1867).

14. For Trumbauer, see Frederick Platt, "Horace Trumbauer: A Life in Architecture," *Pennsylvania Magazine of History and Biography* 125, no. 4 (October 2001), pp. 315–349. See also Horace Trumbauer Collection, ca. 1898–1947, the Historical Society of Pennsylvania; Sandra L. Tatman, "Horace Trumbauer (1868–1938)," Philadelphia Architects and Buildings Database; Roger W. Moss, *Historic Landmarks of Philadelphia* (Philadelphia: University of Pennsylvania Press, 2008), pp. 170–171. For Jacob Otto Schweizer and the Lincoln Memorial Room, see Mitnick, *Union League of Philadelphia*, pp. 150–153.

15. See Richard N. Juliani, "The Consulate General of Italy in Philadelphia: A Bridge between Two Cultures" (unpublished manuscript, Office of the Consulate General of Italy, Philadelphia).

16. Luca Molinari and Andrea Canepari, eds., *The Italian Legacy in Washington, D.C.: Architecture, Design, Art, and Culture* (Milano: Skira Editore, 2007). See also "Ciao, Italia," *The Philadelphia Inquirer*, October 2, 2015; M. Newall, "From Italy to Phila, Con Amore," *The Philadelphia Inquirer*, February 21, 2016; Barbara Ann Zippi, "Canepari's Ciao Philadelphia Event: A Month Long Celebration," *The Delaware Valley Italian-American Herald*, September 7, 2016; Joseph N. DiStefano, "Buon Viaggio: Italian Envoy Leaving Phila with Portfolio of Achievements," *The Philadelphia Inquirer*, May 28, 2017.

17. Barbara Mitnick, roundtable with Daniel L. DiLella, Frank Giordano, and Gregory P. Montanaro, the Union League of Philadelphia, November 28, 2017.

9

David at the Pennsylvania Academy of the Fine Arts

Italian Influences on Curriculum and Art Making

Albert Gury

PAFA, Belvedere Torso, Cast Hall. (Photo: Giò Martorana)

IN 1805, A GROUP OF GENTLEMEN IN PHILADELPHIA founded what is now America's first and oldest art museum and art school, the Pennsylvania Academy of the Fine Arts (PAFA). Their first action, even before having a beautiful neoclassical building constructed to house the new institution, was to purchase fine plaster casts of famous Greco-Roman and Italian Renaissance sculpture. Over 120 fine and rare plaster casts grace the Cast Hall of PAFA.

The current Cast Hall is a component of the historic landmark building at PAFA, the third building to house the institution, built by the firm of Furness-Hewitt and opened in 1876 for the American centennial. Additional state-of-the-art studio, classroom, digital, gallery, and other educational and research facilities adjoin the historic academy building via the Samuel M. V. Hamilton high-rise building to form a unique, urban art school/museum campus.

Sadly, most of these early cast purchases were destroyed in a fire in 1845, but they were replaced throughout the nineteenth and early twentieth centuries. Drawing from the Antique, one of the first courses established in America's new Academy of Art, remains a core foundation course in PAFA's undergraduate BFA college curriculum today.

PAFA also contains one of the largest collections of American art in the world and provides top BFA and MFA degree and related programs to students. For 215 years, the legacy of the Italian Renaissance has been supported by PAFA and integrated into its progressive contemporary approaches to art education.

Whether utilizing the underlying structural harmonies of Italian Renaissance and classical compositional strategies to inform contem-

Students and professors are still inspired by the cast collection during a PAFA open tour in the frame of the Italian cultural month Ciao Philadelphia, 2014. (Photo: Gary Horn)

Students drawing in front of the PAFA cast collection in 1901. (PAFA Archives)

porary art making, or providing the opportunity for PAFA students to visit Italy through its many travel scholarships for students, PAFA continues to nurture its educational roots in the early art academies of Italy. A thoroughly forward-looking institution, PAFA recognizes the firm ground its proactive and comprehensive curriculum is based on, and its Italian connections. One connection is the historic cast collection, carefully restored, cared for, and added to, one of the few great collections in the United States. The objects in the collection are superior in craftsmanship, often being first castings from the original sculptures, and are now very rare. Sister institutions in the United States such as the Slater Museum and Yale University, both in Connecticut, also own fine cast collections. The cast

collection at PAFA has been the subject of much research and information sharing between scholars, curators, and institutions such as the University of Pennsylvania, the Philadelphia Museum of Art, the Royal Academy in London, and the Victoria and Albert Museum in London. PAFA's cast of the Laocoon was recently on loan to the Philadelphia Museum of Art for the exhibition entitled *The Wrath of the Gods: Masterpieces by Michelangelo, Rubens and Titian.*

A centerpiece of the collection, and very popular with students and visitors, is Michelangelo's *David.* The approximately seventeen-foot-tall exact replica of the original, unveiled in Florence in 1504, was a gift to PAFA in 1988. Originally commissioned by the John Wanamaker department store in Philadelphia, the cast was intended to be the focal point of an Italian products exposition at the store. Never used because of its immense weight, over three thousand pounds, the statue was too heavy for the store's floor. The source of the cast is unknown at this time, but it most likely originated in Italy and has found a most appropriate home at PAFA. The beautiful cast was stored in pieces in the department store's basement until it was offered to PAFA. Today, *David* towers over the other casts in the collection at PAFA such as the Winged Victory, the Venus de Milo, the Belvedere Torso, Ghiberti's *Doors,* the Laocoon, and dozens of others.

The *David* cast was recently evaluated and conserved, as was the whole collection, by the Giust Gallery in Boston. Originally named Caproni, the firm has been providing fine casts and cast restoration since the end of the nineteenth century. Many of the casts in the PAFA collection bear the Caproni cartouche.

PAFA's cast of the *David* is assembled in several sections—lower body, upper body, and arms—all held in place by roman pins, an interlocking system of plaster keys and iron rods. Internal, embedded iron rods support the large masses of plaster and provide additional stability. Never having been moved since its installation, little damage has occurred. The cast's surface color is a pale off-white created by an original pale, thin, painted patina of shellac and pigment. Many antique casts were coated with shellac or paint, and restoration often involves removing layers of dirt and modern paints inappropriately applied to casts. Age has given a pleasing warmth to the *David*'s patina. Expert structural and surface evaluation deemed the cast and its patina stable and in excellent condition. Notably, excellent casts of the giant figure grace the collections of the Victoria and Albert Museum in London, the Belgian Royal Museums of Art and Art History in Brussels, and the Pushkin State Museum of Fine Arts in Moscow. The sources of those casts are unknown, but they were probably made in Italy, like PAFA's *David*.

As part of PAFA's ongoing contemporary museum exhibition program, the cast of the *David* presided over the groundbreaking performance in the Cast Hall by the

Several examples of Italian inspirations are found at the Pennsylvania Academy of the Fine Arts. Other than the historic Cast Hall collection, PAFA contains over one hundred sculptures, many of them of Italian origin, and its painting collection includes numerous Italian landscapes painted in the nineteenth century by Thomas Cole, Sanford Gifford, and Jasper Cropsey. Another example is the enigmatic masterpiece *Tasso's Oak*, painted by Peter Blume. Dating from 1957 to 1960, it was named after a tree planted in Rome by the famous sixteenth-century Italian poet Torquato Tasso. (Photo: Giò Martorana / Art © 2019 The Educational Alliance, Inc. / Estate of Peter Blume / Licensed by VAGA at Artists Rights Society [ARS], NY)

contemporary multimedia artist Cassils, entitled *Becoming an Image*, during their exhibition *Melt/Carve/Forge: Embodied Sculptures by Cassils* in 2016–2017.

Not surprisingly, items in the collection are sources of inspiration for contemporary U.S. art students and artists. The filmmaker David Lynch, an alumnus of PAFA in the 1960s, recently posed next to PAFA's *David* for photographers, though his studies at the school predate the arrival of the *David* cast. Contemporary PAFA undergraduate and graduate art students and guests from other institutions draw from the casts, learning both traditional drawing techniques and how to conceptualize and organize the complex visual language and architecture of these intricate objects for contemporary art.

The *David* cast is just one of the many links between PAFA and Italy. Current PAFA students, like generations before them, learn beginning lessons in art making from drawing the casts. Like the youthful Michelangelo drawing objects in the Medici collection, PAFA students learn balance, line quality, harmony, light and shade, composition, and architectural space from these beautiful representations of the art of Italy.

Walking into the Cast Hall at PAFA is like walking into the Italian Renaissance.

Designed by Frank Furness and George Hewitt, the Pennsylvania Academy of the Fine Arts building (1872–1876) reflects the aesthetics of the modern Gothic revival. This includes John Ruskin's appreciation of the richly colored designs of fourteenth-century Venice. (Photo: Richard Barnes)

10

"Pompeii Comes to Philadelphia"

The Wanamaker Bronzes in the University of Pennsylvania Museum

Ann Blair Brownlee

"New Bronzes for Penn" was the headline in the *Philadelphia Inquirer* on May 7, 1905, and the article recorded that "a collection of casts of the best bronzes in the Naples Museum, collected by John Wanamaker, were formally presented by him to the Archaeological Museum of the University of Pennsylvania and placed on exhibition."[1] The bronzes, reproductions of sculpture and objects in the Naples Archaeological Museum from the ancient sites of Pompeii and Herculaneum, had come from Naples to Philadelphia via St. Louis, where they had decorated the Italian Pavilion at the St. Louis World's Fair. The Penn Museum had only been in its grand new home since 1899, and the bronzes took their places alongside recently excavated Roman sculpture in the Graeco-Roman Section in the vaulted William Pepper Hall, named for the Penn provost and one of the new museum's founders.

The donor of the bronzes, John Wanamaker (1838–1922), Philadelphia department store founder and philanthropist, was a prominent supporter, and he was named to its Board of Managers in 1895 and served until the year of his death. Wanamaker was one of the most influential people in Philadelphia, and William Pepper (1843–1898) and Sara Yorke Stevenson (1847–1921), another of the museum's founders and curator of its Egyptian and Mediterranean sections, looked forward to his support and leadership as the new institution began to build its new home and acquire its collections.

The collection of Wanamaker bronzes consists of more than 450 bronze reproductions, and all of them are from the Naples Museum except for a very few, such as the so-called Borghese satyr from the Galleria Borghese in Rome, which has greeted museum visitors at the main entrance for more than fifty years. There is large-scale sculpture from the Villa of the Papyri at Herculaneum, as well as objects associated with daily life in Pompeii: furniture, candelabra, weights, vases,

and musical, medical, and architectural instruments. The bronzes were made by J. Chiurazzi & Fils, a foundry in Naples, which was established in 1870 and became well known for its fine bronze reproductions of ancient objects.

Bronze copies, especially small-scale versions, of famous Roman statues had long been produced, but Chiurazzi, along with a few other foundries, had been given permission to make moulds directly from the originals in the Naples Museum and elsewhere and thereby to produce very close reproductions. Chiurazzi touted this authenticity in its catalogues, where bronze reproductions would be identified by their Naples Museum numbers, thereby calling attention to the faithfulness of the reproductions. Clearly hoping to appeal to a wide audience of both individuals and institutions, Chiurazzi offered their casts in different sizes and finishes. The full-scale versions began to appear in American museums as collections of so-called Pompeian bronzes—even though many were actually from Herculaneum. Bronze reproductions were also exhibited at world's fairs, such as the World's Columbian Exposition in Chicago in 1893, and Wanamaker might have seen them there. He visited a number of world's fairs, and the display of goods from all over the world in the vast halls of the fairs undoubtedly inspired his vision for a new kind of store and gave him the opportunity to see the art of other countries, including Italy.

In 1896, soon after he joined the museum's Board of Managers, Wanamaker gave his support to his first archaeological venture for the museum, excavations at the important Etruscan site of Orvieto in central Italy. Here he could bring together his interest in archaeology and in Italy and his desire to promote the new institution at the University of Pennsylvania. While on a six-month trip that took him to Europe, including Italy and Greece, and to Egypt and to the Holy Land, Wanamaker visited Orvieto with Arthur L. Frothingham, the Museum's antiquities agent in Italy (Chapter 25). Frothingham was also a Princeton professor and associate director of the newly established American School of Classical Studies (now the

ABOVE LEFT: View of Pepper Hall, with the Wanamaker bronzes, ca. 1905. (Courtesy of Penn Museum, image #148681)

ABOVE RIGHT: John Wanamaker, ca. 1890. (John Wanamaker collection [2188]. Historical Society of Pennsylvania)

American Academy) in Rome, and he was anxious to get Wanamaker's financial support for excavations at Orvieto. Ultimately Wanamaker gave a monthly subscription to Frothingham to support excavations, primarily on land belonging to Riccardo Mancini, in the Etruscan cemetery called the Crocifisso del Tufo. Frothingham did not report his progress on a regular basis, however, and Wanamaker, irritated at the lack of communication, withdrew his support and moved on to sponsor other projects at the Museum. But it is thanks to Wanamaker that the Museum has a very important collection of Greek vases found in the Etruscan tombs at Orvieto.

On the way home from another long trip, this time to India, Wanamaker spent several days in Naples, staying at the Hotel Vesuvius on the waterfront near the Castel dell'Ovo, with a dramatic view of Mount Vesuvius. He indulged his archaeological interests in visits to Pompeii and to Vesuvius. It seems likely that he would also have gone to the Naples Archaeological Museum to see the galleries devoted to Pompeii and Herculaneum, including those that were filled with bronzes. This might have brought back memories of the bronze reproductions he had seen in Chicago. He might also have been thinking of the new museum back in Philadelphia and its relatively small collection of classical sculpture. Whatever the inspiration, in early 1902, Wanamaker placed a huge order for bronze reproductions with the Chiurazzi foundry. Their studio was located in the vast Albergo dei Poveri, but there were also two showrooms, one in the Piazza dei Martiri and another in the Galleria Principe di Napoli, a large shopping arcade across from the archaeological museum. One might imagine that he visited the shop close to the museum, where he, along with other foreign visitors, looked at samples and photographs, perhaps with the assistance of Angelo del Nero, who later said that he "directed the making [of the bronze collection] by appointment of the Hon. John Wanamaker."[2]

Chiurazzi shop front in the Galleria Principe di Napoli, ca. 1900. (From *J. Chiurazzi et Fils, Fournisseurs de Cours et Musées. Salles d'Exposition et Vente. Naples*. Milan 1900)

Royal Italian Pavilion at the St. Louis World's Fair. (Courtesy of the Missouri Historical Society, St. Louis)

Interior of the Royal Italian Pavilion. (*Louisiana and the Fair: An Exposition of the World, Its People, and Their Achievements.* Ed. J. W. Buel. St. Louis 1904–1905; v. 6, after p. 2126)

The bronzes were made during the next year or so, and in 1904, they headed to the United States, not to Philadelphia but to St. Louis for the World's Fair. Wanamaker loaned them so they could adorn the Royal Italian Pavilion at the fair celebrating the centennial of the Louisiana Purchase. In 1893, at the World's Columbian Exposition in Chicago, Pompeian reproductions had been exhibited in the Palace of Fine Arts, along with art from many different countries. The St. Louis World's Fair, however, had a large number of foreign pavilions, where individual nations could display their manufacturing, culture, and art. The Italian Pavilion was the work of the Art Nouveau architect

Giuseppe Sommaruga from Milan, and with its large, walled garden and vaulted spaces, it was meant to recall a grand Roman villa. Contemporary commentators particularly remarked on its "Caesarian" or imperial character, an impression no doubt enhanced by the bronze reproductions adorning the pavilion's interior. In the pavilion's main hall, the Borghese satyr took center stage and was encircled by other bronze statues and busts. Marble busts of Roman emperors (also supplied by Chiurazzi), a copy of the Greek vase known as the François Vase from the Archaeological Museum in Florence, and portraits of the Italian royal family completed the decoration of the domed space.

The Chiurazzi firm's work was shown to great advantage in this setting and was introduced to a new group of potential buyers. A catalogue listing 389 examples accompanied the exhibition, and its title page proclaimed, "This collection of bronzes made upon the order of John Wanamaker of Philadelphia for the Archaeological Museum of the University of Pennsylvania."[3] Orders for bronzes could be placed at the fair, and the catalogue noted that "Mr. S. Chiurazzi [Salvatore Chiurazzi, son of the founder] in charge, cheerfully solicits your patronage." The Italian Pavilion was a popular attraction, and when President Theodore Roosevelt and first lady Edith Roosevelt visited the fair in late November 1904, Salvatore Chiurazzi presented Mrs. Roosevelt with a reproduction of the famous dancing faun from the House of the Faun at Pompeii. Wanamaker also visited the German Pavilion, where he acquired a number of objects including the bronze eagle

Faun from the House of the Faun, Pompeii, bronze reproduction. University of Pennsylvania Museum MS3820. (Courtesy of Penn Museum, image #245343)

that became a signature feature of his flagship Philadelphia store. The famous Wanamaker organ had been in the fair's Festival Hall. Wanamaker purchased it in 1909 for his new Philadelphia store. He also acquired much of the fair's Egyptian exhibition for the museum, most notably the painted tomb chapel of Kaipure.

The St. Louis World's Fair closed in December 1904, and the bronzes were packed and shipped to Philadelphia. The shipment of twenty-three cases was delayed, principally because of difficulties with clearances for the Egyptian material, and did not leave St. Louis until early January 1905. Salvatore Chiurazzi wrote to Sara Yorke Stevenson and told her that the bronzes had been loaded onto the train and were on their way to Philadelphia. On January 25, the *Philadelphia Inquirer* announced that "Noted Antiquities Come Here" with the arrival of "seventy-eight big cases" containing the "Wanamaker collection of Egyptian relics" and "many bronze casts of the famous statues unearthed at Pompeii and Herculaneum."[4] And finally, on February 17, Stevenson announced the good news that the "Egyptian collection from St. Louis and the collection of Naples bronzes had arrived."[5]

The bronzes were soon put on exhibition, and they took their place beside other casts of ancient works as well as originals in the Graeco-Roman Section in Pepper Hall and on the landing and stepped parapet of the central staircase. The exhibition was inaugurated in

May 1905 with a lecture in the museum's Widener lecture hall delivered by William Nickerson Bates, curator in the Mediterranean Section and professor of classics. But over time, as the museum's collection of archaeological material grew, and reproductions were not much valued, the bronzes were gradually removed from the galleries. In the 1950s, seven bronzes were placed outside as garden sculpture at the museum's main courtyard. But now, only the Borghese Satyr remains outside, an iconic figure at the museum's main entrance, for the sculpture has come back inside as the value of casts for students and for study has become recognized again.

When John Wanamaker gave the collection to the museum, Sara Yorke Stevenson praised the bronzes: "They enable students and laymen alike to study at home the history and civilizations of foreign regions, and they bring to our own people the very best inspirations of the past, placing them in touch with the artists and artisans of the ancient world to which the new world is indebted for the elements of its own culture."[6] Surely these words echo Wanamaker's own intention in giving this great gift to the museum, and indeed, as Stevenson concluded, "Philadelphia owes a debt of sincere gratitude to Mr. Wanamaker."[7]

ACKNOWLEDGMENT

My thanks to Lynn Makowsky and Alessandro Pezzati at the University of Pennsylvania Museum.

NOTES

1. *Philadelphia Inquirer*, May 7, 1905, p. 6. The correspondence referred to below is in the Archives of the University of Pennsylvania Museum.

2. Letter from Andrea del Nero to Sara Yorke Stevenson, dated only February 10, with no year, but almost certainly 1905. Museum Archives. A sculptor, del Nero served as the Italian Commissioner of Fine Arts at the 1893 fair.

3. See the title page of *S. Chiurazzi & Fils. Naples, Italy. Bronze Foundry. Reproductions of the Bronzes Found at Pompei and Herculaneum ... World's Fair Grounds. Royal Italian Pavilion.* Privately published, 1904. Copy in University of Pennsylvania Museum Archives.

4. *Philadelphia Inquirer*, January 25, 1905, p. 5.

5. Minutes of the Board of Managers, February 17, 1905. University of Pennsylvania Museum Archives.

6. Newspaper clipping from unidentified source in scrapbook, University of Pennsylvania Museum Archives.

7. Ibid.

FURTHER READING

Buel, James W. *Louisiana and the Fair: An Exposition of the World, Its People and their Achievements.* St. Louis: World's Progress Publishing Co., [1904–1906], vol. 6, pp. 2125–2129.

Fucito, Luisa. *Fonderia Artistica Chiurazzi: La Forma dell'Arte.* Naples: Altrastampa, 2001.

Gibbons, Herbert Adams. *John Wanamaker [2 vol. set].* New York: Harper, 1926.

Mattusch, Carol C. *The Villa dei Papiri at Herculaneum: Life and Afterlife of a Sculpture Collection.* Los Angeles: The J. Paul Getty Museum, 2005.

11

"A Dazzling Array"

Italian Art and the Philadelphia Museum of Art

Jennifer A. Thompson

THE PHILADELPHIA MUSEUM OF ART, like the city in which it resides, is recognized for its commitment to Italian art and culture. For over 140 years, the art of Italy has featured in the museum's galleries and programs. The collection today boasts over twenty thousand Italian works dating from antiquity to the present, including paintings, sculptures, prints, drawings, photographs, film, textiles, arms and armor, architectural elements, furniture, ceramics, and glass. The story is not simply one of the acquisition and display of great works of Italian art but also one of engaging local and international communities and building fruitful partnerships with Italian institutions. This essay explores the rich and diverse history of Italian art at the museum in a series of episodes or vignettes that shed light on how acquisitions, programming, exhibitions, and education have shaped the way Philadelphians engage with Italian art.

The Pennsylvania Museum and School of Industrial Art (as the museum was known before its name change in 1938) was founded on the eve of Philadelphia's 1876 Centennial Exposition to show examples of industry and craftsmanship from around the world. Many of the institution's first objects reflected the European origins and interests of its founders and came from the centennial's exhibits. They included Italian maiolica, silk vestments, metalwork, armor, and marble sculptures that were purchased from the fair or given by groups such as the Chamber of Commerce and Art of Siena. The museum's founders looked to the Victoria and Albert Museum in

FACING PAGE: West facade of the Philadelphia Museum of Art with a replica of the "Fountain of the Sea Horses" in Villa Borghese, Rome, in the foreground. It was presented by Benito Mussolini in honor of the U.S. sesquicentennial in 1926 as written in the dedications carved in Italian and English. (Philadelphia Museum of Art)

London—an institution showcasing decorative or "useful" arts—as a model, though the association with a school meant that the Philadelphia collections also served as teaching tools and supported efforts to improve the quality of goods manufactured in the region. Since purchase funds were limited, the fledgling collection was built largely through gifts. Notable early donations included Venetian lace from the Associate Committee of Women in 1894, Greco-Roman objects from metallurgist and engineer Dr. Robert Lamborn in 1903, a cast of Nicola Pisano's pulpit from Siena Cathedral in 1903, and Capodimonte porcelain and ancient Roman glass in 1908.

These objects were presented to students and the public at Memorial Hall, the art building of the Centennial Fair, which had been retained for use as a museum after the exhibition. Initially, the displays were arranged according to materials and techniques regardless of geographic origin. Italian works could be found in rooms devoted to sculpture, woodwork, glass vessels, textiles, and porcelains, among others. This taxonomy of the collection was considered beneficial for industrial school students who tended to concentrate on specific media, but it proved frustrating to collectors and general visitors who were interested in the diverse arts of a region.[1] In 1913 the school augmented its teaching program by offering students a chance to study Italian art firsthand. Three $500 travel scholarships—the first of their kind in the United States—were created to send students to Italy. Funded by Mrs. James Mifflin and Mrs. Joseph F. Sinnott of the Women's Committee and New York financier Mr. Charles Burnham Squier, the scholarships allowed students to visit Naples, Rome, Florence, and Venice to study "art in place . . . to see the hinges and locks on doors, and not torn off and laid on red velvet; to see the bronze bracket attached to the stone and the fountain to the wall."[2] This unique approach was the brainchild of Howard Fremont Stratton, director of the school's Art Department, who accompanied the three recipients to Italy in the summer of 1914: John Ray Sinnock in interior design, Parke Emerson Edwards in wrought iron, and Leon William Corson in decorative modeling and pottery. Stratton guided their study and that of ten other faculty members and alumni who traveled together and spent most of their time in Florence, studying at the Laurentian Library, the Bargello Collection, the Cantagalli Company, the Stibbert Museum, and San Miniato al Monte and other churches. On their return, the scholarship recipients went on to substantial careers: Sinnock became the eighth Chief Engineer of the U.S. Mint and designed the Roosevelt dime and Franklin half dollar, Edwards designed much of the decorative metalwork at Bryn Athyn Cathedral, and Corson was responsible for a revival of Italian sgraffito pottery.

The museum's commitment to providing visitors and students with an immersive experience—like that encountered while studying abroad—took new shape in 1912 with the creation of an Italian alcove. Measuring thirty-three feet wide and twelve feet high, the room contained paneled woodwork inspired by the Gallery of King Francis I at Fontainebleau Palace designed by Rosso Fiorentino and Primaticcio and was filled with examples of Italian Renaissance chairs, chests, mirrors, fire irons, a harpsichord, and other objects. This space, meant to evoke a Renaissance room, had an unexpected counterpart in an Italian-themed amusement park ride popular around the same time. For those unable to travel abroad, the Panadrome in Chestnut Hill Park offered Philadelphians a "120 mile trip through Italy, giving positively true-to-life glimpses from the train window of all the ruins of ancient Roman grandeur and the beauties of modern Italian culture and art."[3] The ride's scenery suggested a breakneck trip from Rome to Naples and was appreciated by adults and children alike. In September 1903, the experience was accompanied by the music of Luigi Chiaffarelli, a visiting band leader considered the "Italian Sousa," and his forty-piece band.

In 1916 the museum hosted its first temporary exhibition devoted to the work of contemporary American artists of foreign birth. Italians were well represented by Nicola d'Ascenzo, Adolfo De'Nesti, Giuseppi Donato, James Novelli, Cesare A. Ricciardi, Onoric Ruotolo, and Luigi Spirrizzi, among others. The exhibition, which showed the work of many European-born artists, was a success and was seen by over thirty-five thousand visitors in January and February 1916. Its intended aim, "to unite the various races and peoples of this country into a single nation," was driven by wartime concerns for unity and a nationalist spirit while demonstrating the talent of local artists.[4]

The arrival of the museum's seventh director, architectural historian Fiske Kimball, in 1926 initiated a concerted effort to acquire fine examples of Italian interiors. Kimball was impressed by German museums in which paintings, sculptures, and decorative arts were integrated into "composite" displays that evoked vivid historical settings.[5] Such spaces, it was believed, gave museum visitors an opportunity to engage with cultures and places they might not otherwise experience and provided context for collection objects. To that end, in the months leading up to the opening of the museum's new building on the Benjamin Franklin Parkway in 1928, Kimball actively pursued the acquisition of interiors from China, Japan, England, France, and Italy. Notable among them was a fifteenth-century bedroom from a Venetian palace. The Palazzo Soranzo Van Axel, located in the Canareggio near the church of Santa Maria dei Miracoli, was built in the twelfth and thirteenth centuries and renovated in the 1470s by Nicolò Soranzo, a merchant who held the important position of procurator of Venice. Kimball appreciated its late Gothic detail and resemblance to the Ducal Palace and the Ca d'Oro as well as its literary and cultural associations; it was speculated that the poets Torquato Tasso and Pietro Aretino, close friends of the Soranzo family, might have written some of their poetry there. Detailed correspondence with Conte Dino Barozzi, a Venetian antiquarian and dealer who acquired the palace in 1920, reveals Kimball's interest in obtaining as many original architectural elements from the second-floor room as possible. He succeeded in purchasing a mantel, a sculpted stone fireplace, and the woodwork and ceiling of a sleeping alcove as the building was being renovated and its interior reconfigured. Venetian craftsmen recreated the windows,

Room from the Palazzo
Soranzo—Van Axel,
Venice, fifteenth, sixteenth,
seventeenth, and twentieth
centuries. (Philadelphia Museum
of Art: Gift of Thomas J. Dolan,
Clarence W. Dolan, and H. Yale
Dolan in memory of their
parents, Thomas Dolan and
Sarah Brooke Dolan, 1929-52-1)

cornice, fireplace hood, and floors, elements that either could not be removed from
the palace or were determined to be later restorations. In Philadelphia, the room
components were adjusted slightly, and it was filled with fifteenth-century furniture from the museum's collection such that "no other interior in this country will
so ably represent the atmosphere and character of Venice during the most important period of her history."[6]

Kimball's pursuit of Italian art was not limited to architecture and furnishings.
In 1929 he oversaw the acquisition of a collection of medieval and Renaissance art
assembled by Edmond Foulc, a Parisian collector and heir to a silk-manufacturing
fortune. Among the two hundred objects acquired in 1930 and paid for over the
next twenty years were extraordinary examples of Italian sculpture, including a
glazed terra-cotta tondo by Luca della Robbia and a marble relief of the Virgin and
Child by Desiderio da Settignano, whose poignant and tender rendering of figures
and drapery in shallow relief astounds. These acquisitions signaled the museum's
shift away from study collections of industrial products and its focus instead on
acquiring and displaying exceptional pieces of Italian art, a pursuit shared by many
American collectors and institutions.

Throughout this period, Philadelphia newspapers extolled the virtues of Italian art galleries and published accounts of tours in Italy.[7] Numerous Philadelphians
traveled to the Italian peninsula, where they admired historic sites and acquired
art. Among them was Isaac Lea, a natural scientist with publishing and mercantile
fortunes who acquired 192 old master paintings, many of them Italian, during a trip

FACING PAGE, TOP:
Desiderio da Settignano
(Italian, 1429/32–1464),
Virgin and Child, ca.1455–
60, marble. (Philadelphia
Museum of Art: Purchased with
the W.P. Wilstach Fund from
the Edmond Foulc Collection,
W1930-1-73)

to Florence in 1852–1853. His son Matthew Carey Lea favored drawings, as did John S. Phillips, a businessman who assembled the largest collection of graphic arts in America in the mid-nineteenth century, including the impressive drawing of *Christ Disputing with the Doctors in the Temple*, attributed to Francesco Salviati and purchased in Italy in the 1850s. The Phillips and Lea collections made their way to the museum a century later, joining others such that the museum's nearly 2,700 Italian drawings make it a prominent place of study in this field today.[8] Other Philadelphians followed suit. In 1881 John T. Morris, a member of a prosperous Philadelphia Quaker family, bought a bronze bell by the Poli Brothers foundry while in Milan and gave it to the museum, encouraging others to do the same by writing, "If each traveler would bring home an object for the Museum, it would help in the good work."[9] These collectors and their successors, including William L. Elkins, John G. Johnson, John McIlhenny, P.A.B. Widener, and George and Henrietta Wurts, benefited from wars and upheavals that caused many noble Italian families to sell their collections of paintings, furniture, and decorative arts to wealthy Americans who were eager to surround themselves with distinguished pieces of the European past.[10]

In the early years of the twentieth century, Philadelphia lawyer John G. Johnson acquired more than 450 Italian paintings and dramatically shaped the city's holdings in Italian Renaissance and baroque art. Johnson made a trip to Italy in

LEFT: Francesco Salviati (Francesco de' Rossi, also called il Cecchino), Italian, 1510–1563, *Christ Disputing with the Doctors in the Temple*, 1539? Pen and brush and brown ink, heightened with white opaque watercolor, on laid paper toned with brown wash. (Philadelphia Museum of Art: The Muriel and Philip Berman Gift, acquired from the John S. Phillips bequest of 1876 to the Pennsylvania Academy of the Fine Arts, with funds contributed by Muriel and Philip Berman and the Edgar Viguers Seeler Fund [by exchange], 1984-56-78)

the early 1870s and documented the occasion by being photographed in Venice by Antonio Sorgato. He returned to Italy at least three more times during summer holidays in 1878, 1884, and 1909. Initially, Johnson was attracted to contemporary Italian paintings by artists such as Tito Conti, Camillo Innocenti, Franceso Paolo Michetti, and Alberto Pasini, and he attended the 1884 Turin Internationale Esposizione, methodically annotating a catalogue with notes on paintings he liked and ones that had been sold.[11] For reasons that are not entirely clear, around 1900 his taste shifted significantly toward older Italian paintings such as fragments of altarpieces and works by artists including Sandro Botticelli, Carlo Crivelli, Duccio, Francesco Guardi, and others in such numbers that the Milanese journal *Rassegna d'Arte* devoted a nine-page article to Johnson's Italian paintings in 1905, calling the collection "one of America's finest in this genre."[12]

Four years later, Johnson embarked on a significant purchase, Titian's portrait of Archbishop Filippo Archinto. The art advisor Bernard Berenson first saw the work in Venice in October 1909 and proposed it to Johnson, writing that "the subject of the picture is so strange that the millionaires will scarcely bid for it. It may be possible to get it at a relatively modest price, in which case it would be just the thing for Mr. Johnson."[13] Acknowledging Johnson's indifference to expensive pictures, Berenson played to the collector's appreciation for works that others might find difficult or atypical. Here the archbishop has a gauzelike veil covering part of his face, producing a subtle and intimate portrait. Berenson suggested that the veil alluded to political troubles that prevented the archbishop from assuming his pontifical office in Milan. Today the work is regarded as a virtuoso example of Titian's mastery of paint and illusion, the veil perhaps an indication that the portrait was painted at the time of the sitter's death in 1558. Berenson highlighted the unique painterly qualities of the work and was not opposed to using peer pressure to encourage Johnson: "It is thus about the date of the Maniago Titian that the Wideners have just got and in every way of as fine a quality … and there is your chance."[14] P.A.B. Widener, a classmate from Central High School as well as Johnson's legal client, friend, and fellow collector, had acquired a portrait of Irene di Spilimbergo, dated 1560, from the Maniago family from the Florentine dealer Elia Volpi a few months earlier, perhaps spurring Johnson's admiration and desire to acquire his own late Titian.[15] With purchases like these, the British critic Roger Fry could claim Philadelphia's growing prestige as a center for Italian art, writing to Johnson that "Philadelphia is becoming a new Rome and your house a Vatican."[16]

At the time of his death in 1917, Johnson's collection totaled 1,279 paintings, 51 sculptures, and more than 150 other objects, of which the Italian pictures represented nearly a third and were complement-

Antonio Sorgato (Italian, 1825–1885). John G. Johnson, 1870s. (Photographs and other images, John G. Johnson Papers, Philadelphia Museum of Art, Library and Archives)

ed by sizable holdings of Dutch, Netherlandish, and French painting. In his taste for Italian art, especially the work of artists such as Sandro Botticelli or Fra Angelico, Johnson was matched only by Isabella Stewart Gardner of Boston or J. Pierpont Morgan of New York, and in bequeathing these artworks to the city, he gave Philadelphia an Italian art collection rivalling that of many European cities.

Johnson intended for his collection to be shown in his home at 510 South Broad Street, a four-story brownstone that he famously packed floor to ceiling, parlor to service stairs, with paintings. The city briefly explored the idea of creating a freestanding Johnson Gallery on the Benjamin Franklin Parkway (the site now occupied by the Rodin Museum), and architect Horace Trumbauer drew up plans inspired the Pazzi Chapel in Florence, designed by Brunelleschi in 1442 for the use of the Franciscan friars of Santa Croce. While the feasibility of this construction was being debated, sixty-two of Johnson's Italian paintings were shown at Memorial Hall in March 1920. It was the first time Philadelphians had had an opportunity to see "characteristic and beautiful examples of the Venetian, Florentine, Umbrian, Milanese, Sienese, and Piedmont schools. . . . One would have to go to the Uffizi and Pitti in Florence or to the Louvre in Paris, or to the National Gallery in London to match the effect of the middle bay in Memorial Hall, with its dazzling array of portraits and sacred subjects," wrote one newspaper.[17] The installation was popular, with 13,387 Philadelphians visiting in a one-week period.[18]

In 1923 Johnson's home on Broad Street was outfitted as a public gallery, Trumbauer's plans having been abandoned as too costly, and the city began to show rotating displays of around two hundred works from the collection.[19] The first installation of nineteenth-century French landscapes was by soon replaced by Italian paintings, heralded for their color, imagination, and brilliance. Ten years later, the Johnson Collection was moved to the Philadelphia Museum of Art, since funds to keep the gallery open were scarce during the Great Depression. When the new Johnson galleries opened in October 1933, they displayed the Italian works first. From the 1930s to the present day, the Johnson Collection has become a necessary stop for art historians thanks to the contributions of generations of curators including Carl Brandon Strehlke, whose 2004 catalogue of Italian paintings from 1250 to 1450 has ensured that the Johnson Collection is well published and a consistent part of art historical discourse. In recent years, the collection has become more inextricably linked with the museum, and since the 1990s it has been installed

Titian (Tiziano Vecellio), Italian (active Venice), first securely documented in 1508, died in 1576, *Portrait of Archbishop Filippo Archinto*, ca. 1558, oil on canvas. John G. Johnson Collection, Cat. 204. (Philadelphia Museum of Art)

The Johnson Collection installed at the Philadelphia Museum of Art alongside architectural fragments, 2011. (Philadelphia Museum of Art)

alongside period architecture and furnishings, helping to provide context for objects now removed from their original settings.

With the Johnson Collection ensuring the city's status as a primary center in America for the study and appreciation of Italian old master paintings, the museum enhanced its commitment to programming, exhibitions, and the display of contemporary Italian works. Museum curators Henry Clifford, Henry McIlhenny, and Carl Zigrosser visited Italy in 1948 to assess wartime museum damage and assisted in efforts to restore monuments. Clifford, the museum's curator of paintings, became deeply involved in the America-Italy Society of Philadelphia, a group that promoted friendship between the two countries through art, science, literature, music, painting, and law. From 1956 to 1964, the museum and the society hosted annual Italian baroque concerts performed by members of the Philadelphia Orchestra known as the Amerita String Orchestra. The concerts were so successful that the museum regularly exceeded the limits of its four-hundred-seat auditorium. The organization also hosted an Italian lecture series and sponsored exhibitions at the museum, such as one in 1964 on the Macchiaioli, a group of Tuscan artists interested in nature, light, and color like the French impressionists.

In the second half of the twentieth century and into the twenty-first, the museum has organized an ambitious calendar of loan exhibitions devoted to Italian art, often introducing influential but less familiar artists and movements to Philadelphia audiences. The graphic work of sculptor Marino Marini, drawings from the Accademia Carrara of Bergamo, Italian maiolica, stage designs, and baroque terra-cotta sculptures have populated the exhibition program alongside focus shows on Giorgio de Chirico, the reconstruction of an early fifteenth-century altarpiece by the Florentine master Gherardo Starnina, and paintings by the nineteenth-century Neapolitan artist Antonio Mancini.

Living artists have been prominent partners in projects, as when fashion designer Elsa Schiaparelli visited Philadelphia in 1969 and was celebrated at a luncheon hosted by the Fashion Group, a museum support committee. To mark the occasion, Schiaparelli presented over seventy gowns and accessories from her 1935–1940 collections to the museum, including a magnificent harlequin coat that juxtaposes a playful pattern and a masculine silhouette. Schiaparelli's contributions to the field of fashion were explored in a 2003 exhibition curated by Dilys E. Blum that addressed Schiaparelli's career from the 1920s to the 1950s and her special relationship with and impact on the American fashion industry. Similarly, Italian leadership in the field of modern design has been highlighted in acquisitions and exhibitions involving Joe Colombo, the Alessi firm, and Gaetano Pesce, whose experiments with unusual materials and forms and engagement with ideas of critical design is evident in his acclaimed "Up 5" chair and "Up 6" ottoman.

The museum's tradition of showing works of different media together was highlighted in *The Splendor of Eighteenth-Century Rome*, a survey of paintings, sculpture, drawings, and architectural models created in the eternal city during the century in which it was the cultural and artistic capital of Europe. Organized by Joseph J. Rishel, Dean Walker, and Ann Percy, curators of paintings, sculpture and decorative arts, and drawings, respectively, the spring 2000 show involved 380 loans and sixty-nine scholars from Europe and America and drew attention to the museum's international stature and distin-

ABOVE: Designed by Elsa Schiaparelli, French (born in Italy), 1890–1973, embroidered by Lesage, Paris, founded in 1922, Woman's Evening Coat, spring 1939. Wool felt, fulled wool, and silk thread embroidery. (Philadelphia Museum of Art, Gift of Mme Elsa Schiaparelli, 1969-232-3)

RIGHT: Designed by Gaetano Pesce, Italian, born in 1939. Made from 1973 to 1981, 1984, and 1994 to the present by B&B Italia, Milan, founded in 1966. "Up 5" chair and "Up 6" ottoman, designed in 1969 and reissued in 1994. Expandable polyurethane foam and stretch jersey fabric. (Philadelphia Museum of Art, Gift of Collab, 2000-151-1,2)

guished holdings in this field. It was followed by the organization of the American pavilion at the 2009 Venice Biennale, where curators Carlos Basualdo and Michael Taylor developed an exhibition devoted to American artist Bruce Nauman that won the prized Golden Lion award and demonstrated the museum's capacity to organize projects on Italian soil.

No less groundbreaking was the exhibition a few years later on the work of postwar artist Michelangelo Pistoletto, whose substantial contributions to the pop, minimalism, and conceptual art movements were relatively unknown in the United States. Organized in collaboration with MAXXI, the Museo Nazionale delle Arti del XXI Secolo in Rome, the ambitious monographic project included Pistoletto's astonishing mirror paintings of the 1960s and his *Stracci* (Rags) series of the 1970s that used humble pieces of cloth in performance. During the Philadelphia exhibition, Pistoletto engaged the city of Philadelphia with a captivating piece called *Walking Sculpture (Scultura da passeggio)*. On Saturday, October 30, 2010, the artist led children, museum staff, and visitors on a walk from the museum to city hall rolling a four-foot-diameter ball created from newspaper strips. The performance recreated a 1967 walk through the city of Turin with a similar ball of newspaper and demonstrated powerfully to participants and curious observers an artist's ability to provoke questions, participation, and dialogue.

The Splendor of 18th Century Rome (March 16, 2000– May 28, 2000). (Philadelphia Museum of Art)

In 2018 the museum embarked on two projects involving collaborations with Italian institutions. A selection of the museum's finest examples of impressionist and French modern paintings were seen for the first time in Italy at the Palazzo Reale in Milan in an exhibition that examined art collecting in Philadelphia. At the same moment, the museum partnered with the Turin-based Fondazione Sandretto Re Rebaudengo and launched the Future Fields Commission in Time-Based Media with a work by artist Rachel Rose titled *Wil-o-Wisp*. The video piece reflects on reality, perception, history, and coincidence in the sixteenth century and was shown in Philadelphia and then Turin as the first in a series of joint commissions by the Italian and American institutions. These initiatives affirm that the Philadelphia Museum of Art's commitment to showing, supporting, and encouraging Italian art is not only thriving but expanding in new directions. Over the last century, the institution's scholarship, acquisitions, and exhibitions have developed an enthusiastic base of collectors, supporters, and visitors for whom Italian art is a vital part of the identity and programs of the museum today and into the future.

Artist Michelangelo Pistoletto rolling *Walking Sculpture* through Philadelphia, October 30, 2010, during the museum's Pistoletto exhibition. (Philadelphia Museum of Art)

ACKNOWLEDGMENTS

The author is grateful to Andrea Canepari and Judith Goode for the opportunity to work on this subject and indebted to Carl Brandon Strehlke, Jack Hinton, and Ann Percy for sharing their advice and perspectives on working with the museum's Italian collections. Graduate student Sarah Junod provided vital assistance in the research for this essay, which was prepared in 2017.

NOTES

1. Kathleen Curran, *The Invention of the American Art Museum: From Craft to Kulturgeschichte, 1870–1930* (Los Angeles: Getty Research Institute, 2016), pp. 173–201.

2. "Industrial Art Scholarships for Foreign Study," *Art and Progress*, vol. 5, no. 10 (August 1914), p. 360.

3. "Chestnut Hill Park Attractions," *Philadelphia Inquirer*, July 5, 1903, p. 5.

4. "Americanization through Art," *The Immigrants in America Review*, vol. 1, no. 3 (September 1915), p. 7.

5. Jack Hinton, Ken Sutherland, and Peggy Olley, "Kimball, Figdor and the Medici: Notes on the Collection and Display of Italian Renaissance Furniture at the Philadelphia Museum

of Art to 1930, Including a Technical Study of a Fifteenth-Century Painted Chest," *Furniture History*, vol. 45 (2009), p. 4.

6. Francis Henry Taylor, "A Venetian Gothic Room," *Bulletin of the Pennsylvania Museum*, vol. 24, no. 127 (April 1929), p. 7.

7. "The Quintet Club," *Philadelphia Inquirer*, August 10, 1891; W. H. Downes, "Famous Art Galleries of Italy," *Philadelphia Inquirer*, July 18, 1900, and July 25, 1900.

8. The John S. Phillips and Matthew Carey Lea Collections were initially given to the Pennsylvania Academy of the Fine Arts. In 1956 they were placed on long-term loan at the Philadelphia Museum of Art, and they were purchased by museum in 1984 and 1985. For more on both collectors, see Ann Percy, "Collecting Italian Drawings at Philadelphia: Two Nineteenth-Century Amateurs and a Twentieth-Century Scholar," in *Italian Master Drawings at the Philadelphia Museum of Art* (Philadelphia: Philadelphia Museum of Art, 2004), pp. 11–101.

9. Kathryn Bloom Hiesinger, *Collecting Modern: Design at the Philadelphia Museum of Art since 1876* (Philadelphia: Philadelphia Museum of Art, 2011), p. 38.

10. See, for example, Carl Brandon Strehlke, "Filadelfia—Roma: George Washington Wurts e Henrietta Tower da Lincoln a Mussolini," in *Voglia d'Italia. Il collezionismo internazionale nella Roma del Vittoriano*, ed. Emanuele Pellegrini (Naples: arte'm, 2017), pp. 49–79.

11. Carl Brandon Strehlke, *Italian Paintings, 1250–1450, in the John G. Johnson Collection and the Philadelphia Museum of Art* (Philadelphia: Philadelphia Museum of Art, 2004), pp. 1–10.

12. F. Mason-Perkins, "Pitture Italiane nella raccolta Johnson a Filadelfia (S.U.A.)," *Rassegna D'Arte*, no. 8 (August 1905), pp. 113–121.

13. Bernard Berenson to John G. Johnson, November 8, 1909, Bernard and Mary Berenson Papers, 1880–2002, Biblioteca Berenson, Villa I Tatti, Harvard University Center for Italian Renaissance Studies, Florence.

14. Ibid.

15. The Widener painting, now at the National Gallery of Art in Washington, DC, is considered the work of a follower of Titian today.

16. Roger Fry to John G. Johnson, August 21, 1909, Correspondence, John G. Johnson Papers, Philadelphia Museum of Art, Library and Archives.

17. "Johnson's Italian Canvases on View," unidentified newspaper clipping, March 10, 1920, Writings, Johnson Collection Curatorial Records, Philadelphia Museum of Art, Library and Archives.

18. "2231 Persons Daily View Johnson Paintings," unidentified newspaper clipping, n.d., Writings, Johnson Collection Curatorial Records, Philadelphia Museum of Art, Library and Archives.

19. For more on the history of the Johnson Collection, see Jennifer A. Thompson, "The John G. Johnson Collection from 1917 to the Present," in *The John G. Johnson Collection: A History and Selected Works*, ed. Christopher D. M. Atkins (Philadelphia: Philadelphia Museum of Art, 2017), https://doi.org/10.29075/9780876332764.

The Italian Legacy in the Gardens of Early Twentieth-Century Philadelphia

RAFFAELLA FABIANI GIANNETTO

AT THE TURN OF THE TWENTIETH CENTURY, the Italian style in landscape architecture was known across the Atlantic thanks to the books on the subject penned by American designers and critics, particularly Edith Wharton and Charles A. Platt. Their writings contributed to spell out the Italian garden's principles of design and the reason behind its timeless charm. Among the many foreign idioms available to American designers, the Italian style was especially appreciated for two reasons: its rigid geometry lent a measure of dignity to civic spaces and institutions that demanded a degree of austerity and decor, and, because its origins pointed to the classic civilization of ancient Rome, rediscovered during the Renaissance, the Italian garden embodied the mark of approval that only the passage of time could bestow. This was important for American families whose wealth had accumulated in the span of a generation and whose progeny lacked confidence in their own identity and place in American society. Architectural critic Herbert Croly wrote about the American millionaire that for fear of being identified as parvenu, he surrounded himself with objets d'art rich in historical association, often imported, and which exuded an atmosphere of time past and stability. The same appreciation of the effects of time on a work of art from a distant and glorious past pervades the rhetoric of Platt and Wharton, who describe for their fellow citizens the magical ambiance of the old gardens of Italy despite their being overgrown and sometimes even crumbling.[1]

Whether meant to dignify public space and institutions or used as foils to sumptuous private residences, the American gardens indebted to the Italian tradition were always an act of translation, effected by means of local materials and hardy plants that would have been foreign to the original model, and with only occasional direct quotations—that is, borrowings of exact forms. This is partly

due to the creative autonomy of the American designer. As Philadelphia architect Wilson Eyre, president of the Philadelphia Chapter of the American Institute of Architects at the turn of the century, argued in an editorial on "Modern Art," modern designers neglect both beauty and the past in an effort to be original. But "denying beauty is like Judas denying the Lord," and "the desperate attempt to be original always fails, but if you use the old forms in *a new way*, that leads to much better results."[2] Incidentally, Philadelphia and its surroundings contain several early twentieth-century gardens that are both eclectic and highly original while being Italian inspired. While discussing some of the most exemplary—such as the gardens of the Museum of Archaeology and Anthropology at the University of Pennsylvania and Longwood Gardens—this essay shows how the Italian influence on the gardens of Philadelphia was very much a matter of style, which at the turn of the century had become disassociated from the moral meanings once tied to land cultivation that early American colonists had learned from Roman classical authors. In this sense, the Italianate gardens of Philadelphia exemplify a trend that was common elsewhere in the country.

The original nucleus of the Penn Museum, designed by Eyre, Frank Miles Day, Walter Cope, and John Stewardson from 1893 to 1923, shows how historical sources, once "thoroughly assimilated," could then be "used unselfconsciously."[3] The architecture of the Penn Museum, formerly called the Free Museum of Science and Art, paid homage to the Romanesque style of northern Italy, inspired as it was by the basilica complex of the "Seven Churches" at Bologna. Yet this clear reference was rendered in the earthy tones of Philadelphia bricks, along with Byzantine and Japanese details that were meant to announce to the museum visitors the character of the collections. While the building's façade showed a dynamic "pointillist sparkle," the adjacent courtyard garden constituted a "most restful feature."[4] The garden was planted between 1896 and 1899. Correspondence in the Museum Archives suggests that Miles Day supervised much of the work on the garden, while Eyre, who authored an evocative watercolor of the garden in 1898, seems to have been responsible for its conception and layout. Eyre's rendering, conserved at the Architectural Archives, shows three elongated compartments lined by sharply pruned hedges, the outer compartments framing rectangular carpets of lawn, the central one containing a grass-fringed pool of water, its reflective surface mirroring the severity of the museum entrance enlivened by floating water lilies. The whole is rendered in subdued shades of green, the only flowering bushes appearing symmetrically within the smaller compartments of the slightly higher terrace. The correspondence between the architecture of the building and its garden is emphasized by their shared axis of symmetry, a feature of many Italian Renaissance villas, here reinforced by the presence of a grand entrance at the top of the double staircase, a smaller arched door at its foot on the lower level, and a water-spouting lion head and stone basin—modeled by Eyre—feeding the pool below. The only trees are reminiscent of Italian cypresses, whose columnar habit of growth punctuates the corners of the compartments, thereby underlining their rigid geometry. The tall, vertical presence of the trees in the foreground leads the eye toward the central body of the building, which juts out as if to reach them and is framed by pairs of equally tall evergreens on both sides. The effect is indeed one of carefully studied proportions that form a balanced composition of mineral and vegetal elements.

The correspondence and integration of architecture and garden were one of the hallmark characteristics of Italian villas according to Platt and Wharton. To understand why an Italian-inspired garden would be the obvious choice of foreground for the museum building, one only has to read a contemporary article published by Wharton's niece, Beatrix Farrand, in *Garden and Forest*. Here the landscape architect explained that a formal garden was needed, and indeed required, "when an imposing or somewhat pretentious building is at the end of it," because "formal work" alone can confer "dignified and quiet delight" to the whole.[5] Indeed, the original scheme for the Penn Museum was going to offer not just one but two Italianate twin gardens; the second was not implemented due to the economic downturn of the late 1920s, when all work came to an end, leaving also the eastern portion of the central, administrative wing of the museum incomplete.

From the earliest museum sketches of 1895 to the final master-plan drawings of 1925, a carriage drive that served as the main entrance to the building was planned in the central forecourt of the museum, around a circular fountain with a single vertical jet of water in its midst and edged by a grass-fringed stone curb. A 1921 red graphite drawing by Eyre in the archives shows the courtyard open to the street, in marked contrast to the enclosed gardens to the east and west. Archival documents record a request made by Eyre to insert a fountain on the interior part of the wall lining the street, facing the museum entrance. But besides this last nod to the Italian tradition, the forecourt was left barren for a long time until its redesign

Laurie Olin, Cortile Museo Nazionale, Rome, 1981.
(Courtesy Laurie Olin)

Laurie Olin, Pincio Fountain, Rome, 1990.
(Courtesy Laurie Olin)

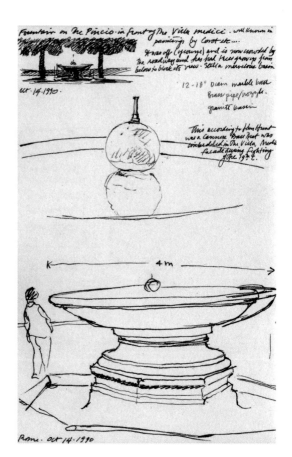

was entrusted, in 1996, to the Olin Partnership. Here, too, a careful observer can perceive an act of translation of the Italian tradition. Laurie Olin chose trees such as *Cryptomeria japonica* to symbolize the Asian art housed by the museum, but at the same time, because of their appearance, the trees bring to mind the cypresses at the center of the courtyard at the Museo Nazionale Romano.

Also Italian is the fish scale of the paving pattern, while the central basin with its water-spouting marble ball quotes a similar detail from the fountain in front of the Villa Medici in Rome. In his initial proposal, Olin would have wanted to keep the sculptural fragments that were scattered on the ground, a practice that was common among wealthy Renaissance connoisseurs, usually members of the church, as recorded in the famous sixteenth-century painting of Cardinal Cesi's *vigna* in Rome by the Flemish artist Hendrick van Cleef III. Art collectors in Renaissance Rome would not have been very different from turn-of-the-century art collectors in Philadelphia in their desire to build appropriate venues to house their objets d'art while also commissioning gardens that would reflect their social status.

Wilson Eyre's client John Worrell Pepper, for whom the architect designed an Italianate garden to complement his residence, Fairacres, north of Philadelphia, was described as a businessman who, as is "typical of third-generation wealth, spent much of his fortune building, collecting, and giving to philanthropic causes."[6] When he retired after thirty-eight years of active business life, Pepper, who was also an avid gardener, devoted his time to the care of his estate. Fairacres gardens, which became one of Philadelphia's most celebrated, were designed in 1897 to complement a half-timbered house Eyre had designed ten years earlier. For this large, rectangular garden, on an axis with the veranda of the house, Eyre used the typical elements of an Italian garden—that is, terraces, balustrades, potted trees, and topiary. These features he also employed in the design of another, more monumental garden not far from Fairacres in Jenkintown, commissioned by Charles Louis Borie. The geometric garden was here composed of a sunken quadripartite terrace with a large pool of water in the center and crisscrossed by equal paths, the two outer and longitudinal ones terminating in twin pavilions with temple fronts, the central one leading to a semicircular upper terrace lined with cypress trees and reminiscent of the well-known belvedere at the Villa Gamberaia in Tuscany. If Eyre's watercolors for both Fairacres and the Borie garden exude an unmistakable Italian atmosphere, however, the photographs of the gardens as actually implemented show that they were rooted in the sites for which they were designed, possibly because of the local materials and plantings used and because they combined details, such as the shallow turf slope, deriving from the Anglo-Saxon and colonial traditions. That this amalgam of influences may have been part of the architect's intended result appears from Eyre's own remarks about the use of historical precedents: "If you know only a little, you reproduce; if you know a great deal, you adapt, combine, in fact, originate, for no imagination, however vivid, can conceive a thing that is not a combination of what he has seen."[7]

Wilson Eyre, *House and Grounds for Mr. Charles Borie*, Jenkintown, Philadelphia. (From Julian Millard, "The Work of Wilson Eyre," *The Architectural Record* 14, no. 4 [October 1903]: 298)

A similar belief was followed by another lover of Italian gardens, the wealthy businessman Pierre du Pont, a keen connoisseur and well-traveled individual, who was responsible for the design of his own grounds at Longwood Gardens, about ten miles west of Philadelphia. These were indebted not only to Mr. du Pont's Italian tours but also to his knowledge of French chateau gardens and of the gardens of Moorish Spain. Du Pont sketched the plan of Longwood's Water Garden—the qualifier "Italian" added only after his death—while on a boat returning from Europe. The proportions and general layout match those of the Villa Gamberaia, whose plan to scale was published by Inigo Triggs in his *The Art of Garden Design in Italy* (1906), which du Pont owned, and which he visited in 1925. As at Gamberaia, du Pont placed the central circular fountain in an eccentric position along the axis of symmetry.

This was an expedient that delayed the foreshortening of perspective so that the farther pair of rectangular pools, which are fourteen feet longer than the nearer ones, appear of the same dimensions when seen from the elevated observation terrace. Also similar to Gamberaia is the exedra of trees terminating the central

axis, the same motif adopted by Wilson Eyre at the Borie estate. Unlike Eyre's clients, however, du Pont was able to commission hand-carved stonework, such as gargoyles and sculpture, directly from Italy, where they were designed and produced before being shipped to the United States by boat. Other Italian details are the jets of water that are activated along the water staircase to surprise the unaware guest for the amusement of the host, a feature that was used both at the villa d'Este at Tivoli and Villa Lante at Bagnaia in the sixteenth century but that originated earlier in Moorish Spain.

Du Pont was unusual as a turn-of-the-century garden enthusiast in that he not only insisted in designing the layout of his gardens himself but also studied the hydraulic mechanisms of his fountains along with the earth moving and grading of the grounds. Even though he hired noted Italian landscape architect Ferruccio Vitale in 1916 to design Longwood's conservatories, which were meant to be architecturally impressive, he specifically instructed him to not concern himself "with any kind of plants . . . nor . . . any landscape gardening."[8] In this du Pont resembled the gentlemen of colonial America, who were designers of their own houses and grounds. In addition, in colonial times those who could master the art of design were also engaged in the farming of their plantations, and the history of Longwood Gardens, previously called Longwood Farms, shows that du Pont (a member of the Farmers Club of Philadelphia) also made an effort to make his estate productive and self-sufficient. But while du Pont's American predecessors followed in the footsteps of ancient Romans (especially the *scriptores rei rusticae*, who equated land cultivation with the cultivation of their souls), and in so doing they were intent on making a profit, the produce and livestock from the 220-acre farm at Longwood supplied only the needs of the house. In fact, du Pont acknowl-

The Italian Water Garden at Longwood Gardens.
(Photo: Larry Albee, Courtesy Longwood Gardens)

University of Pennsylvania
Museum of Archaeology and
Anthropology. (Courtesy of
Penn Museum, 2007. Photograph
by Lauren Hansen-Flaschen)

The Italian Water Garden
at Longwood Gardens.
(Photo: Larry Albee, Courtesy
Longwood Gardens)

edged that his pursuit of husbandry and agriculture was motivated not by profit but by sheer interest, curiosity, and the availability of free manure for the gardens that farming afforded. Eventually the losses persuaded du Pont to say, "I am firmly convinced that the so called 'gentleman farmer' is a menace to the legitimate farmer of his community. The 'gentleman farmer' does not practice economy and offers his product for sale regardless of the cost, all of which is damaging to those who must make a living off their farming efforts. . . . As this community has grown up under my care, I have not taken business from others."[9] Indeed, when he was no longer able to deduct farm losses from his income due to changes in tax laws in the early 1950s, nearly all farming operations stopped at Longwood, except for a small vegetable garden and some orchards. All that remained then of the Italian influence on Longwood Gardens, as on the other Italianate gardens of the early twentieth century in Philadelphia and elsewhere, was a love of beauty for its own sake and for the image it could project of civic institutions as well as private citizens.

NOTES

1. For references and bibliography, I refer the reader to my chapter "The Reception of the Italian Garden in America: The Role of Ancient and Early Modern Italy," in *Foreign Trends in American Gardens: A History of Exchange, Adaptation, and Reception,* ed. Raffaella Fabiani Giannetto (Charlottesville: University of Virginia Press, 2016), 113–139.

2. Wilson Eyre, "Modern Art," *T-Square Club Journal* (1931): 13. Emphasis in the original.

3. The quote is from the draft of an essay on Wilson Eyre's work by Mark Alan Hewitt conserved at the University of Pennsylvania Architectural Archives.

4. George Thomas, *The Book of the School, 100 Years,* Graduate School of the Fine Arts, University of Pennsylvania (Philadelphia: University of Pennsylvania, 1990), 49; Cecil Brewer, "American Museum Buildings," *RIBA Journal,* Third Series, vol. 20, nos. 11–12 (April 1913): 370–372.

5. Beatrix Jones [Farrand], "The Garden in Relation to the House," *Garden and Forest* 10, no. 476 (April 1897): 132–133.

6. Hewitt, draft paper.

7. Mark Alan Hewitt, *The Architect and the American Country House* (New Haven, CT: Yale University Press, 1990), 52.

8. Colvin Randall, "The Fountains of Longwood Part Three: Learning by Doing," *Longwood Chimes* 292 (Winter 2016): 15.

9. Pierre du Pont's quote is in George Thompson Sr., *A Man and His Garden: The Story of Pierre S. du Pont's Development of Longwood Gardens* (Kenneth Square, PA: Longwood Gardens, 1976), 43–44.

13

The Neapolitan *Presepio* at the Glencairn Museum

Joseph F. Chorpenning

ITALY IS OFTEN CONSIDERED THE BIRTHPLACE OF THE CRÈCHE or Nativity scene, a legacy of St. Francis of Assisi (ca. 1181–1226). Undoubtedly, the most popular form of the Italian crèche is the Neapolitan *presepio*. Since 2016, Glencairn Museum in Bryn Athyn, a northern suburb of Philadelphia in Montgomery County, has featured as part of its annual World Nativities Exhibition a magnificent Neapolitan presepio, whose figures and structures were collected over a period of thirty years in the second half of the twentieth century by the late Elizabeth Ann Evans of Bucks County during her annual trips to Naples. Her sisters, Marcia Evans and Suzanne Hoyle-Rhodes, later donated the presepio in their sister's memory to the Samuel S. Fleisher Art Memorial, a South Philadelphia art institution serving the community. Lacking the space required to exhibit this panoramic baroque theatrical staging of the Nativity, the Fleisher initially loaned the presepio to Glencairn Museum. Recently, Marcia Evans has gifted the Evans presepio directly to Glencairn for its World Nativities collection.

While the Neapolitan presepio may be the best known, other Italian cities also have their own distinctive presepio traditions. A cave outside the village of Greccio (about forty miles northeast of Rome) is the birthplace of all presepi. According to legend, Francis of Assisi wanted to replicate the conditions of the Lord's humble birth for Midnight Mass on Christmas Eve 1223. Thus, he made the cave a little Bethlehem, complete with a real ox and ass, as well as real hay on which to lay an image of the infant Jesus, which, according to an eyewitness, came alive in Francis's arms. In the area around Greccio, presepi are sometimes models of Francis's cave, with the saint, rather than the Virgin Mary, holding the Christ Child.

The first permanent three-dimensional presepio in Italy is found in Rome's basilica of St. Mary Major. Its presepio chapel contains one of the famous relics of the Middle Ages—the very cradle in which Jesus was laid—and Arnolfo di Cambio created a five-piece sculptural scene of the Nativity (ca. 1285–1287) for this site. Hallmarks of the Roman presepio are the "glory" of receding clouds, opened for God's timeless decision to send His Son to earth, as well as the tradition of Rome's streets as the Nativity's setting.

Florence contributed to the presepio's iconography of the Three Kings by its grand Magi processions on the feast of the Epiphany, when the Three Kings rode through the city with all the grandeur of the Medici court—dwarfs, monkeys, and actual visitors from the Orient. Genoa also had a processional tradition, with wagons displaying dressed polychrome wood figures depicting not only Jesus's birth but also related scenes, such as the Annunciation, Visitation, and Presentation in the Temple.

While the presepio may owe its origins to the Franciscan tradition, the Jesuits are credited with later baroque developments. During the baroque era, crèche scenes became more and more complex, with the addition of numerous ancillary figures—peasants, horsemen, merchants, dogs, cows, goats, and even water buffalo. The Jesuits contributed to this development by using modeling figures and increasingly intricate architecture and illusionistic landscapes to stage the Nativity story as a teaching device in their churches. It was not long until this practice made its way into the homes of the leading families of the aristocracy, who elevated it to a new level.

At Christmastime, it became customary for the aristocracy to keep an open house so that visitors could come and see their presepi, which would often fill several rooms and be continually added to and rearranged to enhance the effect. The king of Naples, Charles III of Bourbon (r. 1734–1759), and the royal family took the lead, with the king modeling and baking little clay cakes for the royal crèche, arranging shepherds, and devising perspectives. For her part, the queen sewed costumes for presepio figures throughout the year.

The Neapolitan *presepio* at the Glencairn Museum. (Photo: Todd Rothstein, Courtesy Saint Joseph's University Press)

Soon, the best sculptors in Naples were engaged to create presepio figures, ladies of the court vied in dressing the figures, and sets and lighting effects became more elaborate, being changed every year to allow for new "inventions" and hundreds of figures. Still other artists were engaged as "Christmas crib directors." The presepio was conceived of as a theatrical event. The annual ritual of assembling and arranging the figures is called in Italian an *allestimento*—literally "staging," the same term used for the performance of plays and operas.

The section of the presepio that licensed patrons and artists to give free rein to their imagination, unencumbered by the gospel text, was the Magi's retinue. Behind the Magi came a crowd of brightly dressed, exotic travelers, who were symbolic of the homage rendered by all nations to the Divine Child: Mongols and Moors, mingled with Turks and Circassians, advancing on horseback or on foot, carrying colorful trappings, banners, and lances, followed by their camels, attendants, and dogs. These figures are equipped with some of the most elaborate accessories, which were miniature masterpieces produced by Neapolitan silversmiths and other craftsmen: finely chased and gilded scimitars and daggers, silver baskets, and purses. This part of the presepio evokes the *Turquerie* and eighteenth-century opera and ballet more than sacred drama. This comingling of the sacred and the secular exemplifies the porosity that was characteristic of Neapolitan life.

Detail of the Neapolitan *presepio* at the Glencairn Museum. (Photo: Todd Rothstein, Courtesy Saint Joseph's University Press)

So it is that the Neapolitan presepio came to be synonymous with the Italian crèche tradition. Several U.S. museums annually display impressively staged Neapolitan presepi during the holiday season, including the Metropolitan Museum of Art in New York, the Chicago Institute of Art, the Mellon Museum in Pittsburgh, and the Glencairn Museum. The Neapolitan presepio integrates into a single scene four major themes: the birth of Jesus Christ, the adoration of the shepherds, the adoration of the Magi, and the inn at Bethlehem. Apropos of the presepio, Glencairn curator Ed Gyllenhaal explains,

A presepio presents the Nativity scene within the setting of daily life in 18th-century Naples, a bustling port city. This artistic tradition has been called "the translation of the Bible into Neapolitan dialect." The figures are clothed in period costumes typical of the aristocracy, peasants and visiting foreigners. The birth of Jesus is depicted as taking place amid crumbling Roman ruins, signifying the end of paganism and the dawn of Christianity.

In the presepio on exhibit at Glencairn, the Nativity of the Christ Child, which takes place below a host of angels descending from heaven, stands in stark contrast to the mundane life of the inn or tavern. Life at the inn goes on as usual, but the attention of some of the customers has been drawn in the direction of the miraculous event. No figures have been placed in the way of the Holy Family, so the eyes of the viewer move naturally up the steps with the townspeople toward the Nativity.

Detail of the Neapolitan *presepio* at the Glencairn Museum. (Photo: Todd Rothstein, Courtesy Saint Joseph's University Press)

While the Chicago presepio is an enclosed scene of relatively static arrangement, the Glencairn presepio is painstakingly taken apart and reassembled every year, as indeed are those at the Met and Mellon. Planning for the staging of the presepio at Glencairn begins in summer. Bryn Athyn artist Kathleen Glenn Pitcairn, whose background is in stage set design, serves as "theater director" for the presepio as well as for most of the other crèches in the World Nativities Exhibition.

The Glencairn and Mellon presepi especially allow visitors to get up close, giving the viewer the feeling of being part of the scene. Moreover, at Glencairn, the presepio is the largest and core piece in a display of crèches from all continents, thus making it the centerpiece of a vast and impressive multicultural display.

The figures at the Met and Mellon are eighteenth century, while those at Chicago and Glencairn are of more recent vintage. The presepi at the Met, Mellon, and Glencairn were purchased by individuals and later donated by them or on their behalf, whereas the Chicago presepio was purchased by the museum with the help of generous patrons.

Throughout the long history of the Italian presepio, one of its distinctive traits is its malleability and adaptability to the circumstances of the moment. This has contributed in no small part to the presepio's enduring vitality, appeal, and relevance. While the tradition traces its origin to Il Poverello in the mid-thirteenth century, its popularity continues unabated to the present day, as the presepio at the Glencairn Museum—an exquisite example of Italy in Philadelphia—eloquently attests.

SELECTED BIBLIOGRAPHY/SUGGESTIONS FOR FURTHER READING

This essay draws on information and insights from several sources. On the presepio at Glencairn, see Ed Gyllenhaal, "A Nativity from Naples," *Glencairn Museum News*, no. 11 (2016). Glencairn also has numerous resources on the iconography of the crèche available online at https://glencairnmuseum.org. For a lively tour of presepio traditions throughout Italy, see Garry Wills, "The Art and Politics of the Nativity," *New York Review of Books*, December 19,

1996. Wills also provides an informative discussion of presepio exhibitions in several U.S. museums in "Crowding around the Nativity," *New York Review of Books Daily*, December 21, 2016. An early and still valuable contribution to the discussion of the presepio is Olga Raggio, "A Neapolitan Christmas Crib," *Metropolitan Museum of Art Bulletin* 24, no. 4 (December 1965): 151–158. The most comprehensive and in-depth treatment of the presepio available in English to date is Sylvain Bellenger and Carmine Romano, *The Neapolitan Crèche at the Art Institute of Chicago*, with an essay by Jesse Rosenberg and a preface by Ricardo Muti (New Haven, CT: Yale University Press, 2016). Of particular interest is Rosenberg's essay, "Music and the Nativity in Eighteenth-Century Naples," 47–55. For overviews of the history, art, and symbolism of the crèche, see Matthew Powell, *The Christmas Crèche: Treasure of Faith, Art and Theater* (Boston: Pauline Books and Media, 1997), and *Christmas in Miniature: Crèches from around the World*, exh. cat. (Hartford, CT: Knights of Columbus Museum, 2005).

14

The Italian Legacy in Philadelphia

Opera and Instrumental Music

Stephen A. Willier

F ROM THE TIME OF ITS FOUNDING, music played a prominent role in the lives of Philadelphians. Although the Quakers who founded the city believed music to be too pleasurable and worldly, other immigrant groups cultivated it as an integral and necessary element of existence. Both vocal and instrumental music were an important part of the worship service in Philadelphia's various churches. While the most prominent musicians had arrived in Philadelphia from England, Benjamin Franklin also showed a keen interest in music, teaching guitar and inventing musical instruments such as the glass harmonica. English operas and theatrical entertainments abounded, despite the Quakers' objections. In 1793 the New Theatre (later known as the Chestnut Street Theatre) was undoubtedly the most beautiful theater in the land. It seated nearly two thousand people, its design based on the Theatre Royal in Bath.

ITALIAN OPERA AND SINGERS COME TO PHILADELPHIA

Italians in Philadelphia soon began making great contributions to opera and instrumental music. In the eighteenth century, Italian immigrants to the city tended to be upper-class citizens from the Genoa-Liguria area who became leaders in commerce and the arts. Some figures that appear in the eighteenth century include John Palma, who performed a concert in Philadelphia in 1757, and Italian musician and wine merchant Giovanni Gualdo, who, shortly before his death in 1771, sponsored concerts in the city. A Signora Mazzanti was reportedly the first Italian diva to sing in America.

A notable arrival in the early nineteenth century was Mozart's illustrious librettist, Lorenzo Da Ponte, who ultimately settled in New York but spent much time in Philadelphia from 1805 until his death in 1838, where he produced a number of operas (see Chapter 25). It was most probably through Da Ponte that Maria Malibran, the great singer and daughter of the illustrious Spanish tenor Manuel García, first sang for the Musical Fund Society in 1827. García's troupe had come to America in 1825, playing in both New York and Philadelphia.

In 1829 Da Ponte began to negotiate with Giacomo Montresor, tenor and impresario in Bologna, to bring an opera company to America; he began selling subscriptions. Unlike Europe, America had neither state support nor wealthy aristocrats to help support it. The Montresor group finally arrived in the United States in 1832, presenting a contemporary repertoire of four operas Altogether they gave thirty-five New York performances and then twenty-four in Philadelphia. By 1847 Italian musicians had attracted enough interest for a successful season, and the Italian Opera Company was formed. The daughter of two of the singers was Adelina Patti, one of the most famous divas of the second half of the nineteenth century.

Philip Trajetta (1777–1854) was a Venetian-born Italian American composer, teacher, writer, and friend of James Madison and James Monroe, who founded the American Conservatorio, first in Boston and later in New York and Philadelphia. Two of his oratorios, *Jerusalem in Affliction* (1828) and *The Daughters of Zion* (1829), were given their premieres in Germantown, Pennsylvania.

Giulia Grisi, the original Adalgisa in Bellini's *Norma*, became the leading Italian soprano in Europe in the 1840s. After her divorce from an early marriage, she and Mario, the greatest tenor at that time, married and became the first couple of opera. In the early 1850s, a comedian and impresario, James H. Hackett, negotiated with Grisi and Mario to come to America. In the late autumn, the two superstars visited Boston, Philadelphia, Baltimore, and Washington, DC. In Philadelphia, libretti signed by Mario and Grisi were on sale in the theater lobby, perhaps the first time this promotional device had been used.

In the 1850s, the celebrated Havana Opera Troupe made a tour of the principal cities of the United States, generating excitement not experienced since the García company visited earlier in the century. The troupe was organized by Don Francesco Marty y Torres and included two well-known Italian musicians: Luigi Arditi, conductor, composer, and violinist, and Giovanni Bottesini, double bass virtuoso. Singers included Signora Fortunata Tedesco, star mezzo-soprano, who was described as having a beautiful and noble voice. Perelli, the tenor, was an excellent musician and sang well. He settled in Philadelphia, adding greatly to the operatic life of the city, where he did much to educate the public and also elevate their taste.

By the mid-nineteenth century, Philadelphia was a truly international musical city. Operas such as *Der Freischütz*, *La Cenerentola*, *Norma*, *Il Trovatore*, and Charles Gounod's *Faust* all had their American premieres here, a situation calling for a proper "operatic" auditorium, the building of the Academy of Music at Broad and Locust in 1857, at a cost of $250,000. The academy is still in active use today and remains the nation's oldest opera house in continuous existence. An architectural competition for its design was announced in October 1854 and was won by the Philadelphia firm of Napoleon LeBrun, who had previously designed Philadelphia's Roman Catholic Cathedral, and Gustavus Runge, both native Philadelphians. The ornate auditorium has an open horseshoe shape and proscenium columns with elliptical cross sections in order to provide more direct sight lines from the seats in the side balconies. The intention of Philadelphians was to outdo La Scala, the San Carlo in Naples, and other great European theaters. The academy was specifically designed as an opera house, and for this purpose LeBrun visited La Scala, Milan, as an inspiration. The gala opening featured a grand ball and then the American premiere of Verdi's *Trovatore*, then only four years old, performed by the Max Maretzek Italian Opera Company featuring Marietta Gazzaniga as Leonora, Alessandro Amodio as Count di Luna, Zoë Aldini as Azucena, Pasquale Brignoli as Manrico, and Max Maretzek conducting.

Maretzek (1821–1897), composer, conductor, and impresario, who had been producing operas in New York and at the Chestnut Street Theatre in Philadelphia since 1850, returned to the Academy of Music in Philadelphia each year through 1873. Philadelphia saw the premiere in 1845 of the first American grand opera, *Leonora*, by composer and music journalist of the *National Gazette* and the *Public Ledger* William Henry Fry. The opera was written in the Italian style and admired so much that it was performed sixteen times that season. In the late nineteenth century, Philadelphia premieres of Italian operas included Arrigo Boito's Faustian *Mefistofele* (1880), Pietro Mascagni's *Cavalleria rusticana* (1891) and *L'amico Fritz* (1892), and Giacomo Puccini's *Manon Lescaut* (1894), all works still well known and performed today. The Academy of Music was also home to the Philadelphia Orchestra from 1900 until 2001, when the orchestra took up residence at the new Kimmel Center for the Performing Arts.

Another venue, the Philadelphia Opera House, was erected in 1908 at Broad and Poplar by impresario Oscar Hammerstein as the home for his Philadelphia Opera Company. Hammerstein, with his Manhattan Opera House in New York, had been engaged in a rivalry with the Metropolitan Opera for several years. With the Philadelphia Academy of Music serving as the venue for visiting Metropolitan Opera performances, Hammerstein decided to extend the rivalry to Philadelphia. His company appeared in Philadelphia's academy in 1908, presenting *Louise* with Mary Garden and *Lucia di Lammermoor* with Italian superstar Luisa Tetrazzini. From the stage, Hammerstein announced to cheering that he planned to build an opera house in Philadelphia. Construction began in March 1908, and opening night was November 1. The season opened with Georges Bizet's *Carmen*, and other notable performances included *Il barbiere di Siviglia* with Tetrazzini.

Following spread: The Academy of Music, 1855–1857, is the oldest musical auditorium in the country still serving its original purpose, modeled after La Scala in Milan. (Keith Watanabe for Allemann Almquist and Jones)

TWENTIETH-CENTURY ITALIAN AMERICANS AND OPERA IN PHILADELPHIA

In the twentieth century, a number of Italian American singers native to Philadelphia gained international repute. Dusolina Giannini (1902–1986) was born into an extremely musical family. Her father, Ferruccio Giannini, was an operatic tenor who had sung with Patti and had emigrated to America when he was seventeen years old; her mother, Antonietta Briglia-Giannini, was a fine violinist; her brother Vittorio a well-known composer; and Giannini's sister, Eufemia Giannini-Gregory, was a respected voice teacher at the Curtis Institute of Music in Philadelphia and taught Frank Guarrera, Judith Blegen, and Anna Moffo. When only twelve years old, Dusolina sang La Cieca in *La Gioconda* and Azucena in her father's small opera company, suggesting she then considered herself a mezzo-soprano.

Taken up and trained by the Polish soprano Marcella Sembrich, Giannini made her debut in Hamburg in 1925 as Aida. She subsequently sang at Covent Garden and by the early 1930s had proved herself throughout Europe in addition to touring Australia and New Zealand. She made her American debut at the Metropolitan Opera on February 12, 1936, as Aida; the noted New York critic W. J. Henderson wrote of her true Verdian manner. She remained at the Metropolitan until 1941. In 1938, the soprano sang the role of Hester Prynne in the Hamburg premiere of her brother Vittorio's opera, *The Scarlet Letter*. After the end of World War II, Giannini toured Europe. She retired from the opera stage in 1951. She can be heard on a complete recording of Aida from 1928, opposite the noted tenor Aureliano Pertile.

Arthur Cosenza (1924–2005), a Philadelphian of Italian heritage, became a baritone, stage director, and impresario long associated with the New Orleans Opera Association. Cosenza studied at various music and theatrical schools, and in 1948 his friend Mario Lanza introduced him to Armando Agnini, principal stage director of the New Orleans Opera, where Cosenza made his operatic debut in 1954. His most notable role was considered to be Schaunard in *La bohème* from 1959, starring Licia Albanese and Giuseppe di Stefano, conducted by Renato Cellini, a performance released on compact disc in 1995. Cosenza also produced opera in Hartford, Houston, and Pittsburgh, and at the Philadelphia Lyric and the Jackson Opera Guild. He was named a knight in the Order of the Star of Italian Sodality and was an officer in the Ordre des Arts et des Lettres.

Enrico Di Giuseppe (1932–2005) was an operatic tenor who had a long performing career from the late 1950s through the 1990s. Born in Philadelphia, he played the clarinet in school. He studied voice first at the Curtis Institute and then, after serving in the army, at Juilliard. In 1960 he made his debut with the Philadelphia Grand Opera Company as Rodolfo in Puccini's *La bohème*. He sang with the Philadelphia company several more times in the 1960s and 1970s, including Pinkerton in *Madama Butterfly*, Count Almaviva in *Il barbiere di Siviglia*, Cassio in *Otello*, Alfredo in *La traviata*, and the title role in Gounod's *Faust*.

Di Giuseppe then had a distinguished career in New York City, often singing concurrently at the New York City Opera and the Metropolitan, and later with the New York Grand Opera. His NYCO debut was as Michele in Gian Carlo Menotti's *The Saint of Bleecker Street*, and he went on to sing twenty-six roles there. He sang a wide variety of parts during his Metropolitan years (1969–1986) with Joan Sutherland and many others. In 1973 he made his sole appearance with the Philadelphia Lyric Opera Company as Tonio in *La fille du régiment* opposite Beverly Sills as Marie.

Son of Sicilian parents, the Philadelphia-born lyric baritone Frank Guarrera (1923–2007) sang for twenty-eight seasons at the Metropolitan Opera in New York. His large repertory was mainly Italian, but his most popular role was Escamillo in Bizet's *Carmen*, and he was also a notable Valentine in Gounod's *Faust* early in his career. He sang frequently in San Francisco, Philadelphia, and other U.S. cities. Italian roles included Marcello in *La bohème* and Verdi's eponymous Simon Boccanegra, assumed a few days after Leonard Warren's death onstage in 1960.

In 1948, when the twenty-four-year-old Guarrera was participating in the Metropolitan Opera's "Auditions of the Air," which he eventually won, Arturo Toscanini heard him on the radio singing Ford's monologue from Falstaff and arranged for an audition. As a result of Toscanini's intervention, Guarrera sang in two operas at La Scala, Milan, that year, as Zurga in Bizet's *Les Pêcheurs de Perles* (or rather, *I pescatori di perle*) in August and Manfredo in Italo Montemezzi's *L'amore dei tre re* in October. Earlier, on June 10, the thirtieth anniversary of the death of Arrigo Boito, he took part in a concert at La Scala, conducted by Toscanini, of excerpts from Boito's operas. The result was his engagement at La Scala in Boito's *Nerone*, only the first of several performances under Toscanini. Guarrera sang Ford on the conductor's legendary 1950 Falstaff broadcasts, still available on CD.

Guarrera had been admitted to the Curtis Institute of Music as a teenager. His studies were interrupted by a stint in the U.S. Navy during World War II, after which he resumed his studies at Curtis. In 1947 he made his debut at the New York City Opera as Silvio in *Pagliacci* before receiving a contract with the Metropolitan in 1948, where he sang for twenty-eight seasons. Roles that he sang in Philadelphia include Giorgio Germont in *Traviata*, Valentin in *Faust*, Tonio in *Pagliacci*, and Baron Scarpia in *Tosca*. Guarrero sang until 1976. He was honored in his native city with a multi-story mural depicting his most famous roles, found at the corner of Broad and Tasker Streets in South Philadelphia.

Stephen Costello, born in Philadelphia in 1981, is an American operatic tenor and a recipient of the 2009 Richard Tucker Award. Costello has performed in opera houses around the world including Covent Garden, the Metropolitan Opera, and Lyric Opera of Chicago. In 2010, Costello originated the role of Greenhorn (Ishmael) in the world premiere of Jake Heggie's *Moby-Dick* at the Dallas Opera. Costello is a 2007 graduate of Philadelphia's Academy of Vocal Arts, where he performed the Duke in *Rigoletto*, Rodolfo in *La bohème*, Nemorino in *L'elisir d'amore*, Ferrando in *Così fan tutte*, Fritz in *L'amico Fritz*, Roberto in *Le villi*, and Des Grieux in Jules Massenet's *Manon*. His voice teacher at the Academy of Vocal Arts was Bill Schuman.

STARS MADE IN AMERICA: MARIO LANZA AND ANNA MOFFO

Possessing one of the most splendid natural voices ever heard was one of Arthur Cosenza's musical friends, Mario Lanza (1921–1959), who was often compared with Enrico Caruso, whom he would later portray on film. Born Alfred Arnold Cocozza in Philadelphia, he was exposed to operatic singing by his Italian parents, Maria Lanza and Antonio Cocozza. Young Freddie loved listening to the family's Victrola, favoring recordings by Caruso, and by his early teens he knew many arias and opera plots. His first formal music training consisted of violin lessons, although his passion remained with opera, and his mother sent him to study voice with Irene Williams, a local teacher with a good reputation.

By the age of sixteen, he began singing in operatic productions in Philadelphia for the YMCA Opera Company. In July 1942, he was noticed by Serge Koussevitsky, conductor of the Boston Symphony Orchestra. Koussevitsky's immediate

Mural of Mario Lanza. Located on the corner of Broad and Reed Street, South Philadelphia. (© 1997 and 2007 Mural Arts Philadelphia / Diane Keller. Photo © JackRamsdale.com. Reprinted by permission)

reaction was Caruso redivides. The famous conductor provided young Freddie Cocozza with a full student scholarship to the Berkshire Music Center at Tanglewood, Massachusetts, where he studied with Boris Goldovsky and Leonard Bernstein. On August 7, 1942, at Tanglewood he made his opera debut as Fenton in Otto Nicolai's *Merry Wives of Windsor*. At this time he took the masculine form of his mother's maiden name and became Mario Lanza.

After his discharge from the army in 1945, Lanza spent over a year in serious study with Enrico Rosati, the former vocal teacher of the great tenor Beniamino Gigli. After Lanza appeared in Chicago's Grant Park in 1947, the powerful critic Claudia Cassidy praised his "superbly natural tenor" and observed that "he possesses the things almost impossible to learn. He knows the accent that makes a lyric line reach its audience, and he knows why opera is music drama."

In 1947 Lanza signed a recording contract with RCA Victor and, having been brought to the attention of Louis B. Mayer, was asked to feature in motion pictures. Meanwhile, he sang Pinkerton in Puccini's *Madama Butterfly* in April 1948 in New Orleans. His first picture was the 1949 *That Midnight Kiss*, making him an immediate screen star. This picture was followed by *Toast of New Orleans* in 1950, which featured Lanza's first million-seller hit, "Be My Love." The next year it seemed part of Lanza's destiny when he starred as his childhood idol, Enrico Caruso, in *The Great Caruso*, a major triumph. This was followed in 1952 with the film *Because You're Mine*. In 1954 Lanza's voice was used for the soundtrack of the movie version of Romberg's *The Student Prince*. After leaving MGM, he made several recordings and appeared on radio and television shows.

Lanza died of heart disease at the early age of thirty-eight. Nearly sixty years later, his recordings are readily available on CD and video, and his voice has astonished new generations. At the time of his death, Lanza was studying assiduously, planning a return to the opera stage as Canio in Ruggero Leoncavallo's *Pagliacci*. By their own admission, his films, especially *The Great Caruso*, influenced numerous future opera stars including Joseph Calleja, José Carreras, Plácido Domingo, and Luciano Pavarotti. The Mario Lanza Museum is found at 712 Montrose Street in Philadelphia, housing memorabilia from his career such as posters, photographs, costumes, and a terra-cotta bust of the singer.

Anna Moffo was born in 1932 in Wayne, Pennsylvania, the daughter of Italian parents, her father a shoemaker. She studied singing with Giannini Dusolina's sister, Eufemia Giannini-Gregory, at the Curtis Institute and then won a Fulbright scholarship for further study in Italy, where she worked with Luigi Ricci and Mercedes Llopart, teacher of Renata Scotto and others. She made her stage debut at the Spoleto festival in 1955, singing Norina in *Don Pasquale*. The following year she portrayed Zerlina in *Don Giovanni* at the Aix-en-Provence festival. Her first U.S. appearance was at the Chicago Lyric Opera in 1957 as Mimi in *La bohème*, with Jussi Björling as her Rodolfo. Although her career was largely based at the Metropolitan Opera, where she sang for seventeen seasons, Moffo also appeared in

Anna Moffo, 1962.
(Photo: Harry Pot. Creative Commons license CC BY-SA 3.0 NL: https://creativecommons.org /licenses/by-sa/3.0/nl/legalcode)

many of the capitals of Europe, including several music festivals. Her only Covent Garden appearance came in 1964, when she undertook Gilda in *Rigoletto*, which many considered to be an ideal part for her. Another ideal role was Violetta in *La traviata*, and it was as Violetta that Moffo made her debut at the Metropolitan on November 14, 1959. Other significant operatic characters in her career included Massenet's Manon, Liù in Puccini's *Turandot*, and Mélisande in Claude Debussy's masterpiece.

In 1960 Moffo unveiled a new role for her San Francisco debut, Amina in Bellini's *La sonnambula*, also considered perfect for her. Subsequently she portrayed another frail heroine in *Lucia di Lammermoor*, which she sang at San Francisco and the Metropolitan at a time when her rivals in these bel canto roles were Maria Callas and Joan Sutherland. Buffa roles were less frequent, but she displayed a fine sense of comic timing as Adina in Gaetano Donizetti's *Elisir d'amore*, as Serpina in Giovanni Battista Pergolesi's *Serva padrona*, and in the title role of Jacques Offenbach's *La Périchole*.

Moffo's farewell appearance at the Met was on March 15, 1976, when she sang Violetta, as she had done at her debut. Later in that year, she sang the title role in Massenet's *Thaïs* in Seattle and then added Cilea's Adriana Lecouvreur, which she performed in Parma in 1978. In the 1960s, Moffo also began appearing occasionally in Italian films, including roles in the Napoleonic war epic *The Battle of Austerlitz* (1960) with Rossana Brazzi; the comic opera *La serva padrona* (1962), directed by husband Mario Lanfranchi; *Menage, Italian Style* (1965); and the comedy *The Divorce* (1970). She also filmed the operas *La traviata* (1967) and *Lucia di Lammermoor* (1971), both directed by Lanfranchi.

PAVAROTTI COMPETITIONS

Because of his international singing competitions held in Philadelphia during the 1980s and 1990s, Luciano Pavarotti had in fairly recent times a major presence in the city. There were four such competitions, the main prize the opportunity to perform with Pavarotti onstage and possible participation in a full-scale opera production with the then Opera Company of Philadelphia. More than five hundred singers from thirty-three countries entered the first competition in 1980.

THE PHILADELPHIA ORCHESTRA

There was a great deal of orchestral music in nineteenth-century Philadelphia, but the city's major orchestra was not founded until 1900, with eighty-five musicians.

The Philadelphia Orchestra was initially led by Fritz Scheel, who died in 1907. Leandro Campanari, a violinist and experienced leader with much experience conducting at La Scala, assumed leadership but was in that same year replaced by Karl Pohlig, who had been director of the Court Orchestra in Stuttgart. It was Leopold Stokowski who from 1912 to 1941 shaped the orchestra and made it one of the top five orchestras in the United States. Eugene Ormandy had an even longer tenure, from 1936 to 1980. It was Stokowski who fashioned the luscious Philadelphia string sound and Ormandy who preserved it well into the seventies.

An interesting experiment took place in 1930, when Stokowski and Toscanini, director of the New York Philharmonic at the time, switched podiums for two weeks. Two conductors could not have been more seemingly unlike each other: Stokowski was an experimenter with sounds and arrangements such as transcribing organ works of J. S. Bach for orchestra, and Toscanini was a literalist, insisting on the musicians playing the music strictly "come è scritto." Toscanini was a huge success in Philadelphia with both the players and the audiences, playing works such as Mozart's Symphony No. 35 ("Haffner"), Richard Strauss's *Ein Heldenleben*, the first symphonies of Beethoven and Brahms, and several Wagner excerpts. Toscanini returned to the podium of the Philadelphia Orchestra for a total of eight concerts in late 1941 and early 1942.

The orchestra has been immensely enriched through the years by Italian musicians. Frank Costanza, first violinist, himself taught four members of the orchestra. Each October he conducted the Sisters of Mercy Symphony Orchestra, a musical organization of nuns in Merion, and was also active in the Amerita Orchestra, a string group devoted to performing works by Italian composers of the seventeenth and eighteenth centuries. One of his noted pupils was Joseph Primavera (1926–2006), the youngest violist ever appointed to lead the viola section of the Philadelphia Orchestra. Born to a prominent luthier, he began studying the violin at age six with Philadelphia violinists Guido and Joseph Terranova and then with Sacha Jacobinoff. Later, he was a trombone pupil of Pietro Rosano. At the New School of Music, he studied violin with Frank Costanza and viola with Max Aronoff, joining the Philadelphian Orchestra in 1950. After seventeen years with the orchestra, he retired to devote himself to conducting and teaching.

Sometimes the relationships among players were even closer than teacher-student. No family contributed more to the Philadelphia Orchestra over many years than the de Pasquales, sons of a Germantown violinist who wanted all of them to become members of the Philadelphia Orchestra. In 1959 the four sons formed a string quartet with violinists William and Robert, violist Joseph, and cellist Francis. The quartet was in residence at Villanova University, presenting a remarkable chamber music series, performing with such artists as Yo-Yo Ma, Emanuel Ax, Christoph von Eschenbach, and Andre Watts.

Francis de Pasquale joined the cello section of the Philadelphia Orchestra in 1943, the first of the brothers to join the orchestra. William de Pasquale was a student of Vena Reynolds at the Curtis Institute of Music. After studying and performing in Salzburg as a Fulbright scholar, he joined the Philadelphia Orchestra in 1963. He also taught violin at the Esther Boyer College at Temple University and served as a string coach for the Philadelphia Youth Orchestra. William's wife, Gloria de Pasquale, a cellist, was a member of the de Pasquale String Quartet for over two decades and joined the Philadelphia Orchestra's cello section in 1977. She has been very involved over the years with the Philadelphia Youth Orchestra.

Robert de Pasquale, former associate principal second violin with the Philadelphia Orchestra, studied first with his father in Philadelphia and then with Jascha Brodsky at the New School of Music. He has been on the faculties of Haverford College and the University of the Arts. For over forty years, de Pasquale was a part of the de Pasquale String Quartet and Artist-in-Residence at Haverford College and Villanova University.

Joseph de Pasquale was for over five decades active as one of the great violists of the twentieth century. He served as principal violist in two of the nation's most brilliant orchestras, the Boston Symphony Orchestra from 1947 to 1964 and the Philadelphia Orchestra from 1964 until his retirement in 1996. He is credited by his students and other members of the Philadelphia Orchestra with raising the standard of viola playing exponentially. Walter Piston wrote his "Viola Concerto" for Joseph.

There was another string dynasty connected with the orchestra, represented by two brothers, Joseph and Louis Lanza. In 2011 Louis at age seventy-five retired after almost fifty years with the orchestra; brother Joseph joined the orchestra in 1958 and performed until his death in 2006. A native Philadelphian, Louis Lanza studied with his uncle, Michael Pascuccio, and Frank Costanzo. While still in high school, he won a scholarship to the Philadelphia Conservatory of Music, which later became the University of the Arts. After graduating from high school, he entered the Juilliard School, where he studied under Edouard Dethier. In 1964 he joined Joseph as a violinist for the Philadelphia Orchestra. A number of other family members worked as professional musicians.

There was also a father and son of Italian origins among the woodwinds: Anthony Gigliotti (1922–2007) as principal clarinetist for forty-seven years, and his son, Mark Gigliotti, co-principal bassoonist. Gigliotti senior also designed clarinets and mouthpieces, made a number of recordings, and taught more than one generation of young clarinetists. He grew up in Philadelphia and taught at the Curtis Institute of Music and Temple University in Philadelphia, the Peabody Conservatory in Baltimore, and Rowan University in Glassboro, New Jersey, in addition to giving master classes around the country.

Among other "Italians" adding luster to the orchestra have been a number of valuable string instruments with names such as Amati, Guarnerius, Stradivarius, and Gagliano. Double bassists have made a practice of handing down their instruments when they retired. Ferdinand Maresh received his bass from Vincent Lazzaro. Another Italian double bassist was Carl Torello.

Toward the end of Eugene Ormandy's long reign as conductor of the Philadelphia Orchestra, a young Italian musician from Naples, Riccardo Muti (b. 1941), began appearing with the orchestra. He served as music director from 1980 until 1992 and led the orchestra on several international tours. Muti stripped down the orchestra's lush sound, noting that the orchestra would now play each composition with its proper sound and style. Muti's tenure in Philadelphia was marked by several concert performances of operas, including Verdi's *Nabucco* and Puccini's *Tosca*, as he was equally proficient in the opera house as on the symphonic podium.

COMPOSERS

The earliest twentieth-century Italian American composers associated with Philadelphia included Vittorio Giannini (1903–1966), brother of the great singer mentioned above, Dusolina Giannini. Their father, Ferruccio, was a successful operatic tenor who came to America from Tuscany in 1885. In addition to his own singing career, he gathered musicians from Italy to form an Italian American band that toured professionally and made several recordings. A number of these musicians ended up playing in the Philadelphia Orchestra. Ferruccio's wife had also been a professional violinist. Another sister, Eufemia, taught voice at the Curtis Institute for many years, and the youngest brother of the family, Francesco (1908–1982), left his career as a cellist to become a psychiatrist. In 1920 Vittorio composed a *Stabat mater* for soloists, chorus, and orchestra, which he conducted at the Philadelphia Opera House that same year, the first major performance of any of his works. In 1932 he won the Prix de Rome and was able to study in Italy for four years. He produced a full-length opera, *Lucedia*, a symphony, a cantata entitled *La primavera*, and a piano concerto.

One of America's most well-known composers, Vincent Persichetti (1915–1987), was born in Philadelphia in 1915 and died there in 1987. At age five he began studying the piano, then organ, double bass, tuba, theory, and composition, and he wrote his first two works at age fourteen. By age sixteen his organ skills earned him a position at Arch Street Presbyterian Church, which he retained until the 1950s. Persichetti studied at Combs College of Music with composer Russel King Miller while still attending public school, and he received a bachelor of music degree in composition from Combs in 1935. He was appointed head of music theory at Combs immediately after graduating and subsequently began teaching at the Philadelphia Conservatory. In 1947 William Schuman invited him to teach at the Juilliard School, where he had a string of distinguished pupils. In 1952 he became the editorial director of the Elkan-Vogel publishing house. Throughout his career he received numerous awards and honors: three Guggenheim Fellowships, two grants from the National Endowment for the Arts, the Brandeis University Creative Award, the first-ever Kennedy Center Friedheim Award, and the Juilliard Publication award are only highlights.

Persichetti first came to national attention in the 1940s when Eugene Ormandy and the Philadelphia Orchestra started performing his music: *Fables* for narrator and orchestra in 1945 and then Symphony No. 3 (1943) in 1947. After that, his music began to be performed by other American groups. He also managed to write an important textbook on contemporary compositional techniques, *Twentieth-Century Harmony: Creative Aspects and Practice,* and a 1954 biography of composer William Schuman. Persichetti's own compositions showed a wide array of twentieth-century practices, including tonality, atonality, and modality. Among some one hundred commissions were those from the Philadelphia Orchestra, the New York Philharmonic, the St. Louis and Louisville Symphony Orchestras, the Koussevitsky Music Foundation, the Martha Graham Company, Juilliard Musical Foundation, American Guild of Organists, various universities, and individual performers. He appeared as guest conductor, lecturer, and composer at over two hundred universities.

Gian Carlo Menotti (1911–2007) was an important Italian American composer and librettist associated with Philadelphia, as was his eminent composition teacher, Rosario Scalero, who came to the Curtis Institute after an illustrious career in Europe. They are both discussed in detail in Chapter 15, which focuses on the Curtis Institute.

CHAMBER MUSIC

Italians have also done much to further the performance of chamber and orchestral music in the city. The Amerita Chamber Players was founded by Philadelphia Orchestra violinist Frank Costanzo and then–consul general of Italy in Philadelphia, Dr. Giovanni Luciolli. The group presented its first concert in 1956 at the Philadelphia Museum of Art under the auspices of the America-Italy Society.

The Philadelphia Chamber Music Society is currently one of the largest organizations of its kind in America. It was created in 1986 by Anthony Checchia and Philip Maneval and presents several dozen instrumental and vocal recitals each season by the very best international artists.

It is impossible to imagine the great classical music legacy in Philadelphia without the generations of Italian and Italian American musicians, both individuals and families who have made extraordinary contributions to classical music since the nineteenth century.

The Curtis Institute
of Music and Italy

DAVID SERKIN LUDWIG

F ROM ITS FOUNDING, PHILADELPHIA'S RENOWNED CURTIS Institute of Music has had a historic connection to Italy through its instrumentalists, singers, conductors, and composers. The influence of Italian music and musicians shaped the direction of the school from its earliest days, and some of Curtis's most illustrious graduates have had significant connections to Italy—through their personal background, their work with an instructor, or their time spent in the country. These connections extend through the Philadelphia orchestra and conductors of world renown who came into contact with Curtis to influence the students at the school and forever shape its artistic culture.

The Curtis Institute was opened on October 13, 1924, the vision of founder Mary Louise Curtis Bok. Mrs. Bok was the heir of the Curtis Publishing Company (publishers of the *Saturday Evening Post* and *Ladies' Home Journal*), and after partnering to start the Settlement Music School for underserved children she turned her attention to her goal of creating the finest music conservatory in the world. Bok engaged an internationally renowned faculty to teach, and with the artistic input of Philadelphia Orchestra conductor Leopold Stokowski and her new Curtis director, pianist Josef Hofmann, she established the merit-based scholarship that to this day keeps Curtis tuition-free. This combination of top-level instruction and full financial support for its students has made Curtis the most selective institution of higher education (of any kind) in the United States–often only able to accept 3–5 percent of total applicants to its total student body each year. The school has a cohort of roughly 170 students, comprising a full orchestra's worth of instrumentalists, about twenty pianists, twenty-five singers, a handful of organists and composers, two conducting fellows, and a resident string quartet. Despite its small size,

Common Room at the dedication of Casimir Hall.
(Wallace Photography—Courtesy of Curtis Rock Resource Center)

Curtis Institute exterior, retouched, ca. 1924.
(H. Parker Rolfe—Courtesy of Curtis Rock Resource Center)

the school has turned out some of the most influential and well-known figures in the history of music since it was first opened nearly a century ago.

A connection with Italy and Italian music was immediately established when Curtis was still in its infancy. Mrs. Bok hired the Italian violinist and composer Rosario Scalero (1870–1954) in the late 1920s to teach composition, and the impact of his expert instruction was deeply felt among students who worked with him. Scalero was himself an accomplished composer who was born near Turin and studied at the Liceo Musciale there. By his thirties he was a well-known pedagogue in Italy, with an appointment in Rome and important positions Naples and Parma. Just before turning fifty, Scalero emigrated to the United States and taught in New York before two extended tenures at Curtis that ran from the school's founding in 1924 to his eventual retirement in 1946. Among his first and most well-known students were fellow countrymen Gian Carlo Menotti and Giovanni "Nino" Rota, as well as American composers Samuel Barber, Marc Blitzstein, Lucas Foss, and Ned Rorem.

Giancarlo Menotti (1911–2007) was born in the small town of Cadegliano on Lake Lugano. He would become one of the foremost composers of opera of the twentieth century: his *The Medium, The Consul,* and *Amahl and the Night Visitors* are familiar to any opera fan and widely known to other listeners. Menotti was precocious, writing operas for four years during his studies at the Milan Conservatory before coming to Curtis in 1928 while still a teenager. He soon formed a friendship with Samuel Barber that would flower into a lifelong partnership. Among Menotti's many accomplishments include the Pulitzer Prize (the first of two) for *The Consul* and a commission to write *Amahl and the Night Visitors* for NBC as the first opera written for television. The Italian American was gifted in language as well and wrote his own libretti for all of his works—a rarity among composers.

Menotti's colleague Nino Rota (1911–1979) had tremendous success composing for film, collaborating with such legendary filmmakers as Federico Fellini, Franco Zeffirelli, and Luchino Visconti—he wrote an astonishing 150 film scores in his life. After growing up in Milan, Rota came to Curtis in 1930 to study conducting and composition. He then returned to Milan to finish his studies and started teaching at the Liceo Musicale in Bari, where he would eventually become director. Rota distinguished himself as a concert music composer, in addition to his prodigious output of film music. But he is perhaps best known for his scores for the first two of Francis Ford Coppola's *Godfather* films, writing tunes that we hear played by busking musicians on the streets of Philadelphia every day.

Scalero oversaw the education and development not only of Italian composers at Curtis but also of Philadelphia's own Samuel Barber (1910–1981), who is counted among the most important and beloved American composers of the last century. Barber studied with Scalero for nine years, including in the summer in Italy. After his first trip to Italy in 1928, the composer found a great feeling of personal liberation there, and he would return to Europe often to compose. In 1936, Barber—on a trip to Austria with Menotti—wrote his now ubiquitous *Adagio for Strings* as the slow movement of his first string quartet. The *Adagio* was arranged for string orchestra and premiered by the great conductor Arturo Toscanini with his NBC Orchestra just two years later, and the piece remains arguably the most famous work of American concert music to this day.

More recently, subsequent generations of Italian and Italian American musicians have had a great impact on Curtis and music in Philadelphia. Acclaimed conductors Riccardo Muti of the Philadelphia Orchestra (1980–1992) and Corrado Rovaris of Opera Philadelphia (2004–present) worked with the Curtis Symphony Orchestra to collaborate on many symphonic and operatic programs. And the list of Philadelphia Orchestra musicians of Italian descent who attended Curtis and taught at the school is similarly impressive. Names such as DePasquale,

Rosario Scalero. (Albert Petersen—Courtesy of Curtis Rock Resource Center)

Barber and Menotti. (Walter Vassar Collection [MSS 8]; Curtis Institute of Music Archives—Courtesy of Curtis Rock Resource Center)

Lenfest Hall of the Curtis Institute of Music (designed by Venturi, Scott Brown and Associates) located on 1616 Locust St., Philadelphia. (Tom Crane Photography)

Gigliotti, Montanaro, and Montone are revered among musicians and concertgoers as figures who have passed down a musical inheritance through generations of colleagues and students.

A married couple of Italian American Curtis graduates and Philadelphians who have had an enduring and positive influence on music are Anthony Checchia and Benita Valente. Checchia is a Philadelphia native, but his family hails from the Foggia region of Italy. During the tenure of pianist Rudolf Serkin as director of Curtis, Checchia served as Assistant Director at the school. In 1986 Checchia founded the Philadelphia Chamber Music Society as artistic director, and with this initiative he brought some of the finest musicians in the world to the area to play chamber music in venues across the city. Valente is a soprano who built a career of international repute, recording and performing in recitals and operas around the world to great acclaim. She was raised in California, and her family came from the *comune* of Cassino in the southern Lazio region. Among Valente's many teaching and mentoring positions, she is currently an instructor at the summer voice program in Lucca.

The Curtis Institute is one of the legendary musical institutions in the world and remains today a jewel of music education and performance that has had a profound effect on Philadelphia cultural life. It has always had a special connection to the music and musicians of Italy. The contributions of Italian musicians to the school and their subsequent contributions to the world have had a lasting impact on the history of music itself.

16

Italy on Display

Representing Italy in the 1876 Centennial
and the 1926 Sesquicentennial

Steven Conn

FIFTY YEARS SEPARATED TWO GREAT BIRTHDAY CELEBRATIONS in Philadelphia. The Centennial Exposition of 1876 was the largest single event held in the United States to that point, and it has since become a touchstone of nineteenth-century American history. By contrast, the sesquicentennial, held in 1926, has largely been forgotten, though it too richly symbolized the America of its moment.

Those fifty years bracket a remarkable period of immigration that transformed cities like Philadelphia into places of extraordinary ethnic, religious, and linguistic diversity. Italians had been a small community in the city in 1876, but by 1926 they constituted a major part of Philadelphia's social, economic, and political life. In 1876, Italians used the centennial as a way of announcing themselves as a recently united nation alongside other nations from around the world. In 1926, however, Italians took the occasion of the national birthday to stake their own claim to Americanness and help create a new identity: Italian American.

Whatever else the 1876 Centennial Exposition might have been—and it was a great many things beyond marking one hundred years since the Declaration of Independence—it served as an attempt at national reconciliation. The American Civil War had ended just eleven years earlier, and the federal attempts at a just "reconstruction" were still ongoing, though they would end in 1877. In Philadelphia and in cities across the United States, men missing limbs and hobbling on prosthetics were a common sight.

Where better, then, than in Philadelphia, birthplace of the nation, for North and South to come together, to gather around the hearth of shared history while looking optimistically toward a shared future. Never mind that those Southerners who participated in that symbolic joining of hands had repudiated the nation founded in Philadelphia, and never mind that that shared future would come at the expense of African American civil rights and freedom. The millions who came from around the world to see the centennial displays in Philadelphia during the summer of 1876 used history as an excuse to take stock of the present.

Perhaps more than any other nation that sponsored exhibits at the centennial, Italy had some understanding of the American politics at play at the fair. After all, Italians had endured their third war of independence in 1866 and had only achieved full national unification in 1871. Americans have always enjoyed a sense of themselves as a young nation—as if chronological age corresponded to national vigor—but in comparison with Italy, the United States was a venerable nation indeed.

So unity and the connections forged within and between countries were burning topics at the fair, and Italy's contribution would be an important part of that story. But it almost didn't happen.

When the government of the United States issued its invitation to other countries requesting their presence at the fair, the Kingdom of Italy initially declined. Eighteen months before opening day, "the Government has, up to this time, done nothing, and promises to do nothing, to help exhibitors get their wares upon the ground," according to the New York Times's correspondent in Italy. Nor had the impending exposition attracted much attention among Italians. "So far as we know," the Times writer told readers, "nothing has yet been done here to awaken general interest in the enterprise, so that the opportunity may be taken advantage of by the Italians to make their productions better known and extend their commerce with the United States."[1]

The American legation in Rome was fully aware of the situation and communicated urgently with Secretary of State Hamilton Fish to express its concern. On February 10, 1875, George Marsh wrote to Fish saying, "The Italian Government was still not convinced that the industry of Italy would derive, from the active participation of its Government in the Exhibition, any advantage commensurate with the expenditure. . . . At present, then, I have no reason to expect that Italy will take any part in the Celebration beyond the appointment of Commissioners, and even of this I have no assurance."[2]

Perhaps this hesitation resulted from the usual sorts of things that cause governments to move more slowly than they might; perhaps it reflected the challenge of participating in such a celebration of the concept of "nation-state" for a newly formed nation like Italy. In the event, all was resolved by the end of the summer when King Victor Emmanuel II issued a royal decree creating a centennial commission. It met for the first time in October 1875 in Florence. Italy was coming to the fair.[3]

It isn't quite right to say that in 1876 Philadelphians—or Americans more generally—were unfamiliar with Italy. Many had followed the events leading to

Italian unification quite keenly starting in 1847. They cheered when republicanism seemed on the verge of triumph; they lamented when Pope Pius IX turned against the republican movement. They saw Italian unification through the lens of the American Revolution and saw Italians as striving to free themselves from the tyranny of monarchs and clergy just as Americans had.

But it is probably fair to say that most Philadelphians had little familiarity with Italians themselves. A few Italians made it to the city as political refugees after 1848 and its long aftermath. In 1852, Italian Catholics persuaded Bishop John Neumann to establish St. Mary Magdalen de Pazzi, a new parish catering to Italians. Just after the Civil War, Philadelphia's Italian community established the Societa di Unione e Fratellanza as the first Italian mutual aid and fraternal society in the city. Still, by 1870 there were fewer than 1,000 Italian immigrants living in a city that by then had grown to nearly 675,000 residents.

In this sense, the centennial provided tens of thousands of Americans with their first encounter with Italy. What those visitors saw, in keeping with the overstuffed overabundance that characterized the fair as a whole, was something of a hodgepodge. The Italian display occupied space at the far western edge of the fair's main building, and it included everything from samples of marble and alabaster to furniture and yarns to Venetian glass and jewelry from Turin. *Frank Leslie's* guide to the fair, the most exhaustive of any of those produced in 1876, asserted that "the articles of greatest interest and importance in the Italian section are certainly the carved furniture and mosaics, the work in terra-cotta, and a few of the ceramic specimens." But, in fact, *Frank Leslie's* concluded that "the exhibits of Italy are surpassed by those of other countries."[4]

Machinery Hall, which featured displays of the industrializing nations flexing their muscles in steam and steel, was probably the most popular stop at the fairgrounds. The mighty Corliss Engine, a fifteen-hundred-horsepower behemoth, sat right in the center of Machinery Hall, simultaneously on display and providing power for the rest of the exposition. Here, perhaps more than in any other part of the exposition, nations pitted themselves against one another. It was an age of industry, and Machinery Hall offered an opportunity for each nation to show the fruits of its own industry and to measure that against other nations. Italy, alas, did not make much of a showing there—largely, I suspect, because in 1876 Italy had not yet developed an advanced industrial economy of the sort that Germany, Great Britain, France, and the United States had.

Memorial Hall and its annex stood as the counterpart and counterpoint of Machinery Hall on the fairgrounds. The exposition's most architecturally significant building—"the universal critical verdict upon this building places it in the front rank, architecturally, among the more ornate structures existing in this country"[5]—Memorial Hall showcased fine art. Here too was an opportunity for nations to be compared against one another in friendly competition. Art and industry—

taken together, Machinery Hall and Memorial Hall summed up the very definition of *civilization* in the Victorian mind.

In the critics' view, however, Italy presented itself here little better than it did in Machinery Hall. Italian sculpture was shown in Memorial Hall and was judged to be "highly interesting" and "creditable to the modern art school and genius of the country." But the bulk of the Italian art that made its way to Philadelphia in 1876 was shown in the Art Annex, and it did not impress. "In this department," *Frank Leslie's Historical Register* told readers, "one is struck with the lack of the more exalted efforts of inspiration, and with the prominence of simpler and more homely expressions of art than would possibly have been expected from Italy." In a postexposition wrap-up, the *International Review* largely agreed. The *Review's* critic concluded that "of all the countries prominent in art, Italy did itself scantiest justice in the exhibition of paintings." The "best names of to-day" were absent from the Italian exhibit, and what was on display were "pictures seldom rising to a respectable mediocrity."[6]

In fact, the official Italian contributions to the art displays were overshadowed to some extent by the three rooms occupied by the Castellani Collection. The collection of antiquities and some more contemporary jewelry had been assembled by Alessandro Castellani, himself a jewelry maker and scion of a prominent jewelry-making family. Castellani, no doubt hoping to sell some or all of his collection by bringing it to Philadelphia, published his own guidebook to the collection for visitors. The *New York Times* swooned over the "amazing beauty" of the objects Castellani had assembled, and the paper editorialized that New Yorkers should raise the money to buy the collection for the newly established Metropolitan Museum of Art. In the end, the collection was packed up and sent back to Europe, where much of it wound up in London's Victoria and Albert Museum.

That Italy made a somewhat underwhelming impression in Philadelphia in 1876 might well have resulted from the delay the government made in deciding

The art sent by Italy to the 1876 Centennial Exposition did not impress the critics. Art Annex—Italian Section. (Courtesy of the Free Library of Philadelphia, Print and Picture Department, #c011781)

to attend the fair at all and then in the haste necessary to have an exhibit ready for opening day. But it might also have been a consequence of Italy's recent arrival as a unified nation. Regions of Italy, and certainly individual cities, had a sense of their own identity. The Italian nation as a whole, however, struggled to define and present one for visitors to the centennial. That was the sort of question worth debating over a glass of wine—in which case the emporium set up and run by the Italian Enological Committee was the place to go. There you could find a nice selection of Italian wines and vermouths.[7]

Everything that the centennial was, the sesquicentennial was not.

The 1876 fair was universally regarded as a triumph. It was the first major international exposition held in the United States, and its success ushered in an age of ever-bigger, ever-grander events: 1893 in Chicago, 1901 in Buffalo, 1915 in San Francisco. And so fifty years later, Philadelphians tried to recapture the magic when they decided to throw America a 150th birthday party.

It was a flop. When the gates opened on June 1, much of the site, a swampy area at the very bottom of Broad Street, was still a construction zone. By July 5—a day after the symbolic "big day"—fair organizers announced that 90 percent of the exhibits were now complete. The sesquicentennial, like so much else in Philadelphia in the 1920s, was plagued with corruption and controversy. Organizers predicted thirty-six million visitors through the turnstiles; six million actually made the trip to South Philadelphia. It didn't help matters that the summer of 1926 was particularly wet. Of the 184 days the fair was open, it rained on 107 of them.[8]

Disappointments to one side, fifty years after the centennial, the sesquicentennial was held in a different city, in a different nation, and in a different world. All of that was certainly reflected in the Italian presence at the fair.

In 1915 a group of Italian businessmen in South Philadelphia joined to form a merchant's association. The following year, they received their official charter. The association served both a symbolic role in galvanizing the city's Italian American community and a very real role in creating what would be known to generations of Philadelphians as the Italian Market.[9]

That community had grown dramatically since 1876. From the several hundred counted in 1870, the Italian population swelled to 10,000 in 1890, and by 1920 there were nearly 140,000 Italian immigrants and their children living in the city. They were among the millions of southern and eastern European immigrants that

The wine sent by Italians, however, met with a more enthusiastic reception. Alphonse Stevanns Exhibit Agricultural Hall. (Courtesy of the Free Library of Philadelphia, Print and Picture Department, c022244)

came to the United States during those three decades. By 1930, Italian Americans constituted the second-largest ethnic group in the city.

That immigration, to Philadelphia and to the rest of the United States, effectively came to a halt during World War I. After the war, a xenophobic backlash against those southern and eastern Europeans led Congress to enact two restrictive immigration laws—in 1921 and 1924—targeted precisely at immigrants from those areas. Eugenic and other pseudoscientific ideas about race posited that criminality was inherent in Italians and was touted as justification for discrimination against them.

This anti-immigrant backlash went hand in glove with the spread of the domestic terrorist organization known as the Ku Klux Klan out of the South and across the nation. The Klan found targets for their version of white supremacy in Jews and Catholics as well as African Americans. An estimated twenty-five to thirty thousand Klansmen marched proudly down Pennsylvania Avenue in Washington, DC, in 1925, and Philadelphia was home to perhaps as many as thirty-five thousand Klan members during the interwar years. In fact, the KKK petitioned sesquicentennial organizers to be included in the official program, and despite the objections of many, they were granted the use of the fair's auditorium for three days in September.

Things had changed in Italy too by the time of the sesquicentennial. Though Italy had joined the Allies during World War I and was thus on the victors' side at the negotiations in Versailles, the territorial resolutions of that treaty left many in Italy feeling cheated. That sense of grievance, combined with postwar economic turmoil, helped Italian fascists gain political momentum. By 1922, Benito Mussolini had become Prime Minister.

This, then, was the political context in which the Italian presence at the 1926 fair took shape. On the one hand, the planners wanted to celebrate Italy even while distancing themselves somewhat from Italian fascism—after all, the sesquicentennial ostensibly marked the birth of a set of political ideals that Italian fascists had repudiated. On the other, they needed to assert the Americanness of Italian Americans in an environment of toxic racism and ethnic bigotry. All this had to be accomplished within the framework of an event that struggled just to get off the ground.

It seems clear that the Italian participation at the sesquicentennial was organized largely by Italian Americans, not by the Italian government, and largely by Italian Americans in Philadelphia. As early as 1924, sesquicentennial organizers had approached "foreign language speaking groups" in the city to encourage them to organize nationally specific days. These included Poles, Jews, Swedes, and Russians in addition to Italians. In the end, there were three major events to highlight Italy, Italians, and Italian Philadelphia.

The first of these was a grand pageant, held on June 19 in the huge stadium built for the fair. Titled "Italia: An Episodic Spectacle," it served as the climax of Italian Day. The program was printed in both English and Italian and describes an extravaganza in four acts with an epilogue. The first three portrayed three of

Italy's city-states: "Venice, the Magnificent," "Florence, the Beautiful," and "Rome, the Eternal." The fourth act depicted the unification of Italy by Garibaldi and the triumph of Italy's constitutional monarchy, and the breathless language of the program hints at what must have been an over-the-top melodrama inside the stadium: "Far in the distance, gradually growing louder, we hear the sound of marching feet, and as Mazzini and Count Cavour turn, wondering if it be friend or foe, there appears—GARIBALDI!!" The drama went on: "The Liberator is followed by his life-long ideals—Truth, Justice, and Unity. . . . The threatening fore-shadows of 'War,' 'Conquest,' 'Famine,' and 'Death' are scattered to the winds by Garibaldi. . . . Behold! ITALY, the Nation, is born!" After this stirring climax, the pageant ended by celebrating the "bonds of friendship" between the United States and Italy, depicted thus: "Italia and the Spirit of America step to the foreground, followed by their proudly waving banners, and there bursts upon the air the national anthems of these nations united for all time."[10]

Italian Day was one of several such days specifically designated for American ethnic groups at the sesquicentennial. Toward the end of the fair's run, however, came Columbus Day, an American holiday that had taken on a special significance for Italian Americans. The day was another way for Italy and for Italian Americans to stake a claim as part of the founding of the United States. And the Italian government made an appearance at the sesquicentennial's Columbus Day observance in the person of Ambassador Giacomo De Martino.

After he arrived in the city, the ambassador's schedule was laid out with almost military precision. He departed from the Ritz-Carlton Hotel at 9:55 and traveled by car, accompanied by a phalanx of policemen on motorcycles. Straight down Broad Street, he arrived at the gates of the fair at 10:10, where he was met by a cavalry troop.

Columbus Day was not without its small diplomatic kerfuffle. The Spaniards too wanted to claim Columbus's legacy, and they planned their own program of events. In a letter to Joseph Wilson, Director of Foreign Participation, Eugene Alessandroni, president of the Italian Executive Committee of the fair and an Assistant District Attorney, wrote, "The Italian and Spanish groups, in a slightly different way, celebrate the same day." In the end, two lunches were served in the same hotel and at the same time. Philadelphia Mayor Freeland Kendrick shuttled between the two.

Italian Americans did ultimately stake their claim to Columbus and by extension to the foundational moment of what would become the United States, symbolized in the nineteenth century by the feminized figure of Columbia—this despite the fact that the New World was first explored, conquered, and colonized by Spaniards. From then on, Columbus and Columbus Day would have a particular valence for Italian Americans.

This Italianized Columbus Day came toward the end of a fair that, in turn, marked the end of a fifty-year period during which world's fairs served as opportunities for nations to show themselves off. Instead of highlighting the accomplishments of nations, subsequent fairs fantasized about the future. Indeed, the two great fairs of the 1930s—1933 in Chicago and 1939 in New York—were given over more to multinational corporations, rather than nation-states, and the future they promised to manufacture and sell to all of us.

The world's fairs that punctuated the half century between 1876 and 1926 stand as remarkable snapshots of the nation and the world at particular moments in time. They offered an opportunity for this nation and others to put themselves on display, and in so doing they revealed a set of assumptions about just what the nations thought they were and what they hoped to be. In 1876, the newly unified nation of Italy introduced itself, however haltingly, to Americans and to the rest of the world. In 1926, however, Italian Americans used the sesquicentennial to remind their fellow Americans that they too belonged in this nation.

NOTES

1. "Italian Gossip," *New York Times*, January 4, 1875.

2. George Marsh to Hamilton Fish, February 10, 1875, USCC Foreign Bureau Correspondence File, City Archives, City of Philadelphia.

3. See "Italy: The American Centennial," *Chicago Tribune*, October 4, 1875.

4. *Frank Leslie's Historical Register of the United States Centennial Exposition*, (New York: Frank Leslie's Publishing House, 1877), p. 244.

5. *Frank Leslie's*, p. 174. After 1876, Memorial Hall served as the Philadelphia Museum of Art's first home and is still standing today, now as the Please Touch Museum.

6. *Frank Leslie's*, p. 174; "The Late World's Fair," *International Review*, July 1877, p. 497.

7. The committee published a pamphlet advertising its selection. See USCC Foreign Bureau Publications File, City Archives, City of Philadelphia.

8. I have written more about the failure of the sesquicentennial in *Museums and American Intellectual Life, 1876–1926* (Chicago: University of Chicago Press, 1998), chap. 7.

9. I saw an original charter hanging on the wall of Fante's Kitchen Shop on Ninth street in the summer of 2017.

10. "Italia," Sesquicentennial Records, 232-4-5.5, City Archives, City of Philadelphia.

III

Made in America

Immigration, Community Formation,

and Varieties of Creative Italian

American Experience

INTRODUCTION

Judith Goode

R EADERS WILL NOTICE THAT SOME OF THE THEMES discussed in Part II are revisited in Part III from a bottom-up perspective with different actors and processes engaged in the formation of a large Italian American community. Their presence created new Italian influences as industry and the urban economy grew. A new dynamism came from the populations coming to the city to work in the boom in factory production, railroads, and construction, and a significant component were Italian immigrants who (over time) produced a large Italian American community and new Italian American cultural practices.

While John Wanamaker and grand tour collectors brought home the value-laden art objects, crafts, and styles from Italy, between the mid-1880s and 1930, large numbers of Italian craftsmen and laborers came to the United States to work. Italians, some with craft skills in stonecutting, masonry, wrought iron, woodcarving, and carpentry, were important in the expanding residential housing construction for the new elite and middle class who commuted by streetcar and commuter railroad to newly built suburbs and suburban-like city neighborhoods both before and during mass migration (roughly 1880–1920).

This story involves both a clustering of newcomers from Italy in one section of the city—South Philadelphia—and a proliferation of smaller clusters near work. In 1850, the Philadelphia census listed 117 persons of Italian origin, and by 1860, the number had increased to 517. Between 1890 and 1920, over 60,000 people migrated from Italy to the city. The center of Italian American life in South Philadelphia formed two decades before the first mass immigration.

This early settlement from the Liguria-Genoa area before the large, rapid inflow of later immigrants, while small, was important because it formed the foundation for later settlement as described in Chapter 18. Scholars have shown that this early population came predominantly from Liguria and its port city of Genoa on the northwest coast, a major area for transatlantic trade, and because of that trade, diplomatic relations between the city-state and Genoa were the first formal state-to-state Italian links (see Prologue). These immigrants were different from the later immigrants who dominate the narrative of Italian immigration to Philadelphia, which focuses on the post-1880 migration of southern Italian agricultural laborers who worked large estates near the agricultural towns of Sicily and the Mezzogiorno (Campagna [Naples] and "the Boot"). Yet the migrants from the south were themselves diverse. The life stories described in most of the following chapters reveal that there were many differences in experience, skills, and education among the immigrant community and many paths to settlement and careers.

Here we provide the broader evolving political, economic, social, and cultural context in Philadelphia in order to contextualize all the chapters in Part III. The wave of mass immigration stimulated by expanding industry largely came from outside the dominant monarchies and empires of Europe. The restructuring of nations as empires dissolved was creating economic and political insecurity in areas in eastern and southern Europe on the borders of the great powers. It was people from these areas that comprised the bulk of the immigration.

Like many other immigrant groups, single male workers comprised the first waves, but as settlement grew, migration streams of extended families soon followed relatives and friends. For Italians, by the 1920s, a network of institutions—Italian nationality parishes, family-owned enterprises, and mutual aid societies—provided the economic, political, social, and spiritual needs of the community.

The end of mass immigration in the 1920s resulted from national legislation to restrict immigration from southern and eastern Europe immigrants. The nativist movements of this time are well known for their racialization of immigrants. Implicated in these movements are the ideas of racial hierarchy embedded in the "scientific" racial theories of the day, such as eugenics, which placed southern and eastern Europeans in a category below those from "whiter" nations of the north.[1]

The stalling economy of the Great Depression also ended the job and wage incentives of immigrants. Finally, World War II further decreased contact between immigrants and Italy. The Depression stalled investment in housing and consumer goods production, and the war diverted capital and labor to the war effort, creating an appearance of dilapidation and dereliction in many city neighborhoods.

At the same time, Philadelphia had become one of the few very large cities in the United States with a virtual parity of white and black people as a result of the Great Migration from the U.S. South, which increased during the establishment of Jim Crow laws after the Civil War, followed by the labor needs during World Wars I and II.

The first several decades after World War II in Philadelphia were times of economic optimism and upward mobility. After the war, the offspring of the turn-of-the-century immigrants, previously seen as outside the mainstream, found that their shared sacrifice and new social experiences had made their American status more secure. There was no question of belonging to the nation. There were also increasing opportunities to move into the middle class through the GI Bill and FHA mortgages, public policies to address the needs for jobs and housing for the returning soldiers starting families and reentering the economy.

Many of the public programs that created the new middle class were not available to black people, and bias in the real estate markets created increased segregation. Together this meant that suburbanization was not an option for black people. As a result of this, the growing segregated racial structure became an important social, spatial, and political feature of the city through the eras of civil rights and deindustrialization.

In regard to work, collective bargaining rights allowed workers more economic security and career ladders, as did the expansion of access to higher education through the expansion of public universities. At the same time, housing policies privileged new built housing over rehabilitation of old neighborhoods and negatively affected row-house neighborhoods such as South Philadelphia. Policies promoting new highways as well as incentives for new suburban housing led many households to leave the city, although the exodus was less pronounced in South Philadelphia, largely because of the attachment to institutions described in Chapter 18.

By the 1970s, the intertwined processes of deindustrialization and the globalization of the economy were creating a rust belt in the industrial core of the Northeast and Midwest United States. Plants were relocated to the Sunbelt and offshore for cheaper labor and energy costs. Philadelphia—once an industrial powerhouse—lost a large number of industrial jobs in the 1960s and 1970s. The poverty rate has remained the highest among the ten largest U.S. cities even today. Since the 1980s, policy makers have tried to reverse economic decline by restructuring the economy in response to globalization. The effects of these policies are the subject of Part IV.

Part III explores the development of the Italian American individuals and community institutions over the past four to five generations under conditions of depression, war, racial inequality, and public policies promoting suburbanization and new economic opportunities. You will see evidence of all these conditions as you read about the built environment, the settlement, and key institutions of South Philadelphia as well as individual lives and careers and family histories as Italian Americans contributed to city leadership, arts, and culture.

Chapter 17. Jeffrey A. Cohen's "Marking Place: Brief Notes on Building Patterns in Italian American South Philadelphia" looks at the built environment of South Philadelphia for a more material description of the way Italian settlement, attachment to local institutions, and a pattern of postwar resistance to suburbanization and reinvestment in rehabilitating homes created a unique landscape of designs built on the original footprint and row-home stock.

Chapter 18. Judith Goode's essay "How South Philadelphia Became Known as Italian" uses scholarly historical, anthropological, and sociological work on South Philadelphia to examine the foundational institutions of the Italian American community in Philadelphia in order to understand the role of national churches, marketing to provision the community with culturally specific goods, the Italian language press, and mutual aid associations through time. Using a study of Italian-identified families in the 1970s, she and her colleagues demonstrate the ways in which women, through their everyday food activities, created a cycle of events in order to maintain social cohesion. Over time many non-Italian residents were incorporated through community bonds of kinship and friendship into identifying these affiliations as reflecting both Italian and South Philadelphia identities.

Chapter 19. In their essay, "Italian American Leaders in Business and Politics," Scott Gabriel Knowles, Maegan Madrigal, and Isabella Sangaline use archival and oral histories of Italian American leaders in boardrooms and the halls of government to demonstrate that there are many different pathways to mobility in the twentieth century, especially after World War II. The biographies include people who were *prominenti* in the early decades of the twentieth century as well as people of achievement who were born in the 1920s, 1930s, and 1940s. Other chapters such as 8, 14, and 20–30 include more biographies of extraordinary achievements.

ART AND MUSIC

Along with political and economic leadership, there are many stories of achievement in the arts. The next three chapters all deal with Italian American artists and musicians who have had a wide variety of successful careers in the arts in Philadelphia and elsewhere. Some came from families who came to the United States with skills and traditions from the homeland. For others, such skills were developed through opportunities available in the city.

Chapter 20. In "Drawn from the Boot: The Italian Artists of Philadelphia," William R. Valerio discusses several generations of Italian American visual artists and provides insights about the influence of local Italian organized art groups such as the Da Vinci Arts Alliance and other South Philadelphia organizations such as the Samuel Fleischer Arts Center in the training of Italian American artists. Elite institutions such as PAFA and PMA, as well as the mentorship of Albert Barnes and public school art teachers, also often appear in biographies in the identification, training, and mentoring of these artists. We see the broad variety of art styles and new media industries in which Italian Americans participated as well as various ways of relating to Italian heritage among the artists.

Chapter 21. Jody Pinto's "A Family of Italian American Artists" provides an in-depth example of one of the many families of artists by exploring the experience of her own artistic family, one of the several considered by Valerio. She tells the story from her grandparents' time to the experience of her father and his two brothers with Albert Barnes as a patron and mentor who nurtured their talents and through her own career as a PAFA-trained public artist.

Chapter 22. In "Jazz in the Neighborhood and the World," Chris William Sanchirico presents the less well-known but locally recognized contributions and affinities of several important Italian American jazz musicians to this quintessentially America music form. This is especially important because of Philadelphia's recognized jazz venues and academic interest in jazz.

ARCHITECTS: THE PHILADELPHIA SCHOOL OF ARCHITECTURE

The next two essays depict what is known as the Philadelphia School of Architecture, which held sway at the University of Pennsylvania in the latter part of the twentieth century when a group of three architects responded to the earlier modern International Style movement. Two were Italian in heritage, and the third was significantly influenced by Italy.

Chapter 23. Alan Greenberger's "Romaldo Giurgola, Architect: 'The Reluctant Master'" describes the Philadelphia School of Architecture as a movement that was first depicted and named in a journal article in 1963 and was reflected in many important Philadelphia buildings between 1950 and 1980. The contributions of Romaldo Giurgola—who immigrated as an adult after architectural training in Italy—were based on his theories of contextual integration of buildings to their cities and were developed in Philadelphia. He later moved on to international work and acclaim.

Chapter 24. In "An 'Extremely Emotional Love Affair': Robert Venturi, Rome, and Italy," Luca Molinari uses Robert Venturi's own words to look at ways in which he strongly acknowledged the influence of his many experiences in Italy on his work. Beginning with Venturi's year at the American Academy of Rome as recipient of the Rome Prize, Molinari explores these influences on Venturi's work as well as the ways in which Louis I. Kahn, his colleague in the Philadelphia school (who was not of Italian heritage), shared such inspirations from the legacy of Roman urban forms and plans on their theory and practice.

NOTE

1. Daniel Okrent, *The Guarded Gate, Bigotry, Eugenics and the Law That Kept Jews, Italians and Other European Immigrants out of America* (New York: Scribner's, 2019).

17

Marking Place

Brief Notes on Building Patterns in Italian American South Philadelphia

Jeffrey A. Cohen

IN LOOKING FOR THE ARCHITECTURE OF ITALIAN AMERICANS in Philadelphia, one might expect echoes of well-known landmarks from ancient Rome and Renaissance Florence, of medieval Venice and Lombardy, and even of baroque Rome—the staples of art history courses and textbooks. And indeed, one encounters evocations of these historical architectural episodes across Philadelphia and to a lesser degree in the streetscapes settled by the city's Italian Americans beginning in the later nineteenth century—if generally not so monumentally or so literally.

But in the everyday streetscapes in the parts of South Philadelphia that were home to the largest early concentration of Italian immigrants in the decades after the Civil War, one finds something quite different. Beyond the few large institutional structures built for and by Italians, iconic architectural echoes are mostly muted and far outnumbered by the dense urban fabric of smaller residential and commercial buildings. They create streetscapes that are insistently varied, marked strongly by incremental celebrations of hard-won economic successes of individual families at different moments and in different ways.

A widely adopted metaphor likens cities that have grown over the centuries to palimpsests—comparing them to manuscripts on parchment that have been scraped in preparation for new use, but incompletely, so that some older parts still show through. One can usefully think of cities along these lines, finding urban pieces that persist from deeper layers on maps and in time, while neighboring parts have since been built on repeatedly, creating a constructed collage with earlier elements occasionally peeking out amid those several generations younger.

Italian South Philadelphia fulfills this metaphor vividly, but more than most it's a vertical palimpsest, less of map over map than facade over facade. This is the most striking and distinctive thing about these streetscapes, whose houses and small shops often display a staccato rhythm of change every fifteen feet along street fronts, an impatient contrapuntal symphony of building improvement, familial self-representation, and constant change.

Much of this is rooted in the earlier history of the neighborhood into which Italian Americans settled in the second half of the nineteenth century. As the research of Richard Juliani has detailed, there had been early trickles of Italians to the city before 1820, numbering in dozens, and they did not concentrate residentially in a single district until the 1870s and 1880s, when immigration from Italy grew greatly, reaching into the hundreds and then into the thousands each year.[1] A good proportion found their way to what became the core of a growing Italian community in the northeastern part of South Philadelphia. That core area, described by Stefano Luconi as the district between Seventh and Ninth and between Christian and Carpenter Streets, quickly and firmly established itself as the primary center for institutional life and community memory as the Italian population grew.[2]

A critical shaping factor for the streetscapes that would characterize the core of the new Italian district during the late nineteenth-century wave of immigration was the fact that they congregated in a neighborhood that had already been substantially built up during that century's second quarter. As in many American cities of that time, new densely constructed zones expanding the urban edge filled in blocks until then only outlined by planned streets. Then they were quickly transformed by the construction of hundreds of modest houses. These would become home to successive waves of immigrants who were drawn to the dramatically expanding opportunities proffered by the newly rising industrial economies of factories, accelerating

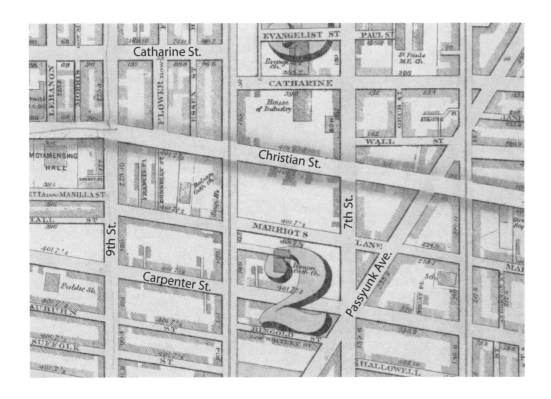

Samuel L. Smedley, *Atlas of the City of Philadelphia* (Philadelphia, 1862), detail of Section 3 (Philadelphia Geohistory Network), with street labels added. The large red numbers identify city wards. (Courtesy of the Free Library of Philadelphia, Map Department)

939–31 League Street.
(Photo: Richard Barnes)

commerce, and the creation of modern infrastructures from new roads to rails and pipes.

As was frequently the case, the new housing was speculatively developed, in street-lining rows of attached red-brick houses. Usually built in series ranging from a pair to a whole blockfront undertaken by a single developer, they were nearly identical, if often mirror images in terms of the position of the doorway along one party wall and chimneys along the other. One street-fronting room wide and two to three rooms deep was typical, but those on narrow midblock alleys and dead-end courts tended to contain just a single room on each floor.

These houses of the 1820 to 1850s could present fronts that seemed spare and utilitarian, with little exterior decoration. But when developers ventured some signs of stylistic currency, they were emulating early nineteenth-century work that was itself quite restrained, with planar brick fronts relieved mainly by elemental semicircular arched transoms or by elements of a laconic Greek Revival classicism that proscribed such arches, instead featuring prominent stone lintels. These marble lintels and pilasters were standard among the grander houses to the north but were less common here, where those lintels were frequently of painted wood.

So the fabric encountered by Italians settling into their new enclave was rather plain and by that point was aging in both stylishness and condition. In many cases, the prior residents were Irish immigrants who had come a generation earlier, often retaining ownership and renting to the new arrivals—nineteenth-century census records seem to reflect Italian surnames years earlier than do deeds for the same properties. Internally, additional partitions and doors, and later additional kitchens and sinks upstairs, reflect the adaptation of what more often had been single-family homes into houses that served more complex constellations of relatives and boarders, including many single men who expected to work and send money back to families still in Italy rather than planning to stay long themselves. For houses on well-traveled streets, the first-floor front was easily adapted to commerce, with a second door and a shop window.

At some point between the 1890s and 1950s, many households had begun to achieve some measure of economic stability and ownership, and proud owners were inclined to show it. The deteriorating wooden lintels would be covered or replaced, the failing front cornice trimmed back, and the front wall reshaped into a crowning parapet. Doorways and doors themselves became opportunities for new decorative elaboration. But most often, the way to improve an old front was by superimposing a new one directly over it, sometimes on just the first floor but often all the way up. Inside, kitchens were modernized, indoor bathrooms replaced outhouses, and winding stairs were often replaced with widened, straighter runs.

By the twentieth century, the new front was often proudly different from the old one. It might be colorfully tinted stucco or brick in a distinctly new color or texture, with grooved surfaces and sometimes laid with thick mortar joints. Rising semioctagonal bays would be added to many fronts. From the 1930s, quilted metal-covered wooden windowsills and masonry-simulating cladding such as "perma-stone" would cover the old brick, long since in need of repointing. After the war, the suburbanizing vocabularies of broken pediments and aluminum screen doors appeared, along with wide parlor windows—sometimes bowed, with diamond glazing—and aluminum or vinyl siding across an entire facade.

These transformations usually came to neighboring houses at different times, and the result was a remarkable matrix of differently treated vertical planes about fifteen feet wide, creating a series of contrasting faces that usually still showed their original rhythms of windows and doors. They present a unity made up of individualized components that reflected a generally shared economic identity. What has become their distinctive historical character lies some distance from their original built form, now seen intact relatively rarely, but often still legibly.

After its initial foothold in South Philadelphia, the Italian population in the area expanded dramatically and spread south and west from the old core. By 1890 the transplanted population and their offspring had grown to more than 10,000, and two decades later, by 1910, it had exploded to almost 77,000, with the enclave spreading north to Bainbridge Street and south to Federal Street. The tide continued strongly into the 1920s, and the footprint of settlement expanded into the adjacent areas further southwest as the city's Italian population reached 150,000 by the end of that decade.

One catches a geographic picture of that expansion in a map from 1934 indicating ethnicity as a "real estate condition" that would inform the decisions of mortgage lenders, effectively providing a tool for discrimination in lending. But as obnoxious as the "conditions" mapped by its maker—J. M. Brewer of Property Services, Inc.—could be in their intent and result, they seem fairly closely observed and can be used to illustrate the remarkable spread of the Italian population, represented in green hatching of three different color intensities to indicate concentration, from "minority" to "predomination" to "substantially complete."

911–19 South Tenth.
(Photo: Richard Barnes)

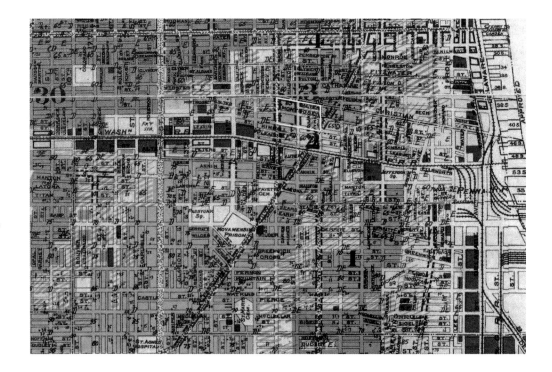

M. Brewer, "J. M. Brewer's Map of Philadelphia" (Philadelphia, 1934), Free Library of Philadelphia (Greater Philadelphia Geohistory Network). The added boxed area in yellow represents the nineteenth-century core enclave of Philadelphia's Italian American community, from Seventh to Ninth and Christian to Carpenter. (Free Library of Philadelphia Map Collection)

The area in light red to the west and north was identified as "Colored," and that in blue in a thin, faint band to the north and a more solid tint to the east was identified as "Jewish." The solidly red areas, especially along Washington Avenue and the waterfront, represented industrial uses. In 1934, Brewer's probably roughly credible impression was that the Italian community had spread a few blocks to the north but far more substantially to the southwest, tracking diagonally along Passyunk Avenue and southward along Broad Street.

In this expanded zone, they increasingly occupied newer row houses that were often more decoratively embellished and spacious than those of the earlier generations yet built in longer rows whose repetitiveness was striking. Nonetheless, owners would continue to find ways to mark their particularity through their house, employing distinctive paint schemes; door, window, and surface treatments. Where set back even slightly from the street, front terrace or yard improvements served as additional forms of self-representation.

In sum, these South Philadelphia houses, strikingly transformed from their earliest form, have become telling visual reflections of this community's very particular history.

NOTES

1. Richard N. Juliani, *Building Little Italy: Philadelphia's Italians before Mass Migration* (University Park: Pennsylvania State University Press, 1998).

2. Stefano Luconi, *From Paesani to White Ethnics: The Italian Experience in Philadelphia* (Albany: State University of New York Press, 2001), pp. 17–25.

18

How South Philadelphia Became Known as Italian

JUDITH GOODE

EW OTHER NEIGHBORHOODS ARE AS DISTINCT in the public imagination of the city as South Philly. Most people associate the space
with Italians, but it has always housed a diverse population. This essay
traces the different views of South Philly over time, as its population composition
changed as a result of major political and economic events, city planning and policies, and the local leadership structures. These processes shaped the representation and local identity of this space as Italian. A well-rounded view comes from
augmenting the official, elite record of formal structures with the rich voices of
informal leaders and structures generated from the bottom up through everyday
cultural practices.

The former borough of Moyamensing, just south of the city's original boundaries (south of South Street), was an early area of nuisance activities—butchering, meatpacking, and other odorous, noisy activities, as well as stigmatized vices.
Around the Civil War, free Black people and Irish immigrants shared tenements
and workplaces. After the war, much of the Seventh Ward, the area studied by
W.E.B. Du Bois in his book *The Philadelphia Negro*, was located in South Philly as
emancipated Black people came north during the postreconstruction era of Jim
Crow laws.

The area served as an early gateway community for the large-scale immigration
of southern and eastern Europeans between 1880 and 1920, mostly Italian, Jewish,
and east European. A century later, journalist Murray Dubin, in his book *South
Philadelphia*, used his own childhood experience just after World War II as well as
life story interviews to describe each of these different groups in separate chapters
on Irish, Black, Italian, and Jewish people.

The identification of this space as Italian American is a relatively late phenomenon. During the turn-of-the-century immigration flow, many newcomer groups speaking different languages inhabited this space. This chapter deals with the process of change, asking how and why this area became a marked Italian space. To answer this, we have to examine the array of Italian institutions—both formal and informal—over time as they serve both local residents and dispersed Italian American clusters.

In the last three decades, the neighborhood has continued to be marked by Italian American institutions and commerce at the same time that new populations are again settling there, including gentrifiers and Asian and Mexican immigrants. Today, South Philadelphia is able to foster the city's claim to valued diversity as important in the appeal of global cities for living global cosmopolitan lifestyles. During the nativist, anti-immigrant years of the 1880–1920 immigration period, the ethnic diversity in South Philadelphia was seen as a threat. One century later, immigrants and traditional Italian cultural commodities and practices help brand this area for consumption and gentrification.

Those who study neighborhoods know that local social fabrics and built environments are not stable but shift rapidly as city planning shapes changes in land use and as people move in and out. In Chapter 17, Jeffrey A. Cohen looks at how the locally constructed environment grew over time to fit the needs of Italian immigrants and how row homes were used in many ways, initially to develop commercial enterprises (artisan food production and commerce) and recently as capital investments through renovations, which signified success and achievement. Here we talk about the ways in which a less visible and obvious Italian marking comes from the concentration of formal enterprises and institutions as well as the informal, invisible, strong patterning of sociality and connections between people in local everyday life.

We explore the settlement, occupations, and upward mobility of Italian immigrants for many generations through key institutions—the church, provisioning enterprises, political ward structures, banks, mutual aid benevolent societies, and fraternal organizations. Much of the historical work on Italians in South Philadelphia[1] is based on official public sources and reflects the point of view of dominant citywide and local institutions, which are governed by men—city elites or local Italian leaders.

When we add work using oral histories or ethnography,[2] we add the voices of nonelites and women. In his dissertation, Richard Varbero through oral histories provides the voices of the working class between the world wars. A book chapter by Judith Goode, Karen Curtis, and Janet Theophano provides data from research with women in 1970 that explores the ways in which women's informal activities and daily, weekly, and annual patterns of celebration create social solidarity linking family, extended family, and friendship networks to create invisible neighborhood bonds through everyday activities.

BEFORE MASS MIGRATION

As we have seen in Part I, the first Italian residents during independence and the early federal period were mostly cosmopolitan, educated Italian elites—scholars, doctors, musicians, artists, and large-scale traders. They shared interests in enlightenment political philosophy. They also shared interests in science, medicine, literature, and the arts with their American friends as evidenced by memberships in learned societies (APS) and social clubs. Richard Juliani, in *Building Little Italy*, describes the Italian presence in the city as an aggregate of individuals rather than a community in formation.

According to Juliani, the formation of an actual community began in the 1860s when the Italian presence increased and became more visible in the census and on the ground. The midcentury migrants came mostly from the region of Liguria, especially the areas around its four major cities. Genoa, on the northwest coast, was where their transatlantic voyages began. Most households were in the area around Ninth and Tenth Streets between Catherine and Christian (see Chapter 17). The concentration of people from Italy in one space and the complete set of institutions that they built later attracted mass migrants, mostly from the agricultural south of Italy between 1880 and 1920.

Juliani uses early census figures to show a variety of individuals and social classes in this period—educated elite as well as commercial and artistic occupations addressed to American consumers. There were also artists and musicians for the popular classes such as street musicians and producers of ceramics and religious figurines (see Prologue for references to the padrone system), many residing in boardinghouses for single male workers.

Archival evidence relating to early Italian institutions represents a top-down view of the role of *"prominenti"* who governed institutions and served as professionals and large-scale business owners. They represented the community to city structures (city government and political parties), to representatives of the Italian state (consuls general), and to the Vatican (through priests and the city's Irish-dominated Catholic hierarchy) in order to shape the community. Significant Italian priests created and sustained Italian national parishes in South Philly.

Networks of Italian American businessmen provided Italian-specific consumer items. The local Italian press provided news. Banks and mutual aid associations provided support and credit. These all created a sense of attachment to this social and physical place, which then attracted the bulk of turn-of-the-century Italian immigrants.

MASS IMMIGRATION (1880–1920)

Who were the Italian immigrants who settled in Philadelphia in the decades just before and after the turn of the twentieth century? Why did they come? Where did they settle? In Chapter 17, Cohen tells us that between the mid-nineteenth century and 1890, the Italian-born population increased from mere hundreds to tens of thousands. They settled in dense tenement housing around the commercial area indicated in Chapter 17 and gradually moved further south and west.

Most Italians in this stream (70 percent, according to Luconi), came from the south—referred to as the Mezzogiorno—with the majority from peasant agricultural worker backgrounds (*contadini*) in Abruzzi, Calabria, Puglia (Bari), Campania (Naples), and eastern Sicily. They spoke different dialects and identified with the place (village, municipality, town, or city) they came from as *paesani*. Social clubs and mutual aid associations were often based on regional identities.

The migrant stream also included town and city artisans who had acquired skills in fabrication, needlework, and construction on estates and in towns and cities. There were different levels of literacy among immigrants as well—often within families and especially for the teachers, professionals, and merchants who came and whose life histories are included in this section. In spite of this variety, most of the immigrants arriving were viewed by potential employers as heavy labor for the manufacturing, construction, and railroad boom. In fact, many industries had sent agents to Italy to directly recruit labor.

Some arrived with skills related to construction and ornamentation, and Italian workers became numerous and active members of several craft unions such as the Granite Cutters' International Association and the Stonemasons' International Union of America. Others had skills in tailoring and were active in the Journeymen Tailors' International Union of America, and Italians were the most numerous members of the Barbers' International Factory Union of America.

Work was often found away from South Philadelphia, leading to a dispersal of Italian clusters. While less visible today, enough Italians worked in the apparel industry in and near Kensington to warrant a nationality parish. Manayunk, an old mill town on the Schuylkill, was the location of a cluster of multigeneration food businesses such as Consolo's Bakery, whose stuffed breads were popular. Other clusters of Italians lived near where new construction was being developed, which related to manufacturing, maintaining railroads, and building elite residences (such as Ambler and Chestnut Hill). Such clusters were also linked to the commerce and mutual aid associations in South Philadelphia.

SOCIAL INSTITUTIONS

As the Italian population grew, anchor institutions developed to provide goods and services. Early examples were the boardinghouses and eating and drinking establishments (pleasure gardens), which were places of informal economic, political, and social activity, especially for early migrants who often came as single males. Frank Palumbo (see Chapter 19) came from a family lineage that had been active in hospitality for several generations. The most critical institutions were Catholic parishes and the many enterprises that provided specific Italian cultural necessities, such as food and elements for life-cycle rituals and the annual round of saints' days and religious holidays.

In *Priests, Parishes and People,* Juliani extends his analysis into the decades of mass immigration as he documents the founding of the first Italian national church: St. Mary Magdalen de Pazzi (see Chapter 30), which is believed to be the first nationality parish in the United States. It was located in the core of South Philadelphia. The shift to national parish churches was intended to serve the new Catholic migrants from southern and eastern Europe whose language and styles of celebration were different from those of the earlier established parishes.

Using church archives, Juliani documents the effects of the shift from serving the initial small Genoan community (the early tenure of Father Mariani) to serving the very robust influx of poorer southern rural farmers through the long tenure of Father Antonio Isoleri, a Genoan priest who astutely led his parish spiritually and pastorally during the transition for fifty-six years from 1870 to 1926, navigating complex relationships between the Vatican, the Irish-dominated hierarchy in Philadelphia, and his parishioners, increasingly from southern Italy. By 1917, there were sixteen Italian parishes in the Philadelphia archdiocese. Only three were in South Philadelphia while the others were in the dispersed clusters.

St. Monica's Church, South Philadelphia.
(Photo: Gary Horn)

Looking at Italian parishes, we get an understanding of the tensions between the archdiocese hierarchy and parishioners regarding liturgical and participatory styles, the economic relationship between the church and the community, and the advantages and disadvantages of Italian national parishes based on national origin versus territorial neighborhoods, since the former—while better providing services (using the Italian language and liturgical style)—would fail to Americanize or incorporate newcomers. Tensions existed between Irish and Italian clergy and between Italians from the north and the south. Important national parishes such as St. Rita and St. Monica, which were not created until the early twentieth century, are discussed later.

Shrine of Santa Rita of Cascia, 1907–1915. The baroque and Roman-inspired facade stands on South Broad Street. (Photo: Giò Martorana)

The work of Stefano Luconi, *From Paesani to White Ethnics: The Italian Experience in Philadelphia,* covers a longer view of the Italian institutional framework and community leadership through the wars of the twentieth century. He too covers the *prominenti,* whose voices are present in the archival data and the citywide and Italian American press coverage. He provides an excellent understanding of the local Italian newspapers and their evolving positions on Italian and American politics.

By the time of the First World War, the families of immigrants who had come at the end of the nineteenth century had two generations of experience in America.

They ranged in class from educated professionals to impoverished heavy laborers and scavengers. Even skilled workers had irregular work and relied on their kin and patrons as well as formal and informal mutual aid.

Regionalism was key to organizing social institutions that provided social services and regional banks clustered on one street that provided loans. Luconi shows how regional boundaries gave way to an Italian national identity. He traces how both U.S. and nativist, anti-immigrant biases as well as the continuing interest in the new unified Italian nation-state helped reduce strong regional boundaries in social life and produced an "Italian" identity. The Sons of Italy was a significant example of the emergence of a new Italian national identity.

Some readers may be surprised to find no reference to a criminal organization that originated in Sicily: the mafia, which looms large in the popular imagination of Americans and has been frequently and often stereotypically sensationalized, romanticized, and exoticized. We already know enough about them to realize that it is their dramatic value that draws so much attention to the mafia in popular culture, and they are pushed to the sidelines here.

SOUTH PHILADELPHIA BETWEEN THE WARS

Varbero provides a glimpse of the social structuring of ordinary residents between the two world wars as generational layers deepened during the nativism of the 1920s and the depression of the 1930s. In line with changes in the discipline of history that put a stronger emphasis on ordinary people's lives and actions, he uses census and statistical data alongside life-history interviews in Italian with older residents to examine both the actual upward mobility and class relations in the community during this time and respondents' perception of social and institutional obstacles they faced. This includes the effects of Americanization policies embedded in the education and church systems in the community.

This work alongside Luconi's work describes the divisions in the community. These divisions were based on the geographic, economic, and linguistic differences between the Italian north and south in general, as well as regional social relations produced by the different governance systems of kingdoms and republics that predated the Italian nation. They were also based on class differences in terms of occupational experience, literacy, artisan skills, and a general distinction between agricultural workers (*contadini*), artisans (*artigiani*), and rich leaders (*galantuomini*).

Varbero describes a style difference between the Irish and Italian churches, which created tension as well. Italian parishioners themselves had a difficult time with the restrained, nonexpressive, and authoritative forms of church practices of Irish priests in contrast to the expressive, participatory processions involved in the attention to celebrating the patron saints. While the hierarchy recruited Italian priests for the national churches, almost all of those selected came from the north (Turin and Milan) in spite of available applicants from the south.

Rev. Dr. Gibbons, with a special class of First Communion children instructed at l'Assunta House, a mission house. (Catholic Historical Research Center of the Archdiocese of Philadelphia)

Finally, there were economic issues between the hierarchy and parishes. Rural Italian churches in the south often had noble patrons and did not depend on parishioners' support. Depression-era parish members could not afford parish schools or large contributions to collections as was expected in Irish parishes. Often, local church missions provided for the life-cycle rituals of children.

Varbero provides a lot of information on the role of schooling in the community as nativist movements and new, restrictive immigrant laws in the 1920s created institutionalized pressures for Americanization in both the church and public school systems. Continuing debates about the value of national parishes led to the diminution of their mission of providing culturally specific Italian social services and an increase in a perceived duty to Americanize and assimilate Italians.

The end of the Second World War produced the ultimate Americanization as Italians participated in the war effort. Over time, intra-Catholic marriage increased, and national parishes became more like ordinary, diverse geographic parishes.

Varbero examines public schools in the 1920s and 1930s as vehicles of assimilation and upward mobility as well. He presents a bifurcated picture. He finds the largest percentage of Italian students at South Philadelphia High School on the "academic" track (college bound) and many Italian students at the magnet Central High School. We see these students as they appear at Penn and Temple in Chapters 25 and 27.

At the same time, a very large percentage of students left school early and are not represented in the data. They entered the work force at fourteen, as they did in Italy. Varbero speculates that these differences reflect those with contadini backgrounds as opposed to artisan and gentry families. It was at the end of the war that opportunities for upward mobility became more widespread.

THE MARKET: FOOD PROVISIONING, SOCIAL MOBILITY, AND SOCIAL RELATIONS

Food provisioning provided a key institution in community life through the Ninth Street market. The original market area—a space of pushcarts and makeshift stalls—was typical of a street market organized by informal agreements until it was officially recognized by the city in 1915 as the Ninth Street Curbside Market. Commerce in this space served all immigrant groups of the mass migration period. Neither vendors nor merchandise sold was limited to Italian needs. Upon city recognition, an official businessman's association was organized as a legal governing board with slightly more Italian than non-Italian members. The board was expected to govern the space and follow city regulations.

The consolidation of the Ninth Street Curbside Market stores under a board that regulated space usage and cleanliness was a major turning point for turning irregular home-based production, pushcarts, and itinerant vendors into registered businesses. This move connected the market leaders to the local party regime of ethnic ward leaders who mediated between the city and all the local communities in the city.

It was not until 2009, when the city officially named the market space "the Italian Market" in a ceremony installing a historic marker, that the long-held, informal, symbolic reputation of this space as Italian was formalized. The story of what happened between the turn of the twentieth century and one hundred years later in many ways provides insight on how South Philadelphia became "Italian" in spite of its continuous and increasing diversity.

The core function of Italian merchants was to provide Italians with culturally specific goods and services. At the same time, the market served as another anchor institution, an important space for everyday life and for important connections. It was the source of a network of relationships between merchants in South Philly and also connected merchants to Italian truck gardens in New Jersey. The market was a space for developing community through important social interaction. It served as a space for everyday sociality and conviviality among women consumers, between merchants and customers, and in local politics.

In *South Philadelphia*, Murray Dubin presents Sal Auriemma's memories of working at the market in first grade to help his father, Claudio, in their store at Ninth Street and Montrose Street. Auriemma recalls how his family moved from a street cart to a store and started specializing in cheese. Auriemma also recalls how his family had very little money but still accepted deferred payment from the community, taking their word as payment. This practice of informal credit based on trust was common. The market also provided opportunities for upward mobility for many Italian entrepreneurs.

Italian owners participating in the market area were involved in providing ingredients and artisan products that were central to the food- and church-based celebrations brought from southern Italy and discussed here. Suppliers included

New Jersey truck gardens for a wide array of greens, vegetables, and herbs. Some necessary foods such as olive oil were imported. Other foods could be locally produced in small artisan workshops, often in row houses with ground-floor shops (see Chapter 17); such products included wine, regional cheeses, cured meats, sausages, pastries, bread, pizza, and pasta. Some householders even produced small batches of these items for family use. Italian butchers and fishmongers provided for community-preferred cuts of meat and a variety of wild game and were prepared for local needs for the annual holidays of the ritual calendar—the odd number of fishes for the Christmas *Vigilia* and sausages made for breaking the fast after midnight (from fall pig butchering), lamb for Easter, and fish for Lent and weekly Wednesday and Friday fast days. They could anticipate and provide for the parish saints days and St. Joseph's Day shared by Italians. The market also sold nonedible goods and services, some for parish-based life-cycle events such as first communion as well as everyday clothes, dishes, cutlery, and linens.

As the Italian population grew, it moved southward and westward, and the market commerce (originally located in the core settlement) extended along East Passyunk Avenue, an area that has recently been revitalized (see Chapter 29). After the establishment of new parishes such as St. Rita (1907) and St. Monica (1911) on the west side of Broad Street drew new residents, Italian merchants operated there as well.

While this volume includes examples of different pathways of upward mobility for later generations of immigrant descendants, the businesses in and around the market provide many opportunities for economic mobility. Small family businesses using family labor and little capital were risky and vulnerable, especially at points of generational turnover. In addition, the circumstances of the period between the wars presented many obstacles to survival. The Depression limited the cash available for both owners and customers. Yet many of them survived and are now celebrating their ninetieth and one hundredth anniversaries in the second decade of

BELOW LEFT: Shoppers on Ninth Street, 1950s. Fresh produce. (Photo: A. Esposito Inc. archive. Used with permission)

BELOW RIGHT: Cookware for sale at the Ninth Street Market. (Photo: A. Esposito Inc. archive. Used with permission)

the twenty-first century. Such venerable businesses emphasize their longevity in terms of their number of generations (four or five). Their histories involve many relocations within the market area as they grew.

Some examples of venerable businesses developed in the first two decades of the twentieth century show common patterns of family ownership and labor, initial row home production, and relocation to bigger spaces. Claudio Auriemma's cheese store sold Maggio's cheese. Maggio's began as an artisan cheese maker founded by two brothers in 1916 on a rented New Jersey farm, moving shortly after to a series of stores near the Ninth Street Market near their customers. They relocated several more times as they expanded. Esposito's Meats was established in 1911 in the market and has similarly expanded in scale.

Marra's, a longtime old-style restaurant, began in 1916 as a home-based pizzeria that sold pizzas from a row-home second kitchen. Today they advertise a pizza oven constructed by the two founding brothers from bricks made of Mt. Vesuvius soil near Naples, claimed as the home of *vera* (true) pizza. Another venerable home-based artisan business is Sarcone's Bakery, which was established by immigrant Luigi Sarcone and his son Louis Sarcone Sr. in his row-house basement in 1918 next door to Ralph's Restaurant. The families behind Sarcone's and Ralph's are both in their fifth generation.

Two market bakeries, Termini Bros. Bakery and Isgro Pasticceria (pastries), who compete with each other for awards, were founded in 1920 and 1913, respectively. The Termini brothers earned their investment capital working at Stetson Hats. They

ABOVE LEFT: Provisioning: salumi, olive oil, and eggs. (Photo: A. Esposito Inc. archive. Used with permission)

ABOVE RIGHT: A social space beyond the kitchen. (Photo: A. Esposito Inc. archive. Used with permission)

Fountain on Passyunk Square, the center of early E. Passyunk commerce recently revitalized.
(Photo: Richard Barnes)

and Gus Isgro had the artisan skills to produce complicated wedding cakes, cookies, and cannoli.

Throughout the two decades (the 1920s and 1930s) between the two world wars, as the community settled in and another generation was born, the market continued to develop to provide for the needs of the population and opportunity for entrepreneurs.[3]

POSTWAR SOUTH PHILLY

After the war, in which the children of the mass immigrant wave of 1880–1920 played a massive role, scholars of social history see that participation in the war led ultimately to feeling like and being recognized as Americans. Luconi describes this as a shift to a white ethnic identity in South Philadelphia. An expanding economy created opportunity as well.

However, two forms of U.S. policy shaped the story in contradictory ways. Wartime deferred investment left neighborhoods physically blighted, and banks were unwilling to invest in mortgages or rehabilitation loans in older neighborhoods. Real estate appraisal forms had a built-in bias against old housing stock at these locations, especially at a time when they sought lucrative profits from public policies that supported subsidized mortgages for new suburban housing and built a new system of roads that made suburban communities possible. Both policies converged to produce the hollowing out of city neighborhoods.

At the same time, the expansion of public higher education for the demobilized soldiers enabled upward mobility. The new middle class produced through affordable education and stronger legal protections for unions flowed into the suburbs to achieve the American dream. The South Philadelphia Italian community experienced this flight—but to a lesser degree than other communities. Many of those who left selected close-by New Jersey suburbs, which could now be easily reached by new roads. This made it easy to return to South Philly for shopping, community events, and extended-family visits and celebrations. Many new middle-class families of all ages, however, chose to stay and reinvested heavily in their homes, especially modernizing kitchens. The social bonds of the women and their role in maintaining and extending the Italian "flavor" of the neighborhood are discussed later. Institutions such as the parish and parish schools were also important to families.

Attachment to market commodities and social relationships also were strong. This meant that the market and the related Italian corner grocery stores further south and west that purveyed community needs were less affected than most other neighborhood shopping strips that served ethnic needs. However, even in South Philadelphia, decades after the war, with professional careers more accessible, often the next generation did not maintain the business. Another limit came from new rules for food and worker safety, which required costly modernization of equipment and space to comply. In an interview, one deli owner who was expanding his catering side business decided against the heavy investment required for the new rules and chose to stay small.

Those who could invest were often forced to expand their customer base by catering across ethnic groups. Di Bruno Bros., founded by two brothers, Danny and Joe, in 1963, whose original neon window sign offered a "house of cheese" and "fancy cold cuts," ultimately targeted a different audience—a new, educated class of "foodies" and corporate customers—with high-end salami and salumi, and imported cheese (Chapter 29).

The businesses introduced here that started in the 1910s and continue today indicate some of the many pathways that entrepreneurs took over generations. In the next generation, one of the Maggio brothers and his two sons moved to a larger factory space with modernized equipment after World War II and ultimately merged with a larger dairy corporation.

The story of Sarcone's Bakery is told in a featured obituary of Louis Sarcone Sr., the son of founder Luigi. Louis Sr. grew up above the store and moved

St. Monica School.
(Photo: Gary Horn)

Esposito's Meats—a retail display. (Photo: Courtesy of Esposito's, used with permission)

to the suburbs (Cherry Hill, New Jersey) to raise his family. Eventually, several of his children came back to the city, and today, Louis Jr. and Louis III co-own the bakery. This well-known bread-baking business supplies "half the hoagie shops" in the city.

Esposito's Meats has flourished for four generations, during which it has expanded to become a major meat wholesaler in the region, supplying both Italian specialties and general quality meats. The late Louis Esposito served on the board of Temple University since the 1980s and was active in the activities related to Temple's Rome campus (Chapter 27). He was also active in the Italian philanthropic community.

Termini Bros. has also built a large workshop nearby, and its retail operations have expanded to four sites. Some have added professionally designed websites and online ordering to their outreach, and others rely on word-of-mouth reputations and media awards. Together with other survivors and new Italian-owned establishments (Chapter 29), these outlets continue to mark South Philadelphia as Italian and to contribute to the social fabric of the community as places of interaction through personal relations with regular customers and through sponsorship of activities.

A recent article about Fante's Kitchen Shop by Ellie Silverman reveals a lot about the continuous social role of the market over time and the web of linked families of owners that emerged. Fante's Kitchen Shop is one of the centenarians with three generations of ownership in the founding family. Mariella Esposito, sixty-seven, worked there in high school and later worked her way up to general manager. She describes the valuable mentoring she received from the third-generation owner, Dominic. When he retired in 1981, he had no family to continue his legacy, so Mariella bought the store, which will continue into the second generation as her daughter takes over. Mariella is married to Lee Esposito, the current owner of nearby Esposito's Meats, described above. The article describes how the store has adapted to new populations and trends in kitchenware.

FAMILY AND COMMUNITY SOLIDARITY THROUGH EVERYDAY LIFE

Throughout the 1970s, my research team studied changes in home-based Italian meal cycles in Philadelphia to explore the role food played in reinforcing and extending community bonds and in creating Italian American identities. Food historian Harvey Levenstein indicates in *The Paradox of Plenty*, a social history of eating in America, that Italians were virtually the only ethnic group in the United States that resisted the Americanization of their food. This Italian exceptionalism is impossible to measure, but the extent to which this is true depends on the same factors that affected the creation of women's networks of extended kin and friends (discussed here) and the rapid spread of Italian gastronomy in the United States and the world (described in Chapter 29). Luconi also provides evidence that Italians in Philadelphia shopped differently, using Italian food outlets rather than the expanded national food market chains. He uses newspaper ads to show that corporate food producers recognized this distinct market niche by creating, naming, and advertising foods as authentically Italian and emphasized Italian food preferences in their marketing.

Examining 250 households through surveys of food behavior as well as conducting in-depth, close-up interviews and observations of a smaller group of 30 extended families, we derived meal patterns related to daily meal planning, shopping, cooking, and eating activities for weekly meal cycles, holidays, and family life-cycle events. The process of creating an Italian American food system is quite complicated. It demonstrates a patterning through which Italian meals and American meals are separately rotated throughout time cycles, thus maintaining a sense of an Italian American household as well as openings for American food and other cuisines to enter.

This research among those who stayed in South Philly yielded an understanding of how the food system reflected identity and the importance of food in the production of local social relations of solidarity. It demonstrated how shared meals and frequent food exchanges helped continue close relationships among households in South Philly and those who had moved away in the moments after suburbanization when gentrification was still merely on the horizon. This led to a small follow-up with related New Jersey households with regular connections to South Philly, which confirmed the pattern of frequent contacts.

Much of the social glue in the community was informal and built from the ground up in everyday life through the webs of multigenerational, extended family and friendship networks. These networks were also the foundation of parish and school celebrations. In addition to shared meals and food exchanges between households, the informal activities relating to horticulture and food processing that had led to many early food businesses before the war continued in older-generation households. Examples include preparing "homemades" (pasta) and making wine. Fig trees, which many old-timers remember fondly and which were featured in a Philadelphia Horticultural Society flower show representation of the South Philly landscape, actually produced figs to be dried. The results of this activity were often consumed in parish events, large extended-family Sunday dinners, and major family life-cycle celebrations.

Most important was the hyphenated identity produced by a community-wide patterning of weekly and annual cycles of meals. In the weekly cycle, almost every survey shared a universal pattern: Tuesday, Thursday, and Sunday were "gravy" nights, and the rest of the week except Mondays were "platters," a word taken from the "main and two sides" model of American meals as exemplified by diners. Mondays followed an old tradition in which easy "one-pots"—soups, stews, or leftovers—allowed a rest after the elaborate Sunday gravy meal. Friday fish (platter) meals followed church meat fast days.

The surveys presented the "ideal" pattern, while the diaries and observations of what families actually ate showed that platters were a flexible category that could adjust to circumstances such as changes in work, school, and leisure activities. Gravy meals, especially on Sunday, were central to the pattern. Some families had only one weekday gravy night instead of two. Gravy nights also were occasions to have guests and to send leftovers to neighbors, relatives, and friends.

Making gravy (red gravy) was a production. It was also a realm of both continuity and creativity. Mothers passed down wooden spoons to daughters and daughters-in-law as they taught them to cook. Daughters-in-law were taught to cook by their mothers-in-law. Gravy, always made from scratch, was produced through a long, slow-cooked ragù in which gravy meats (an assortment of cuts), tomatoes, garlic, onion, and spices melded over time into an essence. Gravy was not supposed to be uniform, and cooks created different combinations, which could be recognized and compared. The freezer allowed working women to produce fresh gravy for Sunday and freeze extras for the one or two weekday nights.

Platters, on the other hand, were quick cooked, and there was rarely anything specific from the Old World food system. These meals were therefore flexible and open to changes in American eating patterns—eating out, taking food out, eating food from new ethnic groups, and so on.

Gravy meals were more elaborate, multicourse meals on Sundays and for extended family dinners on Thanksgiving, Christmas, and Easter. They included several courses, from soup to nuts and dried fruit and a baked gravy dish (e.g., lasagna, ravioli, or more meat—turkey for Thanksgiving and lamb for Easter), and lots of vegetables, both fresh and marinated. In fact, while the amount of greens and vegetables eaten in U.S. households was declining significantly, they had a robust presence in these households.

For larger crowds at parish events and for special anniversaries and birthdays, the meal format was the standard hybrid American sandwich buffet served at parish events across the city's cross-ethnic parishes. Here, aside from the hoagie roll and hot meatball-in-gravy sandwiches, other fillings such as roast beef and sides such as American coleslaw and potato and macaroni salads came from the other side of the hyphen. Thus, the system of celebratory meals in the 1970s consisted of patterned combinations of Italian and American features. Many of the sandwiches produced for these events have become the icons of the city (Chapter 29).

A central symbol of family and friendship bonds at weddings was a tray of cookies. Each table had a composition of carefully arranged and decorated trays. The trays were assembled before the wedding during a get-together of close kin and friends who were "like family." Each participant baked a cookie she was known for. After the cookies were arranged in tiers, the tray was decorated with candies and ribbons.

Collective cooking occurred frequently throughout the year. During our study, we tried to avoid holiday seasons—fall and winter holidays and the season of Lent through Holy Week—to find a "typical" daily pattern. Choosing April, May, and June, we soon discovered that this season of life-cycle events (first communions, showers, weddings, anniversaries, prom nights, and graduations) was full of collective food preparation activities before and after the event that involved the sociality of women's kin and friend networks, reinforcing obligations across families. These occasions not only created solidarity among Italian Americans but also brought in non-Italians, often from the neighborhood and parish, who were invited to gravy nights and became members of groups that prepared food together. They also helped incorporate non-Italian spouses, who had become numerous during the postwar development of marriage among white Catholics.

Among the non-Italian women in the study, all maintained an Italian American kitchen and the Italian American meal cycle. Aware of their own heritages, all the non-Italian wives had been taught by their husbands' mothers to keep the gravy night traditions and to celebrate events as expected. Just as the market became recognized as "Italian," the cycle of red gravy, the seasonal patterns of celebrations, and the exchanges of food were widely practiced across South Philly in the 1970s and contributed to making everyday life Italian in flavor in this social world. Now, four decades later, these patterns have further shifted as eating in America has been transformed. But for the generation raised in the 1970s, they are remembered and selectively retained in many extended families.

A SENSE OF PLACE

South Philadelphia became a marked Italian space over many decades. Visually, this can be seen in the symbols of vernacular housing (Chapter 17), the market space, and turn-of-the-twentieth-century Italian churches. More recent markings include home and business window displays of Italian flags next to Eagles paraphernalia, as well as Italian-themed public murals. The Palumbo name, evoking memories of the old days, is emblazoned on two important institutions near the market: the large expanse of the Palumbo recreation center and the Academy@Palumbo magnet program.

While South Philly, as we have seen, was always diverse in its ethnic composition, critical attributes provided it with an Italian sense of place. Italians were relatively the largest nation represented in Philadelphia's 1880–1920 immigrant population. This factor promoted both national churches and a large customer base and merchant group for South Philly markets and services. After the war, during suburbanization, many Italian Americans stayed and reinvested in the community to which they were attached. They invested in the built environment, commercial enterprises, and the webs of social relationships and exchange. Being Italian had advantages within the parochial school system and machine ward structures, which maintained an Italian flavor as well. Finally, informal networks of family and kin normalized Italian daily and celebratory eating patterns in everyday life and incorporated non-Italians through marriage and sociality. This analysis reveals the way that changes in cultural practices are shaped by major policies of major institutions and by the people themselves.

The next shift occurred when gentrification began in the 1980s and new immigrant populations came to the area. Both were responses to deindustrialization and the restructuring global city. In the late 1980s, a new class of urban professionals moved into South Philly to take advantage of its convenience to the city center and arts and entertainment amenities. Many of these new gentry were returning younger generations of Italian families who had originally settled in South Philly. In the 1990s, an even larger number of newcomers—students, recent graduates, and creative millennial knowledge workers from other cities—joined the earlier "pioneers." It was in the interest of branding the neighborhood as a cosmopolitan destination that the city renamed the Italian Market in 2009. Ironically, by this time, the space was again shared by several streams of new immigrants who had come to Philadelphia after the 1965 immigration reforms. What is happening today in this social space of new diversity is covered more in Part IV.

NOTES

1. Three books—Juliani, *Building Little Italy*; Juliani, *Priest, Parish and People*; and Luconi, *From Paesani to White Ethnics*—provide the major historical and sociological material.

2. Varbero's doctoral dissertation of 1975 presents oral histories of Italian immigrants in South Philadelphia, which focus on the 1920s and 1930s. Goode et al. represents surveys and participant observation of food-related activity in Italian American households of South Philadelphia.

3. Material on venerable businesses comes from articles and obituaries in the *Philadelphia Inquirer* and on enterprise websites. Another significant cluster of venerable Italian American family businesses that is not reviewed in this essay is related to former work and familarity with construction materials. Examples include imported stone and marble enterprises.

BIBLIOGRAPHY

Dubin, Murray. *South Philadelphia: Mummers, Memories, and the Melrose Diner*. Philadelphia: Temple University Press, 1996.

Goode, Judith, Karen Curtis, and Janet Theophano. "Meal Formats, Meal Cycles and Menu Negotiations in the Maintenance of an Italian-American Community." In *Food and the Social Order*, edited by Mary Douglas, 135–199. New York: Russell Sage, 1984.

Juliani, Richard N. *Building Little Italy: Philadelphia's Italians before Mass Migration*. State College: Penn State Press, 1998.

———. *Priest, Parish and People: Saving the Faith in Philadelphia's "Little Italy."* Notre Dame, IN: University of Notre Dame, 2007.

Levenstein, Harvey. *Paradox of Plenty: A Social History of Eating in Modern America*, rev. ed. Berkeley: University of California Press, 2003.

Luconi, Stefano. *From Paesani to White Ethnics: The Italian Experience in Philadelphia*. Albany: State University of New York Press, 2001.

Silverman, Ellie. "Italian Market Stalwart Fante's Banks on Expertise, In-Store Experience to Thrive." *Philadelphia Inquirer*, July 8, 2019, C1.

Varbero, Richard A. "Urbanization and Acculturation: Philadelphia's South Italians, 1918–1932." Ph.D. dissertation, Temple University, 1975.

Concert at Rowan University celebrating Ciao Philadelphia, October 2015. Rowan University historically offered opportunities to the important Italian American community in South Jersey. At the event were Rowan University President Ali Houshmand and New Jersey Senate President—and Italian American—Steve Sweeney. (Photo: Gary Horn)

FROM SOUTHERN ITALY TO SOUTHERN NEW JERSEY

Italian Success in the Garden State

CAV. DR. GILDA BATTAGLIA RORRO BALDASSARI,
Honorary Vice Consul for Italy in Trenton, Emerita

THE 2000 CENSUS INDICATED THAT NEW JERSEY had the largest Italian population of any state in the United States. Most Italian immigrants from 1891 to 1915 were from southern Italy. While large numbers gravitated to the industrialized central and northern counties of New Jersey, others were attracted to its southern region highlighting iconic pine barrens, swamplands, and sandy soil, ideal for cultivating berries, fruit trees, and vegetables. Major agricultural colonies sprouted in Atlantic and Cumberland Counties, where Italians represented 98 percent of the migrant farmers and labor force, including children at harvest time, continuing through World War II. My grandfather and his siblings settled in Mays Landing after they emigrated from Naples, to work as weavers in the Atlantic County Power Company—strictly a cotton mill.

During World War II, Italians suffered discrimination, as did Germans and Japanese living in New Jersey. Internment camps were established for Italian non-U.S. citizens in Gloucester City and outside of Glassboro, New Jersey. Despite these conditions, Italians prospered. After one or two generations, they became the owners of vast tracts of farmland in Vineland and Hammonton. Others distinguished themselves in all spheres of life. Author Gay Talese from Ocean City and talk show host Kelly Ripa are among known artists from the region. All achieved much and contributed significantly to their new homeland.

The Jersey Shore is renowned for its beaches and resorts, transforming the once bucolic south into a bustling, dynamic hub of industry. Although the Italian American journey in New Jersey was fraught with struggle and discrimination, it also offered opportunities. Italians were grateful. They took advantage of them and bloomed in the Garden State.

19

Italian American Leaders
in Business and Politics

Scott Gabriel Knowles, Maegan Madrigal,
and Isabella Sangaline

THE BOARDROOMS AND HALLS OF GOVERNMENT in Philadelphia today have no lack of representation from Americans of Italian descent—but this was not always the case. In fact, for almost the first century of Italian immigration, the highest levels of business and political achievement were closed to Italian Americans. This chapter explores, through the lives of extraordinary individuals, the history of Italian Americans in Philadelphia who broke through barriers and entered the ranks of business and government leadership in the city.

The majority of immigrants arriving in South Philadelphia in the nineteenth century were "unskilled workers" who answered the demand for labor. The previous chapter provided an overview of Italian immigration in the late nineteenth and early twentieth century and the emerging Italian American community in South Philadelphia. Like members of other ethnic groups in Pennsylvania who came at this time, the descendants of Italian immigrants are now integrated into every area and profession in the city.

CHARLES C. A. BALDI JR. (1890–1962)

Charles Carmine Anthony Baldi Jr. lived in the Philadelphia area his whole life and served the city in the Pennsylvania House of Representatives for nine consecutive terms. His father and namesake arrived in the United States from Sicily around 1877, and before the age of twenty-five he was able to work his way from interpreter to pay master for a railroad to owning his own coal yard on Washington Avenue in South Philadelphia. In fact, Baldi Sr. was already an established businessman in Philadelphia when a new wave of Italian immigrants came to the city in the early twentieth century. In a 1997 biographical sketch in the *Philadelphia Inquirer*, Baldi

The only skyscraper in Philadelphia named after an Italian American, G. Fred DiBona Jr., former CEO of the BlueCross. DiBona was President of the Chamber of Commerce of the greater Philadelphia area, he was on several boards (among them Exelon), and he was a lead director of Aqua America. (Photo: Giò Martorana)

is described as a "guide, benefactor, *padrone* to his people."[1] The article continues, "Do you need a job? Go to *Signore* Baldi. A place to stay? See Baldi. Do you want to bring Mama over? Mr. Baldi will see to that."[2] In addition to personal support, Baldi rallied political support for the Republican Party. The "Republican machine" depended on Baldi to deliver the Italian vote.

Born in Manayunk in 1890, Charles Baldi Jr. was raised in a home on 319 Green Lane, now a registered historic landmark. Educated locally, Baldi graduated from

Charles C. A. Baldi. ("The
Pennsylvania Manual," 1935)

Boys Central High School in 1910 and went on to attend the University of Pennsylvania. Continuing the family tradition of civil service in Philadelphia, Baldi served on the city council (then called the Common Council) from 1914 to 1916. The following year, Baldi was elected as a Republican to the House of Representatives, the first of nine consecutive terms. This accomplishment is particularly remarkable considering how few Italians managed to win elections to public office at this time. Before 1933, only six politicians of Italian origin had served in the Pennsylvania House of Representatives; out of those six, one was Charles Baldi Jr. Throughout his time in the House, Baldi proposed a variety of projects to improve the quality of life for people in the city he loved. Baldi introduced a wide range of legislation, including measures to target scalpers and illegal ticket sales, prohibit outdoor parking, hire local teachers, and create a school for mentally handicapped students.

FRANK PALUMBO (1911–1983)

Frank Palumbo was a South Philadelphia restaurateur and nightclub owner. Palumbo was the grandson of Antonio Palumbo and part of the Palumbo family, known as philanthropists for Sicilian and Italian immigrants. Providing shelter for the new immigrants, the Palumbos also helped the immigrants find new work, at the time in manufacturing industries. In 1884, Antonio Palumbo founded a boardinghouse for the newly arrived Italian workers. However, Frank Palumbo made it a legendary supper club at the end of World War II. Palumbo expanded the restaurant-turned-nightclub into a complex labyrinth of buildings. Prior to this landmark institution, Palumbo operated the Click Club on Sixteenth Street and Market.

The network of multibuilding banquet and entertainment halls was the center of Italian American social and political life. The historically famous Palumbo's, located on Ninth and Christian Streets, occupied an entire city block as the buildings expanded. The South Philly location was known to be frequently visited by Mayor Frank Rizzo with occasional performances by Frank Sinatra, Maria Lanza, Dean Martin, Frankie Avalon, Jimmy Durante, Bobby Rydell, Fabian Forte, Frankie Laine, and Sammy Davis Jr. Palumbo's was the premier entertainment destination for Italian Americans along with Philadelphia's politicians and civic leaders.

The historical plaque at the former location of Palumbo's on Ninth Street and Catharine Street, Philadelphia. (Source: Wiki Takes Philadelphia [2009], shared under CC BY-SA 3.0: https://creativecommons.org/licenses/by-sa/3.0/legalcode)

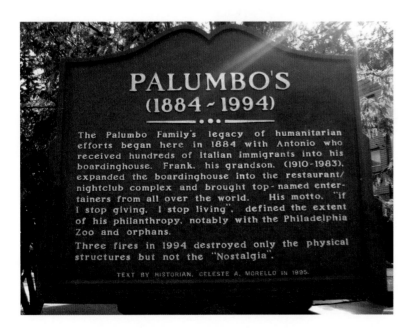

Palumbo was also known throughout Philadelphia as a philanthropist. He helped donate money and animals to the Philadelphia Zoo. He also helped build youth programs and funded parades throughout the city. Mario Lanza once identified Palumbo as an "unsung hero" of Philadelphia because of his work with children and animals.

FRANK RIZZO (1920–1991)

Francis Lazzaro Rizzo Sr., known as Frank Rizzo, was born to Italian immigrants Rafael and Theresa Ermino Rizzo on October 23, 1920. The oldest of four boys, he grew up in South Philadelphia on Rosewood Street. His father worked as a tailor and later became a police officer. In 1938, Rizzo quit high school and enlisted in the navy, though he was medically discharged because of a rare illness related to diabetes. At the age of twenty-two, Rizzo joined the Philadelphia Police Department and quickly rose through the ranks, becoming captain in 1954. Due to his hulking figure at six feet two and 250 pounds, he was referred to as "the General." He continued to be promoted to inspector, deputy commissioner, and eventually commissioner at age forty-six. Rizzo was a polarizing figure. As Philadelphia police commissioner from 1967 to 1971, he frequently incited anger from critics over harsh treatment of political activists and the African American community. But his law-and-order approach to others symbolized security for the people of Philadelphia at a time when crime and poverty rates were high. His approval rating stood at 84 percent in 1967 even after multiple racially charged incidents. In his five-year tenure, Philadelphia's crime rate declined, the lowest crime rate of the nation's ten largest cities.

Statue of Frank Rizzo, former mayor of Philadelphia. (Photo: Giò Martorana)

In 1971, Rizzo resigned as commissioner to run for mayor of Philadelphia and defeated Congressman William J. Green in the Democratic primary and Republican W. Thacher Longstreth in the general election. Running with campaign slogans "Rizzo Means Business" and "Firm but Fair," Rizzo sailed to a win as the first Italian American mayor of Philadelphia. He was reelected in 1975 under the promise to keep taxes low, but he in fact enacted the largest tax increase in city history to fix an $80 million budget deficit. From 1983 to 1991, his life was plagued with defeats as he attempted to come back to city hall, making him the first person to seek the mayoral office in three separate decades. Rizzo lost to W. Wilson Goode, Philadelphia's first African American mayor, in 1983. Rizzo switched from the Democratic Party to the Republican Party in 1986 and won the primary in 1991. Before the election, he suffered a massive heart attack at his campaign office and was pronounced dead later that day at age seventy. Rizzo's clout never stretched beyond Greater Philadelphia—his reputation was tarnished by scandals, police brutality, and the enormous tax hike. However, among his accomplishments as commissioner and mayor, Rizzo is known for beginning a commuter train tunnel through Center City, constructing a high-speed rail line to the airport, building a new city hospital, constructing several major hotels, and building the Somerset Knitting Mills Company, employing mostly African American and Puerto Rican women.

THOMAS M. FOGLIETTA (1928–2004)

Described by the *Philadelphia Inquirer* as "sensitive and intelligent and committed to public service," Thomas M. Foglietta served the city of Philadelphia all his life.[3] Thomas was the youngest of Michael and Rose Foglietta's five children, raised in South Philadelphia, and was a third-generation Italian American. Foglietta attended South Catholic High School and then went on to earn his degree in social science from St. Joseph's College. Foglietta dedicated himself to the study of law at Temple University and graduated in 1952. Three years later at the young age of twenty-six, Foglietta served on the Philadelphia City Council as a Republican and was the youngest person to ever hold the office. Foglietta held this position until 1975 when he unsuccessfully ran for mayor against Frank Rizzo. In 1976, he was appointed by President Ford as regional director of the Department of Labor for Region III, which was headquartered in Philadelphia. In 1980, Foglietta successfully ran for Congress as a representative of Pennsylvania's First District. Although he ran as an independent, Foglietta joined the Democratic Party in 1981. Despite redistricting, Foglietta was elected eight consecutive times. In fact, after the redistricting, Foglietta was the only white representative from a primarily African American district.

Plaque of Ambassador Tom Foglietta in Washington Square. (Photo: Giò Martonara)

During his time in Congress, Foglietta and Philadelphia faced a number of challenges including the closing of the Philadelphia Naval Shipyard and the subsequent effect on the local economy. Foglietta is also remembered for collaborating with Mayor Ed Rendell and the City of Philadelphia's Office of Defense Conversion, as well as labor unions and members of the Pennsylvania, New Jersey, and Delaware congressional delegations to address this issue. He was also active in addressing other problems in the city including sinking homes, the deterioration of Independence Hall, and broader urban economic development issues. Foglietta served on committees including the Merchant Marine and Fisheries, the Armed Services, and the Foreign Affairs Committees as well as the Select Committee on Hunger. In 1997, Foglietta began serving as the United

States' ambassador to Italy, a position he would hold for four years. Considering his long and varied career, it is not surprising that when he was interviewed in 1980 Foglietta stated, "My first love is government."[4]

ANNA VERNA (1931–)

Anna Verna was born and raised in South Philadelphia. She has spent her life as a civically engaged member of the Philadelphia community, spending thirty-six years as councilperson of the Second District. She was chair of the finance committee from 1991 to 1998, where she helped write and implement legislation to prevent the city from declaring bankruptcy. During her time on the finance committee, she also investigated the spending of the Philadelphia Gas Works (PGW). This institution was found guilty of unnecessary spending, and it was under Verna's watch that the PGW underwent necessary reforms.

Portrait of former city council president Anna Verna, made by her former aide Robert Colletti, displayed in the Caucus Room, City Hall, Philadelphia. (Artist: Robert Colletti)

In 1999, she was elected as the first female city council president. She then served three terms as president before retiring in 2012. At that point, she was also the longest-serving city council president. During her political career, she has been known for her support of affordable housing initiatives. She supported reductions for wage and business taxes while also making efforts to support public services and improve public education. To support low-income senior citizens, she supported a tax reform bill that would freeze their tax assessments and assets. Also under her watch, an additional one hundred police officers were added to the force due to an increase in the operating budget for the city. She was committed to seeing that money in the budget was set aside for recreational space as well as fire and police facilities. Investigations were held during her terms that looked at dropout rates and nuisance bars. A citywide ban was placed on public drinking. Verna fought against the trash-to-steam project that she felt would cost the city additional millions of dollars.

Outside of her political career, she has served on the boards of organizations such as the Franklin Institute, Philadelphia Art Museum, Philadelphia Orchestra, Philadelphia Historical Commission, and Board of City Trusts. She has also been involved in the Columbus Day Parade and has acted as chairwoman for the event. She is active in the Order Sons and Daughters of Italy in America and the Grand Lodge of Pennsylvania. Anna Verna is often noted as being a very active member of the Philadelphia community as well as the Italian American community within Philadelphia. To honor her dedication to her civic work, the 1200 block of Philadelphia is named after her: Anna Cibotti Verna Way.

JOSEPH JACOVINI (1940–)

Joseph Jacovini was born and raised in Philadelphia. He graduated from the College of the Holy Cross in 1962 and from Harvard Law School in 1965. He went on to receive his master's degree from Villanova University in 1967. Since then he has had a highly successful law career. He was chairman of Dilworth Paxson LLP, chairman of Drexel University, chairman of the Philadelphia Orchestra, and chairman of the Philadelphia Regional Port Authority. He is now a senior partner in Dilworth Paxson LLP. He has a strong sense of public service and currently serves as a board member for Casa Farnese, Beyond Celiac, Cystic Fibrosis Foundation (Philadelphia

Joseph H. Jacovini as Master of Ceremonies at the opening of the exhibit "Florence . . . with a View" on December 12, 1989. On this date, the City of Philadelphia and Florence celebrated the Silver Jubilee of their Sister City Agreement signed on October 11, 1964. The celebration featured the exhibit presented by the City of Florence. At the request of Mayor Wilson Goode and Italian Consul General Luca Del Balzo, Joseph Jacovini served as the Chairman of the celebration. (City of Philadelphia)

Chapter), and LaFrance Corporation. He is also on the board of trustees for Drexel University, Drexel University Online, the Thomas R. Kline School of Law, and the Philadelphia Orchestra. Jacovini has represented Philadelphia in international matters in China, Korea, Argentina, and Chile and has worked closely with the Italian Consul General in Philadelphia on various trade, educational, and cultural exchanges between Philadelphia and Italy.

Jacovini's mother was a German Lutheran from Germantown and his father an Italian Catholic from South Philadelphia. His grandfather, Pietro, started a bank and an Italian American newspaper. His family also owned a burial insurance company, but because it was difficult for Italian Americans to obtain insurance licenses, the business had to change. The family founded the Pennsylvania Burial Company. The business was taken over by Pietro's three sons, Joseph Jacovini's father and uncles.

Growing up, Jacovini was always encouraged to go in his own direction. He decided to go into law because he saw it as practical intellectual work. After his education, he decided to return to Philadelphia because of family ties, and he joined the socially progressive law firm of Dilworth Paxson. Jacovini feels strongly that it was the work of previous generations of Italian Americans that laid the foundation for him to succeed. According to Jacovini, "There was a sort of perceived moral obligation of the previous generations to make more opportunities for the next generations. It used to be that to get into big law firms, one needed to have a degree from a national law school; however, many Italian-Americans went to local law schools. They would then be elected judges or work in-house for corporations, thus providing opportunities for young lawyers." In reflecting on the traditions of Italian community going forward, Jacovini believes that it is crucial to "preserve the ethnic ingredients that go into the [American] melting pot. Because that's what really makes Americans really special. It's not just those who trace themselves from the American revolution, it's all the other ingredients that have gone into the pot."[5]

MICHAEL DIBERARDINIS (1949–)

Michael DiBerardinis was born and raised in an Italian American community in Downingtown, Pennsylvania—as he recalls it, "between cousins, uncles and aunts and extended families who shared a common hometown in Italy, I grew up, really, in a pretty deep Italian American culture." He remembers, "In that generation most Italians, at least the Italians that I knew and ran with, were working class. My friends, all the kids, everybody worked in the factories. People worked with their hands and their bodies, you know what I mean? Strong arms, strong back." He attended college at Saint Joseph's University, receiving his bachelor's degree in political science. For DiBerardinis, this was a transformative time that led to a life dedicated to public service. Shortly after college, he started being involved with community organizing in Kensington, and then in 1983 he became Philadelphia Chief of Staff for Congressman Thomas Foglietta. He went on to hold public office positions on both the local and state levels. As of 2016, he is the current Managing Director of the City of Philadelphia. He works directly under the Mayor and coordinates the activities of multiple departments. In the past, he has also held the positions of Deputy Mayor for Environmental and Community Resources and Commissioner for the Department of Parks and Recreation. As Commissioner for the Department of Parks and Recreation, he raised $34 million for the department, expanded outdoor recreational activities, and was able to reopen shuttered public pools and playgrounds. With the Free Library of Philadelphia, he was able to expand the relationship between the library and local school districts as well as preserve the after-school program in the local branches. While Secretary of the Pennsylvania Department of Conservation and Natural Resources, he led and oversaw the creation and development of Pennsylvania Wilds. Outside of his political career, he sits on multiple local boards, such as the Philadelphia Board of Pensions and Retirement (ex officio), the Philadelphia City Planning Commission (ex officio), the Philadelphia Industrial Development Corporation (ex officio), the Free Library of Philadelphia, the Mann Center for the Performing Arts, and the Philadelphia Zoo.

Reflecting on the importance of Italian American identity in Philadelphia today, DiBerardinis points to his own efforts to connect with contemporary Italy through travel, study, and involvement with the Philadelphia Italian

Deputy Mayor Mike Di-Berardinis (in the center between Joe Jacovini and CG Andrea Canepari) at the ceremony for the launch of the cultural month Ciao Philadelphia, 2015. Conversation Hall, City Hall of Philadelphia, October 2015. (Photo: Gary Horn)

Interim President Chuck Pennoni at Drexel University College, Medical School Commencement, May 2010. (Courtesy of Drexel University)

community: "What I think is important to sustain that identity . . . is to try to understand Italy today [and also] your ancestors, and the country and its history. So I devote an immense amount of my free time to that idea."[6]

C. R. "CHUCK" PENNONI (1937–)

In the early 1900s, C. R. "Chuck" Pennoni's parents immigrated from the Umbria province of Northern Italy to the United States. They made their way through Ellis Island and straight to Johnstown, Pennsylvania. His father worked in the coal mines, while his mother worked in the garment industry. They worked hard so that their children could live better lives and receive a better education than they had received. The work ethic that Chuck Pennoni's family equipped him with has had a lasting influence. He began working at the age of six in a grocery store and has not stopped working since. All his hard work eventually brought him to college at Penn State and then to Philadelphia. He earned his degree in civil engineering at Drexel University. As a student, Pennoni loved engineering and looked to continue educating himself—taking classes in structural engineering, focused on buildings, bridges, structural steel, and reinforced concrete—while also working as an adjunct professor. On March 1, 1968, he began his own private practice. The first project for the business was the Twentieth Street police station in Philadelphia. As his reputation grew and he began receiving more clients, his company grew as well. He received his first international job in 1966. Now, Pennoni Associates Inc. has its hand in nearly every major construction job in Philadelphia; as well as playing invisible roles in building and maintaining Philadelphia's infrastructure. Two major projects that are credited to Pennoni are the Comcast Tower and the Center City Commuter Rail Connection. In the realm of education, his contributions have been enormous, including two terms as Interim President of Drexel University and a period as Chairman of the Drexel Board of Trustees. The Pennoni Honors College was founded with a gift from the Pennoni family.

Outside of work, Pennoni is very civically engaged. Starting with his time at Penn State, he joined the Student Chapter of the American Society of Civil Engineers. Afterward, he continued volunteering and doing community service. He has served on forty-five boards, eighteen of which were not for profit and nine of which were government appointments at the federal, state, county, and local levels. After all his hard work, Pennoni has since received multiple awards and honors, including the William H. Wisely American Civil Engineer awards, the Robert Morris Citizenship and Excellence in Education awards of the Boy Scouts of America, the National Society of Professional Engineers Professional Development Award, the William Penn Award, and the March of Dimes Service to Humanity Award. He has also been honored by the Sons of Italy as Man of the Year and was inducted into the National Academy of Engineering. Throughout his business and civic career, Pennoni has been proud of his Italian heritage. "My parents are immigrants," Pennoni points out, "and I'm proud of the fact that they are immigrants; my wife's parents are immigrants." He studied Italian, has traveled to Italy to see important sites of family history, and continues to work to create more opportunities for future generations of Italians and the Italian community as a whole. He values how hard they have worked and brought themselves up in America, to the extent that people do not necessarily see Italians as immigrants anymore; they are one key group among many ethnic groups that helped build America.[7]

ROSEMARIE GRECO (1946–)

Rosemarie Greco is the youngest of six children born to Mary DiPaolo Greco and John Greco. Her father was born in Naples, brought to Philadelphia when he was about two and a half years old. All of her paternal grandparents came from Naples. Her mother was the firstborn of seven children, also from Philadelphia; her father was the firstborn of seven children as well. She describes hers as "a very large family, it was pretty typical in terms of Italian immigrants or first-generation. Typical in terms of everybody worked, everybody got together. My dad was active in the community."

"When I was elected by the Board of Directors to the position of President, I commissioned a local artist, Raymond Del Noce. My request was for a painting of the corner of the street where I grew up. The painting depicts a scene from the Italian Market in South Philadelphia, so that every day, I would be reminded of my Italian-American Roots."—Caption by Rosemarie Greco. (Courtesy of R. Greco)

She served as a teacher in Catholic schools in the city and entered religious life, where she stayed for three years, but she left before her first vows and returned home to South Philly. Then, she was hired as a branch secretary at Fidelity Bank before completing her degree magna cum laude at St. Joseph's University.

She describes her career at Fidelity Bank as "a fabulous and blessed journey. I didn't aspire to have a higher title or a higher-level job. I always say I didn't climb the ladder. There were a lot of people who pushed me up the ladder and there were people at the top holding their hand out and pulling me up the ladder." She explains that it was still not fully accepted early in her career for Italian Americans to be in leadership roles—a theme we have heard from other figures in this chapter. According to Greco, "I was reminded more than once that I was a first generation Italian American, an

evening college graduate, a Catholic and from South Philly." Nevertheless, she broke through these barriers.

After twenty-three years, she left Fidelity Bank in 1991 with the titles of president, CEO, and director to become the president, CEO, and director of Core States Bank and president of its parent company, one of the largest and most profitable banks in the United States at that time. Greco was often referred to as the first woman in America to achieve such a leadership position in a large bank. She remembers well those days when "you certainly never found a woman or a Jewish person or a person of color in a vice president position."

In 2000, because of an illness in her family, Greco spent a great deal of time in and out of hospitals, and she came to the realization that patient advocacy, influence, and money could well be the difference between recovery and death for many sick people. When Governor-Elect Ed Rendell asked her to go with him to Harrisburg as Secretary of Banking and Insurance, she remembers telling him, "I don't want a job in government but I do have a cause which government needs to address." On the day of his inauguration, the governor signed his first executive order, naming her as the first Executive Director of the Governor's Office of Health Care Reform. During her six years of leadership, Greco is credited with expanding the C.H.I.P. Program eligibility guidelines; chairing the chronic care commission, which established quality outcome standards for chronic illnesses prevalent in Pennsylvania; enhancing the care options for the elderly to remain in their homes instead of going to a nursing home; and expanding the authority and scope of practice of nurses, dental assistants, and pharmacists.

Among her many appointments to civic boards and commissions, she is most proud of her service as a member of the Philadelphia School Board. She sees definitive parallels between being an effective, challenging, nurturing teacher and being the same type of leader: "Whether you are teaching or leading, you are working to enable, encourage and empower others." Greco cites the Italian word *educare* (educate, train, bring up) of her Italian American family and community as the constant source of her own nurturing throughout her life.

NICHOLAS DEBENEDICTIS (1945–)

Nicholas DeBenedictis, Chairman Emeritus of Aqua America and Independent Director at Exelon Corporation, was born to Italian immigrants in 1945. His parents immigrated from Italy, Naples and Abruzzi on the east coast, in the early 1900s, with his grandparents being the first family members to immigrate.

DeBenedictis grew up with three siblings in the suburbs of Philadelphia. Though not an Italian community, it was a Quaker community where he felt that his Italian American heritage was accepted. He was one of the first to attend college in his family. Growing up in the 1950s and 1960s, college was not expected. DeBenedictis, following in his brother's footsteps, chose to attend Drexel University

Nick DeBenedictis, then President of the Pennsylvania Society, speaking in 2015 at the 117th annual dinner in the Waldorf Astoria, New York, seated near Governor Ed Rendell (D) and U.S. Senator Pat Toomey (R). DeBenedictis was the first Italian American businessman to chair the Pennsylvania Society. The Pennsylvania Society was established in 1899 by Andrew Carnegie and Richard King Mellon and is one of the oldest living civic society organizations in the United States. (The Pennsylvania Society)

because of its affordability and co-op program. During his co-op period, his father unfortunately passed away, and he took over his father's small business. He graduated in management in 1968 with plans to either join the military service or continue on the graduate course.

DeBenedictis took graduate courses and earned an MS in environmental science; this set his career on the path of engineering and science from the business perspective. He became the second Italian to head the Chamber of Commerce for Greater Philadelphia, political exposure he credits to Drexel University. He was also the first Italian American to head Aqua America, a water utility company. Currently, he serves on the Board of Directors of Exelon Corporation and on the boards of Commonwealth Edison Company and PECO Energy Company, which are Exelon subsidiaries. In addition, DeBenedictis has served as a director of MIS-TRAS Group since 2015 and as a director of P.H. Glatfelter Inc. since 1995.

NOTES

With special thanks to Jennifer Cutler (history major in the College of Arts and Sciences, Drexel University) for her help in researching the material for this essay.

1. "History," *Philadelphia Inquirer*, April 27, 1997, 432.

2. Ibid.

3. "Biographical Note," Finding Aid for the Thomas M. Foglietta Collection, St. Joseph's University.

4. Interview with Thomas M. Foglietta, June 24, 1980.

5. Interview with Joseph Jacovini, conducted by Scott Gabriel Knowles and Isabella Sangaline, Philadelphia, February 22, 2018.

6. Interview with Michael DiBerardinis, conducted by Scott Gabriel Knowles, Philadelphia, May 2, 2018.

7. Interview with C. R. "Chuck" Pennoni, conducted by Scott Gabriel Knowles, Philadelphia, May 30, 2017.

FURTHER READING

"Abstract." Finding Aid for the Thomas M. Foglietta Collection, St. Joseph's University. https://sites.sju.edu/library/collections/archives-special-collections/4762-2/.

Avila, Eric, and Mark H. Rose. "Race, Culture, Politics, and Urban Renewal: An Introduction." *Journal of Urban History* 35, no. 3 (2009): 335–347.

"Biographical Note." Finding Aid for the Thomas M. Foglietta Collection, St. Joseph's University. https://sites.sju.edu/library/collections/archives-special-collections/4762-2/.

Blumgart, Jake. "The Brutal Legacy of Frank Rizzo, the Most Notorious Cop in Philadelphia History." *Vice*, October 22, 2015. https://www.vice.com/en_us/article/kwxp3m /remembering-frank-rizzo-the-most-notorious-cop-in-philadelphia-history-1022.

Hevesi, Dennis. "Frank Rizzo of Philadelphia Dies at 70; A 'Hero' and 'Villain.'" *New York Times: Obituaries*, July 17, 1991. http://www.nytimes.com/1991/07/17/obituaries/frank-rizzo -of-philadelphia-dies-at-70-a-hero-and-villain.html.

"Interview with Thomas M. Foglietta, Esq." June 24, 1980. https://libdigital.temple.edu /pdfa1/Oral%20Histories/AOHWMPJZ2014120042Q01.pdf.

Rowan, Tommy. "The Moments That Made Frank Rizzo Philly-Famous." *Philadelphia Inquirer*, updated August 21, 2017. http://www.philly.com/philly/news/pennsylvania /philadelphia/philly-history/frank-rizzo-top-moments-philadelphia-history-20170821 .html.

20

Drawn from the Boot

The Italian Artists of Philadelphia

WILLIAM R. VALERIO

ALTHOUGH WE GENERALLY TAKE IT FOR GRANTED, an impressive work of art that many of us have collected is the United States penny. Designed by Philadelphia-born engraver Frank Gasparro (1909–2001) during his decades-long tenure with the U.S. Mint, a new image on the tails side of the coin was a deliberate surprise to the nation in 1959 on behalf of President Dwight Eisenhower, in honor of the sesquicentennial of President Abraham Lincoln's birth. The composition is a feat in the manipulation of scale.

Gasparro draws the viewer's attention into the interior of the Lincoln Memorial to focus on the tiniest imaginable rendering of Daniel Chester French's colossal sculpture. Gasparro's initials, "FG," appear to the right of the steps in his penny, which was in production through 2008.

Like other Philadelphia artists who were first-generation Italians, Gasparro built a career with the support of city institutions that offered training and an opportunity to develop talent and a creative voice. The program of art instruction in the public schools, the Fleisher Art Memorial, the Pennsylvania Academy of the Fine Arts, and the Da Vinci Art Alliance provided structure and encouragement to the aspiring Gasparro in his youth. Indeed, what makes Philadelphia a unique community in the arts to this day is its array of schools, community arts organizations, and accessible museums. Gasparro also benefited from the tutelage of two distinguished sculptors who served as his mentors: Giuseppe Donato (1881–1965), a distinguished classicist and architectural sculptor, and Walker Hancock (1901–1998), an equally classical modernist best known for the magnificent *Pennsylvania Railroad World War II Memorial* (1950) that presides over the great hall of Philadelphia's Thirtieth Street Station.

Reverse U.S. penny, depicts the Lincoln Memorial. Designed by Frank Gasparro. (Wikicommons, Public Domain. https://commons.wikimedia.org /wiki/File:United_States_penny ,_reverse.jpg)

Joseph Amarotico, American, 1931–1985. *Large Space Dream*, date unknown. Acrylic on masonite, 34 in. × 42⅛ in. (Woodmere Art Museum: Museum purchase, 1974)

To write about artists of Italian descent in Philadelphia from my perspective as director of Woodmere Art Museum, a collecting institution dedicated to Philadelphia artists, is to tell the story of the arts as they evolved in our city in the modern era and were nurtured by our city's great schools and art centers. I could write a similar essay about the paths followed by artists who came to Philadelphia from other European countries. Nonetheless, the pattern of Gasparro's career is in many ways the typical path for Italian artists whose families came to the United States, mostly from southern Italy, in the late nineteenth and early twentieth centuries, uprooted by the economic and social stresses of Italy's post-Unification era. There are instances of Italian artists in Philadelphia in the earlier decades of the nineteenth century, but the pattern of that time was of trained professionals and artisans who came to the young United States to seek opportunity. These were generally educated artists and established specialists in the decorative and architectural building trades who sought commissions and work as the city developed and grew. For example, Piacenza-born Giacinto Riboni worked as a successful artist in Rome for almost a decade and then came to Philadelphia in 1828 to build his career as a painter and portraitist. The combination of refined elegance and whimsy in his *Young Woman Looking in a Mirror* (1836) is the sign of an artist who knows his craft well enough to exaggerate for visual impact. Woodmere is happy to steward the painting in our collection. In 1973 it was restored by Joseph Amarotico (1931–1985), a conservator who is equally known as an artist for his "dream castle" paintings. His *Large Space Dream* (date unknown) is an example of his puzzle-like tableaus of interlocking architectural forms in bright color. Working on *Young Woman Looking in a Mirror*, Amarotico removed a layer of paint that had been applied by a previous owner of the painting, presumably to simplify it, obscuring some of the oddities of the architectural setting and background. Given his own interests, Amarotico must have enjoyed seeing the reemergence of his paysan Riboni's stylizations.

That many artists from Italian immigrant families achieved stature in early twentieth-century Philadelphia is partly the result of good timing. This was a period of both intense immigration from Italy and ambitious architectural growth and civic aggrandizement in Philadelphia, as in other major American cities, with attendant opportunities for artists, including stonecutters, stained-glass makers, ironworkers, and decorative painters. My own maternal grandfather's family had been stonecutters in Italy and immigrated to New York during this time. I was raised with the story that my great-grandfather had cut stones for the Brooklyn Bridge. Though I never met him, I think about him every time I cross the bridge, as I imagine the descendants of Italian artists in Philadelphia think of their great-grandparents when they travel though our city's neighborhoods.

The City Beautiful movement that swept the country from the 1890s into the 1920s gave Philadelphia many grand institutional buildings, homes, and churches, as well as its great boulevard, the Benjamin Franklin Parkway and the grand Beaux Arts buildings that line it. Giuseppe Donato (1882–1966), who as a boy immigrated to Philadelphia with his parents from Italy, trained at the Pennsylvania Academy of the Fine Arts (PAFA) but then returned to Europe on a travel scholarship to continue his studies with the most recognized sculptor of the era, Auguste Rodin (1840–1917). On his return to Philadelphia, Donato enjoyed a career in monumental public sculpture, completing, for example, the pediment of the city's Municipal Court Building, which would become the city's family court building and is currently slated to become a luxury hotel.

A leading American provider of Old World decorative craft was founded in Philadelphia in 1898 by Nicola D'Ascenzo (1871–1954), whose D'Ascenzo Studios, a stained glass and decorating company, is thought to have completed more than seven thousand monumental projects for buildings across the country. D'Ascenzo had immigrated to Philadelphia with his family at the age of eleven, and as a teenager he worked as a mural painter, attending night classes at PAFA and the Pennsylvania Museum and School of Industrial Art (now the University of the Arts). His commissions include the National Cathedral and the Folger Library in Washington, DC, the extraordinary windows and decoration of the Rodeph Shalom synagogue in Philadelphia, and the Washington Memorial Chapel in Valley Forge, Pennsylvania. He also made the famous stained-glass windows of the Horn and Hardart automat chain, including those of the flagship store in Manhattan's Times Square and those of the Chestnut Street Philadelphia eatery. Although the building on Chestnut Street has been repurposed, one of the windows is preserved in Woodmere's collection. The intricacy and brilliance of D'Ascenzo's work is prized to this day (see Sidebar 3).

For artists like Donato and D'Ascenzo, commissions from churches, synagogues, and private clients were branches of the same tree. In Philadelphia today, Anthony Visco (born 1948) has built an international career through projects for an array of secular and religious

Giuseppe Donato, American, born Italy, 1882–1966. *Study for Sans Fin*, date unknown. Plaster, 11½ × 9½ × 9½ in. (Woodmere Art Museum: Gift of Florinda Donato Doelp and David W. Doelp, Sr., 2016)

Anthony Visco, American, born 1948. *Saint Rita in Ecstasy*, 2000. Plaster, 31 × 22½ × 9¼ in. (Woodmere Art Museum: Gift of the artist, 2015)

organizations. His studio, Atelier for the Sacred Arts, has done remarkable work for the Vatican, and visitors to Woodmere are transfixed by his plaster *Saint Rita in Ecstasy* (2000), recently given to the museum by the artist. The sculpture is a fragment of a study for the monumental bronze at the National Shrine of Saint Rita of Cascia on Broad Street. Built in 1907, Saint Rita's has remained at the center of Italian Catholic life, and its architecture and design are spectacular.

The Papale brothers were woodcarvers whose frame shop on Passyunk Avenue in South Philadelphia produced hand-carved and gilded frames that grace the walls of collectors' homes and city museums to this day. Alex Papale, a painter and frame maker, led the effort to found the Da Vinci Art Alliance in 1931 as a social club, exhibition space, and community hub for Italian Philadelphians with an interest in the arts. Inspired by and following in the Papales' footsteps, fellow painter Bernard "Ben" Badura (1896–1986) became a frame maker; his gold and silver arts-and-crafts-styled frames were sought by the artists we know as the Pennsylvania impressionists. Though Badura lived and worked in New Hope, he too was part of the group associated with the Da Vinci Art Alliance.

Another friend and colleague of the Papale brothers and, with them, cofounder of the Da Vinci Art Alliance was photographer Severo Antonelli (1907–1995), who came to Philadelphia in 1921 with his parents at age fourteen. A self-styled American futurist, Antonelli aligned himself with the Italian avant-garde movement, futurism. His exhibitions and activities in Europe in the early 1930s were acclaimed and brought him into contact with fascist dictator Benito Mussolini, who admired the work of the young Italian American. At the encouragement of the United States embassy, Mussolini sat for a portrait by Antonelli, a fine print of which is in Woodmere's collection.

Chilling, the dictator appears in dapper civilian clothing; his emotionless stare should give us pause. Antonelli was no fascist, but his work shows just how close any of us can come to the touch of evil. Back in Philadelphia in 1938, Antonelli founded the photography school and studio that carry his name, the Antonelli Institute, in Erdenheim. Sadly, it is soon to close its doors.

The artists I have thus far described—Gasparro, Donato, D'Ascenzo, Badura, the Papale brothers, and Antonelli—all were active members of the Da Vinci Art Alliance, as was an artist of a younger generation, Peter Paone (born 1936), whose early training included working with the Papale brothers as an assistant framer in their shop. Paone once told me that for a child whose only connection to art at home was a calendar from the church with the face of Jesus that was replaced each year, the alliance was a revelation. The Papale brothers and the other artists he met there offered a window into the larger world of the arts. Paone took classes with Gasparro at the Fleisher Art Memorial, Philadelphia's great free art school, and went on to formal studies at the Philadelphia Museum College of Art (now the University of the Arts), where his teachers included printmakers Benton Spruance and Ben Shahn and painter Larry Day (born Lorenzo del Giorno, a first-generation Italian whose father was born in Salerno; the family Americanized the name). Paone's career has grown on an international scale, and as a teacher at the Pratt Institute and then as founder of the print department at PAFA, he has inspired and given shape to many careers in the arts. He describes his own work as "realism reassembled," and today he serves as a senior speaker and father figure to many of Philadelphia's younger artists. He also works with the imagery of the church, with an understanding that the first "surrealism" is to be found in the Catholic imagery of his childhood.

Larry Day must also be recognized as one of our city's great teachers in the arts, an anchor figure in the painting department at the University of the Arts from 1953 to 1988. A successful abstract painter in the 1950s, Day transitioned to a philosophy-driven, mysterious realism in the early 1960s. His work embraces Italian classicism and mythological subjects, and in some ways he was as much a theorist and writer as a painter. His work is collected and admired worldwide. Of Day, Paone once noted that his teaching method was magical, founded less on imparting the specific techniques or ideas that drove his own work and more on sharing his depth of knowledge in the history and functions of different types of art, building connections, and asking provocative questions.

Other important artist-teachers in Philadelphia have maintained a commitment to classical techniques and practices. Arthur De Costa (1921–2004), a painter of realist still lifes, inspired a following that is loyal to his ideas and technique to this day. Italian-born Italo Scanga (1932–2001) favored unconventional materials and political subjects. He taught at Temple University's Tyler School of Art from 1967 to 1976 and had a solo exhibition at the Whitney Museum of American Art in 1972 before eventually moving to California. Anthony Ciambella (born 1949) also teaches classical methods at PAFA, though his wrapped, life-size figurative sculptures and distorted figurative images are more surrealist

Severo Antonelli, American, born Italy, 1907–1995. *Il Duce*, 1932. Gelatin silver print, 12.75 × 10.125 in. (Woodmere Art Museum: Gift of the artist, 1986)

Peter Paone, American, born 1936. *Flowering Surprise*, 2012. Acrylic on panel, 36 in. × 36 in. (Woodmere Art Museum: Gift of the artist, 2015)

than traditionally classical. His colleague at PAFA, Tony Rosati (born 1947), heads the print department. Longtime PAFA instructor Vincent Desiderio (born 1955) paints haunting, figurative compositions of contemporary life; though he made a strong imprint on the arts of Philadelphia as an instructor at PAFA, he now teaches at the New York Academy of Art.

Fleisher Art Memorial, the Da Vinci Alliance, and PAFA also supported the careers of a trio of brothers, Angelo (1909–1994), Salvatore (1905–1966), and Biagio Pinto (1911–1989). However, the catalyst of their success would be Albert Barnes, the founder of Philadelphia's renowned Barnes Foundation. Born in the early years of the twentieth century, the Pintos immigrated to Philadelphia with their parents and two other brothers in 1909. The talents of the three young artists emerged in grade school, and, while participating in classes at the Barnes Foundation, they were recognized by Dr. Barnes himself. Barnes was committed to changing the world through art and to championing the work of African American artists and immigrants who did not necessarily enjoy—or had not been spoiled by—the privileges of formal education and training. Barnes took the three Pinto brothers under his wing. In the 1920s, he sent them to Paris and the South of France, where they met Henri Matisse, and gave them a scholarship to travel through North Africa. On their return, he employed them as photographers and teachers and championed their unique brands of modernism, giving them a foothold from which each artist followed his own path.

Angelo's daughter Jody (born 1942) continues to carry the family's creative banner as a contemporary painter and sculptor. Her *Fingerspan* (1987) bridge is a favorite experience for many in Fairmount Park (see Chapter 21). Luigi Settanni (1908–1984) was an Italian-born colleague of the Pinto brothers at the Barnes, and he too was a golden child of the foundation. Dr. Barnes described Settanni's work as comparing favorably to that of Renoir.

Salvatore Pinto, American, born Italy, 1905–1966. *Self Portrait with Model*, ca. 1936. Wood engraving, 5 × 5½ in. (Woodmere Art Museum: Museum purchase, in honor of Dianne A. Meyer, Joseph A. Nicholson, and Mary Ann B. [Sally] Wirts, 2011)

Another distinguished family of artist siblings in Philadelphia are the Martinos: Filomena, Francesco, Antonio, Giovanni, Alberto, Ernesto, William, and Edmund, who were born in Philadelphia to Italian-born parents (Carmine, a stonecutter, and Clementina, a buttonhole maker). Antonio (1902–1988) would become a landscape painter allied with the impressionists of the New Hope School, and Giovanni (1908–1998) would become an urban realist; both are recognized as important painters.

Family was the Martinos' support structure, and in the late 1920s they opened the Martino Commercial Art Studios, a successful Philadelphia business that offered a robust array of services in the fine arts, decorative arts, advertising, and promotional design. All of the Martino siblings participated in the business, which had a staff of twenty artists. Of subsequent generations, Eva Martino (born 1929), wife to Giovanni; their daughter, Nina Martino (born 1952); and their granddaughter, Babette Martino (1956–2011) would continue the family's legacy in the arts.

No history of Philadelphia Italian artists would be complete without mention of Raphael Sabatini (1898–1985). Born to immigrant parents in Philadelphia in 1898, Sabatini was encouraged through the system of public school education to pursue the arts, and he was admitted to PAFA. There he became a student of Arthur B. Carles, an influential twentieth-century American modernist and the center of a circle of artists who would be our city's "moderns." Carles encouraged Sabatini to visit Paris and experience European modernism first-

Antonio Pietro Martino, American, 1902–1988. *Winter*, 1927. Oil on canvas, 36 × 40 in. (Woodmere Art Museum: Gift of Marguerite and Gerry Lenfest, 2008)

hand. There he participated in exhibitions, developed his printmaking and design skills, and became part of the international avant-garde in the French capital. Sabatini returned to Philadelphia with his own brand of stylized cubist modernism and began teaching at Tyler School of Art, where he remained for many decades. He also became director of the Philadelphia Art Alliance. Sabatini is known for designing the architectural sculpture on the exterior of the N. W. Ayer Building on Philadelphia's Washington Square, one of our city's most distinguished art deco structures.

I hear you asking, "Were there no women of Italian descent in Philadelphia during this period who made the arts their life pursuit?" Alas, I am describing a sociology of family life and community support that was by and large patriarchal and exclusionary along gender lines. But in the post–World War II era, there are strong voices of Italian women in the arts. Notable among them are Octavia Capuzzi Locke (1929–2011) and Filomena Dellaripa (1922–1990), both of whom taught at Fleisher and prepared young artists for formal studies at our great art academies. Paone, for example, recalls that when he was thirteen years old and taking classes at Fleisher, both women took an interest in ensuring that he pursue further training in the arts. They also imparted a clear understanding that they were both "fed up" with the sexism of both Italian American culture and Philadelphia's art world. Both artists deserve more attention. Dellaripa, whose work is represented in Woodmere's collection, developed a unique voice, exploring an ever-shifting balance between realist subjects and abstract principles.

From the 1940s through the 1970s, Philadelphia was an important home base for the great modernist sculptor and designer of furniture and jewelry Harry Bertoia (1915–1978). The Mangel Gallery sold more of his work than his galleries in New York, Chicago, and elsewhere. Philadelphia's museums were his inspiration. Born in Italy, Bertoia came to the United States at age fifteen. Throughout his career,

N. W. Ayer Building, Washington Square, Philadelphia. Sculptures by Raphael Sabatini on the exterior. (Photo: Giò Martorana)

he insisted that he was neither an artist nor a designer but instead a "metalworker," so closely did he identify with his craft and his material. Bertoia immigrated first to Detroit, where family members had already settled, and he studied at Cranbrook. He then settled in Bally, Pennsylvania, less than an hour outside Philadelphia, where he worked for his friend Florence Knoll. After the financial success of his chair designs for Knoll, he embarked on a career in sculpture. The City of Philadelphia awarded him one of the largest commissions of his career, *Free Interpretation of Plant Forms* (1967), a large, biomorphic fountain for the Philadelphia Civic Center, a hard-edged urban complex that was razed in the first years of the twenty-first century. Now, installed at Woodmere with a ninety-nine-year loan from the City, Bertoia's fountain masterpiece is immersed in the natural beauty of Philadelphia's Wissahickon and is accessible for exploration in new ways. The sounds of church bells in Italy stayed with Bertoia throughout his life, a driving force in the development of his famous "sonambient"—sound-environment—sculpture. He built *Free Interpretation of Plant Forms* with cave-like forms that invite people in to enjoy the sounds of water falling and splattering on its exterior. Bertoia's undulating, wave-like forms also evoke the sculpted draperies of the baroque fountains and antique sculpture of Rome and other great Italian cities.

The 1950s were powerful years of change in the arts, nowhere more than in Philadelphia. If realism and narrative illustration had been the city's mainstream before, now abstraction became a dominant force. A pioneer in abstract painting was Sideo Fromboluti (born 1930), born in Hershey, Pennsylvania, a month after his parents immigrated to the United States from Italy. The pattern of Fromboluti's training will sound familiar: his talent in the Fleisher enabled him to earn a scholarship to attend the Tyler School of Art. An artist who loved the sensuality of thick, rich paint and vibrant color, he moved to New York in 1948 and enjoyed a successful career there.

A prime voice for abstraction in Philadelphia was Group 55 (formed in 1955), a loose coalition of artists (as well as architects and writers) who, inspired by the New York School, mounted exhibitions in storefronts and galleries and held public meetings at the Free Library to describe how new languages of abstraction in the arts could express meaning without being tied to recognizable subjects. Group 55

Sideo Fromboluti, American, 1920–2014. *Trees and Rocks*, 1954. Oil on canvas, 32 × 39 in. (Woodmere Art Museum: Gift of the artist, 2012)

became integrated into the gallery scene of New York, and the broad circle of artists associated with it included women (Quita Brodhead, Jane Piper, and Doris Staffel), a black artist (Paul Keene), Jewish artists (Sam Feinstein and Sanford Greenberg), and Italian artists Larry Day and Michael Ciliberti (born 1935). Part of the goal—an ideal that the group strove for—was to share a language of form, color, gesture, and line that could rise above the particulars of place and time and aspire to the universal, thereby healing a suffering world. Ciliberti's abstraction is characterized by angular forms and gestural patterns with sharp edges. He uses more white than any other color.

As described many times, a combination of family and community supported many first-generation Italian artists in Philadelphia. The path would be different for second-generation artists, such as illustrator Charles Santore (born 1935), whose great-grandfather came to the United States in the 1860s and settled in Buffalo, New York. Upon selling a successful bar there, he relocated his family to Philadelphia in 1868, purchasing a large apartment building at Seventh and Bainbridge Streets in the heart of what was becoming Philadelphia's Italian community. The building would serve as the extended family's home and center of life. Born in 1935, Santore recalls that his father could understand the Italian of his own parents and grandparents, but he himself sought assimilation and could not speak Italian. Fleisher and the Da Vinci Art Alliance were not part of Santore's experience as a young man, though he loved to draw and says that he would have availed himself of these resources if he had known they existed. His high school teachers recognized his talent; he was offered a scholarship to the Philadelphia Museum School of Industrial Art (there, he overlapped with Paone). His career as an illustrator was launched after graduation. He showed his portfolio around and networked his way to his first jobs, finally being hired by Italian American executives at the N. W. Ayer Company to make advertising illustrations. Santore became famous nationwide for his illustrations for the cover of *TV Guide* and was a favored artist of its publisher, Walter Annenberg. Seen by hundreds of millions of subscribers in the 1970s and 1980s, Santore's illustrations for *TV Guide* contributed to the definition of the era's culture. Building on his fame, he became one of the country's most beloved illustrators of children's books.

So much could be said about many wonderful artists of Italian descent in Philadelphia today. Many are part Italian, such as Barbara Mimnaugh (born 1937), whose paintings, such as *Umbrian Nights* (2004), in Woodmere's collection, play with the beauty of Italy as a place of myth and sensuality. Anthony Campuzano (born 1975), Mariel Capanna (born 1988), Salvatore Cerceo (born 1973), Michael Ciervo (born 1982), William DiBello, Billy Dufala (born 1981), Steven Dufala (born 1976), Evan Fugazzi (born 1980), William Gannotta (1945–2009), Ben Passione (born 1987), Keith Ragone (born 1954), Carlo Russo (born 1976), Mary Spinelli (born 1944), and Lucia Thomé (born 1991) are second-, third-, and fourth-generation Italian American artists whose work has been shown or acquired by Woodmere in recent years.

The legacies of grandparents and the search for roots in the Italian cities where forebears lived remain a strong force. It is empowering to feel a special connection to a culture of deep riches in the arts, food, and fashion. However, by and large, assimilation has occurred. To be Italian is no longer a dimension of identity that signifies belonging to a marginalized group. To be of European descent is to be part of the white mainstream in the United States, a mainstream that is increasingly opening its eyes to a dialogue about privilege, on the one hand, and inequalities, on the other, as they pertain to social inclusion, class, race, and gender. Dramatic new patterns of immigration are a global dynamic of our time, and Italy, like the rest of Europe and the United States, is a place where many of the displaced people of our ravaged world would like to be. I would offer that Philadelphia—a sanctuary city—remains a forward-looking, welcoming center of progressive culture.

BELOW LEFT: Barbara Mimnaugh, American, born 1937. *Umbrian Nights*, 2004. Oil on canvas, 34 × 42⅛ in. (Woodmere Art Museum: Gift of the artist, 2007)

BELOW RIGHT: Carlo Russo, American, born 1976. *Yarns in Orange and Blue*, 2009. Oil on linen, 23 in. × 28 in. (Woodmere Art Museum: Museum purchase, 2013)

THE D'ASCENZO STUDIO

Jean M. Farnsworth

Nicola D'Ascenzo (1871–1954) was born in Torricella, Italy, and immigrated to the United States in 1882. He attended the Pennsylvania Academy of the Fine Arts, the Pennsylvania Museum and School of Industrial Art (later the University of the Arts), and the New York School of Design. D'Ascenzo began his career as a mural painter and interior decorator, and by the early twentieth century he also promoted himself as a stained-glass artist. His interest in stained glass led him to study medieval windows in Europe, and although D'Ascenzo often worked in a painterly mode and even produced windows in opalescent glass, his studio is best known for windows in antique glass reflecting a medieval aesthetic.

The D'Ascenzo Studios' better-known national commissions include windows for the Cathedral of St. John the Divine, New York City; the Washington Memorial Chapel, Valley Forge, Pennsylvania; and the National Cathedral and Folger Shakespeare Library, both in Washington, DC. Some of the Roman Catholic churches in the archdiocese of Philadelphia with windows from D'Ascenzo Studios are St. Francis of Assisi; St. Philomena, Lansdowne; St. Francis de Sales; Shrine of Our Lady of the Miraculous Medal, St. Vincent Seminary; John W. Hallahan Catholic Girls' High School; Church of the Gesù (1868–1993, now associated with St. Joseph's Preparatory School); Holy Child (1909–1993, now Our Lady of Hope); and St. Joseph Church, Collingdale.

D'Ascenzo's accomplishments were recognized with a variety of prestigious awards, including the Columbian Exposition, Chicago, medalist, 1893; Philadelphia T-Square Club, gold medal, 1897; the Architectural League of New York, gold medal, 1925; and the Pennsylvania Museum and School of Industrial Arts, most outstanding alumnus, 1927. He was also an honorary member of the American Institute of Architects.

The work of D'Ascenzo is featured in this volume in Chapter 20 and in the discussion of the Rodeph Shalom synagogue in Chapter 30.

(Excerpted and adapted with the permission of Saint Joseph's University Press from Jean M. Farnsworth, "The D'Ascenzo Studios," in *Stained Glass in Catholic Philadelphia*, ed. Jean M. Farnsworth, Carmen R. Croce, and Joseph F. Chorpenning [Philadelphia: Saint Joseph's University Press, 2002], 432–433).

FACING PAGE, TOP:
St. Stanislaus Kostka, stained-glass window, 1912–1913. The D'Ascenzo Studios, Philadelphia. Principal artist: Nicola D'Ascenzo. St. Stanislaus Chapel, the domestic chapel for the Jesuit Community of Saint Joseph's College and Saint Joseph's Prep, located on the campus of Saint Joseph's Prep. (Photo courtesy Saint Joseph's University Press)

FACING PAGE, BOTTOM:
St. Ignatius Loyola, stained-glass window, 1912. The D'Ascenzo Studios, Philadelphia. Principal artist: Nicola D'Ascenzo. St. Stanislaus Chapel, the domestic chapel for the Jesuit Community of Saint Joseph's College and Saint Joseph's Prep, located on the campus of Saint Joseph's Prep. (Photo courtesy Saint Joseph's University Press)

TOP: Congregation Rodeph Shalom, details of the exterior. (Congregation Rodeph Shalom/Photographer Graydon Wood)

LEFT: Congregation Rodeph Shalom, details of the decoration. (Congregation Rodeph Shalom/Photographer Graydon Wood)

21

A Family of Italian American Artists

JODY PINTO

OUR PARENTS WERE ARTISTS WHO MET IN PHILADELPHIA. Our mother (Gertrude Dwyer), whose father immigrated from Ireland during "the troubles" and became a glass-blower, illustrated her best friends' column, "On a Shoestring," which gave women inexpensive design ideas for the home and clothing in the *Philadelphia Inquirer* in the 1940s through the 1960s. Dad was a painter (reverse painting on glass), printmaker (wood engraving and etching), set designer, and photographer.

On my father's side, our grandparents, Luigi and Josephine Pinto, came from Casal Velino in the province of Salerno (region of Campania). Grandma, who was pregnant at the time, nearly died during the passage. Arriving with three children—Aunt Grace, Uncle Salvatore, and our father, Angelo (one year old)—they were processed (as were all immigrants at the time) at Pier 53 (now Washington Avenue Pier) in 1909.

Luigi and Josephine lived near South Ninth Street in the Italian Market. Luigi sold fruit and produce from a horse and cart in South Philadelphia. His five sons helped by going to the docks on the Delaware River and picking up shipments of produce.

Encouraged by their mother, Dad and his brothers Salvatore and Biagio began to follow their passion—painting. They went to the free "Sketch Club" (now the Fleisher Art Memorial) after school. Dad said they would wait until the students had gone and then collect any charcoal and paper that was left. Soon the three brothers won scholarships to the Pennsylvania Museum and School of Industrial Art.

One day they heard students talking about a place out in Merion where there were unusual paintings and a man who lectured about art—and it was free, if you

ABOVE: "Fingerspan Bridge" in Fairmount Park, Philadelphia, by Jody Pinto. The watercolor *Fingerspan (yellow hand)* was made in 1987, the same year the bridge was installed. (Courtesy Jody Pinto)

LEFT: Angelo Pinto. Photograph. Albert C. Barnes holding Angelo Pinto's painting *Icarus*, ca. 1946. Pinto Family Donation, Barnes Foundation Archives.

One day Dr. Barnes asked our father to take his portrait. Dad was about to take the photograph when Dr. Barnes walked over to Dad's painting, took it off the wall, and held it, saying, "Now you can take the photograph."—Caption by Jody Pinto. (Photograph Collection, Barnes Foundation Archives, Philadelphia, PA. Image © 2019 The Barnes Foundation)

Land Buoy on the Delaware River, by Jody Pinto, 2014. Galvanized steel, fiberglass, solar illumination.

Philadelphia's Washington Avenue Pier (Pier 53) was an immigration alternative to Ellis Island from 1873 until 1915. During that time, the Washington Avenue Immigration Station received over a million immigrants from England, Ireland, and southern and eastern Europe.

Buoys are navigational markers for ships. *Land Buoy* is a celebratory marker for land and sea—a structure for watching, waiting, and remembering the long, great journey. (Photo: Bradley Maule)

were invited to attend. They followed the students and arrived at the Barnes Foundation. Dr. Barnes was impressed by the three young boys and invited them to his classes from 1928 to 1932. He gave them scholarships to travel and study in Europe (in 1931, 1932, and 1933). As children we heard the wonderful stories. The first scholarship to Europe came as they were in class listening to Dr. Barnes speak about the influence of Titian on another painter; suddenly, Barnes stopped and said, "But you will understand when you are in the Louvre, so pick up your tickets tomorrow!" On one trip they met Matisse, who invited them to his studio in Nice, where he was working on his mural *Danse* for the Barnes Foundation. He encouraged them to go to Morocco and Corsica. In Corsica they were arrested while painting a landscape of concealed armaments. The brothers told the police they were traveling with Dr. Barnes and Matisse. Matisse vouched for them, saying they were "nice young boys."

Dad and his brothers began to exhibit paintings in New York, Paris, and Philadelphia during the 1930s, often winning awards. Dr. Barnes purchased nine Angelo Pinto paintings, most of them reverse paintings on glass. During the 1930s, Dad's work in wood engraving and etching entered the collections of the Metropolitan Museum of Art, the Whitney Museum of Art, the Library of Congress, the Louvre, and the Philadelphia Museum of Art. The subjects were his personal experiences—stage sets, backstage, carnivals, shooting galleries, dart throwers, carousels, streetcars, and train tracks from unusual vantage points or extreme perspectives.

In the mid-1930s, the brothers' interest in photography took them to New York. They opened a studio at 38 West Fifty-Seventh Street between Fifth and Sixth Avenues. The area was a beehive of artistic activity, heavily populated by musicians, artists, photographers, and dancers. They did some of the first color on-location photography essays for *Life*, *Look*, and the *Saturday Evening Post*. Dad began teaching at the Barnes Foundation, and a few years later he began the first of his reverse paintings on glass.

When America entered World War II, the brothers gave up the studio and offered it to our parents. Mother and Dad were just married and looking to move to New York. The studio became our home. The theater of New York was part of that home. My sisters Maria and Anna and my brother Angelo Antonio grew up on Fifty-Seventh Street while Dad continued to teach at the Barnes. Then in 1961 I moved to Philadelphia to live for a short time with my uncle Biagio and his wife, Ruth. My short stay grew into twenty years. Every Tuesday Dad and I would have dinner with the relatives in South Philly. In 1964–1968, I attended the Pennsylvania Academy of the Fine Arts and was awarded a Cresson Traveling Scholarship. Going to Europe was like stepping into my father's stories, his talks about the great artists and how the light of their country affected the color and perception of their subjects. My work has been influenced by the experience of parents who were artists and by the city I grew up in as an artist—Philadelphia. My parents were curious about people and life, and they encouraged us to open our eyes to the world.

My gift to them, and to the over one million immigrants who made the great journey to this country, began when I first learned during a public art project that I was standing on the same pier on which my grandparents, Luigi and Josephine (for whom I am named), had touched land after their long journey.

Eddie Lang (born Salvatore Massaro) is remembered in a mural located at Seventh and Fitzwater Streets in Philly, not far from Lang's boyhood home on St. Alban Street. The mural was created by the Mural Arts Program of Philadelphia and Richard Barnes, the Blackbird Society Orchestra of Philadelphia. The ceremony on October 23, 2016, was attended by Councilman Mark Squilla, City Representative Sheila Hess, and CG Andrea Canepari. It was in the framework of the cultural month Ciao Philadelphia 2016. (© 2016 City of Philadelphia Mural Arts Program / Jared Bader. Photo © Richard Barnes. Reprinted by permission)

Jazz in the Neighborhood and the World

CHRIS WILLIAM SANCHIRICO

THE STORY OF JAZZ IS COMPLEX, ORGANIC, and, unfortunately, often unrecorded, much like the best improvisations of the players. Yet certain points are fairly clear. One—it must be said up front—is that the wellspring of jazz is the African American experience; that unique struggle is jazz's central dynamo. Another is that Italian immigrants and their descendants also played and continue to play an important supporting role, one that is sometimes underappreciated. Yet another is that a remarkable portion of the Italian American chapter in the history of American jazz comes out of South Philadelphia, its pieces interconnected like the stories of a neighborhood.

Those stories begin sometime around 1910 in the violin section of a Philadelphia school orchestra, where Eddie Lang and Joe Venuti are said to have shared a music stand.[1] By their late teens, Lang had switched to guitar, Venuti was still on violin, and the two were playing together in Philadelphia clubs. According to legend, they had "tossed a coin to see who would play which of two instruments they had bought from a Philadelphia pawn shop. Lang got the guitar."[2] Apparently, chance was on their side: each went on to become "the premier player on their instrument from the early days of jazz," producing many seminal recordings, several as a duo.[3]

Eddie Lang was born Salvatore Massaro in Philadelphia. His father was from a small village in Molise, a mountainous region east of Rome. Lang died at the young age of thirty, after what should have been a routine tonsillectomy. Nevertheless, his short career was rich enough to earn him the title "father of jazz guitar"[4]—a title that, in truth, he shares with others. More concretely, Lang seems to have been largely responsible for the guitar's supplanting of the banjo in both larger jazz bands and smaller ensembles.[5] He is also said to have paved the way for the guitar's emergence as an instrument for soloing rather than only for accompaniment.[6]

On Lang's recordings, such as "Stringing the Blues" (freely available online), one hears Lang's rhythmically steady, chord-chomping style and his liberal use of chromatic chordal slides.[7] To the modern ear, the playing has a vintage feel. Yet the virtuosity is evident, and there are clear glimpses of the guitar's future as a spotlighted instrument.

Since 1991 Lang's father's village in Molise has hosted an annual jazz festival in Lang's honor, drawing top jazz performers from around the world.[8] Every year Lang's own hometown, Philadelphia, celebrates Eddie Lang Day—thanks to the hard work of Richard Barnes and the generous support of the Italian Consulate in Philadelphia.[9] A commemorative plaque for Lang is displayed at the corner of Seventh and Fitzwater Streets in the Bella Vista neighborhood of South Philadelphia where Lang grew up. At the same corner is a classic Philadelphia mural depicting Lang seated with his guitar.[10]

Lang's earliest and most important partner, Joe (born Giuseppe) Venuti, is "considered the most important violinist in early jazz, with a full tone, a jocular style, and a strong sense of rhythm."[11] Mischievous about his personal history, Venuti sometimes claimed to have been born in Lecco in Italy's Lombardy region, sometimes in Philadelphia, and sometimes on the boat in between. Whatever his true starting point, we apparently find him a decade or so later seated next to Lang in the school orchestra.

One important commentator asks, "Who can listen to the string music of Joe Venuti and Eddie Lang without hearing echoes of the Italian lyric tradition?"[12] But the more important flow of influence may be the one that runs back to Italy. The pair's recordings "were highly influential in Europe, serving as a model for Django Reinhardt and Stephane Grappelli in Paris."[13] Venuti, in particular, "served as an important link between the developing swing traditions in the United States and Italy."[14] *The King of Jazz* (1930), a movie featuring Venuti and Lang among others, remains controversial in the United States for its glaring omission of African American contributions. Yet the movie "drew record crowds [in Italy] when it was released under the title *Il re del jazz*. Italian audiences were especially excited by the film's inclusion of featured performances by well-known Italian American musicians: most notably Joe Venuti [and] Eddie Lang. For many, *Il re del jazz* . . . served as a visual example of what modern European jazz might be."[15]

These early influences bore fruit for American jazz musicians of all backgrounds. The jazz scene in Europe is now perhaps the most vital in the world and remains a welcoming outlet for American musicians, who often find themselves more appreciated (and better paid) on the other side of the Atlantic.[16] Italy alone boasts three hundred annual jazz festivals.[17] And jazz fans will recall the many great recordings of American artists with a European city or festival in their titles.

Lang was the first in a line of jazz guitarists of Italian descent from South Philadelphia. Perhaps the greatest in this line is Pat Martino (aka Azzara), whose career spans the last several decades. Martino plays jazz guitar in the modern style and, along with Wes Montgomery and others, is responsible for defining what that means. While Lang's playing is steadily rhythmic and mostly chordal, Martino emphasizes improvised single-note melodic lines, often with fast, precisely executed runs. Chords are also important in Martino's playing—during both solos and accompaniment. But unlike Lang, Martino spaces his chords with an improvised, though still rhythmic, irregularity. Furthermore, Martino's chords are more compact, and he replaces some of the usual chord tones with related notes to add subtler shades of color.

In his autobiography, Martino reports a personal connection to Lang himself: "He [Martino's father, Carmen 'Mickey' Azzara from Palermo] was a guitar player and a singer. As a young man he had a great interest in . . . the great jazz guitarist Eddie Lang, who was from the neighborhood. . . . In fact, at some point, Dad actually spent two weeks with Eddie Lang learning how to strum a guitar. That's how he learned how to play the changes [i.e., chords] when he would serenade my mother [Genoveffa Orlando]. He would sing all these romantic Italian love songs to entice my mother into a smile."[18]

Martino has a global reputation and is considered by many to be among the greatest living jazz guitarists.[19] He still plays around Philadelphia and for several years running has appeared Thanksgiving weekend at Chris' Jazz Café on Sansom Street near Broad.[20]

Jimmy Bruno, another jazz guitar great born and bred in Philadelphia,[21] reports that he "first saw Pat [Martino] play in 1969. I was sixteen when my father took me to Grendel's Lair [on South Street in Philadelphia] to see him. He had dark glasses on. He was just a major force . . . not only his music, but his presentation." Bruno himself went on to become another towering virtuoso of the jazz guitar. Bruno is particularly noted for his ability to cleanly and quickly play compelling, seemingly impossible, almost baroque patterns. Like Martino, he is a musician of world renown, and, like Martino, he plays regularly in Philadelphia.[22]

The guitar is a particularly important instrument in the history of Italian American jazz in Philadelphia. But there have been many other great artists on other instruments.

Joey DeFrancesco, the premier jazz organist of his generation, was raised in a family of jazz musicians in Delaware County, just outside of Philadelphia. DeFrancesco, whose grandfather immigrated from Sicily, attended the Philadelphia High School for the Creative and Performing Arts and was "playing out" around Philadelphia by age ten.

DeFrancesco's improvisations convey an enormous sense of drama and excitement. This is evident, for instance, in his solo on the tune "El Hombre" on Pat Martino's album *Live at Yoshi's*.[23] Starting with a sparse melodic line, by the last chorus he has let out all the stops (figuratively, and possibly literally). DeFrancesco has also made several important recordings with Jimmy Bruno, including on Bruno's well-regarded album *Like That*.[24] DeFrancesco is credited with "introduc[ing] a modern harmonic vocabulary to the playing of the Hammond organ, and his success helped to fuel that instrument's revival among new and established players in the 1990s."[25]

The vibraphone—a kind of reengineered xylophone with a warm, woody sound—has always been central in jazz. The vibraphonist Tony Miceli grew up near Philadelphia in Burlington County, New Jersey, studied at the University of the Arts on Broad Street, and currently lives and teaches in Philadelphia. Miceli is a leader in the world community of vibraphonists and is rapidly becoming one of the most sought-after players around the globe. He is a master of a particular four-mallet technique of his own design, which enables him to play rich chords without diminishing the intricacy of his melodic lines.

Miceli's playing combines a compelling sense of rhythm with a deep probing of chordal textures, and he is just as much at home playing the most tranquil ballads as the most off-balance high-speed passages of Thelonious Monk.[26] Miceli's freely available YouTube recording of "Whisper Not" is an excellent example of his mastery.[27]

It's probably true that most of these great musicians, most of the time, consider (or considered) themselves musicians, not Italian American musicians—ready to play with anyone who can keep up or, even better, lead the way, and open to all appealing influences. Moreover, it should always be kept in mind that one of jazz's most admirable traits is that it is among the social spheres least burdened by the barriers that can arise from differences in background. And yet it is still interesting to note, especially in this celebration of links between Italy and Philadelphia, that Italian Americans—from the neighborhoods of South Philadelphia, in particular—were so ready to embrace and so capable of carrying forward America's distinctive musical tradition.

NOTES

1. Gioia, 270.
2. "Joe Venuti," in *Encyclopedia of Popular Music*.
3. Gioia, 270.
4. Ferguson, 78.
5. Dapogny.
6. "Lang, Eddie," in *Encyclopedia of Popular Music*.
7. "Stringing the Blues," Discography of American Historical Recordings.
8. *Il Giornale del Molise*, July 21, 2016.
9. "Eddie Lang Day in Philadelphia—Official Website."
10. "Mural Dedication: Eddie Lang, Mural Arts Philadelphia."
11. Robinson.
12. Gioia, 136.
13. Robinson.
14. Celenza, 111.
15. Celenza, 176.
16. Gioia, 704.
17. Gioia, 704.

18. Martino with Milkowsky, 35.

19. Martino with Milkowsky, 261 et seq. (reporting impressions of other guitar players).

20. Timpane.

21. "Bruno, Jimmy," in *Encyclopedia of Popular Music*.

22. For example, he recently appeared with guitarist Sonny Troy at a Jazz Bridge event in Center City. See http://www.jazzbridge.org/event/jimmy-bruno-sonny-troy-in-center-city/.

23. On Pat Martino, *Live at Yoshi's*, Blue Note (2001).

24. See Jimmy Bruno, *Like That Featuring Joey DeFrancesco*, Concord Jazz (1996).

25. Gilbert.

26. Schermer.

27. https://www.youtube.com/watch?v=NhvTBgUe1OI.

BIBLIOGRAPHY

"Bruno, Jimmy." In *The Encyclopedia of Popular Music*, 4th ed., edited by Colin Larkin. Oxford, Oxford University Press, 2006 (last updated 2009). No separate author is listed for this entry.

Celenza, Anna Harwell. *Jazz Italian Style: From Its Origins in New Orleans to Fascist Italy and Sinatra*. Cambridge, Cambridge University Press, 2017.

Dapogny, James. "Lang, Eddie." In *The New Grove Dictionary of Jazz*, 2nd ed. Oxford, Oxford University Press, 2004.

Discography of American Historical Recordings, s.v. "Columbia Matrix W142697. Stringing the Blues/Eddie Lang; Joe Venuti." Accessed April 18, 2017. http://adp.library.ucsb.edu /index.php/matrix/detail/2000032458/W142697-Stringing_the_blues.

"Eddie Lang Day in Philadelphia—Official Website." http://eddielangdayinphiladelphia .blogspot.it.

"Eddie Lang jazz, grandi nomi anche quest'anno." *Il Giornale del Molise*, July 21, 2016. http:// www.ilgiornaledelmolise.it/2016/07/21/eddie-lang-jazz-grandi-nomi-anche-questanno/.

Ferguson, J. "Eddie Lang: Father of Jazz Guitar." *Guitar Player* 17 (1983): 78.

Gilbert, Mark. "DeFrancesco, Joey." Grove Music Online. 2003; Accessed 16 Dec. 2020. https://www-oxfordmusiconline.com.

Gioia, Ted. *The History of Jazz*. 2nd ed. Oxford, Oxford University Press, 2011.

"Lang, Eddie." In *The Encyclopedia of Popular Music*, 4th ed., edited by Colin Larkin. Oxford, Oxford University Press, 2006 (last updated 2009). No separate author is listed for this entry.

Martino, Pat, with Bill Milkowsky. *Here and Now! The Autobiography of Pat Martino*. Milwaukee, Backbeat Books, 2011.

"Mural Dedication: Eddie Lang, Mural Arts Philadelphia." https://www.muralarts.org /events/mural-dedication-eddie-lang/.

Robinson, J. Bradford. "Venuti, Joe." In *The Grove Dictionary of American Music*, 2nd ed. Oxford, Oxford University Press, 2015.

Schermer, Victor L. "Tony Miceli: Mallet Magic." All About Jazz, 2006. https://www .allaboutjazz.com/tony-miceli-mallet-magic-tony-miceli-by-victor-l-schermer.php.

Timpane, John. "Pat Martino and Friends Make Thanksgiving Weekend Memorable at Chris' Jazz Café." *Philadelphia Inquirer*, November 29, 2015. http://www.philly.com/philly /entertainment/music/20151130_Pat_Martino_and_friends_make_Thanksgiving _weekend_memorable_at_Chris__Jazz_Caf.html.

"Venuti, Joe." In *The Encyclopedia of Popular Music*, 4th ed., edited by Colin Larkin. Oxford, Oxford University Press, 2006 (last updated 2009). No separate author is listed for this entry.

South Philly Musicians Remix mural, located on Broad and Tasker Streets, celebrates south Philadelphia's music icons, depicted in the mural: Eddie Fisher, Fabian Forte, Bobby Rydell, Frankie Avalon, Jerry Blavat, Chubby Checker, Charlie Gracie, and James Darren. (© 2016 City of Philadelphia Mural Arts Program / Eric Okdeh. Photo © Steve Weinik. Reprinted by permission)

SOUTH PHILLY MUSICIANS REMIX MURAL

JEREMY GOODE

OF THE EIGHT MUSICIANS ON THIS MURAL, five have Italian heritage on both sides. Jerry Blavat's mother was Italian. While Al Martino represented earlier singers usually referred to as "crooners" of traditional popular music of nightclubs, radio, and early TV, the others were part of a postwar explosion in TV variety shows, recordings, and movies.

Al Martino was born to Italian immigrants in Philadelphia in 1927. Martino worked as a bricklayer growing up. Seeing his childhood friend Mario Lanza's success as an opera singer, Martino began singing in local night clubs, leading to his leaving for New York City. Martino found quick success, winning the Arthur Godfrey's Talent Scouts show, which ultimately led to Martino's record deal with BBS, a Philadelphia independent music label. Several of Martino's singles became quite popular, including "Here in My Heart," "I Love You Because," and "Spanish Eyes."

From the 1950s to the mid-1960s, South Philadelphia was known for its contribution to the teen idol phenomenon. The teens in this mural were all nurtured in South Philly and used local televised dance shows such as *American Bandstand* and talent competitions as well as contracts to launch entertainment careers. The proximity to New York TV and record companies helped them attain fame and success in popular music careers, and many moved on to Hollywood movies and television appearances on variety shows and sitcoms.

Throughout their intertwined careers, common South Philly roots helped produce the iconic singer-actors that they became. In the mid-1960s, the "British Invasion" of rock stars took over the scene and ended the era, and although most continued to perform into the new millennium, their position in the music scene was muted.

Jerry Blavat was born in South Philadelphia in 1940 to a Jewish father and an Italian mother. Blavat's key role was not as a singer or actor but as a host-DJ-producer, building on his successful appearances on *American Bandstand* in the early 1950s. Blavat's success led to his producing and hosting *The Discophonic Scene*, a dance show for teenagers that took place in Philadelphia, similar to the earlier *American Bandstand*. He is still active in the music scene in Philadelphia today, where he is still known by his nickname, the "Geator with the Heater."

James Darren was born in 1936 in the city and named James William Ercolani. He grew up in Philadelphia in an Italian American family. Darren's father often had him accompany him to bars and nightclubs in Philadelphia where he would sing a few songs. He left for New York to study acting and attracted the attention of Columbia Records. He then acted in his first film lead, *Rumble on the Docks*. He is best known for his role as Moondoggie in *Gidget*, one of the first beach-party-era movies. Darren's acting career also involved popular songs, as he sang the title track, "Gidget." Darren went on to record pop hits including "Goodbye Cruel World" and "Her Royal Majesty," among others.

Frankie Avalon was born in Philadelphia in 1940 and christened Francis Thomas Avallone. He made his first television appearance as a trumpet player on *The Jackie Gleason Show* when he was twelve. In 1959, Avalon's "Venus" and "Why" earned the number-one spot on the Billboard Hot 100. Avalon's acting success began with an appearance in *Jamboree*, singing "Teacher's Pet" and playing the trumpet. He also appeared in *Guns of the Timberland* and *The Alamo* with John Wayne. He is still involved in the entertainment industry.

Fabian Forte was born in 1943. He appeared on *American Bandstand* in 1957 as a fourteen-year-old when Bob Marcucci, owner of Chancellor Records, sought him out in his search for "good looking teenage talents" in South Philadelphia. Fabian attended South Philadelphia High School while receiving finances from Chancellor Records. Hit songs of Fabian's include "Turn Me Loose," "Hound Dog Man," and "Tiger." Twentieth Century Fox saw potential stardom in Fabian and signed him to an acting contract. He was featured in *Hound-Dog Mad*, *High Time*, and *North to Alaska*, as well as several television series.

Bobby Rydell was born in 1942 and christened Robert Louis Ridarelli. Rydell rose to fame as an eight-year-old after appearing on *Paul Whiteman's TV Teen Club*, ultimately winning their talent show. He would later go on to sign a record deal with Cameo Records.

At eighteen, Rydell went on tour in Australia with several prominent musical groups, including the Everly Brothers, the Champs, and the Crickets. His first successful single, "Kissin' Time," hit the charts in 1959 and led to his first album release, *We Got Love*. Throughout the 1960s, several singles of Rydell's found themselves on the Billboard Hot 100 record chart, including "Wild One," "Volare," and "Swingin' School." After signing with Capitol Records in 1964, although his career slowed after the British Invasion, Rydell continued to perform into the 2000s.

Rydell had an especially significant impact on influencing other creative music and theater arts. In the musical theater and film versions of *Grease*, the high school, Rydell High, is named in tribute to Rydell. Additionally, Paul McCartney acknowledged that "She Loves You" was inspired by a Rydell song.

Charlie Gracie was born Charles Anthony Graci in 1936. His career took a different route from the teen idols. A guitarist, he worked across the genres of blues, gospel, and country and toured in the United Kingdom, Europe, and the United States into the 1990s and 2000s. He was inducted into the Rockabilly Hall of Fame in 2011. He was well known in the United Kingdom and Europe, where he most actively toured, and he was the subject of a documentary film rather than a feature film star.

Jackie Robinson, Duke Snider, and Roy Campanella (*left to right*) of the National League dominating Brooklyn Dodgers. (John W. Mosley Photograph Collection, Charles L. Blockson Afro-American Collection, Temple University Libraries, Philadelphia, PA)

TWO ICONIC SPORTS FIGURES

JEREMY GOODE

KNOWN AS "CAMPY," HALL OF FAMER ROY CAMPANELLA is regarded by many as one of the best catchers ever in the game of baseball. Using statistical records alone, he ranks as the third best in major league history. Campy was born in Germantown in 1921. His father, John, was the son of Sicilian immigrants, and his mother, Ida, was African American. His parents and three older siblings soon moved to the Nicetown area of North Philadelphia, which was then a racially diverse working-class neighborhood. Campanella's father was a salesman of fresh produce and fish, trucking his commodities daily from the central food distribution center to be sold from the truck in the neighborhood. He later owned a grocery store. His mother was a housewife.

Campy was an outstanding and popular athlete at Simon Gratz High School, an integrated school. While there was some racial tension, his remarkable athletic prowess made him a team captain in several different sports, but baseball was his passion. Because of the segregated nature of baseball, he established a successful career in the Negro League and the Mexican League before becoming the second Black player hired in the Brooklyn Dodger system after Jackie Robinson. His outstanding major league career as a future Hall of Famer was established between 1948 and 1957. In 1958 he was seriously injured and became a quadriplegic in a career-ending automobile accident, but he remained in sports communications.

Neil Lanctot's book *Campy: The Two Lives of Roy Campanella* tells the moving story of how Campanella dealt with the two significant challenges in his life: discrimination based on race and handicap. The MacGee Rehabilitation Center in Center City where Campanella experienced most of his rehabilitation contains a small exhibit that documents his career and relationships to the city and to the center.

Vince Papale, who played for the Philadelphia Eagles for only three years, is nationally known largely because of his extraordinary accomplishments as a "walk-on" player for the Eagles at age thirty after never having played college football. His achievements are well documented in his book *Invincible* and the movie of the same name, which was drawn from it. Papale was born in Chester, Pennsylvania, and grew up and went to school in Pennsport in South Philadelphia. He specialized in track and field and was awarded a track scholarship at St. Joseph University, where he was an especially notable pole vaulter. There was no football at St. Joe's. His life has been an inspiration for many other athletes seeking careers outside of normal career routes.

23

Romaldo Giurgola, Architect

"The Reluctant Master"

Alan Greenberger

THE GOLD MEDAL OF THE AMERICAN INSTITUTE OF ARCHITECTS is the highest honor the profession confers on an individual for lifetime achievement. Since 1907, the institute has awarded the Gold Medal to seventy-seven individuals from around the world. Six of them practiced in Philadelphia. Two of them are of Italian descent. And one of them, Romaldo Giurgola (AIA Gold Medal 1982), was born in Italy and emigrated to the United States.

Aldo, as he was universally known to family, friends, and colleagues, was born on September 2, 1920, in Galatina in the Apulia region of Italy (the "heel of the boot"). He was raised in Rome, where he attended college and received the equivalent of a Bachelor of Architecture degree. His interest in architecture was undoubtedly piqued by his father, who was a set designer for the theater. Aldo emigrated to New York City in 1952 to attend Columbia University, where he received his Master of Architecture degree and where he subsequently taught.

In 1954, Dean Holmes Perkins of the School of Fine Arts at the University of Pennsylvania invited Aldo to join the faculty of what was to become one of the leading intellectual and creative centers for architectural education in the country. Perkins had assembled other leading practitioners and theorists, including Louis Kahn (AIA Gold Medal 1971), Robert Venturi (AIA Gold Medal 2016), and Ian McHarg (noted landscape architect).

Together, they were dubbed the "Philadelphia School" by Jan Rowan in an article in the journal *Progressive Architecture* in 1963. Though each of their work differed in intent and emphasis, their commonality was in the rejection of the modernism characterized by what was then known as the International Style—an approach to architecture largely born in Europe and made famous by such architects as Walter Gropius, Le Corbusier, and Mies Van der Rohe. That approach emphasized the universality of modern design in any culture or context. It rejected the neoclassicism and ornamentation of previous eras and instead developed a sparer design aesthetic that characterized so many of the commercial and institutional buildings built in this country, including in Philadelphia, between 1950 and 1980.

In 1958, having known each other through their employment at the Philadelphia firm Bellante and Klaus, Aldo and Ehrman Mitchell (Mitch to his friends and colleagues) formed the firm Mitchell/Giurgola Associates, regularly referred to as M/G.

M/G became internationally known primarily through their winning entries in national and international design competitions. Aldo was the guiding design force of the firm. Mitch gave the firm its professional ethos. Aldo articulated his philosophical position most clearly in an article in the journal *Yale Perspecta* in 1963. In that article, he described something called the "partial vision." By that, he meant that architecture exists as a fragment of a larger context. As such, the architect has obligations in his or her designs to that context. The context may be the urban fabric, the surrounding historical buildings or natural landscape of the site, or, as is sometimes the case, a combination of two or three of these important characteristics. Aldo believed strongly that all building design should respond to and honor its context while enhancing the quality of the life that the building is intended to accommodate.

It was this philosophical statement that earned Aldo and M/G a place in Jan Rowan's description of the Philadelphia School. However, years before the idea of a Philadelphia School was articulated, Aldo's early design work was demonstrating the practical result of his philosophy.

No better place was this demonstrated than in the design of the Wright Brothers Memorial in Kill Devil Hills, North Carolina, in 1958. The commission was part of a nationwide program developed in the late 1950s by the National Park Service to improve the visitor experience of national parks and monuments throughout the country.

The memorial is at the long, sandy, ocean-side site at which Wilbur and Orville Wright experimented with the construction of an airplane and eventually successfully flew one. When they were there in the early 1900s, the place was quite isolated and hard to access. However, its relative isolation, smooth terrain, and local wind conditions proved to be a great advantage to the Wrights' endeavors.

In addition to providing various visitor facilities, the new building was to house the original airplane. Given the stature of the achievement, the building could have been designed as a large monument itself and could have been given a position of prominence in the site. Instead, the siting and the design were comparatively modest so that the remembrance of what had happened there would be the dominant experience.

The pavilion is positioned to take advantage of the sweeping view of the landscape on which the early airplane taxied and ultimately took off. The room in which the airplane is exhibited is modest in scale, consistent with the small scale of the airplane itself. With its lifted domed roof to allow more sunlight and view of the sky, there is an intimacy to the experience of seeing the airplane that reminds the visitor that this seminal achievement was done by the handicraft and inventiveness of two bicycle makers working in a drafty shed in a remote environment. Far from being a pristine and bold example of modern architecture, the building recedes into the land and becomes a fragment of a much larger experience that the architects intended to emphasize.

Where does such an approach come from, especially given the large ego structure that is often associated with architects and was on full display in Ayn Rand's book *The Fountainhead*, first published in 1943? Aldo, ever the modest gentleman in his personal manner, never really explained the origins of his philosophical approach to design, at least not to this author. But knowing something of the environment in which he grew up, particularly in Rome and not coincidentally reinforced by his time in Philadelphia, it is possible to surmise the origins of his experience and thinking.

The Italy in which Aldo grew up and in fact the Italy that we all enjoy to this day is one in which the pleasures of place are more public than they are private. The streets of Rome are lined with buildings both ordinary and extraordinary. Decorated or undecorated, they support the street as a public room in which daily life is on display. When they are ornamented, it tends to be not for the sake of declaring their presence above all others but to offer the celebration of artistry and craft at a given place in a given moment. Even the special buildings of Rome—the great churches and public buildings—are given greater weight by their relationship to the surrounding streets and public places. St. Peter's Cathedral—a great building by any estimation—is made greater by the sequence of public space that leads to it and even by the presence of its great dome on the Roman skyline.

There exists in Rome a very powerful sense of how the parts work together to create profoundly moving public experiences that do not rely solely on the greatness of individual architecture. Aldo loved Philadelphia because it was one of the few American cities where he was able to see the same thing, though of course rendered in an American vernacular. He was taken with the colonial scale of Philadelphia and the way the row houses created the public rooms of the city that led you from place to place. In a 1979 show called Roma Interotta (Rome Interrupted), he proposed the fabric of the row-house streets as a way to both complement and bring new order to a Roman neighborhood.

These experiences grounded him in a sensibility that looked to the larger context of place as a basis for how the architecture of a single building might work best. Shortly after the completion of the Wright Brothers Memorial, the firm entered the Boston City Hall design competition and placed second. Their proposal—a muscular U-shaped office building with a very public appendage that contained the City Council chamber aligned with Quincy Market and Fanuiel Hall—was

United Way Building.
(Courtesy Melissa Romero)

carefully woven into the irregular street pattern of Boston. Its great courtyard was a public room that openly received the energy of the surrounding public realm.

The winning proposal by another talented firm—Kallman McKinnell of Boston—was an equally muscular building whose presence on the City Hall plaza was always more of an object in space than an integral part of the fabric of Boston. It is not uncommon for second-place finishers in major architectural competitions to gain special notice for their work. So it was for M/G, who began to attract major clients in the financial and insurance industries in Philadelphia. It was through these commissions that Aldo was to leave his greatest mark on Philadelphia and to assert his unique version of what by then was known as the Philadelphia School.

The first of these major commissions was a new headquarters building for the United Fund (now United Way) Building on the Benjamin Franklin Parkway. As the most prolific charitable organization in Philadelphia with an extraordinarily prominent site, the United Fund was especially conscious of not building something that was "showy." However, the site they had acquired couldn't be more visible and would serve as an effective reminder to the Philadelphia community that the United Fund was the premier place for charitable giving.

Aldo responded positively to these apparently conflicting interests by crafting a very simple glass box that would have four different walls. The east wall was a party wall and would be largely invisible anyway. The north wall received little to no direct sunlight and so was left as all glass. But for the west and south walls, Aldo conceived of concrete screens over the glass that would respond in form to the needs for sunscreening, particularly in the hot Philadelphia summers, which, combined with office lights and machinery, could render very unpleasant conditions.

The west wall became a series of horizontal strips with deep overhangs in order to block out the low-angled western sun. The south wall—the only wall to face the parkway—creates a monumental scale on one of Philadelphia's only monumental streets and at the same time screens the glass from relatively high-angled sun. These simple but brilliant ideas were arguably one of modern architecture's earliest forays into sustainability, though it was not called that at the time.

While United Fund was in construction, the firm won a commission to design a major addition to the headquarters of the Penn Mutual Insurance Company on the south side of Independence Square. Leaving aside the singular visual importance of designing a prominent building that would serve as a backdrop to Independence Hall, Aldo approached the project with a very keen respect and appreciation for his own opportunities in a country of immigrants.

Many of the same principles of sustainability that were used in the United Fund were employed here as well. But the most innovative idea involved the question of what do with a building on the site that was owned by Penn Mutual and had been designed by noted Philadelphia architect John Haviland in 1838. That building was done in what was known as the Egyptian Revival style, a short-lived movement made popular by the public's awareness of Egypt as a result of conquests by Napoleon in the late eighteenth century.

Penn Mutual Building. (Bruce Anderson on WikiCommons [2007]. Licensed under CC BY-SA 3.0: https://creativecommons.org/licenses/by-sa/3.0/legalcode)

The four-story facade, built in a white marble, was the only significant facade to what was an otherwise a straightforward office building of its day. Unfortunately, it sat squarely on the site of the proposed much larger addition and could not be retained in any reasonable way. It had also been designated as a Philadelphia Historic Landmark in 1962, and as such, any change to it—let alone demolition—had to be approved by the Philadelphia Historical Commission.

Aldo's sensitivity to context and his willingness to allow factors outside of the project program itself to influence design resulted in an extraordinary idea. The building was to be taken down, but the Egyptian Revival facade was not only to be retained but to be disassembled, cleaned, and put back on its own free-standing concrete frame. The result was not just the incorporation of an old facade into a new one. The plan reimagined the facade as a piece of art that had intrinsic value and retained the scale and rhythm of the street, especially as it was seen under the arching branches of the great trees on Independence Square.

In effect, Aldo conceived of a building that would have two distinct characters. The one at and near the ground level would be dominated by the historic facade (and its neighboring buildings, which were to stay in place). The other—a tower—would be visible largely from a distance. As it was directly behind

Independence Hall, it was conceived as a simple, dark glass curtain wall that would frame the white steeple of the hall. Once above the steeple, the building had a simple concrete crown that led to a museum devoted to William Penn on the top floor. An elevator with a window and view of the mall took visitors up directly from the street to the museum.

Other, more subtle aspects of the design all paid homage to the dominant lines and scale of the existing Penn Mutual headquarters. In the end, the key facade of the building was an amalgamation of responses to the context of the site. But through Aldo's skill as an architect, these disparate elements were united into a very satisfying whole.

By the time United Fund, Penn Mutual, and several other Philadelphia buildings were done, a Mitchell/Giurgola office was established on the Upper West Side of Manhattan to allow Aldo convenient access to Columbia, where he was asked to lead the architecture program. Though he lived there continuously from 1968 through 1980, he continued to commute to Philadelphia weekly to work on projects here.

Perhaps the project that meant the most to him in Philadelphia was the small pavilion that was to house the Liberty Bell. In expectation of large crowds visiting Philadelphia in the bicentennial year of 1976, the National Park Service decided to move the Liberty Bell out of Independence Hall to a spot on the mall where the bell and the hall would be in clear view of one another. Mitchell/Giurgola was hired to design the pavilion.

And once again, though faced with designing a building for one of America's most treasured icons, Aldo's instincts were to subsume the architecture to the experience and meaning of the bell itself. He designed a pavilion that he hoped would feel like a series of walls and roof that created an outdoor room—a symbol for him of the accessibility of American freedoms. He situated those walls and roofs to create shelter for people waiting in line and to create opportunities to view the bell without ever having to go inside.

The walls were also arranged to create a processional to the bell: a room for gathering, a narrower passageway—perhaps reminiscent of a church nave—to approach the bell, and then a sunlit larger room in which the bell could be viewed with the full backdrop of Independence Hall beyond. Though not an overtly religious man himself, Aldo designed the pavilion with a reverence that is reserved for religious experiences.

The pavilion was not without its critics. By its position on the mall, it obstructed the long view of Independence Hall from blocks further north of Market Street. And the need to create a full glass enclosure ultimately took away from some of the feeling of an open-air pavilion in a park that Aldo tried to replicate. The pavilion was demolished in 1998 and was replaced with a much larger building to the side of the mall that allowed for exhibits and queuing inside.

For those who remember the Liberty Bell Pavilion, there is debate about its value relative to the larger building that took its place. But separate from that debate,

Liberty Bell Pavilion in front of Independence Hall. (Jack E. Boucher [2004], Library of Congress, Prints and Photographs Division [HABS PA-6712-5])

there is no question that the pavilion that Aldo designed was a wonderful example of his willingness to submerge the ego of the architect in the cause of something greater to life's experiences. And at the same time, his love of craft and place supported the firm's elegantly detailed pieces of architecture.

It would be appropriate to end this chapter of Aldo's story here as he began to spend less and less time in Philadelphia. But no story about this Italian immigrant can be complete without recalling his ultimate work—his opus—in, of all places, Canberra, Australia, where he lived out his life to age ninety-five.

In 1979, the government of Australia conducted an international design competition to design the new Parliament House of this emerging country. It was to replace the provisional Parliament House that was completed in 1929 in what at that time was a relatively new capital city. Canberra itself had been the result of an international design competition won by American architect Walter Burley Griffin of Chicago. The plan, considered a clear expression of the City Beautiful movement of the late nineteenth century—exemplified by Philadelphia's own Benjamin Franklin Parkway—created a city of wide boulevards and axial relationships set in a landscape of eucalyptus-treed hills and river valleys.

In Griffin's plan, one of the hills was reserved for the permanent parliament. It was positioned at the end of diagonal boulevards that connected this hill to the downtown and government centers of the city. The provisional parliament had been built immediately below the capitol hill so as to reserve that space for the permanent seat of government.

The competition was done in 1979 when Aldo was fifty-eight. At this point in his career, his analytic and design skills were at their peak. With tremendous assurance in his sensitivity to context, Aldo envisioned a building that was built into the hill, not on top of it. Its formal order that responded directly to the fabric of the city was created by two great curving walls that further defined the essential functional areas of the government. And in a breathtaking gesture that came to represent Australia to the world, the building was to be topped not by an enclosed space but by a pyramidal flag mast that made the views to the land beyond the reinterpreted "capitol dome."

Over the next nine years, the Parliament House was realized by a team of nearly 125 architects working in Canberra, as Aldo commuted back and forth between New York, Philadelphia, and Australia. The Parliament House opened to great acclaim in 1988. It was at that time that Aldo decided to permanently live in Canberra and began the process of withdrawing from the firms in the United States, which were maturing into their own independent entities.

After the Parliament House project, his wife, Adelaide, and his daughter, Paola, moved to Australia to join him. He was made an honorary citizen of Australia, where he completed several smaller projects. One was a modest country house for himself. The other was a neighborhood Catholic church where, upon his death in 2015, his funeral service was held.

Aldo's design sensibilities—a product of his upbringing in Italy, further cultivated and refined here in Philadelphia, and ultimately played out on the other side of the world—created not only a legacy of buildings but also a legacy of firms that are still practicing today in Philadelphia as MGA Partners, in New York as Mitchell/Giurgola, and in Canberra as Guida Moseley Brown.

In a lecture at the University of Melbourne, Luigi Rosselli, a former colleague of Aldo's, referred to him as the "Reluctant Master," a tribute to Aldo's quiet ways. Though this humble man was Italian by birth, his experiences made him, by his own admission, a world citizen.

CHRISTOPHER COLUMBUS MONUMENT

Architects: Venturi, Scott Brown and Associates, Inc.
Location: Philadelphia, PA
Client: America 500 Anniversary Corporation
Construction Cost: $1,050,000
Completion: 1992

VSBA was asked to design a monument, located in
the International Sculpture Garden at Penn's Landing,
Philadelphia's old seaport, to commemorate the 500th
anniversary of Christopher Columbus's voyage and to
celebrate the role of all immigrants in the development
of Philadelphia and the United States.

Our design utilizes steel technology to create a
modern representation of a traditional Italian symbol—
the Obelisk, which punctuates Roman plazas. Instead of
being hewn from solid stone, the monument is fabricated
from thin stainless steel panels cantilevered from an
internal stainless steel structure. The base of the three-
sided monument is granite with polychrome inscriptions
and dedications resting on a granite and brick plaza in
the shape of a compass rose.

The obelisk rises to the height of 106 feet and
is capped by a sphere and weathervane/banner
representing the national colors of Italy and Spain.
The large, open joints between the panels create deep
shadows during the day and are illuminated at night
by beams of light projected up through the obelisk and
into the sky.

Award: 1993 Design Award for Excellence in
Architectural Design, The Pennsylvania Society of
Architects

(Photo: Gary Horn)

24

An "Extremely Emotional Love Affair"

Robert Venturi, Rome, and Italy

Luca Molinari

"ROME, AS I FIRST SAW THAT CITY THAT SUNDAY in August 1948, as I walked on air—this time in a place rather than an institution—discovering unimagined pedestrian spaces and richness of forms bathed in the 'golden air of Rome.' The American Academy in Rome, as a Fellow where within its community, headed by its easy and supportive hosts, the director and his spouse, Laurence and Isabel Roberts, and by means of its location, I might exist every day in architectural heaven, and learn new lessons via Michelangelo, Borromini, Brasini, hilltowns, and other historical mentors and places, and where I discovered the validity of Mannerism in art for our time, and from whose perspective as an expatriate I could better perceive my own country and the genius of its everyday phenomena, to see the Piazza Navona and Main Street. Louis Kahn, profound teacher of mine, and ultimately, in some ways, as all teachers become, a student of mine—I trust now I can acknowledge how my son informs me through his sensibility as I simultaneously guide him."[1]

When delivering the above acceptance speech for the Pritzker Prize in 1991, Robert Venturi, one of the most important and influential North American architects of the twentieth century, generously and meticulously extended a series of thanks and acknowledgements to those people and institutions that had helped give expression and substance to his theoretical and design path, as if to say that his receipt of the most prestigious architectural award in the world was owing to the influence of many people, places, and institutions that had helped shape his original vision. Balanced and considerate, his speech went to the heart of the change in architecture that occurred in the 1960s—one in which Venturi himself played a crucial role—but it did so with grace and with the same lightness and character

that he has shown over the last several decades, transforming them with his subtle irony and middle-class radicalism.

This short text is an elemental yet richly referential source that identifies Italy, and Rome particularly, as a kindred place for Venturi, an inevitable lifelong reference, an "extremely emotional love affair," attested by the fact that he continued throughout his life to celebrate the anniversary of his first trip to Rome in an attempt to demonstrate its significance.[2] The 1948 trip to Europe, a truly first European "grand tour" for Venturi, led to his application for a fellowship at the American Academy in Rome, where, after two failed attempts, he eventually succeeded in obtaining a place for the period of 1954–1956.

His second, decisive trip to Rome confirmed an unconventional intellectual path with respect to the modernist training in vogue among young American architects after World War II,[3] one that reflected the familiar environment of Venturi's training at Princeton University from 1944 to 1950, as well as his relationship with the other great teacher of North American architecture, Louis Kahn, whom he would often quote.

It is interesting that Philadelphia was both birthplace and professional home to two of the artists who most profoundly marked an American way of looking at modern architecture, a way so deeply different from the northern European influence associated with the Congrès Internationaux d'Architecture Moderne (CIAM) circles, and one that would become a hallmark of the professional and academic architectural scene from New York to Boston and Chicago.

It is equally interesting that both these artists, despite their belonging to two different generations, nurtured such a genuinely meaningful and personal relationship with Italy and the Mediterranean cultures. This relationship reached beyond

ABOVE LEFT: Robert Venturi seated in Piazza Navona. (The American Academy in Rome. Image used with permission)

ABOVE RIGHT: Annual exhibition of the American Academy in Rome, 1955. The far panel shows architectural drawings by Robert Venturi. (The American Academy in Rome. Image used with permission)

the stereotypes of classicism that a Beaux Arts training had imposed on the first generation of North American "modern" architects, to search out in the villages of Italy and in the vernacular culture, as well as among the folds of Renaissance and Mannerism, those references that would mark these artists' design paths.

The two architects not only had both held, within a few years of each other, fellowships at the American Academy of Rome but were also in tune with one of the most vital and interesting moments of Italian architectural culture of the twentieth century, thanks to the experiences of neorealism and to the central role of *Casabella-continuità*, the prominent architectural journal headed by Ernesto Nathan Rogers from 1953 to 1964.[4] Their shared interest in the Italian Renaissance and in the uncanny and visionary scope of Giovanni Battista Piranesi's drawings solidified a relationship of extraordinary importance for both,[5] while their respective creative and theoretical paths led to their being considered among the last heroes of modernist culture and among the first of that conceptual and linguistic reform that would later be called postmodernism.[6]

It was also in Philadelphia, in the suburb of Chestnut Hill, where Vanna Venturi asked her son to design a house—a provocative manifesto of a new world that departed from the traditional iconic American house and just two blocks away from the Esherick House, designed only a few years earlier by Louis Kahn and best known for its symmetry and clear modernist orientation.

The Vanna House is one of twelve projects mentioned by Venturi in the appendix of *Complexity and Contradiction in Architecture*, a volume, published in 1966, of seminal theoretical importance for its rethinking of modern architecture. This book, together with *Learning from Las Vegas*—another volume, published in 1972, with Venturi's wife, Denise Scott Brown, and Steven Izenour—can be credited with changing the theoretical horizons of the international debate by signaling key words and themes that were to decisively influence the way in which architecture was viewed by generations to come. Both books are strongly indebted to the Roman and Italian experience of Robert Venturi, an experience that is revised and expanded through a rereading of the notion of Mannerism[7] not only as a historical moment of rupture with respect to the Renaissance but above all as a way of reinterpreting reality in its imperfect and commonly known form, one capable of producing new and unexpected shapes and languages more closely in tune with a profoundly changing world.

The original debate that Venturi initiated with the concept of tradition, and through the long series of examples developed in *Complexity and Contradiction in Architecture*, considers the concept of history as a living material to be questioned consciously and used actively in the design process: "This book deals with the present, and with the past in relation to the present. It does not attempt to be visionary except insofar as the future is inherent in the reality of the present."[8] It is no coincidence that the last page of the essay in this book ends with a picture of a typical

American Main Street, recalling the greatness of Italian urban public spaces together with the debate sparked by Jane Jacobs on the life and death of American cities.[9]

Upon Piero Sartogo's invitation to participate in the conference and exhibition *Roma Interrotta* (Rome Interrupted) in 1978, the symbolic and cultural relationship of Venturi's theoretical work with the Italian capital was further instated.[10] Within the quadrants of the Nolli map with which he was entrusted, the Philadelphian artist intervened not with a project but rather with a superimposed image of the Cesar Palace in Las Vegas, taken from his 1972 book.

The autobiographic character is testified at the very beginning of the text: "Las Vegas is the apotheosis of the desert town. Visiting Las Vegas in the mid-1960s was like visiting Rome in the late 1940s. For young Americans in the 1940s, familiar only with the auto-scaled, gridiron city and the antiurban theories of the previous architectural generation, the traditional urban spaces, the pedestrian scale, and the mixtures, yet continuities, of types of the Italian piazzas were a significant revelation. They rediscovered the piazza. . . . Each city is more an archetype rather than a prototype, an exaggerated example from which to derive lessons for the typical."[11] The Italian street and piazza continued to be necessary references for the elaboration of Venturi's theory and poetics, which, in the work on Las Vegas, finally led to a conceptual union between city and architecture through the scale of the commercial and ordinary street, in which monument and language come together to define an unprecedented contemporary epos.

The Vanna Venturi House. (Photographs in the Carol M. Highsmith Archive, Library of Congress, Prints and Photographs Division)

The street, and its most subversive and visionary postmodern version, became yet another fragment of the fruitful relationship between Venturi and Italy when he was asked by Paolo Portoghesi, along with another team of architects, to contribute to the *Strada Novissima* project at the First International Architecture Exhibition of the Venice Biennale of 1980. Venturi's presence in the Italian architectural culture remained an important constant by way of his participation in other Venice biennales, conferences, and publications and by his steady collaboration with the international magazine *Zodiac*,[12] headed by Guido Canella from the 1980s to the 1990s, with the publication of projects for the Theatre of Philadelphia, the Sainsbury Wings of the National Gallery in London, and a series of university buildings that illustrate the activities of a long-established and internationally recognized firm.[13]

His "love affair" was not solely sentimental and private but viewed the relationship with Italy and its cultures as a valuable and vital source for looking at the contemporary in unexpected ways.

NOTES

1. Robert Venturi, "Acceptance Speech," *Zodiac*, no. 12, September 1994–February 1995, p. 208.

2. Martino Stierli, "In the Academy's Garden: Robert Venturi, the Grand Tour and the Revision of Modern Architecture," AA Files, no. 56, p. 45.

3. Joan Oackman and Avigail Sachs, "Modernism Takes Command, 1940–1968," in *Architecture School: Three Centuries of Educating Architects in North America*, ed. Joan Oackman with Rebecca Williamson (Cambridge, MA: MIT Press, 2012), pp. 121–159.

4. Luca Molinari, *Continuità: A Response to Identity Crises—Ernesto Nathan Rogers and Italian Architectural Culture after 1945* (Delft, Netherlands: TU Delft, 2008); Stierli, p. 49.

5. "Unlike his commissions for actual buildings in these years Kahn's visionary proposals for Philadelphia that he now initiated for his own provided space for dreams. *Perspectives of Philadelphia* show a fantastic landscape of powerful forms reminiscent of Piranesi's Rome. The Roman quality, in fact, seems stronger here than in earlier work and may reflect the influence of Robert Venturi." Sherri Geldin, "The Mind Opens to Realization: Conceiving a New Architecture, 1951–61," in *In the Realm of Architecture*, ed. David B. Brownlee, David G. Long, and Louis I. Kahn (New York: Rizzoli, 1992), pp. 85–86.

6. Charles Jencks, *The Language of Post-modern Architecture* (New York: Rizzoli, 1977); Terry Farrel and Adam Nathaniel Furman, *Revisiting Postmodernism* (London: Riba, 2017).

7. See note 1 on Mannerism; Stierli, p. 54.

8. Robert Venturi, *Complexity and Contradiction in Architecture*, vol. 1 (New York: Museum of Modern Art, 1977), p. 14.

9. Jane Jacobs, *The Death and Life of Great American Cities* (New York: Random House, 1961).

10. *Roma Interrotta* was the first occasion on which all the major artists of what would come to be known as the postmodern movement participated: Costantino Dardi, Antoine Grumbach, James Stirling, Paolo Portoghesi, Romaldo Gurgiola, Colin Rowe, Michael Graves, Robert Krier, Aldo Rossi, Leon Krier, and Robert Venturi.

11. Robert Venturi, Denise Scott Brown, and Steven Izenour, *Learning from Las Vegas: The Forgotten Symbolism of Architectural Form* (Cambridge, MA: MIT Press, 1977), p. 18.

12. Venturi, Scott Brown, and Assoc., "Philadelphia Orchestra Hall," *Zodiac*, no. 4, 1990, pp. 74–109; Venturi, Scott Brown, and Assoc., "The Sainsbury Wing of the National Gallery, London," and Robert Venturi, "From Invention to Convention," *Zodiac*, no. 6, March–August 1991, pp. 77–135; Robert Venturi, "Some Words Concerning Designing for Architecture on American Campuses," *Zodiac*, no. 7, March–August 1992, pp. 72–93; Venturi, Scott Brown, and Assoc., "The Charles P. Stevenson Jr. Library, Bard College, NY," *Zodiac*, no. 10, September 1992–February 1994, pp. 218–235; Venturi, Scott Brown, and Assoc., "Restoration and Renovation of Memorial Hall, Harvard University," *Zodiac*, no. 19, March–November 1998, pp. 196–204; Venturi, Scott Brown, and Assoc., "Mielparque Kikko Kirifuri Resort," and Robert Venturi and Denise Scott Brown, "Learning from Tokyo and Kyoto and Nikko," *Zodiac*, no. 20, January–June 1999, pp. 118–135.

13. Stanislaus von Moos, *Venturi, Scott Brown & Associates, 1986–1998* (New York: Monacelli, 1999).

IV

CONTEMPORARY PHILADELPHIA

Experiencing the Italian Legacy in

the Branded Global City

INTRODUCTION

Judith Goode

THE FOURTH SECTION COVERS A NEW SET of relationships between Philadelphia and Italy in the late twentieth and early twenty-first centuries in the post–World War II era. The convergence of expanding economies, independence movements in former colonies, and the civil rights movement in the United States alongside emerging international structures of credit, trade, and law ushered in a new global system that included the nations of Asia, Latin America, and Africa.

By the 1970s, the concept of globalization was widely used to describe the increased flows of capital, people, ideas, and goods across borders. The effects of these changes in Philadelphia were first experienced as deindustrialization as plants moved offshore to find cheaper labor. This produced concomitant population loss in Philadelphia's industrial neighborhoods, further exacerbating the earlier suburbanization that had left former industrial cities smaller and poorer.

Air transportation and changing media and communication technology sped up the movement of people, ideas, investment capital, and commodities, which traversed space faster, easier, and with lower cost. New U.S. immigration and refugee laws were passed that reduced exclusionary quotas for some European nations and expanded access to the new postwar ex-colonial nations. By 1970, new immigrant and refugee populations from many world regions were coming to Philadelphia. The new immigration consisted of both high- and low-wage workers. The high-wage workers with higher education came to work in corporations, finance, and the "eds and meds" discussed below. Other immigrants served in the expanding hospitality, tourism, and cultural industries that further attracted millennial creative knowledge workers as well as university students, the future creative knowledge workers.

The city, like others in the rust belt, used a common playbook to restructure the economy from manufacturing to professional service or technical jobs based on highly educated workers. Recognizing that the largest group of employers in the region were the many institutions of eds and meds, higher education became prominent—arts, humanities, and sciences with a special emphasis on medical and pharmaceutical research and health care. These institutions formed the foundation of a knowledge-worker economy, which could spin off many opportunities for jobs and entrepreneurship in the hospitality and culture industries to serve the lifestyles of new residents and destination tourists.

Strategies for attracting creative workers and tourists included branding the city as diverse and cosmopolitan in the lifestyles it offered. Through the context structured by colleges, universities, and supportive urban development programs that were publicly funded with private partners (such as the creation of the convention center and the Avenue of the Arts development), the city brand was upscaled. Older downtown neighborhoods were reclaimed as hip new landscapes (gentrification), and new links in art and culture between Italy and Philadelphia were forged.

Universities have been continuously significant in relationships between the city and Italy, but the nature of the links has changed as universities have evolved. For the first century, colleges in the United States were elite institutions. With the notable exception of the University of Pennsylvania, founded by Benjamin Franklin, most were tied to religious institutions. They tended to serve and reproduce a prosperous, literate population. In the late 1800s, new types of higher education institutions developed for new populations. This was the era of publicly funded land grant schools to provide new, useful research knowledge through extension services disseminating knowledge in the public interest, especially in agriculture and health. Access for new kinds of students proliferated—for example, women's colleges and schools addressed to working-class residents such as immigrants and formerly rural or mining workers who aspired to middle-class status. This greater inclusivity and access accelerated after World War II with the growth of state-supported institutions, which created a vast middle class and served the nation as it prospered and built a booming postwar economy.

While Penn was always an institution with a cosmopolitan faculty and student body (see Chapter 25), today it is a key local center for current globalization due to an increase in recruitment of international faculty and students as well as the international collaboration in the production and dissemination of research. The same can be said for Jefferson (Medical) University (Chapter 26), Temple (Chapter 27), St. Joseph's (Chapter 4), and Drexel (Prologue). At the same time, local universities were always sites for cosmopolitan diversity even before the contemporary moment.

Chapter 25. Chris William Sanchirico's "Italy, Philadelphia, and the University of Pennsylvania" provides an account of several kinds of Italian influence at Penn prior to the present global moment during earlier periods of Penn's engagements with Italy. Each is the product of the historic moment in which it occurred. The value of the Italian language for Europe-oriented U.S. educational elites was strong early in the nineteenth century—recall Jefferson's knowledge. It remained strong at Penn as depicted by the story of the Da Pontes. The founding of the Penn museum later in the nineteenth century recalls discussions of collecting classical and Renaissance collections (Part II), while the role of Penn in the education and mobility of Italian American immigrants with means and the case of the Italian American who funded Italian studies both recall the Italian American university experience in Part III. Today, Penn is an institution with a very large population of international students and faculty. This is reflected in the data of a Brookings Institution report on immigration in the Delaware Valley, based on the 2010 census, which indicates that the wealthy census tracts surrounding Penn and Drexel contain the largest concentration of people born outside the United States in the metropolitan region.

Chapter 26. In "Dr. Gonnella's Journey from the Mountains of Basilicata to the Medical Wards of Philadelphia," Salvatore Mangione builds on Philadelphia's history as the earliest center of medical education under Benjamin Rush with more medical schools than other U.S. cities. He provides a life history interview of Dr. Giuseppe (Joseph) Gonnella, an immigrant from the agricultural south. Gonnella was a national-award-winning medical educator known as a recruiter and mentor. Over his career, he was especially successful in recruiting and mentoring medical students from Italy as well as Italian Americans in a way that created lasting bonds between medical institutions in Philadelphia and Italy.

Chapter 27. In "Temple University and Its Italian Connection," Judith Goode shows how Temple was an example of a late nineteenth-century university created in 1884 for material and cultural uplift of the working class that was accessible in terms of tuition and schedules (such as night school). Like Penn, it served new Italian immigrants and their children. Goode demonstrates how Temple's main contemporary links to Italy come through its campus in Rome. Goode shows the many ways in which Temple University's Rome campus leads to deep and lasting bonds in Italy for students, faculty, alumni, and their parents and leads to continued immersion in Italian culture. She includes the ways that the descendants of earlier immigrants attend the Rome campus and are able to reconnect with their extended families and their regions, and how they and their parents incorporate Italy meaningfully into their lives. Temple Rome also links institutions in both cities, especially those in the arts and medicine.

The next three chapters focus on ways to experience the Italian legacy in global Philadelphia. Most residents and visitors would follow the visitor's guides to South Philadelphia and the Italian Market. The city provides guides and tours that emphasize diversity and events such as Mural Arts Bus Tours and festivals, including special events at the Italian Market. The last chapters all provide different ways of experiencing the Philadelphia-Italy relationship. The final essay provides commentary by a contemporary Italian journalist as he reflects on his perceptions of the Italian legacy in the city.

Chapter 28. Fred Simeone's essay, "The Simeone Foundation Automotive Museum," focuses on the ways in which the foundation's auto museum provides encounters with elegant modernist design through models of cars throughout the twentieth century. While the award-winning museum features race cars designed and manufactured in many countries, it is at the same time an exceptional site for experiencing the spirit of Italian racing. Besides auto design, the museum also focuses on the sensory experience of twentieth-century auto racing through exhibits of famous auto races throughout the Italian countryside, and its internal track offers opportunities to experience driving these cars. In 2018, the museum was ranked the number-one automotive museum in the world.

Chapter 29. In "Italian Gastronomy and Its Many Roles in a Cosmopolitan City," Judith Goode demonstrates how Italian gastronomy is central to many aspects of the contemporary city of Philadelphia. Globalizing cities compete to make themselves food destinations for visitors as well as desirable places to live for corporate leaders, professionals, and students. Food is a major component of this competition, as "foodie" creative knowledge workers focus on food taste, authenticity, creativity, sociality, local sourcing, and health. Italian food plays a role in each of these dimensions and serves as an exceptional domain for observing the reinvention and fusion of the traditional.

Chapter 30. In "Recalling Italy in Bricks and Mortar," Inga Saffron identifies ten Philadelphia buildings that evoke Italian arts and culture. She uses her long accumulated knowledge and insight about Philadelphia's built environment to make connections between Italy and the city. Dividing the buildings into three categories—those inspired by Italy, homages to specific Italian structures, and those made by Italian Americans in the United States—she provides a blueprint for designing an architectural "tour" that demonstrates the many ways in which Italian influences have played a significant role in the architecture of the city.

Chapter 31. Paolo Valentino, deputy editor of the historic Italian newspaper *Corriere della Sera*, came to Philadelphia to cover the first edition of Ciao Philadelphia in 2014. This essay, entitled "From Rocky to Botticelli, Italian Philadelphia: Concerts, Shows, Exhibits, and Conferences in a City in Pennsylvania Where the 'American Dream' Speaks Our Language," is a sign of renewed attention to Philadelphia in Italy, which had known the city only through the film *Rocky*. The title links the city to a broader image of Italy's beauty and culture. The chapter then shows how Italian cultural heritage has been part of the connective tissue of the city, describing events and people exemplifying this relationship.

25

Italy, Philadelphia, and the University of Pennsylvania

CHRIS WILLIAM SANCHIRICO

THE UNIVERSITY OF PENNSYLVANIA has been an important presence in Philadelphia for nearly 275 years. Yet during its most optimistic periods, it has aspired to become even more, a university for all places and times. And quite naturally, during those propulsive episodes Penn has often reached out toward Italy and its pervasive and timeless history and culture.

A DA PONTE FOR PENN

By the year 1830, Philadelphia—which had been the second largest city in the British empire and had served as capital of the United States during its first postconstitutional decade—had fallen behind not only New York but also Baltimore in population.

As its collegiate session was opening in September of that year, the University of Pennsylvania was half a century old. It had just moved into a pair of new buildings at the corner of Market and Ninth Streets, one for the medical school, one for the college. Under the leadership of Provost William Heathcote DeLancey— namesake of Center City's Delancey Place and Street—Penn was in the midst of reinvigorating its "collegiate department" after several years of decline. Although the medical school had continued to thrive, wealthy Philadelphians had been sending their sons elsewhere for college.[1]

Across the Atlantic, the Italian peninsula was a patchwork of political entities: Tuscany was an independent grand duchy; the Roman Catholic Church ruled Rome and a broad swath of land stretching across the peninsula and up the Adriatic seaboard; Venice, Milan and the surrounding territory was controlled by the

UNIVERSITY OF PENNSYLVANIA.

Austro-Hungarian empire, Sicily and the southern mainland were ruled by the Bourbons, a branch of the Spanish royal family. "Italy," as a modern political entity, was still an idea—a dangerous, yet powerful idea. Many of the advocates of unification were imprisoned or executed; others went underground or into exile. Nevertheless, the movement to unite the peninsula was starting to gain traction, and the founding of the modern Italian state was not far off. Animating the drive toward political unification was the conviction that the peninsula was already substantially unified culturally, and that these shared artistic and literary traditions ought to be the source of pride—national pride.[2]

Back in the United States, the cultural side of Italy's resurgence was heralded by a small but prominent set of Italian immigrants who sought for Italy a place in the intellectual life of the new nation. These individuals were often fleeing political or economic difficulties in their homeland. Nevertheless, they apparently brought with them a proud attachment to Italy—along with obvious talent and a keen eye for opportunity.[3]

One of the most prominent among these freelance attachés—certainly by his own account but also that of many historians—was Lorenzo Da Ponte.[4] Best remembered today as the librettist for several of Mozart's operas, Da Ponte was born near Venice into the Jewish faith and was later ordained as a Catholic priest. He fled Venice to the Austro-Hungarian empire to avoid charges of unpriestly behavior, eventually worked his way to London setting up shop as a purveyor of Italian-language books, and then immigrated to the United States in 1805 apparently to flee creditors.

By 1818, Da Ponte was living in Philadelphia and attempting to support himself and his family by teaching Italian and continuing to sell Italian-language books. Yet, discouraged by the lack of interest for his wares, Da Ponte shortly thereafter decamped to New York. His move north was beckoned by Clement Clarke Moore, a former student, who would later become president of Columbia College. Moore helped Da Ponte settle in New York and establish himself as a successful teacher of Italian. In 1825, Da Ponte was appointed professor of Italian language at Columbia College. Though he maintained a connection to Philadelphia, Da Ponte remained based in New York for the rest of his life.[5]

By 1830, as Penn was settling into its new location at Ninth and Market, Da Ponte was engaged in efforts to bring Italian song and opera to audiences in New York and Philadelphia. In 1832, for instance, he helped bring an Italian opera company to the Chestnut Street Theater in Philadelphia (see Chapter 14). Though not always financially successful, efforts like these helped to engender interest in Italian culture, while also bolstering Da Ponte's reputation as a cultural ambassador.[6]

Back at Penn—it is fair to speculate—Provost DeLancey and his colleagues decided that if they were going to compete with Columbia, they too would need to offer Italian language classes, and for that they would need their own version of Da Ponte. And so in 1830, Penn appointed as its first professor of Italian Da Ponte's son, Lorenzo L. Da Ponte.[7]

Lorenzo L. was already a scholar and teacher in his own right. He had apparently acted as his father's informal teaching assistant throughout his teenage years. He was also his father's official translator in several cases—for instance, on the libretto for *Don Giovanni*. By 1830, Lorenzo L. had been teaching at Washington College in Maryland.[8]

Unfortunately for Penn, six months after his appointment, in June 1830, Lorenzo L. resigned in favor of a position as an English teacher in New York at Columbia Grammar, then a prep school attached to Columbia College. Lorenzo L. explains in his letter of resignation to Penn that finances were the driving force in his change of plans.[9] And there are reasons to take him at his word.

First, the position teaching English at Columbia Grammar probably paid a definite salary. By contrast, college teachers of modern languages at that time were some mix of adjunct faculty and franchisee. They were paid per student, and their students were charged fees over and above tuition.[10] (Lorenzo senior himself had tried to renounce the "decorative title of professor" at Columbia. "I have neither pupils nor salary!" he wrote. His friends at Columbia ignored his resignation.[11]) It is thus quite possible that Lorenzo L. found too few students in Philadelphia to make the Penn position viable.

Second, the Da Pontes' efforts to bring Italian opera to American audiences appear to have greatly strained the family's finances. One case involved Da Ponte senior's Italian niece, a singer of uncertain quality. When she did not arrive from Italy on time in the spring of 1830, the Da Pontes were forced to forfeit rent on the Bowery Theater in New York, which is said to have swallowed up half of Lorenzo senior's savings.[12] It was that same June that Lorenzo L. resigned from Penn.

In any event, Lorenzo L. appears to have maintained no connection to Penn, and for the next twenty years Penn employed no teacher of Italian.[13]

ETRUSCOPHILIA IN PHILADELPHIA

The resurgence sparked by Provost DeLancey in the early nineteenth century had reenergized the University of Pennsylvania and sent it searching for ways to bring Italian culture to campus. The same story was repeated in broad outline at the end of that same century—though with greater success.

By the late 1800s, the University of Pennsylvania had again been reinvigorated after having, again, suffered through a period of decline. And once more the charge had been led by a dynamic provost, Dr. William Pepper. During Pepper's term (1881–1894), Penn added thirteen new departments, twenty new buildings, and greatly expanded its curriculum.[14] This is the Pepper who sits in bronze on the landing of the main stairway of the Free Library, an institution that he founded in 1891. Pepper was also one of the founders in 1887 of what is now known as the University of Pennsylvania Museum of Archeology and Anthropology, or simply the Penn Museum. (Chapter 12 discusses the museum's gardens.)

At least as important as Pepper to the museum's founding and early development was Sara Yorke Stevenson, the museum's first curator of the Egyptian and Mediterranean Sections, later secretary of the museum under Pepper, and finally herself president of the museum. Stevenson wrote and lectured in Egyptology as an independent scholar. She was the first woman to receive an honorary doctorate from Penn (1894) and the second to be admitted to the American Philosophical Society. She was a central figure in Philadelphia's social and intellectual life and, along with Pepper, a member of the influential Mitchell-Furness Coterie, an influential group of writers and scholars. Stevenson and Pepper operated as a team in advancing the museum's interests.[15]

As Pepper and Stevenson were getting their museum off the ground, news of the ancient Etruscans and their rich burial complexes was beginning to spread outside of Italy. The Etruscans, from whom Tuscany takes its name, were the strongest and richest civilization on the Italian peninsula in the several centuries around the year 500 B.C., just as the city of Rome was getting underway. They flourished in twelve major cities, allied as the Etruscan League, dotting the region stretching north-south between Florence and Rome and east-west between the Apennine Mountains and the western coast.[16] (Chapter 10 discusses one of these cities).

Etruscan civilization held great sway over ancient Rome both directly and indirectly. The last three kings of Rome preceding the founding of the republic in 509 B.C. were Etruscan. Key elements of Roman religion and architecture are thought to be of Etruscan origin. The emperor Claudius—of *I, Claudius* fame—was so enthralled by this precedent culture that he is said to have complied a twelve-volume history of the Etruscans as well as a dictionary of their language.[17]

The Etruscans were eventually conquered by the Romans. But they continued to exert a strong influence over the peninsula even after Rome's decline. In the Renaissance, for instance, Florence and Mantua, seeking suitably ancient origins, took pains to establish their Etruscan roots, emphasizing the precedence to Rome. In the eighteenth century "Etrusophilia" was a fashion among northern Italian scholars who sought a greater role for their own region in the origins of Italian history and culture.[18]

For the English-speaking world, however, Etruscan civilization did not start to come into focus until the middle of the nineteenth century when two events sparked interest: the publication of *Cities and Cemeteries of Etruria in 1848* by the British explorer and self-taught scholar George Dennis, and the founding in 1889 of the National Etruscan Museum at Villa Giulia in Rome. The Etruscans left behind elaborate hillside burial grounds called *necropoli*. In these "cities of the dead," tombs were often lined up along streets, each tomb having rooms and decorated walls and containing treasures such as bronzes and vases. The museum at Villa Giulia took the scientific step of presenting the artifacts grouped according to the tomb in which they were found, with tomb groups arranged chronologically.[19]

As Pepper and Stevenson were looking to expand the collection of their new museum, Etruscan tombs were a natural possibility. In 1895 the museum engaged for that purpose Arthur Frothingham, founder of the *American Journal of Archeology* and a lecturer at Johns Hopkins and Princeton. Frothingham, who had been raised in Rome, was back there again that year as associate director of the American School of Classical Studies, now part of the American Academy in Rome.

As a sideline to his directorship, Frothingham had simultaneously solicited several American university museums, proposing to act as their agent for collecting Etruscan tomb artifacts. His appeal to the Penn Museum was compelling and well tailored: "I ask you," he wrote to William Pepper, "in your own interest and for the glory of Philadelphia if you will not see to it that Philadelphia should take the lead in America in establishing a great museum of originals, for which these excavations will furnish the nucleus."[20] An important subtext was that the collection of New York's Metropolitan Museum of Art, like those of most American museums at the time, was almost entirely composed of casts and copies.

Having secured funding from the likes of John Wanamaker (see Chapter 10), Pepper and Stevenson took Frothingham up on his offer. Frothingham, in turn, engaged several Italian citizens to complete the actual work, including most notably Francesco Mancinelli-Scotti, apparently the chief excavator, and Count Lorenzo Cozza, who took several photographs of individual tomb groups that proved invaluable in later analysis.

Frothingham's arrangement with Penn had been that he would supervise and provide plans of the tombs, lists of the items uncovered, and records of where each was found. But given his duties back at the school in Rome and with several different excavations going at once for several different university museum clients, Frothingham had difficulty fulfilling his promises.[21]

In early 1896, Stevenson wrote to Frothingham, "What I would like to understand from you is your business arrangement with these various people [other museums] and also upon what term you propose to deal with the representatives of other institutions."[22] Josephine Fitler, wife of Mayor Edwin Henry Fitler of the eponymous square in Center City, was also involved and wrote to Frothingham, "I earnestly beg you to put the matter upon a definite business basis with regular satisfactory reports with some show of personal interest and attention to [Wanamaker]."[23]

Frothingham ultimately purchased several tomb groups that had been excavated before his arrival on the scene; for only one of these had a plan been drawn up. He then had Mancinelli-Scotti newly open several tombs at Narce. In the end, the museum received twenty-nine tomb groups from three different sites. For quite a few of the groups, the information is insufficient. To be sure, Mancinelli-Scotti is thought to have diagramed the tombs and made appropriate lists, as contracted, and to have taken scientific records during the excavation. But apparently much of this documentation never made it through Frothingham to the Penn Museum. Only twelve of the twenty-nine groups have any tomb diagrams at all, and these are generally not carefully drawn layouts.[24]

Fortunately, however, Count Cozza's photographs of the tomb groups, taken on shelving in an Italian warehouse before shipment to Philadelphia, proved crucial in sorting out what finally arrived at the museum. Although it would have been preferable to know where each item had been found in each tomb, there is at least reliable information on which items were found together in the same tomb.[25]

Most of the tomb groups that arrived at Penn came from Narce, an ancient Faliscan city and a member of the Etruscan league, that existed for the two millennia leading up to 300 B.C. on a group of hills north of Rome.[26] Among the tomb groups from Narce, one of the most notable is that of the "Narce Warrior." The tomb dates from around 700 B.C., close to the legendary date of Rome's founding (753 B.C.). It can be seen on display at the Penn Museum and is featured on the museum's website.[27]

CIRCOLO ITALIANO

During the years that Stevenson and Pepper were proactively engaged in securing pieces of Italy's past for the Penn Museum, Italy's present was making its own way into Philadelphia, person by person. In 1870, as Pepper was just beginning his career at Penn, there had been only three hundred Italians in Philadelphia—probably not much more than in Da Ponte's day as a proportion of population. By 1898, the year Pepper stepped down as Penn Museum president, the number was approaching eighteen thousand. By 1910, a few years after Stevenson's term as museum president, the number was seventy-seven thousand—a 250-fold increase relative to 1870, while the full city population merely doubled.[28]

What did this wave of migration mean for the University of Pennsylvania? It is safe to say that few of those who themselves arrived as adults, many from the rural south, had much connection to the university, other than perhaps as stone masons or general laborers.[29] But what about their children, those born in the years surrounding 1905, of college age in the mid-1920s?

Penn in the mid-1920s was a different place from the Penn we know today. If an observer back then had described Penn as an undergraduate business school with appendages in dentistry, law, medicine, engineering, and education, that would have been a bit unkind but not especially inaccurate. The spring commencement program for 1924 lists about five hundred names for receipt of a bachelors of science in economics, the degree conferred by Wharton. That amounts to about 55 percent of the undergraduate laureates in that year (as compared to 15 percent in 2017). The 1924 program also lists about 220 dental school graduates. The next largest groups were doctors of medicine and bachelors in the science of education, each with about 150. Next there were 95 engineers. After them about 55 lawyers, with the rest of the program spread widely across other, smaller departments.

The Penn yearbook, *The Record*, provides a window into the world of Italian Americans at Penn during those years. One finds in several volumes from the teens and twenties a page dedicated to the Circolo Italiano, the Italian Club. In the images of those pages from 1921 and 1923, one sees photos of about twenty to thirty young men (no women) and, underneath, lists of fifty to sixty names, almost all distinctly Italian. A casual cross-check against commencement programs and single-student yearbook portraits supports the inference that nearly everyone at Penn with an Italian last name was a member of the club. Since at that time nearly everyone with Italian heritage had an Italian surname, it would appear that almost every Italian American at Penn signed on to the Circolo Italiano.

Who were those students, and what happened to them after leaving Penn? Thanks to the Penn Archives and its director, Mark Frazier Lloyd, the question is in many cases answerable.[30]

The secretary of the club in 1923 was Henry Salvatori, who graduated that same year in electrical engineering. He is also apparently listed on the 1921 page as "Henry Salvatore." Salvatori was born Ercole Salvatori in 1901 in the hill town of Tocco da Casauria, in Abruzzo, about two hours by car east of Rome, on the other side of the Apennine range as the land begins to level off toward the Adriatic Sea. His family immigrated in 1908. His father founded

University of Pennsylvania, *The 1921 Record: Published by the Class of 1921*, p. 262. (University Archives and Records Center, University of Pennsylvania)

CIRCOLO ITALIANO

President . . . . . . Pasquale Torraca
Vice-President . . . Francis Pugliese
Treasurer . . . . . . Antonio Mazza
Secretary . . . . . . Harry Dragonetti

Nicholas Gallucci
John E. Sindoni
Henry Salvatore
A. Joseph Rinaldi
Louis A. Torraca
Michael Aria
Philip J. Franzese
Enrico Coscia
Samuel J. Saso
Alfred W. Accetta
Angelo Perri
Michael Stalfo
Theodore Cianfiano
Frank Siano
Edward Bevelacqua
Frank Morgarero

Antonio Mazzara
Frank Travaline, Jr.
Dante Pigossi
Claude A. Florio
Andrew Secondo de Masi
William A. Lell
Dr. Paolo A. Cresta
M. Adam D'Alessandro
Dr. Edward Chiero
A. W. Demio
Albert Di Lauro
Vincent E. Padula
John Di Bello
Ernest Magaro
Joseph D'Emilio
Aniello Di Givanno
Dr. Domenico Vittorini

Joseph Napolitano
P. F. Lucchesi
F. P. Ingenito
N. Dunno
Albert D'Orazio
Roddy Dennio
Francesco Di Pasquale
Saverio M. Flemma
M. F. Mantia
W. Crallo
Michael Di Vette
James Palumbo
Anthony D'Angelo
Frank J. Granforte
Thomas Chianese
Vincent C. Lentin

and ran a successful wholesale grocery business. Salvatori worked in his father's business while attending South Philadelphia High School.[31]

Sixty years after the club photo, in 1985, Penn awarded Salvatori an honorary doctorate. A chaired professorship in computer and cognitive sciences still bears his name, as does a research fund administered by the Center for Italian Studies to support investigations of Italian culture and society.

Salvatori was an innovator and entrepreneur in the use of seismic technology to locate oil deposits. In 1933, in the middle of the Great Depression, he struck out on his own and founded a company, Western Geophysical Corporation, which he then ran profitably for nearly three decades, turning it into one of the world's largest petroleum-exploration companies.

After selling his company, Salvatori became an important supporter of Republican causes: "He was considered a conservative kingmaker and member of Mr. Reagan's 'kitchen cabinet' of intimates. . . . Such was his influence in California politics that one detractor, Mayor Joseph Alioto of San Francisco, once charged that it was Mr. Salvatori, rather than then-Governor Reagan, who wielded the real power in Sacramento."[32]

Among the other students appearing on Circolo Italiano's member lists is Guy Gretano de Furia, a college (1925) and law (1928) graduate. De Furia, who had attended Chester High School, went on to become assistant counsel to the special U.S. Senate committee that censured Joseph McCarthy. Later he was senior partner in his own law firm. He was Chester man of the year in 1969 and served on the board of SEPTA. In 1960, according to archive records, de Furia donated to the University Library several volumes in Italian. Worthy of mention in his giving record, these books were presumably of some value. One cannot help wondering whether they included books that Lorenzo Da Ponte had been brokering a century and a half before.

Another name on the lists is C. Thomas Chianese (Wharton 1923). Chianese graduated from Trenton High School, was student ROTC commander at Penn, and retired from the U.S. military as a decorated colonel having fought in seven major battles in the two world wars.

Frank Speno, also Wharton 1923, appears on the list as well (though as "Spino"). He invented the Speno Rail Grinding Train for smoothing bumps in railroad tracks and was president of the Speno Railroad Ballast Cleaning Company.

Also listed is Frank Travaline (Wharton 1923, Law 1926). Travaline arrived at Penn from Camden High School. To support his studies, he worked as a professional trumpeter (trombonist according to one source) and played for major big bands in the region. Shortly after graduating from law school, he was an instructor in political science at Penn. He went on to be elected to the New Jersey General Assembly and was one of the first Italian Americans to serve in that body.

Dr. Domenico Vittorini, whose name is at the bottom of the 1921 list, was the faculty sponsor of the Circolo Italiano. Vittorini was a professor of romance languages at Penn, and his career at that institution spanned nearly forty years. He was born in 1892 in Preturo outside the city of L'Aquila in Abruzzo, northeast of Rome. He received a doctorate from the University of Rome in 1916 and a master's from Princeton in 1917. In 1918 and 1919, he taught at Temple University (see Chapter 27), and from 1919 until his death in 1958, at Penn.

Vittorini was apparently a mild yet energetic and charismatic figure. A memorial tribute describes his "impeccable Italian" and "the kindly look in his bright blue eyes highlighted within the velvety olive framework of his face."[33] Speaking of his reviews of others' work, the tribute says, "No matter how many reservations he has on the character or importance of the book in question, these are unfailingly couched in courteous and objective terms and they are almost always offset by words of praise and encouragement that have been heart-warming to the authors he has examined."[34] Vittorini's character may be part of the reason for the Circolo Italiano's popularity with Italian American students.

As a teacher of Italian language, Vittorini was credited by colleagues for his ability to instill in his students an unusually high level of listening comprehension and speaking ability. Vittorini was nationally prominent in Italian language pedagogy, serving in 1948 as president of the American Association of Italian Teachers.[35]

As a scholar of Italian literature, Vittorini had two chief focuses. The first was the work of the modern Italian playwright and Nobelist Luigi Pirandello. Pirandello himself wrote the forward to Vittorini's 1935 *The Drama of Pirandello*. Vittorini's second concentration was Dante. Over the course of thirty-five years, he completed *The Age of Dante: A Concise History of Italian Culture in the Years of the Early Renaissance*, which was published in 1957, the year before his death.

Vittorini was also a public figure and in that capacity a great advocate not only for Italian language and culture but also for Italy the nation. Penn's archives contain copies of his editorials and notices of his public lectures. In 1933 he was honored by the Italian government for his efforts in advancing Italian culture in the United States.

Being a vocal supporter of Italy and all things Italian was a complex proposition in the 1920s and 1930s—in two regards. In the first place, the American public's impression of Italy and Italians at that time was not characterized by the same positivity, receptivity, and warmth as today. During the opening decades of the twentieth century, the massive influx of Italians into places such as Philadelphia started to take its toll on public opinion, and a nativist sentiment gained political traction. Around the time the photos from 1921 and 1923 were taken, Congress passed immigration restrictions that greatly curtailed the influx of Italians into the United States. An advocate for Italy in those years—even one whose message was Pirandello, Dante, and the subjunctive mood—faced a powerful populist headwind.

The second complexity was that to advocate for Italy in the 1920s and 1930s was to advocate, at least in part, for the government of Benito Mussolini. Vittorini, in his lectures and writing in the 1930s, was indeed an apologist for Mussolini's policies, including the invasion of Ethiopia in 1935. In assessing this unfortunate fact,

Dr. Domenico Vittorini.
(University Archives and
Records Center, University of
Pennsylvania)

it should be kept in mind that Vittorini was hardly alone in painting an optimistic picture of Mussolini's Italy. At the time most of the Italian American press—an important institution in those years—was pro-Mussolini. Supporting or at least apologizing for Mussolini may have been more an expression of national pride than an endorsement of fascist principles—a pride that was perhaps in part a reaction to nativism, and a pride that Mussolini was expert at exploiting. It must also be recognized that American support for Mussolini in the prewar era was hardly confined to Americans of Italian descent. Until fairly late in the game, Mussolini was regarded by prominent American politicians and intellectuals as a positive force in Italy and, internationally, a useful bulwark against the spread of communism.[36] In any event, Pearl Harbor put a firm stop to any lingering condonation. During the war, Vittorini used his public stature to support the American war effort. In radio announcements he expressed regret at the conflict between Italy and the United States, but he reminded Italian American citizens of their loyalty to the United States, encouraging them to buy U.S. war bonds.

Over the years Penn has celebrated its connection to Vittorini in several different ways. A 1978 memo written for Penn's Arts and Sciences dean in anticipation of a visit by the Italian ambassador refers to Vittorini as "THE great Italian presence on the campus in recent decades."[37] Letters from Penn's development office soliciting donations—from Henry Salvatori, for instance—make frequent reference to Vittorini's memory. In the years following his death, a Vittorini Scholarship encouraged careers in teaching and researching Italian language and culture. And since 1979, the Vittorini Prize has been awarded to Penn students for excellence in Italian coursework.

Finally, there is the important and surprising story of Mariano DiVito. Though he immigrated to Philadelphia at the same time as those so far considered, DiVito's tale is quite different. He was not a member of Circolo Italiano. Nor was he a student or teacher at Penn—or at any other university. Even so, DiVito played a crucial role in solidifying Penn's scholarly connection to Italy.

DiVito immigrated as a child from the town of Fallo in Abruzzo in 1907—one year earlier than Salvatori, from a spot about thirty miles to the southeast of Salvatori's origin. He landed in Philadelphia at age twelve and over the next several decades worked his way up from newsboy to the manager of the vast staff at the Bellevue Strattford on Broad Street. DiVito oversaw the Bellevue during its reign as one of the country's preeminent hotels, when its guests routinely included queens, presidents, and other prominent personages.[38]

DiVito was apparently as good at managing his savings as he was at managing the Bellevue. He also had a keen interest in Italian culture and a deep fondness for Philadelphia. When he passed away in 1987 at the age of ninety-two, he left $1.25 million to Penn to endow a professorship in Italian studies. After almost a decade of fits and starts, and with much prompting and guidance from Dr. Edmund Forte and other prominent Italian Americans, Penn filled the position by appointing Dr. Millicent Marcus, a respected scholar of Italian literature and film. Marcus held the position for its first seven years. In a letter to Forte upon receiving the appointment, she writes that she is delighted to be "moving to a city with a large and dynamic Italian American community" where her "commitment to spread the wealth and beauty of the Italian cultural heritage will be supported by two constituencies—one within the University and one within the citizenry of Pennsylvania—each of which can reinforce and enrich the other in profound ways."[39]

CONCLUSION

In Penn's early years, establishing a connection with Italy required some persistence. Among the first endeavors was the university's attempt, frustrated in the end, to forge a connection with the Da Ponte family, those ambassador-entrepreneurs of Italian language and culture in early nineteenth-century America. More fruitful, though also somewhat fraught, was the Penn Museum's procurement of Etruscan tomb groups as that institution was just beginning its long and continuing career as a leading institution of its kind.

The most lasting, significant, and successful connections between Italy and Penn, however, may turn out to be those that required of the university no extraordinary measures, nothing beyond its core mission. These are the students of Italian birth or descent that have passed through Penn, nurtured and coached by faculty like Vittorini, before being launched on successful careers—starting with the children of the great wave of Italian immigration and continuing to the present day.

ACKNOWLEDGMENTS

With special thanks to Mark Frazier Lloyd (director, University Archives and Records Center, University of Pennsylvania) and Alessandro Pezzati (senior archivist, University of Pennsylvania Museum of Archaeology and Anthropology).

NOTES

1. Richardson, p. 224.
2. Duggan, pp. 87–116 ably summarize these events.
3. Ragusa, pp. 276–277 mention a few such individuals.

4. See, generally, Lorenzo Da Ponte, *Memoirs*; Ragusa, p. 275 suggests a skeptical reading.

5. See Lorenzo Da Ponte, *Memoirs*, p. 386, and Hodges, Chapter 7 for a description of these events.

6. Hodges, p. 214.

7. *Philadelphia Inquirer.*

8. Washington College.

9. Lorenzo L. Da Ponte, *Letter to the Trustees.*

10. University of Pennsylvania, Website of the University Archives, http://www.archives .upenn.edu/histy/features/1700s/charter1791.html; Lorenzo Da Ponte, *Memoirs*, p. 468; Hodges, p. 198.

11. Da Ponte, *Memoirs*, pp. 438–439 (see especially translator's note).

12. Hodges, pp. 206–207, 211.

13. Dallet (pages unnumbered).

14. Burt and Davies, p. 500; Pezzati, p. 6; Danien and King, p. 41.

15. Pezzati, p. 8; Danien and King, pp. 38–40, 43; see generally Van Ness.

16. Beard, pp. 196–198.

17. See generally Hall.

18. Bule, pp. 312–314; DePuma, p. 220; Sparkes, p. 21.

19. DePuma, pp. 220, 223; Potter, pp. 916–921; Dohan, p. 1.

20. Rosasco, p. 31.

21. Rosasco, p. 40.

22. Rosasco, p. 52, note 243.

23. Rosasco, p. 40.

24. Dohan, pp. 2, 3; White et al., p. 2.

25. Dohan, p. 2.

26. DePuma, p. 222; Davison, p. 4.

27. University of Pennsylvania, Website of the Penn Museum, https://www.penn.museum /on-view/galleries-exhibitions/etruscan-gallery.

28. Burt and Davies, p. 490.

29. Burt and Davies, p. 490.

30. Unless otherwise noted, the information on the individuals discussed in this section comes from their respective files at University of Pennsylvania Archives and Records Center, generously made available to the author by director Mark Frazier Lloyd.

31. Holpin and Robinson, p. 125.

32. Saxon.

33. Fucilla, p. 78.

34. Fucilla, pp. 78–79.

35. Fucilla, p. 77.

36. Diggins, pp. 82–83, 106 et seq; see generally, Migone and also Tooze.

37. Dallet (pages unnumbered).

38. See generally Forte.

39. Forte, p. 12.

SELECTED BIBLIOGRAPHY

Baxter, Kathleen, Larry Rose, Valentina Follo, and Alessandro Pezzati. "Arthur L. Frothingham Records from the Etruscan Tomb Groups Excavation." University of Pennsylvania,

Penn Museum Archives, July 2009, last updated March 1, 2017, http://hdl.library.upenn
.edu/1017/d/ead/upenn_museum_PUMu1040

Beard, Mary. *SPQR: A History of Ancient Rome*. New York: Liveright, 2016.

Bolt, Rodney. *The Librettist of Venice: The Remarkable Life of Lorenzo Da Ponte, Mozart's Poet, Casanova's Friend, and Italian Opera's Impresario in America*. New York: Bloomsbury, 2006.

Bule, Steven. "Etruscan Echoes in Italian Renaissance Art." In *Etruscan Italy: Etruscan Influences on the Civilizations of Italy from Antiquity to the Modern Era*, edited by John F. Hall, pp. 307–336. Provo, UT: Museum of Art, Brigham Young University, 1997.

Burt, Nathaniel, and Wallace E. Davies. "The Iron Age, 1876–1905." In *Philadelphia: A 300-Year History*, edited by Russell F. Weigley, Nicholas B. Wainwright, and Edwin Wolf II, pp. 471–523. New York: W.W. Norton, 1982.

Dallet, F. J. "Penn and the Italians," attached to Memorandum to John S. Price, Jerre Mangione, and Judge Lisa Richette, November 30, 1978, available from Penn Archives.

Danien, Elin C., and Eleanor M. King. "Unsung Visionary: Sara Yorke Stevenson and the Development of Archaeology in Philadelphia." In *Philadelphia and the Development of the Americanist Archaeology*, edited by Don D. Fowler and David R Wilcox, pp. 36–47. Tuscaloosa: University of Alabama Press, 2003.

Da Ponte, Durant. "Whitman's 'Young Fellow Named Da Ponte.'" *Walt Whitman Review* 5 (1959): 16–17.

Da Ponte, Lorenzo. *Memoirs*. Translated by Elizabeth Abbott. New York: New York Review of Books, 2000.

Da Ponte, Lorenzo L. "Letter to the Trustees of the University of Pennsylvania," June 17, 1830, available from Penn Archives.

Davison, Jean M. *Seven Italic Tomb-Groups from Narce*. Firenze: Leo S. Olschki, 1972.

DePuma, Richard D. "The Etruscan Legacy: Early Collecting and Bucchero Pots." *Archaeology* 29, no. 4 (October 1976): 220–228.

Diggins, John Patrick. *Mussolini and Fascism: The View from America*. Princeton, NJ: Princeton University Press, 1972.

Dohan, Edith Hall. *Italic Tomb-Groups in the University Museum*. Philadelphia: University of Pennsylvania Press, 1942.

Duggan, Christopher. *A Concise History of Italy*. Cambridge: Cambridge University Press, 1994.

The Evening Post, August 4, 1929, p. 1.

Forte, Edmund J. "The University of Pennsylvania Makes an Appointment to the Marian DiVito Professorship in Italian Studies: After a Nine Year Delay and Intervention by the Dante Commission on Education/Culture of the Grand Lodge of Pennsylvania." Undated manuscript on file with author.

Fucilla, Joseph G. "In Memoriam: Domenico Vittorini." *Italica* (June 1958): 77–82.

Harrsch, Mary. Photo: "Etruscan Faliscan Commanders Crested Helmet 8th Century BCE." Photographed at the University of Pennsylvania Museum of Archaeology and Anthropology on September 17, 2005. https://www.flickr.com/photos/44124324682@N01/58268051.

Hodges, Sheila. *Lorenzo Da Ponte: The Life and Times of Mozart's Librettist*. Madison: University of Wisconsin Press, 2002.

Holpin, Nicole, and Ron Robinson. *Funding Fathers: The Unsung Heroes of the Conservative Movement*. Washington, DC: Regnery, 2008.

Kaminski, Alyssa. "Etruscan Helmet [Object of the Day #72]." Penn Museum Blog, September 27, 2012. https://www.penn.museum/blog/collection/125th-anniversary-object-of-the-day/etruscan-helmet-object-of-the-day-72/.

Lesko, Barbara S. "Sara Yorke Stevenson 1847–1922" (PDF). https://www.brown.edu/Research/Breaking_Ground/bios/Stevenson_Sara%20Yorke.pdf.

Levi, Carlo. *Christ Stopped at Eboli: The Story of a Year.* Translated by Frances Frenaye. New York: Farrar, Straus and Giroux, 2006.

Migone, Gian Giacomo. *The United States and Fascist Italy: The Rise of American Finance in Europe.* Translated by Molly Tambor. Cambridge: Cambridge University Press, 2015.

Pezzati, Alessandro, with Jane Hickman and Alexandra Fleischman. "A Brief History of the Penn Museum." *Expedition* 54, no. 3, accessed January 2018. http://www.penn.museum/documents/publications/expedition/pdfs/54-3/a_brief_history.pdf.

The Philadelphia Inquirer, January 9, 1830, p. 2.

Potter, T. W. "Dennis of Etruria: A Celebration." *Antiquity* 72, no. 278 (December 1998): 916–921.

Ragusa, Olga. "Lorenzo Da Ponte at Columbia College." In *Atti del Convegno Lorenzo da Ponte, librettista di Mozart: New York, Columbia University, Casa Italiana, Piccolo Teatro, 28–30 marzo 1988,* edited by Marina Maymone Siniscalchi and Paolo Spedicato, 275–283. Rome: Ministero per i beni culturali e ambientali, 1992.

Richardson, Edgar P. "The Athens of America: 1800–1825." In *Philadelphia: A 300-Year History,* edited by Russell F. Weigley et al., 208–257. New York: W. W. Norton, 1982.

Rosasco, Betsy. "The Teaching of Art and the Museum Tradition: Joseph Henry to Allan Marquand." *Record of the Art Museum, Princeton University* 55, no. 1/2 (1996): 7–52.

Saxon, Wolfgang. "Henry Salvatori, G.O.P. Adviser and Oil Company Founder, 96." *New York Times,* July 13, 1997.

Sparkes, Brian A. *The Red and the Black: Studies in Greek Pottery.* London: Routledge, 1996.

Titus Livius (Livy). *The History of Rome.* Book 1, chapter 2. Perseus Digital Library, www.perseus.tufts.edu.

Tooze, Adam. "When We Loved Mussolini." *New York Review of Books,* August 18, 2016. http://www.nybooks.com/articles/2016/08/18/when-we-loved-mussolini/.

Turfa, Jean MacIntosh. *Catalogue of the Etruscan Gallery of the University of Pennsylvania Museum of Archaeology and Anthropology.* Philadelphia: University of Pennsylvania Museum of Archaeology and Anthropology, 2005.

University of Pennsylvania. *The 1921 Record: Published by the Class of 1921.*

———. *Record of the Class of 1923.*

———. Website of Penn Arts and Sciences, Italian Studies. https://www.sas.upenn.edu/italians/, accessed December 2020.

———. Website of the University Archives and Records Center. www.archives.upenn.edu, accessed December 2020.

———. Website of the University of Pennsylvania Museum of Archaeology and Anthropology (Penn Museum). https://www.penn.museum, accessed December 2020.

USC News. "Trustee Henry Salvatori Dies at 96." September 1, 1997. https://news.usc.edu/11494/Trustee-Henry-Salvatori-Dies-at-96/.

Van Ness, Christine Moon. "The Furness-Mitchell Coterie: Its Role in Philadelphia's Intellectual Life at the Turn of the Twentieth Century." Ph.D. dissertation, University of Pennsylvania, 1985. https://repository.upenn.edu/dissertations/AAI8523463.

Vittorini, Domenico. *The Age of Dante: A Concise History of Italian Culture in the Years of the Early Renaissance.* Syracuse: Syracuse University Press, 1957.

———. *The Drama of Luigi Pirandello*. Philadelphia: University of Pennsylvania Press; London: Milford, 1935. Second edition, New York: Dover, 1957.

Wainwright, Nicholas B. "The Age of Nicholas Biddle: 1825–1841." In *Philadelphia: A 300-Year History*, edited by Russell F. Weigley et al., 258–306. New York: W. W. Norton, 1982.

Washington College. Website of the Revolutionary College Project. https://staging.washcoll.edu/centers/starr/revcollege/300years/giovanni.html, accessed December 2020.

White, Donald, Ann Blair Brownlee, Irene Bald Romano, and Jean Macintosh Turfa. *Guide to the Etruscan and Roman Worlds at the University of Pennsylvania Museum of Archaeology and Anthropology*. Philadelphia: University of Pennsylvania Museum of Archaeology and Anthropology, 2002.

VITTORINI'S *THREADS OF LIFE* LIVES ON

Pietro Frassica

Most of the Italians who immigrated to the United States within the last two centuries were limited to speaking the dialects they had grown up with in their individual regions of Italy. In contrast, Domenico Vittorini's Italian was empyrean. Vittorini spoke an Italian that resounded as a perfect academic standard taught to him by some of the most outstanding scholars (Vittorio Rossi and Cesare De Lollis) at the University of Rome. Such an impeccable knowledge of Italian perhaps granted him great success in teaching and scholarship, but it also vested him with a cosmopolitanism, diffusing his influence beyond the boundaries of his academic career.

His Italian may be one reason why Vittorini will always be remembered for his excellent career as a professor of Italian language, literature, and culture, initially at Temple University and later at the University of Pennsylvania. Indeed, he left an industrious and indelible mark on the cultural life of Philadelphia.

Apart from his teaching career, Vittorini's critical essays on Dante and Pirandello will always be valued as his significant contribution to his academic field. Vittorini's essay on Pirandello's literary corpus deserves particular attention for his innovative analysis and interpretation. His book *The Drama of Luigi Pirandello* is among the first comprehensive studies about the Sicilian author. Although today, nearly one hundred years after its publication, to some it may appear somewhat passé due to the critical and theoretical shift of recent Pirandello scholarship, at the time of its publication this four-hundred-page volume stood as a monolith of literary criticism.

It should also be remembered that Pirandello himself was so impressed by Vittorini's interpretation that he wrote a humorous and theatrical letter as a foreword to the book. Over the years, the acute observations of the playwright—elucidated by this letter—had been essential in clarifying many aspects of Pirandello's complex views on the human condition:

New York 30 VII 1935 XIII

Dear Vittorini,
    The world of literary criticism has been crowded with numerous Pirandellos—erratic, insane, obscure—in whom I cannot recognize myself. You too have now decided to present your own Pirandello. Indeed, you have done just the opposite of this, and as you can well

imagine, I am very grateful to you because, among many who think they
know so well what I am, I, who have no conception of what I am, find in
you one who grants me as much hearth as a I need to love and pity this
poor humanity of ours, both when it is rational and when it is irrational;
one who tries to explain that if so many believe me erratic, it is because I
move in my own way and not as others would like me to.

I have tried to tell something to other men, without any ambition,
except perhaps that of avenging myself for having been born. And yet life,
in spite of all that it has made me suffer, is so beautiful!

I thank you for the mirror of this book which you place before me, in
which I can behold myself with so much gratification.

Pirandello

Besides his major contribution to Pirandello and Dante studies, it seems appropriate to recognize the remarkable creativity that emerged during the latter years
of Vittorini's life. In this respect, one should remember that his collection of Italian
folktales, initially titled *Old Italian Tales for Children*, was published in 1957, just
one year before his death.

Although this book is far removed from his critical works such as *The Age of
Dante*, *The Drama of Luigi Pirandello*, and *The Modern Italian Novel*, it merits recognition simply for its exemplary creativity and prose. *Old Italian Tales for Children*
reveals how successfully he can shift from the serious studies of his scholarship
(Dante and Pirandello) to a more imaginative way of writing. This shift may ultimately reveal his ambition to elaborate a new and modern literary form. The collection of twelve folktales is not merely a transcription or translation of old fables;
Vittorini recreates the stories with an original and creative touch. The stories reproduced in the collection are well known (for instance, Cinderella) and are mostly
set in small villages that are intentionally unrecognizable—all of the details of the
masterfully executed collection by Vittorini are successful in captivating today's
young readers. When Vittorini cites these old tales, it is as if each word invites
the reader to find new expressions. It is a style that stimulates the imagination to
think beyond the mere words on the page; perhaps these are the reasons the book
was reissued in 1995 under the new title *The Threads of Life*. This version notably
includes artwork by renowned artist Mary GrandPré, famous for her illustrations
of the Harry Potter series.

From a faraway Italian land, such folktales filled with wisdom have found their
way to America—thanks to this creative scholar, whose imaginative insight has
given these stories an entirely new audience.

26

Dr. Gonnella's Journey from the Mountains of Basilicata to the Medical Wards of Philadelphia

SALVATORE MANGIONE

PHILADELPHIA OCCUPIES AN IMPORTANT PLACE in American medical history. It was here that the first hospital was established in 1751 (the Pennsylvania Hospital), the first anatomy school in 1762, the first medical school in 1765 (the Medical College of Philadelphia), the oldest medical society in 1787 (the College of Physicians of Philadelphia), the first mental hospital in 1813 (Friends Hospital), the first pharmacy college in 1821 (Philadelphia College of Pharmacy), the first eye hospital in 1832 (Will's Eye), the first women's medical school in 1850 (Female Medical College of Pennsylvania), and the first pediatric hospital in 1855 (Children's Hospital of Philadelphia). Soon a student at the Medical School of the University of Pennsylvania could justifiably boast to a Bostonian friend that Philadelphia was "decidedly the city of the Union for doctors."[1]

Still, the Italian American contribution to medicine became evident only in the second half of the twentieth century; in fact, it almost parallels the personal journey of the protagonist of this chapter. Thus, the life of Giuseppe Salvatore Gonnella is an inspiring Philadelphia story, a wonderful piece of Americana, and a great example of how Italians have enriched medicine. It's also a sort of "hero's journey," as Joseph Campbell described it in 1949: a wondrous inner and outer adventure, full of challenges, discoveries, and guides.[2]

Born in 1934 in Pescopagano, a hamlet of 2,000 souls in the mountains of Basilicata, Joe was separated at birth from his father, who was forced to return to the United States for work. Then, the outbreak of the Spanish Civil War, the Italian invasion of Ethiopia, and ultimately World War II caused Joe to be raised in Italy by his mother and grandparents before eventually reuniting with his father at age twelve. He knew no English, but in less than six years he was at Dartmouth to earn his AB, then at Harvard to complete his medical education, and lastly in Chicago

Dean of Jefferson Joe Gonnella, painted by Dean L. Paules, on display at the Bluemle Life Sciences Building of Thomas Jefferson University. (Painted by: Dean L. Paules/Permission granted by Thomas Jefferson University)

to train in internal medicine. Dr. Gonnella came to Philadelphia in the mid-1960s to work in the dean's office of Hahnemann, but by 1967 he had already moved to Jefferson Medical College, where in 1984 he became one of the longest-serving deans in American medical history. Dr. Gonnella has enjoyed an amazing career as a researcher, administrator, and inspiring role model. He has received multiple awards and honorary degrees, including the prestigious Flexner Award from the Association of American Medical Colleges. He has forged international bonds among medical schools and studied the relationship between knowledge, capabilities, and clinical performance. He has also created instruments widely used to evaluate educational programs, measure severity of illness, and assess quality of care and costs. Yet, as a sort of Johnny Appleseed of medicine, Dr. Gonnella has primarily served as a talent scout. Finding and nurturing bright young people—many from Italy—has been his lifelong passion. One could even say that without Dr. Gonnella, the role played by Italian physicians in Philadelphia would have been very different. I know this from personal experience, since I was lucky enough to run into Joe as a wide-eyed medical student in Rome. Dr. Gonnella had come to Italy to give a lecture, and that was his first time back in thirty years. So, he was thrilled. But he was also Joe and thus generous with his time and wisdom. That encounter changed my life. Like me, many young and bright Italians were similarly touched.

I recently spent several hours talking with Dr. Gonnella, who is now eighty-four but still traveling the world to offer wisdom and advice. Since I have an interest in understanding creative genius, I tried to unlock the secrets that made him such an effective educator and leader. I tried to deconstruct Joe. This is not idle curiosity, since medicine has been accused of curbing creativity. If we could understand what makes creative people tick and then nurture those traits in our educational practices, we might be able to produce more creative physicians. A close look at Dr. Gonnella's personal history reminds us of the benefits of adversity, the advantages of being an outsider, and the blessings of unconditional love and humor. Lastly, his story provides a sweeping panorama of fifty years of Philadelphia medicine, plus the revisiting of some crucial themes in the immigrant's experience.

You have blue eyes, a light complexion, and fair hair. Are you sure you are a southern Italian?

As you know, lots of people have honored our South by visiting it over the centuries. Greeks, Romans, Germans, Byzantines, Arabs, Normans, French, Spanish, and lately even the Americans have all come and left genes. My Gonnella ancestors were from the Italian northwest. Some went to Florence and in the process either dropped one *n* (becoming *Gonella*) or acquired a *u* (becoming *Gunnella*). From Florence they went to Rome and became bankers and diplomats. Finally, some went to Benevento and became architects. It was that branch of the family which was invited to Pescopagano in the early 1700s, since an earthquake had destroyed the local church and my great-great-great-grandfather was asked to rebuild it. He brought his wife, fell in love with the town, and decided to stay. Later the Gonnellas became stonemasons, and that's what my grandfather and father were: talented craftsmen. In many ways, I too became a builder, but of people.[3]

Pescopagano has a time-honored history that goes back to the Greeks, the Samnites, and the Punic Wars, yet it's also a small "paese sulla collina." What was it like growing up there?

I had none of today's distractions: no TV, no smartphones, and no Internet. But I had a mother who valued culture, and I had Suora Emilia. She was a Franciscan nun, very tough but very loving, and she was probably my most influential teacher. She took only five boys, all children of her former students, and she taught me throughout elementary school. She made me work really hard (I even read

Homer!), but she also gave me a lifelong love for books. My two maternal uncles also enriched my education. One taught physics in Perugia but came home during the summer, while the other was a geometer who prepared me for the admission exam to Ginnasio. I took it in Avellino, and that was my first time out of Pescopagano. We left in the morning with my grandfather, mother, and a driver. If you passed that exam, you went to study in a convent near Castellamare di Stabia, but then we came to America, and so that was the end of my Italian education. Teachers play a fundamental role during the formative years, and Suora Emilia was that kind of teacher. When I went back to Italy in 1976, she had already died, but what an enormous influence! Still, I didn't only study; I also played soccer. One time I fell on a rock and got a nasty laceration. The local GP stitched it, but that led to a bad infection. Thank God my grandfather took me to a certain Dr. Orlando, who didn't practice much but was distinguished and wise. He immediately realized the problem, opened the wound, and saved my life. Maybe it was Dr. Orlando who first gave me the idea of becoming a physician.

You were born in 1934, a very good year for Italy. We won the World Cup, Pirandello won his Nobel Prize, and Fermi carried out the experiment that led to his own Nobel. Here in the U.S. the mint restarted production of the beautiful Peace Silver Dollar, which Italian immigrant Antonio De Francisci had based on his Neapolitan wife, Teresa. Yet for you 1934 was the year that your father left for America before you were even born. Adversities are not uncommon in the life of brilliant people (your fellow paesano Horace used to muse that "adversity reveals genius, prosperity conceals it"), yet what did it feel like?

It forced me to grow up with my grandparents, and that was the best thing that could have ever happened. My paternal grandfather had emigrated to America in 1898, worked in construction, and returned to Italy in 1924 with fifty thousand dollars. And so my mother, sister, and I lived in his big house, where he even built a terrace for me so that I could ride my tricycle. Underneath he made his wine, and we all stayed together. Yet my maternal grandparents were only a mile away, and so I saw them almost every day. We also had a maid, Carmela, who took me to school in winter by holding me in her arms. My two maternal uncles were a presence too, and so was a paternal uncle. Plus, there were cousins. So I had lots of love and lots of father figures. I still had an absent father, though, and I often wondered whether I suffered or gained. The plus was that I spent a lot of time with my grandparents, and that was a gift. If you look at the animal world, the father gives you the physical strength, but it's the grandparents that give you unconditional love and wisdom. My maternal grandfather was a notary with a planning mind. He would have made a great chess player. My paternal grandfather was instead an extrovert who loved life and loved people. I see both traits in me.

Then at twelve you go to Naples, board a ship, and leave for the U.S. What do you remember?

We left in May 1946 on the first American transport bringing civilians. My most vivid memory has to do with my favorite dessert: apples dipped in wine. The first day on board, I looked down into the kitchen and saw a big pot with what I assumed were wine and apples. I was eager to taste it, but then I ate the stuff and realized that it was *beets*. Since then I've always hated beets. I guess that was my first disillusionment.

What was it like meeting your father?

Odd. Our relation was limited. I was twelve when I first saw him and eighteen when I left for college. He was kind and firm but not very warm. Yet he was a provider, and so when he knew we were arriving he did something astute: he put us in Mountainside, New Jersey—a town with no Italian Americans. That forced us to learn English. Then through the Red Cross he got us summer tutors, so that by September I knew enough English to be placed in fifth grade. My father had only an elementary school diploma, but he valued education. Yet my mother valued it even more. She was the one who was never satisfied with our achievements. Her love was full of expectations. You had to make something of yourself.

Who were your role models in the U.S.?

They were my teachers. From the very beginning, I *loved* culture, the power of ideas and the capacity to dream. I also loved how books make you *travel*. Still, my great love was diplomacy. One of my heroes was Marco Polo, and if I had stayed in Italy I would have undoubtedly gone into either medicine or diplomacy.

How was college?

Not easy. It was my first time away, and I felt lonely. I still remember my first meal in the cafeteria: pasta on a steel tray with a scoop of mashed potatoes and a glass of milk. It was a culture shock. But then adversity provides resilience, since if you can survive you'll become a better person. I wanted to be a doctor, but I also wanted to be a *cultivated* doctor. In Dartmouth there was a young history teacher who nurtured my love for history. There was also a brilliant refugee from Nazi Germany who nurtured my love for math and problem-solving. And so my education was not mainstream premed but included history, current events, critical thinking, the art of debating, plus lots of competition. Then for the clinical years I went to Harvard, and there I had wonderful teachers too. In surgery I rotated through Boston City Hospital, where I did my first appendectomy under Dr. Dunphy, a giant of American surgery. Yet it was residency that shaped my life.

Did you ever feel discriminated against, either in college or medical school?

I never felt inferior. If they tried to make me feel like that, I didn't give them a chance: I was always an honor student. And I was very proud of being Italian.

Of course, the first time I was called a "wop"[4] I felt insulted, but instead of getting angry I reacted by getting smarter and better. Plus, being an outsider gave me two different viewpoints, and that was a big strength.

You went to medical school thinking of becoming a GP but then ended up in academia. How?

I initially wanted to be a practicing internist, which I saw as the pinnacle of medicine. Yet in residency I met a few mentors who saw in me something I hadn't seen and gave me an opportunity to develop it. That is why teachers are so important. My first attending at the University of Illinois was Dr. Kellow, who later became dean at Hahnemann and brought me to Philly. Another important mentor was Dr. Roberg, who as vice-chairman of the department of medicine chose me as chief resident. That chief year was so seductive that I gave up my plans of becoming a practicing physician and instead pursued a fellowship in medical education. So, Dr. Roberg changed my life. Later we became good friends. He had married a brilliant Roman socialite, and they were in love. When he retired from medicine, they moved to Rome and lived near Campo di Fiori. They had no children, and his wife was his world. So when she died he became so heartbroken that two weeks later he committed suicide. He was a good man.

How did your parents react to your decision of going into academia?

They had mixed feelings. They were proud, of course, but to them the only real doctor was a practicing physician. For years I tried to convince them I was still a doctor, but then gave up.

Famed Italian American bioethicist Edmund Pellegrino used to say that a well-rounded physician must be competent, compassionate, and cultured. What do you think makes a good physician?

I actually knew Dr. Pellegrino. Curiously enough, his family came from Calitri, which is only seven miles away from Pescopagano. And even more curiously, he and I went on to win the prestigious Flexner Award on two consecutive years, which is remarkable but not much considering that the first medical school in the world was in nearby Salerno. I guess some propensity for medicine must have lingered in the genetic pool. As for what makes a good doctor, I agree with the need for personal traits, but to me a good physician has also to be a detective, a teacher, and a manager. That is the framework I've used for my research and also the kind of framework I've used for recruiting people.

How did you get to help so many Italian physicians?

The opportunity came only when I had power and thus a chance to exercise influence. I was an associate dean when I was asked to do an accreditation for the New York Polyclinic Medical School, and that's how I met its dean, Dr. Colosi. We immediately liked each other. Natale was born in Messina, and his father owned lemon groves. But after his father's death, Colosi had to take care of the family. So he came to New York, went to college, became a microbiologist, and ultimately dean. He was also cofounder and dean of the Institute of Continuing Biomedical Education, which prepared foreign medical graduates to work in the U.S. That is how I first got back to Italy in 1976. Natale had got himself involved with the medical schools of Perugia, Bologna, and Rome, and through him I made important connections, including Professor Manzoli, director of the Istituto Superiore di Sanità, and later Dr. Francesco Taroni. Together we were able to create collaborative projects that eventually opened the floodgate for the arrival of many Italian researchers. I was then able to recruit Carlo Croce, and Carlo brought so many Italians to Jefferson that in our research building the most spoken language was Italian. I also traveled extensively, since in the same way as American physicians of the 1800s had to go to Germany and France to learn their trade, now it's our turn to help others. I'm very proud that I was able to influence medical education in Japan, China, Malaysia, and Portugal.

You epitomize the concept of servant leadership. Can you elaborate?

Maybe it was my grandfathers' influence that made me interested in people. Still, I've always drawn satisfaction from helping others become the best they can be. In this regard, power is just a mean to a larger end. Power per se is instead self-defeating, since in order to lead you need to earn *trust*. And that only happens when people know that you are there to help them.

Part of your charm is self-deprecating humor. Were you born like that?

No, I developed it. Maybe being an immigrant taught me the importance of defusing conflict, since if you choose to attack, your options are limited: you either kill or you let the enemy escape. Yet humor is a wonderful tool to defuse tension. And so I developed it.

How has medicine changed in the past fifty years?

In some ways I don't see progress but regression. Technology has now started to interfere with how we interact with students, and that is a mistake. We have become so seduced by simulation to believe we can replace the teacher. Yet technology can only *assist*. Ultimately, what is needed in medical education remains the direct connection between student and teacher. Medicine has also become *larger* but in many ways *narrower*, and that is another mistake. Lastly, our obsession with guidelines, algorithms, pathways, and electronic medical records is killing critical thinking. And that is another big mistake.

Your office has many pictures; which is your favorite?

My picture with Joe DiMaggio. When I came to America, I learned English from school and private tutors but also by listening to Mel Allen's baseball radio

Joe and Joe—Dr. Gonnella with DiMaggio in 1989.
(Photograph provided by Dr. Giuseppe Gonnella)

broadcasts. Of course, being Italian, I became very proud of the Italian players. And since I lived close to New York, I became a fan of Phil Rizzuto, Yogi Berra, and above all Joe DiMaggio. I loved Joe, and in 1989 I was finally able to dine with him. I felt like a teenager!

NOTES

1. Steven J. Peitzman, "City of Medicine," *The Encyclopedia of Greater Philadelphia*, https://philadelphiaencyclopedia.org/archive/city-of-medicine/.

2. Joseph Campbell, *The Hero with a Thousand Faces* (New York: Pantheon Books, 1949).

3. Probably the most famous Italian stonemasons in the United States were the Piccirillis: a Tuscan family of a father and six sons who fought for Garibaldi and then went on to carve many American landmarks, including the colossal statue of Abraham Lincoln in the Lincoln Memorial, the lions of the New York Public Library, much of the Washington Square Arch in New York, and the Tomb of the Unknown Soldier in Arlington Cemetery.

4. A racial slur aimed at people of Italian heritage. Probably from the Neapolitan *guappo*, i.e., "ruffian."

27

Temple University and
Its Italian Connection

JUDITH GOODE

TEMPLE'S MAJOR CONNECTIONS TO ITALY STEM from two historic moments: the founding in 1884 and the initiation of campuses abroad toward the end of the twentieth century. The founding was based on Russell Conwell's vision of an institution that would provide access to education to the working class of the expanding industrial city. Italian immigrants were one population served. Temple University Rome, founded in 1965, was the first campus abroad and has linked Philadelphia to Italy in many significant ways for over fifty years. Through the Rome campus, Temple has created links between individual faculty, students, alumni, and their families as well as administrators and trustees who move back and forth and establish lifelong contacts in Italy while expanding the flow of ideas and cultural practices. Campus activities also link institutions in Philadelphia and Italy.

Temple was founded to provide uplift and opportunity for the new industrial working class. Its founder, Russell Conwell, a Baptist minister, was a famous motivational speaker whose "Acres of Diamonds" speech promoted the view that the city was full of aspiring people such as immigrants from Europe and offspring of farmers and miners from Pennsylvania and New Jersey. Analogous to unpolished nuggets (diamonds in the rough), they could be polished into educated professionals and managers needed in the expanding metropolis with its growing economy. Making higher education accessible required keeping tuition and fees at a minimum, and the speech was used to raise funds.

James Hilty, in his comprehensive volume *Temple University: 125 Years of Service to Philadelphia, the Nation and the World*, describes Conwell as a tireless fundraiser who approached well-known Philadelphia philanthropists such as John Wanamaker and Anthony Drexel for his educational mission, but in most cases, he was not suc-

"Acres of Diamonds" was a famous lecture used by Russell Conwell, the founder of Temple University, to raise funds for the education and uplift of the urban working class. His mission was to create an accessible institution for higher education of the children of industrial workers. Metaphorically, he spoke of potential students as diamonds in the rough who could be found in the neighborhoods of the city and polished into professionals and managers. (Temple University Press)

cessful. Wanamaker became a benefactor of the Penn Archeology and Anthropology museum (see Chapter 10), and Drexel founded his own university with a similar mission to Temple's.

Temple is a recent institution in comparison to Penn. Temple graduated its first class in 1892 at a time when Penn was going through its second period of revitalization and Pepper and Stevenson were developing the Penn Museum (see Chapter 25). Temple's foundation was built by Russell Conwell, who especially relied on Laura Carnell as an administrator and leader as they joined a national trend to develop urban schools to provide local professionals.

While Penn saw itself as a venerable, prestigious school competing for the sons of the East Coast national elite and preparing its graduates for the higher tiers of management and professional practice, Temple was one of many schools founded in the late nineteenth century that aimed to train local professional practitioners not only in traditional academic fields such as medicine and law but also the newer credentialed fields such as teaching, pharmacy, dentistry, and management. From the beginning, Temple recruited the children of the working class and immigrants, whose parents often had little formal education. They offered degrees attainable through night school as well as day school, and they charged much less than other schools, which made constant fundraising an absolute necessity.

The 1880–1920 wave of Italian immigration had been represented at Penn by the Circolo Italiano in the 1920s (Chapter 25). A parallel Circolo Italiano was also active at Temple in the decade before World War II. Many Temple faculty held doctorates from Penn, which might explain the parallels. In fact, Dr. Domenico Vittorini, who sponsored Il Circolo at Penn, taught at Temple in 1918–1919 and may have played a role in establishing the club. In the 1928 yearbook, *Templar*, a page is devoted to the Circolo. There are fifty-four members, seventeen of whom are women. All have Italian surnames, while the two male faculty advisors do not. Below the picture, a statement tells us,

> *Il Circolo Italiano* was organized for social and literary purposes. For the acquisition by its members of a better knowledge of the Italian tongue, and for the development of a spirit of amity among the students of Italian parentage. The Circolo made rapid progress in all these aims and in athletics. In the season of 1925 the Circolo won the Intramural League Championship in basketball and baseball.

In the 1930s, a Circolo Italiano existed at the College of Pharmacy with seventeen members, all male. At the same time, the undergraduate group was coed.

In 1965, Temple (and the University of Pittsburgh) became state related, joining Penn State, already a state-affiliated land grant institution. This was Pennsylvania's response to the demand for state investment in a more accessible system of universities engendered by the educational benefits of the GI Bill of Rights to meet the demand of postwar economic growth and the need to absorb the mass of returning veterans. This period of state investment saw a burst of building expansion for labs, classrooms, and dormitories as Temple aspired to become a residential campus with an enhanced academic appearance (new architecture and landscaping) to replace the original repurposed structures. However, in a period of economic retrenchment in the 1970s, state investment began to shrink; today, it is less than 20 percent of the total budget. In its public role, Temple continued to serve a diverse, regional population of mostly first-generation college students.

TEMPLE ROME

Temple at this transformative moment also launched an early and successful push toward global study abroad for students and increased recruitment of international students in Philadelphia. Encouraging the early entry into global education was the new university president, Marvin Wachman, who, in his 2005 autobiography, *The Education of a University President*, describes how his experience while serving as a U.S. postwar military attaché had engendered his interest in internationalism and education for global citizenship. Under his stewardship, Temple established campuses in Rome and Tokyo. Wachman's successor, Peter Liacouras, was equally enthusiastic about international education and expanded the number of campuses abroad.

Beginning in 1965, connections were forged with Italy as a result of the development of a Temple University campus in Rome (henceforth, TUR). In the first years, the campus was part of the Tyler School of Arts. The concentration in the arts resembled the traditional elite school "semester abroad" idea, which resembled the grand tour goals of acquiring aesthetic discernment and inspiration from the old masters. As public higher education expanded access to first-generation college students, in the postwar 1960s, Temple's program became an early attempt to democratize access to opportunities to study abroad.

In the beginning, TUR was the initiative of Dean Charles LeClair of Temple's Tyler School of Art, who gained support from President Wachman and the trustees. LeClair, a grandson of French-speaking immigrants, originally planned to develop the Tyler extension in Paris, but during a brief trip to Rome while on sabbatical in France, he was inspired by the friendliness he found in Italy and relocated the planned campus to Rome. He reports, "In spite of my physical heritage, I felt my soul was Italian."[1]

The first group of students numbered thirty-six. They arrived in Italy by boat in 1966, before the era of mass commercial aviation. Today, as many as 650 students have studied at TUR in one year. Originally a small and intimate community of art history majors and artists or architects in training, the costly program often recruited students from elite schools. But over time, scholarships supported by program alumni and the university made this opportunity more available to first-generation college students. The curriculum also expanded to include skills for cosmopolitan global participation, international business, law, governance, and multinational and global institutions (NGOs) and contemporary issues such as immigration.

Critical to the success of TUR is its continuous home, the Villa Caproni, located on the Tiber near the Piazza de Popolo and the Spanish steps, and the relationship with the Caproni family.

Reflecting on the early days, LeClair talks about the luck of encountering the Caproni family—"an unusual family with an interest in modern art" whom he credits with the program's success. The villa was owned by Count Gianni Caproni de Talcedo, who developed and manufactured airplanes in the 1920s. A propeller from one of his two-engine planes greets people at the door of the villa. A new twenty-year lease was recently signed, extending TUR's location in the villa to seven decades. Over the first fifty years, the villa's teaching facilities including classrooms, studios, and labs have been remodeled twice, both times using Italian designers and architects. The contessa and principessa, daughters of the count, still live in part of the villa and maintain cordial relationships and mutual interests with the program.

By the 2000s, TUR had developed a critical mass of alumni and had become recognized as one of the earliest and largest study-abroad programs in Rome. The celebrations of the fortieth anniversary made this network visible through events in the academic year 2006–2007. The fiftieth anniversary in 2016–2017 marked success through a well-attended yearlong series of events in both Philadelphia and Rome. Today, TUR continues its influence in old and new art practices, including filmmaking and digital photography. It is a year-round campus that offers courses in broader humanities, law, business, and even engineering and develops perma-

Villa Caproni, Temple University in Rome. (Temple University in Rome)

nent social and intellectual connections to Rome, Italy, and the broader Mediterranean basin as well as EU and UN agencies.

The individual Philadelphia-Italy connections built over five decades are personal and professional. They were forged and carried back and forth by students and their families as well as by faculty. The stories of alumni and faculty captured in the annual *Postcard*, a newsletter for alumni, showcase a maintenance of interest in Italy through prolonged residence, continued language learning, and frequent trips and visiting. Many met their spouses in Italy. Alumni often continue their connections to TUR by sending their children there and visiting them frequently. A parents' weekend at TUR also brings families to Rome who have never traveled abroad, making them familiar with Italy.

Many TUR alumni and U.S. faculty living in Rome have gained the knowledge and the language and culture skills for careers as diplomats, experts on Italy in many economic and political fields, and key actors in the burgeoning Italian sites for U.S. study-abroad programs. In addition, a vast number of TUR alumni are producers of multiple forms of art, from painting to digital photography and filmmaking. They too may live in Italy or move back and forth, creating ongoing connections and new worldviews. This experience has been very important to those students who had never left the country or even the state of Pennsylvania before coming to Temple. Other alumni and faculty met their spouses and stayed in Italy, returned to the United States, or moved back and forth, bridging two worlds. Similarly, many students develop strong ties to Italian friends and visit each other regularly.

Exhibition of Temple University Rome Faculty (a Ciao Philadelphia event),
October 2016. This exhibit, located in the Tyler School of Art Atrium foyer, is just one
event in the year-long celebration of the fiftieth anniversary, and this is the first time
Temple Rome faculty artwork is being presented at the same location. Several TU
professors in attendance with Temple University Executive Vice President and Provost
JoAnne Epps and Italian CG Andrea Canepari. (Photo: Richard Barnes)

Ribbon cutting of renovated
facilities at the fiftieth
anniversary celebration
at Rome Campus, 2015.
Third from the left is the
project architect, Cinzia
Abbate. Among others in
the picture are President
Richard M. Englert, Provost
JoAnne A. Epps, and Hilary
Link, Dean of Temple
University Rome. (Courtesy
Temple University)

Some Italian American students are drawn to TUR by their interest in heritage. Often, they rekindle their contacts with their hometowns and extended families, which were attenuated during World War II. For example, one family sent their three daughters to TUR. They were each Temple students who had never been abroad before. They visited with their Campania family and continue today to visit back and forth. A faculty member who teaches filmmaking has reconnected with his extended family in Abruzzi and returns to teach every few years so as to maintain these strengthened ties with family and place.

The alumni newsletter is full of references to how Philadelphia students are taught to make a "simple red sauce" during orientation on *la cucina Italiana*. Rosemarie Tran, a Vietnamese American from Philadelphia, remembers this lesson when she recalls her experience. Soon after the lesson, she met Gianluca Demotis, and today they are married and co-owners of a Tuscan BYOB that opened in 2003 and draws people from the mid-Atlantic region, as well as university students from Italy, to its Tuscan specialties. It features homemade pasta and wild mushrooms, and game dishes such as a favorite wild boar ragù and quail stuffed with dried fruit and nuts with pomegranate reduction.[2]

Faculty, administrators, and board members connected to TUR also forge links between themselves and colleagues at other institutions in Rome, in turn creating links between U.S. and Italian institutions such as universities, disciplines, and political and economic institutions. The first act of Dean LeClair was a gallery to display art, and for fifty years there have been continuing and expanding connections to the art, film, and photography communities through formal collaborations between schools and through explicitly comparing and discussing different art practices. Pia Cardenas, who served as the librarian for decades, organized colloquia on women's issues, among others, which brought the TUR community together with Italian intellectuals.

Rosemarie Tran and Gianluca Demotis, co-owners of Melograno. (Courtesy Rosemarie Tran)

The examples of faculty who teach often at the Rome campus include many who find research and writing inspiration in Italy and create collegial relationships with their disciplinary colleagues and collaborators throughout Rome. They bring home new knowledge and materials to enrich the main Philadelphia campus.

Professor Justin Vitiello (professor emeritus of Italian language and literature) taught for two separate multiyear periods, 1977–1979 and 1995–1997, and returned in 2003. During those times, he developed tours to ancient sites on the mainland in Sicily, his primary academic focus. Being in Italy allowed him to publish a book on Sicily and to publish a body of poems inspired there. He was able to present his work to Italian scholars as well. In 2003, he ran an International Women's Day multimedia program featuring Italian public intellectuals. In between, he brought this knowledge back to the main campus.

Professor Lawrence Venuti (English) is an internationally known scholar in translation theory—studying how differences in meaning affect the translation process. Not only was this an interesting perspective for TUR students, but living immersed in an Italian-language environment also generated new insights for his work.

Professor John Pron (architecture) taught several times at TUR and developed a lifelong and intense interest in things Italian. His two daughters later attended TUR, and he and his family visit often. In spring 2018, Pron co-organized an innovative exhibit at the Da Vinci Art Alliance, which played an important role in art training for first-generation Italian Americans (Chapter 20). The exhibit featured local artists and was called *Rocky (re)Runs*. It examined the lives and locations in Philadelphia that grounded the *Rocky* film (Chapter 31).

Alice Abreu, a law professor in the law school program in Rome, is a Cuban American who was already living a bicultural life. She not only developed scholarly relationships with Italian legal colleagues; back home in Philadelphia, she takes courses in Italian language and literature at the America-Italy Society of Philadelphia, an organization founded after World War II that provides classes and a venue for concerts, films, and other projects.

Louis Esposito, a member of the Temple Board of Trustees whose expanding family meat enterprise is discussed in Chapter 18, has helped develop the Italian connection between the South Philadelphia community, TUR, and Italy through his participation in the anniversary celebrations as well as through other fundraising events.

The following story illustrates the nature of back-and-forth travel and the maintenance of both face-to-face and virtual networks between coresearchers in the medical community and between universities in Philadelphia and Italy. In 2015, the Mayor of Rome, Ignazio Marino, was selected for the honor of presenting the provost's lecture at TUR. Mayor Marino was formerly a professor of medicine at Jefferson and head of the transplant unit. He was introduced by Antonio Giordano, the head of Sbarro Institute for Cancer Research and Molecular Medicine and the Center for Biotechnology at Temple. Giordano's work produced discoveries of the molecular mechanisms governing cell proliferation, and the institute was supported by a donation from Mario Sbarro, owner of the Sbarro restaurant chain. Giordano, who is also a professor of pathology at the University of Siena, Italy, established a solid virtual bridge connecting Italian and U.S. researchers, and this event underscored many overlapping links between Philadelphia, Rome, and medical training and research in the city (see Chapter 26).

INTENSIFYING ENGAGEMENT AND PARTICIPATION IN ROME

Students at TUR are encouraged to immerse themselves in Italian life and institutions rather than observing them from a distance in order to garner self-knowledge of their place in the world. Through these experiences, students not only can devel-

Engineering students
visiting the DaVinci
Museum in Rome. (Courtesy
Temple University)

op an understanding of Italy but also may grasp the in-between-ness of their own situations. Since the beginning, the program has included trips to learn about the past (historic and ancient sites), and today this is augmented by experiencing Italy as the third largest European economy through visits to the fashion and car industries. Internships are available that involve contemporary issues such as immigration, inequality, sustainability, and mobility.

Continuous engagements through working side by side in everyday life in service learning courses, internships, and volunteering activities bring TUR students together with secondary school students and their communities in Rome, which provide cultural exchange, college preparation, tutoring, mutual language learning with oral practice, and athletic competitions. TUR students have hosted film festivals for Italian schools and have in turn been hosted in the regions that Italian students come from for holidays. TUR students who participate in community engagement feel that they are contributing to the city that has given them so much new understanding of themselves in the world. By broadening its goals from the grand tour to learn an idealized past to one that grapples with the present to learn other points of view, individuals who experience TUR have an array of futures to choose from as well as many opportunities to follow new possibilities. At the same time, Temple as a global institution is enriched and reinforced in its global outlook.

ACKNOWLEDGMENTS

I would like to acknowledge the generous help from Denise Connerty, the former director of the Temple Office of International Programs; Suzanne Willever of the study abroad program; and Hillary L. Link, former dean of Temple University Rome.

NOTES

1. These reminiscences come from excerpts from Dean Charles LeClair in an article entitled "Ambitious Experiment" in the program's newsletter, *Postcard: News from Temple University Rome*, fall/winter 1992–1993, published by Temple University International Programs.

2. In addition to Melograno, the couple have recently opened another Center City restaurant, L'Anima, with a different concept.

BIBLIOGRAPHY

Hilty, James. *Temple University: 125 Years of Service to Philadelphia, the Nation and the World.* Philadelphia: Temple University Press, 2010.

Postcard: The Newsletter for Temple University Rome. Office of International Programs, Temple University, 1975–2016.

The Templar, 1928; Pharmacy Edition, 1931. Yearbook published by Temple University.

Wachman, Marvin. *The Education of a University President.* Philadelphia: Temple University Press, 2005.

Joseph V. Del Raso, chairman of the NIAF during the 2013–2017 term. (© NIAF/Andy DelGiudice)

NIAF AND ITS LINKS TO PHILADELPHIA

JOSEPH V. DEL RASO

WHEN THE NATIONAL ITALIAN AMERICAN FOUNDATION was organized in Washington, DC, on April 1, 1976, a prominent Philadelphia scholar and poet, Rose Basile Green, was elected to serve as secretary of the board. Other founding board members included Nicholas Giordano, CEO of the Philadelphia Stock Exchange, and Frederick D. Tecce, inventor and successful businessman.

The local board members sponsored various events in Philadelphia, the most notable taking place at the Union League of Philadelphia. At the time, the Union League dinners focused on honoring successful Italian American families. Two events in particular come to mind. One honored the Pasquariello family for medicine, and the other honored the Genuardi family, operators of a regional supermarket chain. Another Union League dinner celebrated the success of Villanova University basketball coach Rollie Massimino's 1985 national championship.

In 1985, a group of Philadelphia businessmen supported the NIAF efforts to bring the Carabinieri Orchestra to the city. Louis Esposito and Vincent Del Raso underwrote hosting the orchestra while in Philadelphia. Louis Esposito sponsored several Italian American senior citizens resident in local congregate living facilities by purchasing concert tickets and arranging transportation to the Academy of Music.

In later years, Philadelphians would ascend to the leadership of NIAF. Three chairs of the foundation are natives of Philadelphia. The late Dr. A. Kenneth Ciongoli grew up in Philadelphia and was the first Philadelphian to serve as president and then chair of NIAF. He was known for his commitment to higher education and scholarly projects. Joseph V. Del Raso also served as president and then chair. He focused his efforts on strengthening ties with Italy and hosted several Italian government and business leaders in Philadelphia. The current cochair of the NIAF is Gabriel Battista, a native-born Philadelphian who maintains close ties to Philadelphia through his involvement with NIAF, local universities, and the Union League.

The current NIAF board officers and directors from Philadelphia include Frank Giordano, Philip Rinaldi, Dr. Antonio Giordano, and Anthony DiSandro. Joseph Del Raso currently serves as chair of NIAF Italia and is chair emeritus of the NIAF board.

Gabe Battista, cochairman of NIAF at an event of the Italian cultural month, Ciao Philadelphia, held by American University of Rome (AUR) at the Consulate General of Italy in Philadelphia in October 2015. Mr. Battista was then Chairman of the Board of AUR. (Photo: Gary Horn)

28

The Simeone Foundation Automotive Museum

Fred Simeone

THE SIMEONE FOUNDATION AUTOMOTIVE MUSEUM was founded in 2008. The story of the museum is very much related to my family's story of immigration from Italy and settlement in the United States and to our cultural roots. My grandparents came to Philadelphia during the great immigration at the turn of the twentieth century. They came seeking a better life and brought with them a strong commitment to their cultural heritage.

ITALIAN HERITAGE: FROM MEDICINE TO CARS IN AN ITALIAN AMERICAN FAMILY

My father, a first-generation family physician in the Italian community, mentored me, and I became a neurosurgeon. From him, I also acquired a passionate interest in beautifully designed and technologically proficient racing automobiles and their historical development. Through him, I began to refine my taste and appreciation for the modern design influenced by Italian art forms inherent in the artisanship manifested in exciting vehicles, which had gained fame on racing circuits.

During my career as a practicing neurosurgeon, using the small automotive library that my physician father put together, I accumulated a collection of the most evocative sports racing cars of an earlier era. I began to seek cars that, though recognized as special in their efforts, had not yet become central icons for automotive connoisseurs. As such, they could still be found in barns, in an unrestored state or carefully preserved by aging collectors. In one instance, I followed a one-line comment in a twenty-year-old automotive magazine, a reference to a great car in a race in Argentina, and traced the race driver, whose ramshackle garage still housed a priceless historical racing 1937 Alfa Romeo. This and other Alfa Romeos that had

led the racing world throughout most of the 1920s and 1930s were acquired and preserved. The great 1938 Alfa Romeo Mille Miglia winner was acquired from a collection in Scotland. Known as the Holy Grail of Ferraris, the first twelve-cylinder Testa Rossa was acquired in a complex trade for four other cars.

When I retired from practice, I opened this carefully curated collection to Philadelphians and visitors. The site of the museum was chosen to fulfill its mission— to entice people's interest in and understanding of motorsport through education and experience, to increase their appreciation of the aesthetics of design and technical proficiency exemplified by the cars themselves, and to allow them to see the cars as they developed through time in form and function.

The building provides the world's largest instructional display for the seventy automotive treasures. Exciting diorama displays present the cars in their periods and are arrayed in chronological order. The site selected, in a somewhat remote part of Southwest Philadelphia, was large enough to also afford an opportunity for the actual exercise of cars on a large three-acre adjacent track. This provides an opportunity for engaging broader feelings and senses in order to understand the sport and its spirit of competition. The underlying theme by which these vehicles were curated was based on the excitement of road racing in cars, which any driver can relate to, not necessarily only professionals.

A major feature in the collection is the impressive number of the core reference documents that were used in the nascent days of the collection, the 1950s. With

Fred Simeone driving a 1933 Alfa Romeo on October 6, 2016, at an event called "Demo Day at the Simeone Museum—Targa Florio!" in the frame of Ciao Philadelphia. (Photo: Richard Barnes)

Brooklands was the first custom-built banked track in the world. Shown here are a 1933 Alfa Romeo Spider (*left*) and a 1925 Alfa Romeo RL Super Sport that actually raced at Brooklands (*right*).
(Andrew Taylor)

few authoritative books yet produced, we relied on scattered but detailed primary historical information on automotive history, particularly racing. Among these, the original literature produced by the manufacturers to tout their current cars as well as their great history became a principal source of information for cars produced before and immediately after World War II. Although hard to get, these documents became the source of an intensive search so that the museum library has the country's largest collection of factory-printed literature, dating back before the turn of the twentieth century. In this library, one can generate the history of each of these automobiles and their relationship to their immediate antecedents and their successors.

ITALIAN HERITAGE: DESIGN AND ARTISANSHIP

In many ways, the museum is connected to my Italian heritage. The endurance of Italian style, creativity, and artisanship flourishes today in many forms of modern luxury, from fine furniture and exciting shoes to couture and jewelry that adorns the stars. In the field of motor sport and in the design of amazing racing cars, Italian aesthetic design and technical developments have been key.

While many nations are represented among the seventy cars in the exhibition, Italian spirit and excellence can be found in the Ferraris, the Maseratis, and America's largest exhibition of historic Alfa Romeo race cars, which hold pride of place in the museum. There was something special about the Italian automobiles, especially before the era of giant corporations when the designers and artisans were given free rein to use their talents unrestricted.

By featuring the great Italian automobiles side by side among America's and Europe's finest, this museum contributes to Philadelphia's increasing globalization and multiculturalism. I consider them as representative of the development of modern Italian design. There is no practical compromise to good design. When one raises a bonnet over an engine to see the beautifully fluted manifolds, the gently curved suspension parts, and the polished valve covers, we understand one visitor's comment: "The search for beauty is in every part."

What better way to understand this than through the visual presence of automotive old masters? The famous 1958 Ferrari Testa Rossa set a new paradigm for the sports racing car, and the chassis itself won the international championship for sports

cars three times, racing against the world's most refined. Also illustrated is the beautiful 1933 Alfa Romeo Monza, and out-and-out race car refashioned by the Zagato Carrozzeria into a beautifully fendered sports car capable of entering that great Mille Miglia race, coming in second place to another Alfa Romeo. Refinement in design, lightness, aerodynamics, and sheer excitement are exemplified by the world champion 1956 Maserati 300 S, the magnificent product of a small company struggling to beat competitors from the world's largest companies. And finally, we illustrate our Mona Lisa: the 1938 Alfa Romeo that won Italy's most famous race, a car the British motoring press describes as the greatest vintage racing sports car ever made.

The Academy Awards of the historical automobile world are given annually by the International Historic Motoring Awards at a gala in London. Competition includes every automotive museum in the world. The Simeone Automotive Foundation Museum won the organization's first award in 2011 and won for an unprecedented second time in 2017. It was also listed as the most popular automotive museum in the United States by *USA Today* in 2016. In a celebration in Paris in

MILLE MIGLIA

The Mille Miglia ("Thousand Miles") started in 1927 and was one of the most popular races in Europe. The cars departed from Brescia on the *partenza*, as shown in the diorama, and raced down the east coast of Italy to Rome, making a circle back to where they started, a distance of about a thousand miles. Shown are a 1933 Alfa Romeo 8C 2300 Monza (*left*) and a 1937 Alfa Romeo 8C 2900A (*right*). Both cars finished second in the race. (Andrew Taylor)

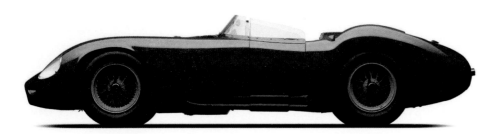

ABOVE: TARGA FLORIO

In 1906, Vincenzo Florio devised a race through the hills of Sicily. At that time, sports car racing had become popular in Italy, and the Targa Florio was the most important race in Europe until Le Mans and the Mille Miglia were started in the 1920s. The car in front is a 1975 Alfa Romeo 33-TT-12 that was part of the World Championship team. The car on the right is a 1926 Bugatti Type 35 that may have competed in the Targa Florio. (Andrew Taylor)

CENTER: 1956 Maserati 300 S. (Michael Furman)

BOTTOM: 1938 Alfa Romeo. (Michael Furman)

FACING PAGE: Ferrari Testa Rossa 0710. (Photo: Giò Martorana)

June 2019, the prestigious Classic Car Trust, after a review of one hundred collections, voted the Simeone number one.

It is hoped that the many messages in such a collection can be conveyed to the students and visitors to the museum. In addition, the foundation itself is a contribution to Philadelphia's cultural fabric and a reminder in some small way of the Italian influence on the best parts of our way of life.

29

Italian Gastronomy and Its Many Roles in a Cosmopolitan City

Judith Goode

THIS ESSAY EXAMINES THE IMPACT of Italian food on the city's post-1970 aspirations to be a global city in economic terms and a great place to live or to visit as a tourist. Italian food has played a major role in the city's food renaissance beginning in the 1970s, which included a proliferation of new and exotic cuisines, a new world of star chefs and entrepreneurs, and the trend toward imaginative innovations and fusions. Italian food helps brand the city by providing popular food icons in addition to following new food movements with a shift to healthier and high-end cuisine. Italian cuisine creates destinations, marks Italian space, and helps produce increasingly valued diversity. We contextualize these dynamics within the nature of global food cosmopolitanism and food movements in the United States, Italy, and the world. The particulars of Philadelphia's neighborhood gentrification also shape this process. As we will see, the Italian food legacy travels through many routes, through Italian American food enterprises, increased travel between the United States and contemporary Italy, and the new post-1965 Italian immigration of students and professionals.

In the contemporary United States and Italy, as well as global cities throughout the world, the consumption and enjoyment of food has become a culturally elaborated focus of life. We not only eat; we read about food in the proliferating market of cookbooks, food magazines, and restaurant reviews and more recently in online sources such as food blogs and Yelp customer reviews. We watch performances of cooking on the food networks and social media. We also participate in food movements that relate to the health of ourselves and the planet's ecosystem, to ethical issues of hunger and overconsumption, and to the related themes of waste and the parallel virtues of foraging, local sourcing, and opposing animal cruelty. Finally, post-1970s globalization has led to the movement of cuisines, ingredients, and dishes throughout the United States and the world as people travel as immigrants and tourists.

Food has become a key focus of aesthetic evaluation and a field of late twentieth-century creativity and innovation. Many contemporary changes in food are reactions to modern life and laud tradition and heritage. The slow food movement (and journal, *Slow Food*) began in Italy in response to industrial processed food and fast-food trends seen as degrading the health, social, experiential, and symbolic significance of food preparation and consumption. In the 1980s, Julia Child, one of the first celebrity cooks, and vintner Robert Mondavi created the American Institute of Wine and Food and a journal, *Gastronomy*, to raise the academic profile of food studies related to aesthetic, social, and symbolic experience.

ITALIAN FOOD IN THE UNITED STATES AND PHILADELPHIA

Throughout these processes, Italian food has held a continuous but evolving role in most national and local food trends, moving from the enclave to the mainstream in terms of both widespread popularity and new "foodie" trends.

In Philadelphia before World War II, while Italian foods were visible to other immigrant populations who shopped at the Ninth Street Market, food differences were largely used to reinforce ethnic community boundaries in early generations. Life histories reveal Italian disparagement of Irish soft bread, mayonnaise, and bland bologna, alongside Irish disparagement of garlic and hot spices. The generally enclaved nature of ethnic community eating was reflected in a National Research Council study in the 1940s to help to prepare for war and the possible evacuation of new immigrants.[1]

After the war, food consumption in the United States was heavily influenced by mass production and distribution (supermarkets) through which Italian food entered popular food culture. Italian food became popular through trends in mass production and marketing of industrial, standardized products. Chef Boyardee (Hector Boiardi) introduced canned versions of spaghetti and ravioli available in supermarkets in 1938. Later, frozen Italian food became available. In U.S. supermarkets, Italian foods are the only "ethnic" food to have their own labeled shelf section in contrast to a generic "international" section shared by the rest.

Pizza and pasta became mainstream food categories. School lunch programs often featured pizza and pasta as well. Companies mass-producing dried pasta and Italian cheese were able to market by disseminating recipes to newspapers and women's magazines. Urban areas on the East and West Coasts where Italian American enclaves were large were the spearheads of this spread, while less dense regions with few Italian enclaves had to wait for the spread of corporate chains such as Pizza Hut. Thus, many Americans became acquainted with mass-produced Italian food rather than the artisan and homemade foods available in South Philly (see Chapter 18).

However, a reaction to mass-produced food occurred in the 1960s, and media representations of food cosmopolitanism developed in the United States as well. Julia Child disseminated an understanding of authentic everyday French cuisine on TV. Craig Claiborne, the *New York Times* food critic, began to write more about international food in the 1960s and 1970s as New York received a postwar influx of new immigrants.

VALUING ITALIAN FOOD

Today, Italian food is seen as "good" in many ways.[2] It is valued as part of the healthy plant- and olive-oil-based Mediterranean diet, low in animal fat, and full of complementary proteins such as *pasta e fagioli* (pasta and beans)—foods that in combination provide all necessary amino acids required for vegetarian and vegan diets. Travel to Italy and experience with family-owned trattorias and their conviviality, combined with U.S. media representations, associated such food with strong sociality, warm relationships, and cheer. Italian food also closely aligned with what is good for the planet—farm-to-table freshness and a low carbon footprint.

Most importantly, there is an association with nature, authenticity, and artisan skills. Another alignment with the critiques of modern life comes from the frequency of foraged and hunted foods (greens, mushrooms, and wild game), which create associations with nature and rusticity, while the artisan aspects of handmade processing and daily bread baking cater to a similar preference for authentic lives. Vineyards and farm restaurants evoke regional terroir or the notion that local ecologies produce differences in the taste and essence of locally produced food.

Today, the desire for creativity and innovation in the contemporary world of foodies leads to new imaginative changes in Italian food. Looking at the transforming foodie scene in Philadelphia, we can identify the processes of continuity and innovation in the Italian food legacy. The term *foodie* has been used since the 1970s to describe people for whom the qualitative evaluation of ingredients, dishes, and menus and the seeking of an extensive knowledge of cuisines are an important part of identity and a way of achieving social distinction.[3]

ITALIAN FOOD AND THE PHILADELPHIA BRAND

Today, the Italian food legacy is manifested by both plebian and high-end foods. In the realm of popular foods, locally developed sandwiches serve as brands for the city, representing its blue-collar, gritty side. Today's foodies search for quality and taste across social hierarchies, from the upscale restaurant dynasties to the lowly food truck and hole-in-the-wall. Philadelphia's signature food icon, the cheesesteak, is one of the hybrid creations made in South Philly for large event buffets (Chapter 18). The cheesesteak can be found at the airport and the ballpark, with upscaled versions in high-end places as well. Almost always identified as the Philadelphia or

The reputational rivalry in ranking the "best" cheesesteak between Pat's and Geno's in the heart of South Philly is the oldest in the city. (Photo: Richard Barnes)

Philly cheesesteak, it can be found on many national menus. In 1987, I found a drive-in called Philly Cheesesteak in Bogota, Colombia, begun by returning Colombian migrants who had acquired a taste and nostalgia for cheesesteaks. Ex-Philadelphians in Los Angeles have their pick of many outlets that advertise their Philly cheesesteaks. Projected by national and international tourist media, such foods are consumed by tourists as well as newcomer young professional hipsters who have gentrified South Philadelphia. The relative merits of recipes and tastes of different outlets are endlessly debated through rankings and word of mouth.[4] Eating cheesesteaks is a mandatory photo op for visiting political candidates.

Other well-known local Italian sandwiches that represent the popular quick food of the working man include roast pork with broccoli rabe, found at the airport, at the ballpark, and even in hip Brooklyn, where a local Philadelphian began a two-venue business out of his walk-up apartment.[5] There are different stories of the origins of these particular sandwiches, but the hot sandwiches are connected to large, collective celebrations produced by women or by the large deli-caterers that developed after the war. The hoagie, a ubiquitous Philadelphia brand that also lends itself to competitions for ratings as "the best," is linked to early working men's carried lunches.

PHILADELPHIA'S FOOD RENAISSANCE

Today, Italian food holds a privileged position in the high-end world of foodies as well. It is a major component of the media-driven competition between Philadelphia and other aspiring global cities to brand themselves as special places to live and experience valued culture through history, art, architecture, music, and food. Chef-driven Italian restaurants are proliferating as places to experience new food creations.

When I moved to Philadelphia in the mid-1960s, the city had a reputation as a conservative food backwater where the sidewalks were rolled up before midnight. On the eve of the first restaurant renaissance in the 1970s, the available options for upscale and celebratory eating were old country inns and city hotels, which served what was then referred to as "continental" style—European dishes such as veal Oscar. There were also several seafood venues, Bookbinders being the best known. All were known for their regional fish and seafood, such as shad from the Delaware River and Chesapeake blue crabs, all seasonal delicacies. Snapper soup, a nineteenth-century delicacy from the great turtle trade, was a favorite. Afro-Caribbean and Creole dishes such as "pepper pot" were served as well, stemming from the city's role as a port connected to the Caribbean. When my department recruited new faculty to Temple, in order to provide a more interesting place to eat, we took them to Villa di Roma in the market. I also was advised to serve fresh stuffed breads from Consolo's in Manayunk, as I did for parties.[6]

The first downtown restaurant renaissance occurred during the 1970s and accompanied early gentrification driven by the desire to reverse suburbanization and revitalize the city center. It was spearheaded by innovative chefs locating in storefronts and elegant townhouses. When economic development stalled in the 1980s, the stage was set for the millennial food scene ushered in by a second restaurant renaissance in the 1990s under new conditions. The transformations have continued through the first two decades of the millennium as eds and meds, scientific and medical research, and arts and amenities such as the Avenue of the Arts grew and a new diversity and cosmopolitanism emerged from increased travel and living abroad as well as the new ethnic communities.

New food creativity was linked to new residential populations in Center City and its surrounding gentrified neighborhoods near the many universities including arts, music, and theater schools. Such newcomers ranged from recent university graduates (millennials) to retired regional empty-nest executives and professionals. Creative workers included New York artists and musicians drawn to a cheaper housing market by campaigns touting the city as New York's "sixth borough" as well as suburban returnees and transferring workers from other U.S. cities. Transnational migrants (including Italians) coming to Philadelphia for higher education or knowledge work jobs also increased. For all these consumers, the second food renaissance evolved over time as celebrity chefs aspired to national and international rankings.[7]

Finally, the food scene in the city has increased in its diversity and moved farther away from European dominance as many restaurants in new ethnic communities from Asian, Latin American, Middle Eastern, and African nations are now attracting mainstream consumers. Within this competitive environment, Italian food has held its own in the new food scene in the city where the upscale food landscape appeals to the new food-centered lifestyles of both established Philadelphians and newcomers across generations.

THE CONTEMPORARY FOOD SCENE

The second renaissance raised the food profile for the city. In the era of chef-driven Italian restaurants, there are many connections to Italy and to Italian Americans living in South Philadelphia. We now examine the pathways that Italian chefs have taken to get where they are. Among the chefs are those who grew up in venerable restaurant families and other homegrown South Philadelphians who were workers in the earlier South Philly food scene. There are also many restaurateurs and chefs who are Italian born and raised. The scale of operations runs from star chefs hoping to launch restaurants in New York or Las Vegas to rising stars to mom-and-pop trattorias, which can also serve exquisite food. Training comes from a combination of formal cooking schools and on-the-job training in kitchens, which now serve as artisan workshops that launch new chefs. Training in Italy is common. These sources can all sustain classical and authentic artisan techniques drawn from regional differences, the traditional emphasis on the wild and natural, and the current Italian-based interest in nose-to-tale butchering.

At the same time, new chefs also emphasize creativity, imagination, playfulness, and constant reinvention. In the next section, we illustrate the new Italian food scene through the career of Marc Vetri, a star chef, and through key spots in the geography of Greater South Philadelphia (especially East Passyunk and Queen Village) plus the adjacent zone on South Broad, which is linked to western South Philadelphia on one end and the Avenue of the Arts at the other. We explore Italian food over time and catch glimpses of a variety of chefs and owners, the camaraderie of kitchen teams, and the dense network of creative kitchen workers as they are mentored, eat after-hours meals together, and move frequently across an array of establishments and highly ranked kitchens, producing a vibrant and dynamic scene.

MARC VETRI, STAR CHEF

Marc Vetri is Philadelphia's star of Italian cuisine, sharing the highest ratings and prices with Philadelphia's top chefs aspiring to awards, past and present, such as

Michael Solomonoff, Ellen Yin, Jose Garces, and others who compete for national and local James Beard awards. Like many of today's celebrity chefs, he writes books. Vetri, rather than looking down on the common pizza and pasta categories, instead plumbs their depths through creative thought and technique. He has written four books about mastering pizza, pasta, and rustic Italian food. Vetri was the first local Italian chef to aspire to a national profile. In 2018, he opened another Vetri Cucina on the top floor of a new Las Vegas casino. The original Philadelphia flagship is located in the former townhouse of Georges Perrier's famous Le Bec Fin, the first and only nationally reputed local chef in earlier days.

Vetri was raised in South Philly. After spending six years training, half in Bergamo Italy and in high-end New York kitchens, he opened Vetri Cucina, followed by Osteria, Pizzeria Vetri, and others that are now run by protégés who have risen up the ranks in the kitchen training centers. He recently added a pasta venue, Fiorella Pasta, in the Italian Market as a new chef-driven site for himself.

Lineages of workshop-trained sous-chefs start out on their own as aspiring stars. One of them is Joey Baldino, also a South Philadelphian, who trained with the Vetri team and has achieved his own reputation through two restaurants with different brands. The first was Zeppolo, a well-ranked Sicilian place in Collingswood, New Jersey—a suburb where a satellite cluster of chef-driven places serve customers from Philadelphia and southern Jersey. In 2017, he opened Palizzi Social

Vetri Cucina, 1312 Spruce Street, Philadelphia.
(Photo: Richard Barnes)

Club, which is inspired by his South Philly upbringing and features reproductions and reinventions of dishes such as spaghetti and crabs designed to recreate memories, nostalgia, and the social vibe of his youth. The original club was one of the many long-closed exclusive private eating places based on regional/municipal identities.

Turning to the South Philadelphia and Avenue of the Arts zone, we find a dynamic story through time. Queen Village upscaled its restaurants as it gentrified, mostly through new American food, and it became a food destination in the 1980s. In the 2000s, the East Passyunk area, the home of some venerable Italian restaurants, underwent a revival. Lynn Rinaldi was one of the early drivers of this restaurant renaissance with her regional Italian place, Paradiso. She grew up in South Philadelphia, worked in restaurants as a server, and studied art at PAFA and food at the Restaurant School in West Philadelphia. She was an active leader in the group of chefs and owners who energized the revival, which was not limited to Italian American food by any means, but it was most prevalent.

Chef Joe Cicala was part of this revival. He had spent some time in the Abruzzi with friends and family and dug into regional shepherd's foods, following an interest in *cucina povera* (rural southern Italian). He built his brand of cooking on wild and foraged ingredients as an homage to authentic regional cooking. Today, he is referred to as a "genius with the pig" by critic Craig LaBan. He has turned his attention to *salume* (cured meats) and his company Salumificia.

While Marc Vetri and the East Passyunk revival signaled a new generation, we can trace the staying power and the upscaling of the old, venerable enterprises that have sold and served prepared food since the first two decades of the twentieth century. Since the first renaissance in the 1970s when Queen Village began to gentrify, restaurants have been volatile, shifting domains, always changing as enterprises adapt by relocating, rebranding, and reinventing dishes. Branches in upscale, easy-to-reach suburbs followed populations settling outside the city. At the same time, many long-term enterprises were able to retain their traditions, which appealed to new audiences.

The Victor Café, one of the centenarians, is still operated by the Di Stefani family and has maintained its popularity through word of mouth and through the persistent popularity of live opera. In this world where sociality, fun, and experience are important again, the periodic performance of opera students and singers from the large community of vocalists still attracts.

Other families have adapted by appealing to tradition and authenticity. Such establishments are run by children and grandchildren of multigenerational enterprises, and we have seen some of the adaptations they have made in Chapter 18 (Sarcone Bakery, Termini Brothers, Isgro Pastries, etc.). Today, they still produce delicacies coveted across many class and ethnic groups in the city who argue about the relative value of bread or cannoli. Isgros today is still using (and tolerating) the nuisance of matriarch Cruciferia's giant table, placed in the middle of the kitchen in 1904. Her husband, Gus Sr., would not allow it to be moved, and it is still a work space.

The De Lucas, who have run Villa di Roma since the war, emphasize their new handmade meatball techniques and take-out red gravy as they remain in the market location near regular and tourist customers. The DiBrunos (five cousins), who ran a deli of cheese and cured meats in the market since the war, now have several catering venues, a restaurant in the downtown area, and a mail-order business that serves a national market. Bill Mignucci Jr., the CEO, participates in events promoting the national American revolution in food.

Family-owned trattorias, many of them BYOBs, create affordable good food for regulars from the local neighborhood residents who eat out frequently. Scannicchio's, newly opened on South Broad, is the reenactment of a venerable Atlantic City restaurant owned and operated by the South Philadelphian father of the new owner, who had commuted daily from South Philly to the larger hospitality market there. Opened by his son, the location

is ranked highly by Craig LaBan and has a large old-time South Philly following, including Marc Vetri's parents.

There are many BYOBs owned and operated by Italian restaurateurs in the Avenue of the Arts entertainment zone, where clientele include tourists, convention visitors, and suburbanites. Examples of places operating for more than ten years include two storefronts, La Viola East and West, which advertise a friendly Italian staff. Melograno, the Roman BYOB owned by the couple who met through Temple University Rome (Chapter 27), has now been joined by a sibling, L'Anima, based on a broader concept. These are just a few.

The Iovinos, a Neapolitan couple, operated a respected upscale venue in the entertainment zone for more than a decade but have recently downsized. In 2017, they opened a small trattoria in the South Philly zone, Angelina's, which has been well reviewed. The Italian-raised and -trained restaurateurs as a rule bring with them urban Italian trends, bringing them Italian residents and Americans who frequently travel to Europe. The authenticity of their Italian origins is an important selling point.

Top: Termini Brothers pastries display. (Photo: Giò Martorana)

Bottom: Most of the centenarian enterprises have displays of mementos, family members, and celebrity visitors to verify their success, tradition, and authenticity. This display comes from Terminis. (Photo: Giò Martorana)

In 2018, a Roman pizza chain opened Alice Pizzeria and Restaurant, its first expanded-menu restaurant in the entertainment zone, with a local Philadelphia partner, signaling a new multinational corporate link.

BACK TO QUEEN VILLAGE

Between 2016 and 2019, Queen Village–Bella Vista, one of the key sites of the 1970s food renaissance, was revitalized by experienced chef couples. Most of the new enterprises bear an Italian brand, but their chefs have worked in other cuisines, and many have neither Italian nor South Philly backgrounds. This reflects the fact that Italian cuisine knowledge and technique has become a critical part of much chef training and work experience in most food scenes. Their shared goals are to be creative and to make eating a transformative sensory experience. Most of the following received three bells (excellent) ratings from Craig LaBan, the highest rank below the rare four bells received by Vetri and other nationally ranked celebrity chefs.

One couple with local interests and experience with Irish and Portuguese food have renovated Judy's, the landmark 1970s breakout Queen Village eatery. Now Crybaby Pasta focuses on state-of-the-art technology for handmade pasta. Res Ipsa, which serves dinner and is branded Sicilian, is run by four chefs—two from Italian backgrounds and one an expert in Asian noodles. Another entrepreneur opened a restaurant that was struggling. In response, his move was "scrapping menu plan #1 [their original concept] and just serving Italian food,"[8] opening Trattoria Carina. The implication was that such cuisine is always a winner.

New York chefs are also coming to Queen Village. In 2019, Fiore (three bells) was opened by a non-Italian couple from New York. In the review, the first paragraph says it all: "New York is a place where young chefs go to prove themselves. This [Philadelphia] is where many come to find a home." Thus, the Italian food legacy has traveled through many routes and in different forms to Philadelphia, from earlier Italy to South Philadelphia and from modern Italy to the city. It is now again being re-created by aspiring chefs of different ethnicities in one of the first gentrified areas of South Philadelphia.

While this reinforces the Italian markings of the South Philly space, at the same time it must be remembered that South Philadelphia is also a place of new immigrant diversity and a proliferation of diverse markets. The July 2019 theme of *Philadelphia Magazine* was "South Philadelphia Is Changing," and the food map emphasizes the variety of cuisines in the neighborhood. There are Asian markets and restaurants along Washington Avenue south of the Italian Market. Mexican restaurants have grown up around the market, and there is at least one example of a Mexican sous-chef at Scannicchio's, which is not surprising since some of the Mexican migration in the 1990s were restaurant workers from Chicago. Crème Brulee, a popular Mexican pastry shop, has a sideline producing pizza dough for many high-end pizza makers.

Given the new mix, there is a flurry of experimentation with fusing cuisines. At least three places serve a cheesesteak eggroll. These aspects of food fusion are part of the ever-changing landscape of the Italian food legacy in Philadelphia, which has persisted in holding its own in a cosmopolitan world. Italian food checks all the foodie boxes. People take the iconic sandwiches seriously. Pizza and pasta are everywhere—from chain eateries to the highest artisan craft kitchens. Inspiration comes from traditional agrarian Italy, modern Italy, and South Philly's past. The new chefs of Queen Village demonstrate the ways in which the Italian food legacy is broad and deep in the contemporary, cosmopolitan city.

ACKNOWLEDGMENTS AND SOURCES

I am deeply indebted to the food writing of Craig LaBan, the food critic of the *Philadelphia Inquirer*, who has chronicled these changes, told the backstories, and provided wonderful insights not only about the food and ambience of each venue but also about the world of the kitchen, the training, the lineages, and the careers of aspiring stars. He does the same for the histories and lineages of family-owned venues as well.

Other *Philadelphia Inquirer* food writers such as Michael Klein were also important sources used for the contemporary period, as was the restaurant coverage in *Philadelphia Magazine*.

NOTES

1. Famous anthropologist Margaret Mead led a team to study the eating habits of immigrant groups in major U.S. cities in the early 1940s in the event of a necessary evacuation of cities during the war. The U.S. National Research Council sponsored the research.

2. Since the initial contact with Italian food was through its mass production, it was first disparaged as too heavy in carbohydrates and fat and too low in protein through a lack of awareness about the actual eating patterns and assumptions that pasta and pizza were daily fare (see Chapter 18).

3. Previous ideas about "refined palates" and being a gourmet focused only on things associated with high-class status and the shared definition of the specific rules for using highly ranked dishes and foods. The term *foodie* implied a more intense and engaged role of food in one's life and contextualized food curiosity from the acquisition of ingredients to processing to composing and experimenting.

4. As an example of the intensity of interest, one blog begun in 2018 by Jim Pappas documents close to three hundred cheesesteaks in a year in the region according to their qualities (roll, cheese, meat, lettuce, tomato, etc.) in his search for the ultimate cheesesteak. A rideshare driver, he gets his referrals from his customers.

5. Dave Federoff grew up near Pat's and Geno's. He knows his sandwiches and carefully searched for the right roll. He moved to New York as an adult and found a need to fill. He has two storefronts today, one in his Brooklyn neighborhood and a tiny one in the Manhattan financial district.

6. Some dishes were derived from links to the colonial ports of the Caribbean and New Orleans. For example, pepper pot soup (an early Campbell's favorite), snapper soup, and a Philadelphia platter of fried oysters with chicken salad were popular local foods.

7. The second renaissance occurred as the nature of the U.S. high-end urban restaurant business restructured in response to the need for large-scale capital. Management structures were rearranged in terms of the division of financial and creative roles in restaurant teams and groups. Expansion to high-end suburbs or national food meccas such as New York and Las Vegas was contemplated. While not discussed here, the choices made in this competitive context provide interesting stories.

8. Craig LaBan, dining review of "Trattoria Carina," *Philadelphia Inquirer,* December 17, 2017, p. H11.

30

Recalling Italy in Bricks and Mortar

INGA SAFFRON

AMERICA HAS ALWAYS BEEN AN ARCHITECTURAL MAGPIE, sampling styles from around the world. But there was something about Italian architecture, which descended from the architecture of ancient Rome, that must have struck a chord with the young republic. Scholars were rediscovering the accomplishments of classical antiquity right around the time that America was beginning its democratic experiment, and the new nation saw a reflection of itself—or the self it hoped to become—in the stately forms of the Roman republic.

Philadelphia, of course, was hardly the only American city to mimic classical and Renaissance architecture. But, as one of America's first great cities, it had the sophistication and financial means to realize them at a high level. It helped, of course, that the city became an early haven for Italian immigrants. Without their extraordinary construction skills and deeply embedded architectural memories, many of the buildings described in this chapter would not have been possible.

Philadelphia has many great classical buildings. Rather than focus on the most famous, I selected the ten described here because of the way they reflect their heritage. They are Italian to their core. I start with a group of modest, almost vernacular buildings that Italian immigrants constructed for themselves, perhaps as a way of easing their dislocation from their ancestral home. The second section is devoted to civic monuments that derive their appearance directly from classical precedents. In the final section, my goal is to show that the essential qualities of Italian architecture are present even in the most modern of buildings. In the three centuries since Philadelphia's founding, it has experienced a series of architectural infatuations, from its early fling with Greek Revival to its embrace of Parisian city planning. Yet, through it all, it has returned again and again to the Italian peninsula for inspiration. If we're lucky, those traditions will continue long into the future.

ITALIANS MAKE THEIR MARK ON PHILADELPHIA

America's First Italian Church

If you told a Philadelphian in the 1850s that Italian Catholics needed their own parish, they might have asked, "What Italians?" Until the first great wave of immigration got underway in the 1860s, there were so few Italians living in the city that they could easily be accommodated at Old St. Joseph's in Society Hill, which was then a mainly Irish church. But the city's Catholic bishop, John Neumann, sensed that a new wave of immigration was coming. In 1852, Bishop Neumann, who was fluent in Italian, decided to establish an Italian parish in South Philadelphia to help new arrivals adjust to life in America. Bishop Neumann bought a former Methodist burial ground on Montrose Street and recruited two Italian priests to oversee the construction of a new church, which was given the name St. Mary Magdalen de Pazzi.

The church that opened a year later was a spare, classical-style building. Pushed toward the back of the site, the building was capable of accommodating a modest-size congregation, perhaps two hundred worshippers. In just a few years, however, Philadelphia's small Italian community would explode, just as Bishop Neumann had predicted, partly as a result of the upheavals following Italian unification in 1861. South Philadelphia became the epicenter of Italian life.

It soon became clear that the neighborhood's expanding Italian community would need a bigger worship space. Rather than make do with a purely functional building, this time the parish hired a well-known church architect, Edward Forrest Durang, to design its sanctuary on the Montrose Street property. Completed in 1891, the second St. Mary Magdalen is a far more assertive building than its predecessor. Instead of hiding the church in a garden at the back of the property, Durang took the building up to the sidewalk, giving it a strong civic presence. Finished with crisp, white stone (no doubt cut by Italian craftsmen), the facade immediately stands out from the neighboring red-brick row houses. While there are no lavish sculptures on the exterior, Durang used a mix of columns, pediments, pilasters, and lintels to animate the surface. The result is a disciplined Renaissance-style composition that suggests a small but prosperous urban church in Italy.

Bishop Neumann intended St. Mary Magdalen to be a refuge for Italian immigrants, and Durang expressed that welcoming quality in the architecture. The arched main door is huge. Durang surrounded the entrance with an elaborate stone portico flanked by Corinthian columns and shielded by a classical pediment. Right above the entryway, a large Palladian window calls your eye to the second floor. Tall, narrow arched windows on the ground floor emphasize the building's height, which was tall enough to allow for two balcony levels inside. That verticality is further accentuated by the pilasters (flat columns) placed on either side of the entrance.

The only thing missing from Durang's design was a bell tower. That would come a decade later. By 1901, the parish had succeeded in raising the funds to build

TOP: Saint Mary Magdalen de Pazzi Roman Catholic Church on Montrose Street. (Photo: Giò Martorana)

BOTTOM: Saint Mary Magdalen de Pazzi as seen from Beulah Street. It shows the church in the context of a tight block, and it is an interesting vision, since huge churches stumbled upon in unexpected places look more Italian than American. (Photo: Giò Martorana)

a slender tower on the east side of the building. It's not a particularly tall tower, but it is crowned by an elaborate circular cupola that is clad in copper, painted an avocado green, and topped with a gold-colored cross. The church would remain the heart of Italian life in South Philadelphia until after World War II, when assimilation, prosperity, and the suburbs began to beckon. As children of the original immigrants moved away from the neighborhood, the number of parishioners dwindled. In 2000, the archdiocese of Philadelphia decided to consolidate the parish by merging St. Mary Magdalen's and St. Paul's into a single congregation. The original church, which is listed on the city's Historic Register, was preserved as a worship site where occasional masses and funerals are held. Although St. Mary Magdalen's balcony no longer pulses with choir song on Sundays, its bulbous, green dome is still visible above South Philadelphia's row houses. Even without its own congregation, St. Mary Magdalen's remains a monument to the powerful impact of Italian culture on Philadelphia's history and physical development. St. Mary Magdalen de Pazzi is located at 714 Montrose Street.

South Philadelphia's Bankers' Row

As thousands of Italian immigrants streamed into South Philadelphia in the late nineteenth century to start new lives, Seventh Street was transformed into a bustling bankers' row. By 1897, there were twenty-five row-house-size banks between Bainbridge and Washington Avenues, all competing to provide newcomers with loans, money transfers, and railroad and steamship tickets.

The fierce competition for customers produced its own distinctive architectural form, one that adapted Italian traditions to Philadelphia's street grid. Because the immi-

Banca d'Italia in the Bella
Vista neighborhood.
(Photo: Giò Martorana)

grant banks wanted their operations to stand out in Philadelphia's tight street grid,
they preferred to locate their buildings on corners so that they would have two visible frontages. The main door to the bank was typically placed at the corner, which
became almost a third facade. The entrance and the upper floors were dramatically
curved in response to their context. But they also served as a pleasing come-on to
approaching customers. One of the most seductive of these corner banks is Banca
D'Italia, designed by Watson and Huckel in 1903.

Although Banca D'Italia is hardly bigger than the neighboring row houses
that box it in at Seventh and Pemberton Streets, it has the swagger of a major civic

building. The curved, bull-nose entrance is decorated with classical stone carvings, including a large frame around the door that resembles something you might see on a Roman chapel. The portico is crowned by a curved stone balcony, chiseled with the bank's name. The balcony is held up by a pair of spiraling stone brackets, which in turn rest on flowery, Corinthian column capitals. Lest a potential Banca D'Italia's customer walk by without noticing the entrance, the architects punctuated the third floor with a soaring clock tower. The bank's founder, Gennara Di Genova, was so proud of the architects' work that he took out a special supplement in the South Philadelphia newspaper *L'Opinione* in 1906 to tout the beauty of the building.

Banca Calabrese on the corner of Seventh and Christian. The name of the bank—in Italian—it is still readable on the facade. (Photo: Giò Martorana)

Banca D'Italia's design inspired a long list of copycats. Three years after it opened, another ambitious businessman, Lorenzo Bozzelli, erected an equally lavish corner bank a few doors away, at the corner of Fitzwater. (Today it houses a dry cleaner.) Banca Calabrese did the same at the corner of Christian Street. Knowing that the banking business might not last, their canny immigrant owners included apartments upstairs in all three buildings. It's a good thing, too. The 1929 stock market crash was not kind to small banks. By the time Philadelphia had recovered from the Great Depression, Seventh Street was no longer a crowded bankers' row. While many of the former banks have been converted to other uses, from the aforementioned dry cleaner to private homes, it's impossible to walk by without noticing and admiring their decorative, curving corners.

The Flying Church

Most Catholic churches in Philadelphia look to the past for their design inspiration. Not Our Lady of Loreto in Southwest Philadelphia. Built for the Kingsessing neighborhood's tight-knit Italian community, this little parish church exuberantly embraces modernity with a facade that evokes an early, art deco airport terminal.

To appreciate how radical the church's design is, it helps to know that air travel was only just becoming commercially viable when architect Frank L. Petrillo received the commission for Our Lady of Loreto in 1938. Only a year earlier, the city had broken ground for a municipal airport in southwest Philadelphia, and the public was captivated by the potential of air travel. What was then the main road to the city's primitive airfield—called Lindbergh Boulevard after the pioneering aviator—ran through the Kingsessing neighborhood. The new airport promised to become such an integral part of Kingsessing's identity that the parish decided to dedicate their new church to the figure who had been adopted as the patron saint of aviation.

As with so many religious narratives, this one is built on layers of meaning. According to Italian legend, the Virgin Mary's childhood home in the Middle East had been transported to the town of Loreto in the fourth century, carried aloft by winged angels who were concerned it would be damaged in religious wars. But many Italians in Kingsessing had experienced their own version of flight. Nearly everyone in the neighborhood had emigrated from the town of Nusco, near Naples, to Philadelphia in the early twentieth century. By the 1930s, Kingsessing's Italian population had swelled to twelve hundred families, enough to justify building their own church.

The architecture of Our Lady of Loreto celebrates the miracle of flight in both its religious and secular forms. Petrillo, who worked on many projects for Philadelphia's Italian community, designed the church in the streamlined modern style, an offshoot of art deco that was associated with new forms of high-speed travel, such as ocean liners, electric trains, and airplanes. While it's not unusual to see streamlined modern hotels and steamships, it is rare to see the flamboyant style adapted for a religious building. Petrillo employs the style in an almost whimsical fashion, brilliantly fusing the emerging imagery of air travel with the traditional imagery associated with Our Lady of Loreto.

At the center of the small church is a stubby belfry that looks like a miniature version of the air traffic control towers that were going up in the late 1930s. The connection to commercial air travel is reinforced by the openwork metal cross on top of the tower, which resembles a radar antenna. Instead of sending instructions to pilots, the tower broadcasts a religious message and suggests God is wired directly into the church sanctuary. On the face of the bell tower, a tile mural depicts Our Lady of Loreto being borne aloft with her house. In a conflation of tradition and technology, Mary is surrounded by a swirl of angels and prop planes. Above the door, Petrillo carved a winged crest. While the emblem is a references to the angels, its form is nearly identical to the pins that Pan Am flight crews wore in the heyday of air travel.

Like other streamlined modern buildings, Our Lady of Loreto's smooth sandstone facade seems molded from one continuous sheet of stone. But look around the corner, and you'll see that the side walls are made of Philadelphia's distinctive red brick. The walls are laid with randomly protruding "clunker" bricks, giving them a rough, artisanal texture that contrasts sharply with the smooth and refined public facade. After all, Our Lady of Loreto was a parish church for a modest immigrant community that hadn't forgotten its roots in the Italian countryside. That community has now moved on, and today the flying church is the home of Grace Christian Fellowship. The former Our Lady of Loreto is located at 6208 Grays Avenue.

Our Lady of Loreto.
(Photo: Richard Barnes)

Our Lady of Loreto.
(Photo: Richard Barnes)

PHILADELPHIA'S HOMAGES TO ITALIAN ARCHITECTURE

Philadelphia's Bridge of Sighs

Tourists come to Venice's Piazza San Marco to admire the lacey stone arches of the Doge's Palace and the picturesque gondoliers on the lagoon. After taking in these postcard views, they invariably turn their attention to the small bridge that vaults across the adjacent canal, connecting the doge's courtrooms with a prison. The Bridge of Sighs (Ponte dei Sospiri) owes its poetic name to the English poet Lord Byron, who imagined the convicts sighing at they took their last look at Venice through the bridge's grated windows. The white marble structure is considered a masterpiece of Renaissance design.

Philadelphia has its own loving replica of the Bridge of Sighs, but it is unlikely to attract any tourists, for reasons that have nothing to do with its architecture. Philadelphia's Bridge of Sighs is tucked away in a gritty alley on the edge of what was once the city's main shopping district. Completed in 1912, it was built to make it easier to haul men's suits and ladies' dresses between the former Lit Brothers department store on Market Street and its warehouse on Filbert Street.

What made the architects, Stearns and Castor, choose the famous Venetian landmark as the inspiration for their prosaic, twentieth-century bridge? The simplest explanation is that they were trying to keep its style consistent with the Lit store on Market Street, which resembles a massive Renaissance palazzo. Although that huge store spanned an entire block between Seventh and Eighth Streets, Lit continued to hunger for space. In 1912, the company acquired a Renaissance Revival building around the corner on Arch Street to use as its warehouse. Because

Bridge of Sighs on Lits Alley, behind the Cast Iron building in Center City (Market and Eighth Streets), Philadelphia. (Photo: Giò Martorana)

Filbert Street separated the main store from its new building, Lit decided it needed a bridge to make it easier to move merchandise between the two structures. Searching for a Renaissance precedent to inform their design, Stearns and Castor selected the well-known Bridge of Sighs.

While stylistic integrity was probably the original motivation for spanning the street with such an ornate design, the architects may have also been expressing some sly humor. A bustling service alley filled with delivery trucks, Filbert Street supports a steady flow of people and goods, much like a busy Venetian canal. It's also possible that Stearns and Castor were influenced by the architecture theories of John Ruskin. In his hugely influential treatise, *The Stones of Venice*, Ruskin urged architects to embed Renaissance forms and values in everyday buildings and not just save them for civic monuments.

Whatever their reasons, Stearns and Castor were extremely faithful to the original, even while adapting their bridge to Philadelphia's architectural traditions. Rather than build their span out of expensive white limestone, they chose red brick, a more modest material that is the city's vernacular. While the architect of the Bridge of Sighs called attention to the span's graceful arch with a series of elaborately sculpted heads, Stearns and Castor substituted simple keystones that are more in keeping with Philadelphia's sensibility.

A close examination reveals several other intriguing differences: The Roman god of justice appears on the crest at the top of the Venetian Bridge of Sighs to communicate its connection to the law courts. Since there isn't a corresponding god of retail in America (although maybe there should be), the Philadelphia architects mark the midpoint with an ornate stone window modeled on a Roman temple. In standard classical fashion, the pediment of that temple is supported by a shield and garlands. Two smaller windows, fitted with carved stone grilles, bracket the composition. Like the poor prisoners being led to their cells in Venice, one imagines Lit's busy stock clerks pausing in their labors every time they passed those windows to gaze longingly at the great city beyond. Even with all its variations, the very existence of this bridge has allowed a small piece of Venice to be magically transported to Philadelphia.

The Lit chain ceased operations in 1977, but its magnificent Renaissance Revival store on Market Street survives today as an office building, as does its old warehouse. The bridge is no longer used, except perhaps by the occasional ghost from Philadelphia's retail heyday. Philadelphia's Bridge of Sighs is visible on the 700 block of Filbert Street.

A Florentine-Style Palazzo for a Philadelphia Medici

If you were a wealthy Philadelphia banker in the early decades of the twentieth century, you probably thought of yourself as a modern-day Medici. Having made a fortune from investments in railroads, coal, and steel, you could spend your free

time amassing a fabulous art collection or constructing Renaissance-style mansions in places like the Main Line and Palm Beach. Edward T. Stotesbury did all
that. But he went a step further and built himself a Florentine palazzo in Center
City. It just happened to be based on one that belonged to the Medici family's great
rival, Filippo Strozzi the Elder.

Stotesbury got his start working for Anthony Drexel, the founder of Drexel
and Co. (as well as Drexel University). In the late nineteenth century, the firm
established a relationship with J. P. Morgan, the ruthless and successful New York
banker. After Drexel's death, Stotesbury became Morgan's main partner. While
Morgan reigned in New York, Stotesbury remained in Philadelphia to oversee that
part of their empire. In 1925, he commissioned Day and Klauder to design a new
Philadelphia office for Drexel and Co. to reflect the company's financial might.

Palazzo Strozzi, Florence, Italy. Picture taken before 1908, when it was the inspiration for the Drexel and Co. Building. (Image from page 78 of "La casa fiorentina e i suoi arredi nei secoli XIV e XV" [1908], available at https://www.flickr.com/photos /internetarchivebookimages /14778817945/)

With their deep knowledge of European architecture, Day and Klauder could have easily made the Palazzo Medici their model. Instead, they chose a less famous precedent.

Both palaces were constructed in the late fifteenth century, so maybe it is not surprising that the Medici and Strozzi palaces are actually quite similar. They are both crafted from enormous blocks of stone—rolled, chiseled, and rusticated at the base to give them a natural appearance. Both are strong forms that convey strength as well as an air of impenetrability. Their double-arched windows are set high above the street on the second-floor piano nobile, beyond the reach of prying eyes. Yet there are differences. Although the Medici name is more famous, the Strozzi palace is much more graceful and vertical in its proportions. And because there is only a single entrance on the main facade, the energy is concentrated toward the center.

The Strozzi's more efficient form was also better suited to Drexel's location at Fifteenth and Walnut. Like the Strozzi palace, the Drexel and Co. headquarters sits at a corner where it is seen from only two sides, while the Medici palace stood alone and could be seen in the round. In the 1920s, that stretch of Walnut Street was evolving a miniature version of Wall Street and was lined with handsome limestone brokerage houses and banks. Built of light gray granite, the design by Day and Klauder improves on the Strozzi palace in certain ways, adapting it to life in a modern city. Although it sits on a high base, marked by a rounded ledge, it has large ground-floor windows. At six stories—twice Strozzi's number—it also appears more statuesque. The architects modulate the height by inserting stone balustrades at the top of the first and third floors and setting back the top two levels.

Filippo Strozzi, as it turns out, never got to live in his palace. After he died in 1491, it was confiscated by Cosimo I de' Medici, and, consequently, construction was never finished. Stotesbury had similarly bad luck. Although Drexel and Co. did get to occupy their Florentine palazzo, the company was hit hard by the Great Depression and was dissolved in 1930. Like the Strozzi palace, it was passed on to new owners and never played the magnificent role in the city's cultural life that its original client envisioned. Philadelphia's Strozzi palace can be found at 1435 Walnut Street.

A Florentine Cathedral on Broad Street

Built half a century and an ocean apart, Philadelphia's Rodeph Shalom and the Great Synagogue of Florence are architectural siblings, born of common ideas and influences. You might not be aware of the relationship simply by looking at the exteriors. But once you enter their sanctuaries, the family resemblance becomes apparent.

The synagogue in Florence was built as a direct result of the new civil rights that European Jews gained in the nineteenth century. Although Jews had lived in Europe for centuries, they suffered from continual repression and were forced to minimize the presence of their synagogues. After the social and political upheavals of the French Revolution, many of those restrictions were loosened. In 1840, the walls of the Florence ghetto were demolished. Almost immediately, the city's Jews began making plans for a prominent new synagogue that would sit among Florence's architectural treasures.

The challenge was to find an architectural language that expressed the building's Jewish identity and would not be confused with one of Florence's many churches. Like other newly liberated Jewish communities in Europe, Florentine Jews sought inspiration by looking back to those periods in their past when Jewish culture had flourished. The design of the Florence synagogue mashes together two different styles: Moorish and Byzantine. You enter through stylized arches straight out of the Alhambra in Spain and emerge into a sanctuary whose massive dome is borrowed from Istanbul's Hagia Sophia. The ceiling, walls, and floors are all decorated with interlocking Moorish vines and flowers. The construction of the magnificent synagogue took eight years and was finally completed in 1882.

While American Jews were never repressed in the way Italian Jews were, they wrestled with the same architectural problem that faced Florence's community: How explicitly should the synagogue assert its Jewish identity? How much should it assimilate into its architectural surroundings? Rodeph Shalom's congregation may have felt these issues more acutely than most because it is the oldest and largest Ashkenazic group in Philadelphia. In 1873, they moved the congregation to a prominent site just a few blocks north of City Hall. They hired the famous Philadelphia architect Frank Furness to design their new home. He produced a strongly Moorish design, similar in some ways to the synagogue in Florence.

But for a variety of reasons, the congregation wasn't entirely happy with Furness's Moorish building. Less than half a century after it opened, Rodeph Shalom decided to replace the Victorian temple with a more modern design. Once again, they struggled with how their new building should communicate its Jewish identity.

The new design, built by the architecture firm Simon and Simon in 1926, cleverly balances the congregation's competing impulses by making it Western on the outside and Eastern on the inside. The building's simple, boxy form and its art deco detailing reflect the transition to modernism taking place in architecture in the 1920s. Unlike the Furness design, there is no bell tower or spire set off to the side. Instead, the three-story-high limestone facade, with its crenellated cornice and narrow archers' windows, suggests an ancient Middle Eastern fortress. Like the Florence synagogue, the entrance is marked by three soaring arched portals. Their shape is more classical than those in Florence, but the intricate swirls of the mosaics above the bronze doors gives them a Moorish flavor.

The references to the Florence synagogue and, by extension, the Hagia Sophia become more pronounced once you enter the building. From the outside, the

Rodeph Shalom Synagogue. (Congregation Rodeph Shalom/ Photographer Graydon Wood)

Rendering of the sanctuary at Rodeph Shalom by Nicola D'Ascenzo. (The Athenaeum of Philadelphia)

rooftop crenellations obscure the existence of the large dome that hovers over the three-story sanctuary, similar to the one in Florence. Once you step into the enormous room, your senses are overwhelmed. Every inch of the walls and ceiling is intricately stenciled with stylized vines, leaves, and medallions that recall the patterns on an oriental carpet. The colors are bright: cobalt blue, tomato red, and shimmering gold. Rodeph Shalom also owes this rich display to the skills of an Italian immigrant, Nicola D'Ascenzo, a celebrated craftsman who was responsible for decorating the main sanctuary. With his work we see the architectural ideas perfected in the Florence synagogue, reinterpreted for an American congregation. Rodeph Shalom is located at 615 North. Broad Street.

A Pantheon for an American Hero

The practice of honoring gods and emperors with works of architecture is as old as humankind. The Egyptians gave us the pyramid. The ancient Greeks perfected the columned temple. And the Romans improved on their designs by perfecting the use of concrete. With better engineering, the Romans were able to create enormous vaulted domes that could span a large structure without the support or interruption of heavy crossbeams. To this day, the vaulted roof of Rome's Pantheon remains one of the largest self-supporting domes in the world.

Philadelphia completed its own version of the Pantheon in 1934, designed by John T. Windrim. Unlike the original, which is dedicated to the Roman gods (or, some argue, a single god), the Philadelphia Pantheon memorializes a mere mortal: Benjamin Franklin. By choosing this well-known Roman temple as an architectural precedent, Philadelphia effectively elevated the American scientist, statesman, and founder of the nation to the level of a secular deity. Every year, tens of thousands of people pass through the Philadelphia Pantheon, which serves as the entrance to the Franklin Institute Science Museum.

Of course, Philadelphia was not the first city to copy the Pantheon. Since its completion by the Emperor Hadrian in A.D. 126, the Pantheon has been widely imitated and has become a template for many important civic buildings. In the United States, Thomas Jefferson was the first to recognize the monumental power of the Pantheon's soaring dome. He based the main library at the University of Virginia on the temple, fashioning the great drum of the rotunda in red brick. Variations in white stone can be found at Columbia University, MIT, and the National Gallery of Art in Washington, DC. When the United States finally got around to erecting a memorial to Jefferson in Washington, DC, the design was based on the Pantheon.

Why are we so drawn to this particular Roman temple? The main facade looks like any number of classical temples. But after stepping through the immense Corinthian columns, you find yourself enveloped in a vast cavern of open space. Light pours in from a round opening at the apex of the dome, called an oculus. Because the rotunda is essentially an immense, open-plan room, it can be easily put

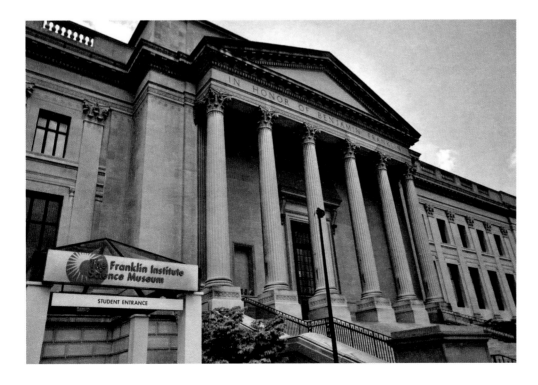

The main entrance of the Franklin Institute in Philadelphia. (The Franklin Institute)

Franklin Hall contains a statue of a seated Benjamin Franklin, and it is based on the Pantheon in Rome. (The Franklin Institute)

to any number of uses. In Philadelphia, the rotunda serves as a setting for a twenty-foot-high marble sculpture of Franklin created by the sculptor James Earle Fraser. He depicted Franklin seated in a chair, perhaps contemplating his next scientific experiment or political speech.

Proposals for building Philadelphia's Pantheon were first discussed in the 1920s, after the Benjamin Franklin Parkway had been cut through the northwest quadrant of Center City. The parkway had been envisioned as a cultural corridor lined with neoclassical buildings housing museums devoted to the arts and sciences. A site on the west side of Logan Square was reserved for the Franklin Institute, the city's oldest science museum. The lobby was intended to serve as the national memorial to Franklin.

You enter the building from Twentieth Street and proceed through a three-story-high, columned portico reminiscent of the Pantheon's temple-like facade—

but with only six Corinthian columns instead of eight. The portico leads directly into the dramatic rotunda. Faced in milky white marble and lit with modern lighting, the Philadelphia version seems less moody than the original. The huge volume of space is capped by an immense coffered ceiling designed by the Spanish architect Rafael Guastavino, who specialized in domes. The walls of the rotunda are punctuated with arched niches and other classical details similar to those in the original. The Philadelphia arches all have skylights near the top, further adding to the brightness level. As sunlight filters in from the oculus, Franklin's statue is bathed in a halo of light. What better honor could our secular democracy bestow on one of its heroes than to treat him like an ancient Roman god? Find Philadelphia's Pantheon at 271 North Twenty-First Street.

ITALIAN INSPIRATIONS

When Tuscan Architecture Was the Official Style of America's Middle Class

The Italianate style became popular just as America was creating its first suburbs in the mid-nineteenth century, and it reflected the aspirations of the country's newly emerging middle class. The development of streetcars and trolleys had made it possible for affluent businesspeople, enriched by the country's rapid industrialization, to leave the congested central city for greener neighborhoods. Because the new streetcar suburbs were neither city nor country, they posed an architectural challenge. Searching for an appropriate building style that wasn't too countrified, housing developers looked to an earlier generation of suburban pioneers: the medieval Tuscan merchants who also built country villas on the outskirts of the city.

Today, you can see blocks of flat-roofed Tuscan-style houses throughout West Philadelphia and Chestnut Hill, two of the city's first streetcar suburbs. As with so many borrowed styles, their resemblance to actual Tuscan villas is fairly casual. The central portion of the house is generally a boxlike form that is surrounded by a deep porch and accented with Italian features such as cupolas, loggias, and overhanging cavetto cornices. Unlike the interconnected townhouses that these new industrial barons left behind, Philadelphia's Italianate villas were surrounded by lawns and gardens, similar to those occupied by their Tuscan predecessors.

It wasn't just middle-class homeowners who associated their new prosperity with the country houses built by prosperous Tuscan merchants. So did the retailers who catered to them. When Jacob Reed's Sons clothing store moved its operations to Fifteenth and Chestnut in 1903, it infused the design with elements of the Italianate style even though it was a thoroughly urban building.

Founded in 1824, Jacob Reed's had started out near the Delaware waterfront, selling humble, ready-made clothing for working men and soldiers. But by the end of the nineteenth century, it had gone upmarket and was turning out finely tailored men's clothing for the new business elite. As Philadelphia's business district shifted

The present store at 1424-26 Chestnut Street

Jacob Reed's Sons.
(From *One Hundred Years Ago: Jacob Reed's Sons, Founded 1824*, by Jacob Reed's Sons, published by Jacob Reed's Sons, Philadelphia, 1924)

west from Old City to the new political hub around city hall, Jacob Reed's followed the men in suits.

By the start of the twentieth century, Jacob Reed's was the premier men's haberdasher in Philadelphia, so it was natural to want to be close to Philadelphia's magnificent city hall, which was completed in 1901. It picked a site on Chestnut Street just a block from city hall and chose William L. Price, of Price and McLanahan, as its architect. Price was an early advocate of the Arts and Crafts movement, which rebelled against the homogenizing effects of industrialization by incorporating earthy, handmade elements into buildings. His design for the Jacob Reed's store weaves together the aspirational message of Italianate architecture with a wealth of handcrafted details, which help communicate the brand's devotion to high-quality craftsmanship.

Built with dark red brick and limestone, the four-story building is richly detailed, starting with the two-story-high Palladian arch on the ground floor. The arch serves as a gateway into the retail emporium. By setting back the store entrance under the arched portal, Price created a civilized transition from the noisy street to the store's elegant interior. Customers could pause to admire the colorful Mercer tile mosaics that decorate the underside of the arch. Each circular image depicts a different stage in the manufacture of clothing. Along with promoting Jacob Reed's brand with colorful murals, Price made sure there was plenty of space to show off the company's clothes. A pair of Corinthian columns stand like sentries on either side of the arch, creating two vitrines for displaying merchandise.

At the second level, Price added two smaller arched windows with romantic Juliette balconies. As the building rises, the window arrangement changes, growing lighter and lighter, as if to escape gravity. The fourth floor features a delicately sculpted loggia, or porch, surrounded by more Mercer tile mosaics produced at the Moravian Pottery and Tile Works in Doylestown. The factory was one of the main suppliers of the colored tiles prized by Arts and Crafts architects. The little building is crowned by an overhanging eave, which unfurls over the facade like a gently cresting wave. All the architectural themes were continued inside the store, where Gothic arches spring from Doric columns and divide the space into intimate nooks for displaying Jacob Reed's clothing.

The specular craftsmanship continues around the back of the building on Sansom Street. An enormous, arched stained-glass window mirrors the Chestnut Street Arch and originally let natural light filter into the store. While there are endless Arts and Crafts details to admire, Price also embraced modern technology for the store's construction. Jacob Reed's was the multistory building in the city constructed with reinforced concrete.

As the suburbs moved further out of the city in the 1970s and 1980s, Jacob Reed's lost its clientele. The store closed in 1983. Today it houses a drugstore that caters to a mass market of rich and poor alike. Jacob Reed's Sons is located at 1424 Chestnut Street.

How Tuscan Towers Inspired a New Approach to Architecture

Louis Kahn made two extended trips to Italy, and his experiences there transformed his approach to architecture. Like other architects who came of age in the 1930s, Kahn had been a committed, if occasionally skeptical, adherent of Corbusian modernism. But a three-month fellowship at the American Academy in Rome in 1950 reacquainted him with ancient landmarks and fired up his imagination. As he traveled through Tuscany, Umbria, and the Veneto, he was entranced by the stately stone and brick architecture, both the timeless landmarks and everyday structures. Kahn filled his notebooks with evocative black-and-white sketches that emphasized the light and shadows cast by their heavy masonry forms. The medieval tower houses he saw in San Gimignano made a special impression on him, and he produced a series of Cezanne-like paintings in addition to numerous pencil sketches.

Even before his stay in Italy, Kahn had been growing increasingly dissatisfied with certain aspects of modernism. He especially disliked the International Style and its emphasis on slick, generic glass buildings. As his career began to take off in the early 1950s after his return from Rome, he would often refer to the sketches he made in Italy for inspiration. When he received a commission in 1956 to design a pair of buildings for the University of Pennsylvania, the towers he had seen in San Gimignano provided the starting point.

Located on an important pilgrimage route in Tuscany, San Gimignano had been a wealthy trading post during medieval times. For defensive reasons, the town had been built on top of a hill and surrounded by protective wall. But because the wall limited the amount of land available for housing, prosperous merchants who wanted to establish family compounds were forced to build up, creating an unlikely skyline of some seventy stone towers. Although the town fell on hard times after the plagues of the fourteenth century, more than a dozen of the vertical mansions were still intact when Kahn visited. His paintings, executed in shades of ochre and gold, depict the towers as if they were a single, interlinked organism.

Kahn's design for Richards Medical Research Laboratories (which includes the attached Goddard Research building) is not an exact copy of San Gimignano but an abstracted interpretation that captures the spirit and heft of those statuesque forms. Although the two red brick research facilities are really a single building, they have been segmented into six discrete towers ranging from six to nine stories. Each of the six is bisected by a narrow brick shaft that rises above the roofline, forcing the eye upward and further accentuating their verticality. Kahn arranged

Louis Kahn's Richards Medical Research Laboratory. (Photo: Giò Martorana)

the towers on the site in a pinwheel formation rather than in a straight line. Set back from Penn's Hamilton Walk, the group evokes San Gimignano's jumbled skyline as it might have been seen by pilgrims making their way up the hill.

Kahn didn't segment the buildings into towers just to create a visual effect. Each tower was intended to perform a specified role. Some contain labs, while others house the services—ventilation, cooling, and water—needed to operate them. By dividing the building this way, Kahn was able to create a hierarchy of uses, which he called the "served" and "servant" spaces.

Kahn's formal and structural innovations made Richards a sensation even before it was completed in 1965. But those aren't the only reasons why the labs are considered one of the most important designs of the twentieth century. Unlike many modernists from that period, Kahn recognized the value of creating new buildings that responded to their surroundings. Penn was and still is a red brick campus. Kahn's labs are bordered by three classic collegiate buildings whose red brick facades are accented by gables and turrets and trimmed in limestone. Describing the Richards-Goddard project in 1959, Kahn wrote that he envisioned the building as a "massive, raw-boned structure" that would complement the traditional architecture of Penn's campus "in a way that no shimmering tube of glass and steel could."

While Kahn would never consider emulating the gables on the older buildings, he believed that modern designs needed to acknowledge that they were part of an architectural continuum. Before he started work on Richards, he had struggled to develop a style that fused a modern sensibility with the timeless quality of older masonry structures. With a trip to a medieval town in Tuscany, Kahn found the inspiration he needed to push American architecture into the future. The Richards Labs are located at 3700 Hamilton Walk.

The Sons of Italy's Modernist Lodge

South Philadelphia is often thought of as a bastion of tradition, but there is nothing the least bit traditional about the building that once served as the home for the Grand Lodge of the Pennsylvania Order of the Sons of Italy in America. Set amid South Broad Street's nineteenth-century brownstones and churches, the flat-roofed International Style structure is an assertive—even aggressive—statement of modernity.

Order of Sons of Italy,
1200 South Broad Street,
designed by Carroll,
Grisdale, Van Alen, 1954.
(Photo: Richard Barnes)

The Sons of Italy was formed in the early twentieth century to help immigrants adjust to life in America. Along with providing practical help with banking, insurance, and language instruction, they operated meeting halls that became the social heart of the community, hosting weddings, funerals, and feasts. After the end of World War II, the Sons of Italy decided to expand its presence in South Philadelphia, optimistically expecting the Italian population to grow. In 1954, the group selected one of Philadelphia's top modernist firms, Carroll, Grisdale and Van Alen, to design a new Grand Lodge at Broad and Federal Streets. Although the firm would later go on to create inventive and sculptural forms, such as the Rittenhouse Labs at Penn, at this point they were still adhering to a functionalist vision of modernism. The result is that the Grand Lodge is about as far from a typical Italian social club as one could imagine.

Built around a generous landscaped courtyard that is accessed from Federal Street, the two-story, glass-and-stone building is low and long and might easily be mistaken for an anonymous high school or government building from the period. What saves it is the architects' decision to emphasize the vertical. Thick columns of golden limestone—similar in color to the stone at the Philadelphia Museum of Art—divide the regimented grids of glass into a series of bays. The push and pull of the horizontal grids against the vertical bays helps give the building a sense of movement.

The large complex was a massive undertaking for the Sons of Italy, and the building was designed to provide revenue-generating opportunities. The bays along Broad Street were sized to accommodate shops. Inside there were two social halls—one equipped with a stage, the other with a curved bar—that could be rented out for events. In a lavish gesture, the Sons of Italy installed a six-lane Brunswick bowling alley in the basement. The rest of the building housed offices to provide social services.

But it appears that the Sons of Italy misjudged the need for its programs. The group was also unable to generate the revenue it expected. In 1968, the organization worked out a deal to sell the building to the state, which was looking for space for a new kind of training center for the intellectually disabled. The federal government had just passed the Community Mental Health Act in 1963, which began the process of deinstitutionalizing care. The Grand Lodge proved to be perfect for its new task. In 1972, a group called Programs Employing People (PEP) moved in and converted the banquet halls to classrooms and workshops, places to provide training and adult day-care services.

They kept the architects' original design largely intact but greened the courtyard, adding lush plantings and new trees. The bowling alley—now called Pep Bowl—was opened to the public. It is now a popular spot for birthday parties. The bowling alley and banquet halls also generate nearly 10 percent of PEP's revenue. Half a century later, the functionalist Grand Lodge designed by Carroll, Grisdale and Van Alen is doing exactly what they intended: housing social services and celebratory events under one flat, modernist roof. The former Grand Lodge can be found at 1200 South Broad Street.

31

From Rocky to Botticelli, Italian Philadelphia

*Concerts, Shows, Exhibits, and Conferences in
a City in Pennsylvania Where the "American Dream"
Speaks Our Language*

Paolo Valentino

The bronze statue of Rocky stands at the foot of the steps of the Philadelphia Museum of Art. An icon of American pop culture and a "must" destination for every tourist visiting the city, both the statue and the steps incite a strange fascination as a monument celebrating a fictional hero, but they pay homage to a true ideal—the American dream.

If we begin our tour of Philadelphia, known as the birthplace of the United States of America, there at Rocky's steps, it's for a specific reason: the Italian American origins of the boxer brought to life on the screen by Sylvester Stallone. Because—and here the cinematographic fiction ends and reality begins—very few regions of the United States have the same presence, influence, and contribution of the Italian community, in all aspects of the social fabric, as Philadelphia.

It is starting from this fact that Andrea Canepari, the Consul General of Italy, one of those diplomats that Italy should have as a model, came up with the idea of Ciao Philadelphia (ciaophiladelphia.com). He went knocking at every door: government offices, private companies and corporations, museums, foundations, universities, and cultural organizations.

The result was a unique endeavor, which for the first time brings together all the pieces of "Italianicity" of this metropolitan area. For the entire month of October, Philadelphia speaks and thinks Italian: concerts, exhibits, film screenings, conferences, university seminars, and architectural tours. "The influence of Italian-Americans has been huge. *Ciao Philadelphia* highlights this bond," said Democratic Mayor Michael Nutter at the launching of the event—so enthusiastic about Italy that when there were proposed plans about possibly closing the Italian Consulate,

FOLLOWING SPREAD:
The map of an Italian journey in Philadelphia as seen through the eyes of the *Corriere della Sera*, journalist Paolo Valentino, during Ciao Philadelphia in October 2014. (Drawing by Antonio Monteverdi)

il Philadelphia Museum of Art d.

AUTOMOTIVE MUSEUM

Fred Simeone Foundation

Passyunk
Avenue

GENO'S STEAKS

GENO'S STEAKS

PIZZA

Antonio Monteverdi

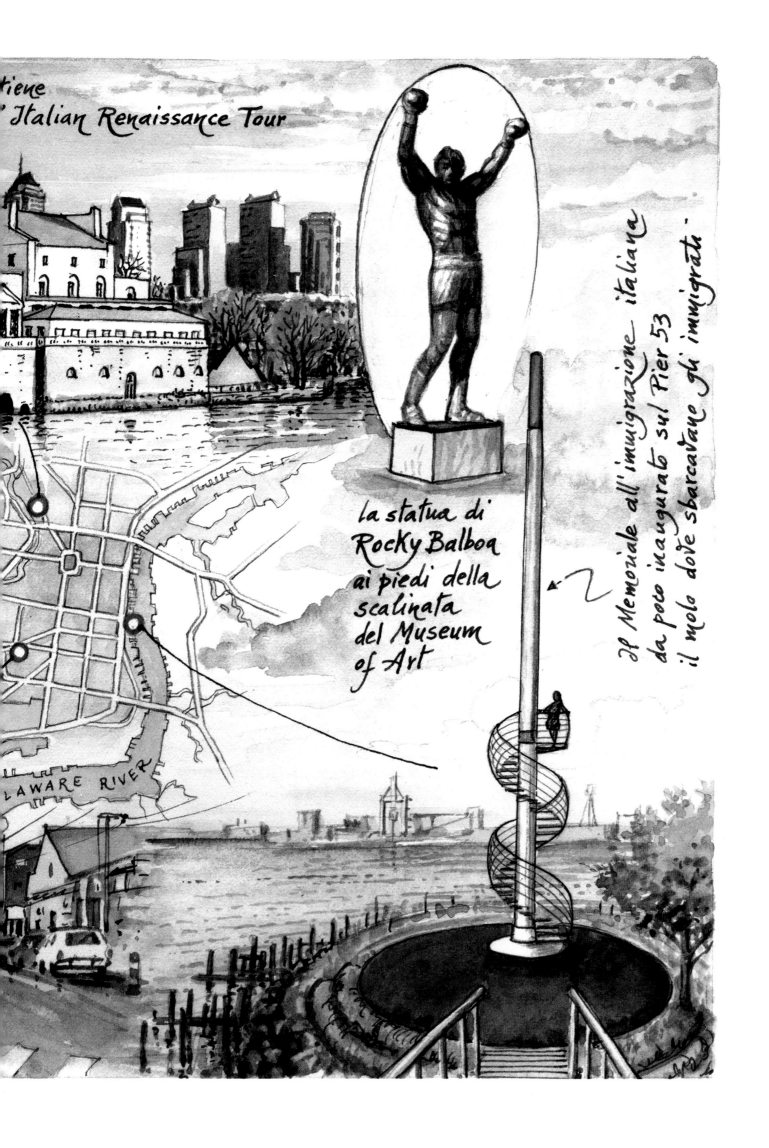

tiene
' Italian Renaissance Tour

la statua di
Rocky Balboa
ai piedi della
scalinata
del Museum
of Art

Il Memoriale all'immigrazione italiana
da poco inaugurato sul Pier 53
il molo dove sbarcavano gli immigrati -

LAWARE RIVER

he didn't hesitate to act immediately to prevent it by calling Italian Prime Minister Matteo Renzi, whom he knows personally as the former mayor of Florence, Philadelphia's sister city.

But let's go back to the beginning, the starting point. Let's go back up the Rocky steps and take a jump back in time to the Renaissance. The museum (philamuseum .org) dedicates a "not to be missed" road to the Italian Renaissance, displaying from its permanent collection the masterpieces of the great and grand masters from Masaccio to Botticelli and from Bellotto to Tiepolo. Also, in the framework of Ciao Philadelphia, the Philadelphia Art Museum hosts an exhibit dedicated to Paul Strand, one of the masters of modern photography, and Italy is among the focal points of the exhibit. The height of Italian immigration to Philadelphia between the end of the 1800s and early 1900s is now memorialized at Pier 53 on Washington Avenue, which was the second major port of entry to America after Ellis Island: at Pier 53 a million people arrived by boat, almost two hundred thousand Italians. Here Jody Pinto, Italian American artist, installed a very suggestive memorial, a metal landmark with an illuminated top piece, marking the place where so much hope and suffering was concentrated.

The major cultural institutions in Philadelphia speak Italian, such as the prestigious University of Pennsylvania, where Fabio Finotti directs the Center for Italian Studies, or Temple University, where oncologist and geneticist Antonio Giordano runs the Sbarro Institute for Cancer Research and Molecular Medicine and is about to launch a new master's program in bio-innovation, which combines the disciplines of medicine and business. For Ciao Philadelphia, Drexel University College of Media Arts and Design organizes an exhibit dedicated to eighty years of Italian shoe design ranging from Ferragamo to Prada. Meanwhile, Villanova hosts another beautiful photographic exhibit, with panoramas and sights of Pavia from the 1800s to the present day.

It is certainly worth traveling just a short distance from Center City Philadelphia to visit the Automotive Museum, housing an incredible collection of vintage race cars that an Italian American entrepreneur, Fred Simeone, acquired in the course of forty years (simeonemuseum.org). In 2011 named the best automotive museum in the world, it houses sixty-five legendary automobiles, half of which are Italian: original race cars, winners of Mille Miglia, Targa Florio, Le Mans, extremely rare gems not to be found elsewhere, such as the 1929 Alfa Romeo Super Sport and a 1958 Ferrari Testa Rossa.

Philadelphia's architecture is also Italian—just take a stroll through the heart of the historic area, the birthplace of American democracy, to find buildings such as the First Bank of the United States, the Athenaeum, and Carpenter's Hall, the gathering place of the First Continental Congress of the thirteen original colonies—all of these buildings are Palladian style.

The popular soul of the Italian American heritage is found in South Philadelphia, along the very streets where Rocky trained by running amid the encouraging cheers of the locals. The new waves are now found on trendy Passyunk Avenue, full of local restaurants, lounges, and pastry shops, full of younger crowds. Perhaps no other city in the United States more than Philadelphia brings us inside the Italian soul of American identity. "I hope that Ciao Philadelphia becomes an annual event," declares Deputy Mayor Michael "Michele" DiBerardinis.

Translation of an article published by the historical Italian newspaper *Corriere della Sera*, October 24, 2014, on pages 30 and 31. Reprinted with permission.

ROCKY BALBOA

Icon of the City

JUDITH GOODE

PAOLO VALENTINO'S ARTICLE (CHAPTER 31) DEMONSTRATES the central significance of Rocky Balboa as a symbol of the city. The hero of six Rocky films made between 1976 and 2006 and a major figure in the two Creed spin-off films (2015 and 2018), the franchise reflects the city in several ways.

Its creator, Sylvester Stallone, is of Italian descent. While he is from New York, he is treated as an "adopted" native son. The films' characters and scenes represent the material city. The central characters and the local spaces allude to Italians and South Philadelphia.

Yet Rocky's story resonates with people all over the world who are familiar with the films. In the movie franchise, Rocky and later others are portrayed as underdogs with vision, determination, and a strong work ethic. It inspires individual aspirations. It also serves to symbolize an important aspect of Philadelphia's late twentieth-century reputation as an underdog, a gritty, blue-collar city. Seeing Rocky running up the PMA steps for a moment of triumph and gazing at the beautiful view of the city from the steps has helped the Rocky story become connected in symbolic terms to both individual triumph and the identity of the city itself.

Rocky statue by A. Thomas Schomberg, 1980, at the footsteps of the PMA. (Photo: Giò Martorana)

The films and the relocated bronze statue on the steps represent the city to residents and visitors alike. The contradictions between the elite high-culture museum built to symbolize the city as an industrial and cultural powerhouse of the gilded age and the declining underdog city of popular culture is represented by the conflicts over the placement of the statue. A series of relocations of the Rocky statue from the museum to various athletic venues and finally back to the museum steps—but in a lower, decentered position—was the result of an agreement worked out between Stallone and the Philadelphia Art Commission.

The steps are an iconic place, and Eakins Oval has become a central ceremonial space for recent major events such as the Pope's visit, holiday musical events, and the completion of parades and races. Conquering the steps in triumph is an almost mandatory experience for visitors and many residents alike. Another way to celebrate Rocky is to go on tours of the territory through which Rocky ran to train, which connect Rocky's grit to the material landscape of South Philadelphia.

Ciao Philadelphia

Creation of an Italian Cultural Initiative and Volume

Andrea Canepari

A FEW MONTHS AFTER MY ARRIVAL IN PHILADELPHIA as Consul General of Italy in August 2013, I participated in the traditional celebration in honor of Christopher Columbus during the month of October. On the Sunday preceding Columbus Day, I attended the parade organized by the 1492 Society in South Philadelphia. On Columbus Day, I joined the Sons of Italy in a ceremony in front of the obelisk dedicated to Christopher Columbus, created by Robert Venturi in 1992, on the five hundredth anniversary of his arrival in the New World.

There were not as many people at that ceremony in front of the obelisk as I would have expected, since, as written by Stefano Luconi in "Italians and Italy" in *The Encyclopedia of Greater Philadelphia*, "By 2010, the U.S. Census identified the Philadelphia metropolitan region as home to the second-largest Italian-American population in the United States."[1] I figured there would be a larger turnout. I began wondering about the lack of participation at the ceremony. Maybe Italian Americans were becoming more and more assimilated into American society and therefore no longer felt a strong connection with Italy as their motherland and among themselves as a group. Or maybe they did not feel the need to show those links.[2] I was in Philadelphia, a city with so many Italian influences that it does not even have a central business district called "downtown," as in the majority of U.S. cities, but a "center city" that reminded me of the Italian *"centro città."*[3] Every day I was discovering different segments of the Italian community and getting in touch with economic, political, and cultural leaders of Italian origin. Furthermore, I was meeting with several people not ethnically linked with Italy who showed a strong attraction to contemporary Italy for its culture and way of life. I would call them the "friends of Italy," an idea grounded in the concept of "Italicity"—that is, the transnation-

FOLLOWING SPREAD: Image composition of the PECO Skyscraper celebrating Ciao Philadelphia, October 2014. (Photo: Gary Horn)

al spirit of Italy that sees the heritage of Italy as part of the heritage of humanity.[4] While I was using the idea of the friends of Italy more as an evocative term for my speeches and a way to communicate a public diplomacy message[5] rather than as a specific conceptual category, I was aware of the fact that Philadelphia was an example of Italian cultural richness created through centuries of relations. This richness was the basis for the Italicity of the city and the region.

Councilman Mark Squilla and John Oliano (State Lodge of Pennsylvania, Order Sons of Italy in America) with the Italian Consul General at the Wreath Laying Ceremony on Columbus Day 2015, in front of Robert Venturi's Columbus Obelisk, Columbus Boulevard, Philadelphia.
(Photo: Gary Horn)

How was it possible, then, that all these connections, even appreciated by non-Italian Americans in Philadelphia, were not reflected in the level of participation at events such as the one on Columbus Day? I started reflecting on this question and talking with leaders and several members of the Italian American community who could help me understand. I felt it was important to improve the awareness of the links between Italy and Philadelphia, and I decided to start my reflection with Columbus Day, given the importance this celebration has for Italian Americans throughout the United States, as highlighted by Steven Conn in Chapter 16 of this book. Conn explains how on the occasion of the sesquicentennial exhibit—celebrating the 150th anniversary of U.S. independence in Philadelphia in 1926—Italians used the celebrations "to stake their own claim to Americanness and help create a new identity: Italian American." According to Conn, Columbus Day was an American holiday that became more Italianized because of the sesquicentennial fair held in Philadelphia and the involvement of Italian Americans, mainly from Philadelphia, when Columbus Day became an occasion for Italian Americans to "stake a claim as part of the founding of the United States." Italian Americans of 2013 did not feel the same urgency to prove their Americanness as their ancestors of 1926 did. Was this another reason for the small number of people in front of the obelisk?

I started thinking about the controversies that were arising throughout the United States around the Columbus Day celebrations. However, the theme did not seem to me as sensitive in Philadelphia as it was in other parts of the United States. To this point, a couple of years later in 2015, a petition organized on change.org to remove the Columbus obelisk from its position in Philadelphia collected only 543 signatures from a metropolitan area of almost six million inhabitants.[6] In Philadelphia, the majority of people felt that the Genoese explorer—and his celebration on Columbus Day—was essentially identified with his Italianity,[7] as explained by Charlene Mires in her essay entitled "Columbus Day" in *The Encyclopedia of Greater Philadelphia*.[8] Rather than viewing him as a conqueror or as an abstract American hero, by commemorating Columbus, "Italian-Americans embraced the navigator as their countryman, celebrated Italian culture, and called attention to their American loyalty and identity. While the practices and places for observing Columbus Day changed over time, the holiday in Philadelphia and its suburbs retained a distinctively Italian flavor." For these reasons, Philadelphians did not always join passionately in the American debate questioning the role of historical monuments that include Civil War testimonies.[9] Philadelphians seem to recognize that monuments to Columbus, such as the Venturi obelisk at Penn's Landing, are ways of celebrating the Italianity of the city and the importance of emigrants for its development. In Chapter 21, Jody Pinto describes, among her creations, a monument *Land Buoy* (inaugurated in 2014) dedicated to her grandparents' crossing of the ocean and to more than one million immigrants who made the same great journey. The Christopher Columbus monument in Marconi Plaza (South Philadelphia), the Venturi obelisk, *Land Buoy*, and other monuments in the city, such as the one dedicated to Octavius Catto, an African American, unveiled in 2017, are ways of recognizing the role of minorities, not oppressing them. In fact, over the last century, the celebration of Columbus in Philadelphia has been one of the measures of the rise of Italian Americans from the status of a denigrated minority; the celebration of this Italian hero in America and Venturi's 1992 obelisk were, in a sense, a step in the broader revision of history that is now underway in favor of minorities and not against them.

Columbus Day Parade on Broad Street in Philadelphia, organized by the 1492 Society, October 2014. Ciao Philadelphia stresses the importance of the parade, aiming to bring together the traditional Italian American community, the new immigrants from Italy, and friends of Italy in the region. (Photo: Gary Horn)

As Consul General of Italy in Philadelphia, one of my responsibilities was to strengthen the relationship between the consular jurisdiction and Italy. In Philadelphia there was a powerful tool available to increase awareness and strengthen connections: the Italian legacy of the city. When I started, I felt like an archeologist in front of a treasure that needed to be rediscovered in its fullness from the dust of time. I felt the importance that an increased attention for the Italian legacy in the city would have for the relationships between the consular jurisdiction and Italy. I started thinking about the idea of creating a series of cultural events meant to create bridges between the Philadelphia region and contemporary Italy around the occasion of Columbus Day, a celebration so dear to Italian Americans. My aim was to bring together the descendants of Italians who immigrated decades ago, recent Italian settlers, and friends of Italy in the region—that is, those Philadelphians who, although not linked by heritage, had fallen in love with "Italicity."

I believed that linking Philadelphia to contemporary Italy would allow the newest generations of Italian Americans to find a new way to connect with their ancestors. The majority of young Italian Americans that I met told me how important their bond with Italy was for their cultural identity, but often they were referring to everyday family traditions such as "Sunday dinner" and "gravy" (Chapter 18), the very Philadelphian way to indicate tomato sauce. However, these young generations did not feel personally connected to other internationally renowned dimensions of their Italianity such as art, science, design, opera, architecture, and fashion. The more popular dimension of the Italian and Italian American culture, developed through popular media after World War II, had lost its connection with the high formal culture, and it was important to bring them back together. To put it in a more evocative way, I felt that it was important to unite Rocky (the popular Italian American icon impersonated by Sylvester Stallone) with Botticelli (the

Councilman Mark Squilla and the Italian Consul General, with the leadership of the 1492 Society and a news anchor for ABC 6, Alicia Vitarelli, at the society's Citation Ceremony at City Council Chambers in Philadelphia City Hall on October 10, 2014.

(Photo: Gary Horn)

Renaissance paintings at the Philadelphia Museum of Art), as effectively summarized in the title line of the article published in *Corriere della Sera* by Paolo Valentino, "From Rocky to Botticelli: Italian Philadelphia," and printed in this book as Chapter 31. In Chapter 31, Valentino reports about Philadelphia rediscoveries, the Italian and Italian American soul of the city, through the Italian cultural initiatives created under the umbrella of Ciao Philadelphia. In Philadelphia, Rocky had already interacted with Botticelli when the popular movie star Sylvester Stallone filmed part of its training on the steps of the

Philadelphia Museum of Art, where Renaissance art from Italy is on display (see Sidebar 8). Today, near these same steps, there is a statue of Rocky Balboa.

The reconnection between the two cultural dimensions, the popular dimension celebrated at Columbus Day and the formal dimension expressed inside museums, academies, and universities, would offer Italian Americans a way, different from the previous generations but without neglecting traditions, to publicly manifest the bond with their Italian heritage. Furthermore, it would offer non-Italians who were familiar with Italy through popular culture an appreciation of the Italian classic, Renaissance, and Enlightenment culture.

During my tenure as Consul General of Italy, I continued joining the Italian American community in the traditional celebrations of Columbus Day, not only in Philadelphia and all Pennsylvania but also in other parts of the consular jurisdiction, places such as Delaware, South Jersey, and Maryland. In my opinion, it was useful to bring together new groups and new interests around the celebration of Columbus, marking its Italianity even more and linking Italian Americans to contemporary Italy, thus recreating a moment of inclusion and openness to all. Moreover, an interesting lesson comes from the same Venturi obelisk, which had been viewed by its creator as a way to "celebrate the role of all immigrants in the development of Philadelphia and the United States."[10]

In order to share my idea and create consensus about expanding the number of events around Columbus Day, I organized a meeting at my residence with several key members of the Italian American community in the region: longtime U.S. congressman and chairman since 1986 of Philadelphia's Democratic Party, Bob Brady; Deputy Mayor of Philadelphia, Mike Di Bernardinis; City Councilman, Mark Squilla; the leadership of the 1492 Society (organizers of the Columbus Day parade on South Broad Street in Philadelphia every year); the National Italian American Foundation national chairman and Philadelphian, Joe Del Raso (also author of Sidebar 7); and philanthropists and entrepreneurs such as former Union League

Italian National Day and presentation of Ciao Philadelphia in 2017 in the Lincoln Memorial Hall at the Union League of Philadelphia. From left to right: State Treasurer for the Commonwealth of Pennsylvania, Joe Torsella; Consul General, Andrea Canepari; then-U.S. Congressman, Bob Brady (Italian American and chairman of the Philadelphia Democratic Party since 1986); Mayor's Office of Grants, Ashley Del Bianco; and City Representative, Sheila Hess, on behalf of Mayor Jim Kenney. (Photo: Giò Martorana)

President and Philly Pops Chairman Frank Giordano (see Chapter 8). In that meeting, I found great support and the willingness to work together to highlight the international richness of the city of Philadelphia through Italian lenses. In fact, it was with that meeting that the idea of creating a series of Italian-themed events called Ciao Philadelphia was born. It was planned as a three-day Italian cultural event to emphasize the Italianity of the city, but the enthusiasm grew tremendously, and the envisioned three days became first a week and then the whole month of October 2014.[11] Starting in 2015, Ciao Philadelphia naturally evolved into an annual celebration with dozens of events highlighting the richness of cultural ties with Italy that exist in Philadelphia and in the region, coupled with the even more important desire to create new opportunities. The Ciao Philadelphia celebrations were also appreciated and supported by those who did not have any ethnic ties with Italy[12] but who enjoyed Italian culture or saw these events as a means of promoting the region of Philadelphia at the international level.[13] To this point, I remember that the first sponsor of Ciao Philadelphia was not an Italian company but a global company, American Airlines, which regarded the Ciao Philadelphia project as a means to promote exchanges and highlight the rich cosmopolitan dimension of Philadelphia.

Interest about Philadelphia rose in Italy as well, thanks to reports like the one by Valentino from the prestigious Italian paper *Corriere della Sera* (Chapter 31), portraying the city as a tourist destination with all the qualities of a cosmopolitan and sophisticated place (Chapter 29), complementing its grittier portrayal in movies such as *Rocky*. The beautiful drawing by Antonio Monteverdi that accompanies Valentino's article (and is reproduced in this book) visually creates an Italian itinerary, a web, linking several places in Philadelphia that were highlighted through the Ciao Philadelphia events to create a cultural unity, the same unity later reproduced in this book on the Italian legacy in Philadelphia. Interest in Italy about Philadelphia was also echoed in the Italian economic press. On April 15, 2015, Francesco Cerisano published in *Italia Oggi* (the second business paper in Italy) a one-page article titled "Philadelphia's Comeback" highlighting the excitement in the city for being chosen for international events such as the Democratic Convention of 2016, the Pope's visit for the World Meeting of Families, and the possibility to connect the region with Italy, thanks to Ciao Philadelphia. In the article, Nick DeBenedictis, speaking as chairman of the Philadelphia Convention and Visitors Bureau, explained the agency support of Ciao Philadelphia as a way to strengthen economic and political ties between Pennsylvania and Italy.[14]

Philadelphia was on the verge of a transformation. From being internally perceived as a former industrial city too often overlooked and underappreciated, the city was becoming a global destination. I thought that highlighting the Italian legacy was in line with the ongoing renovation process and could help support it. Mike Newall published an article in the *Philadelphia Inquirer* on February 21, 2016, about my presence as Consul General of Italy in the city entitled "From Italy to Phila., Con Amore." He wrote, "A big part of this column has always been about

The Union League created
tours open to the public called
"Italian Art and Inspiration
at the Union League of
Philadelphia." In the picture,
a Ciao Philadelphia tour on
October 8, 2016.
(Photo: Richard Barnes)

In the framework of Ciao Philadelphia 2016,
The Laundry Project, Panni Stesi. Installation
by Pia Brancaccio's Exhibition of Photography
dedicated to Napoli and Italian urban areas,
with works by Stuart Rome, Blaise Tobia, and
Stefania Zamparelli. Displayed in October
2016 at Drexel University URBN Center
in collaboration with Julie Mostov, Senior
Vice Provost for Global Initiatives, Drexel
University. The venue has an Italian connection,
as well. Venturi, Scott Brown and Associates
Inc. designed the Institute for Scientific
Information (ISI) headquarters in University
City in 1979. Today, it is Drexel's URBN center.
(Photo: Richard Barnes)

celebrating Philly for the city it's becoming—about how although we still have far to go, we've come a long way. About seeing ourselves a little differently—as a place we can be proud of. Well, the Consul General is onboard. Fully."

A few years after the first edition of Ciao Philadelphia, in 2016, I started to think that the Italian web, the wealth of Italian heritage throughout the city that Ciao Philadelphia helped showcase, needed to be shared in a structured manner through a book written by scholars and experts belonging to the most prestigious cultural institutions of the

region. My first inspiration for the creation of a book came from the experience that I had during my posting at the Italian Embassy in Washington, DC, from 2006 to 2010 when I had the privilege to be working on the volume *The Italian Legacy in Washington, D.C.: Architecture, Design, Art and Culture*, published in 2008 by Skira in Milan. The book was conceived during a meeting between then Italian Ambassador Giovanni Castellaneta and then Speaker of the House Nancy Pelosi. The book was imagined as a public diplomacy tool among the initiatives spearheaded by Luca Ferrari, the Head of Public and Legislative Affairs at the Italian Embassy. The book, which contained a foreword by Speaker Pelosi, was presented at the National Gallery in Washington, DC, in front of representatives of the Italian community, and launched at a reception hosted by the Speaker on Capitol Hill with the bipartisan Italian-American Caucuses of the House and Senate. On Capitol Hill, it is where the beautiful rotunda ceiling, painted by Costantino Brumidi and displayed on the cover of the Washington, D.C. book, can be found. Brumidi's frescos, described in the Washington, D.C. book by then Architect of the U.S. Capitol Barbara Wolanin in the essay "Italy's Presence in the U.S. Capitol,"[15] appear again on the cover of this book about the Italian legacy in Philadelphia, which portrays the Cathedral of Philadelphia dome, another of Brumidi's work, here described in Chapter 5.

The idea of creating a book on the Italian legacy in Philadelphia was received with great interest. Participation in the project was enthusiastic from the start, and it could count on a wealth of amazing authors with different backgrounds covering the richness of the Italian legacy in the city. The enthusiastic involvement in the book mirrored the level of support enjoyed by Ciao Philadelphia from all the most prestigious cultural institutions in the city, including the Philadelphia Museum of Art (Chapter 11), the University of Pennsylvania Museum (Chapter 10), and the Pennsylvania Academy of the Fine Arts (Chapter 9). I envisioned the book as a symphony of Italian and Italian American themes through words and pictures, a symphony as harmonic as the relationship between Philadelphia and Italy.

ABOVE: "International Archaeology Day: Spotlight on Italy." Italian archaeology and ancient Italian culture are the focus of the family-friendly International Archaeology Day celebration. This was a Ciao Philadelphia event at the University of Pennsylvania Museum of Archaeology and Anthropology, October 15, 2016. (Photo: Richard Barnes)

FACING PAGE: Since 2014 in the framework of Ciao Philadelphia, the Philadelphia Museum of Art (PMA) has offered a series of tours of the Italian Art Collection called "The Art of Italy," promoted by Gail Harrity, President of PMA. In the picture, concert of Giada Valenti in June 2016 at the presentation of the next edition of Ciao Philadelphia on Italian National day. (Photo: Richard Barnes)

RIGHT: The gala and opening night for the Philadelphia Opera performing Giuseppe Verdi's *La Traviata* at the Academy of Music, Conductor Corrado Rovaris, October 2, 2015. An event part of Ciao Philadelphia 2015. (Photo: Gary Horn)

BELOW: The State Lodge of Pennsylvania (Order Sons of Italy in America) in partnership with the Munier Mandolin and Guitar Orchestra presented a concert as part of Ciao Philadelphia on October 11, 2015, at the Venice Performing Arts and Recreation Center, Philadelphia. In the picture, tenor Frank Tenaglia joins the Munier Orchestra for a tribute to the music of Mario Lanza. (Photo: Gary Horn)

October 9, 10, and 11, 2015—"Sinatra: A Centennial Celebration," Philly Pops, Verizon Hall—Kimmel Center. Organized by the Chairman of the Philly Pops, Frank Giordano, in the frame of Ciao Philadelphia 2015. (Courtesy The Philly Pops)

Mosaic Concert (Il Mosaico) at Temple Performing Arts Center on October 10, 2014, as part of Ciao Philadelphia. The Boyer College of Music and Dance concert included the works of Italian composers in honor of the Italian cultural month. They played Ottorino Respighi's "Pine of Rome." In the picture, the introductory speech by Hai-Lung Dai, Vice President for International Affairs of Temple University. (Photo: Gary Horn)

The Philly Pops recreated in Philadelphia the legendary 500 Club, originally from Atlantic City, New Jersey. Frank Sinatra, Dean Martin, and other top Italian American artists used to perform in the club. In the picture, taken October 10, 2015, is Deanna Martin singing "That's Amore," one of Dean Martin's classics. The event was organized by the Chairman of the Philly Pops, Frank Giordano, in the frame of Ciao Philadelphia 2015.

(Courtesy The Philly Pops)

Some aspects of this relationship were evident, while others needed to emerge in their entirety through the powerful analysis conducted by some of the scholars in the book. The Italian architectural influence in the city is highlighted in the chapters by Giannetto (Chapter 12), Cohen (Chapters 1 and 17), Greenberger (Chapter 23), and Saffron (Chapter 30). Italian influence is also present in music, as described by Willier (Chapter 14), Ludwig (Chapter 15), Sanchirico (Chapter 22), and Jeremy Goode (Sidebar 4). Grey (Chapter 6), Colletta (Chapter 7), and Chorpenning (Chapter 13) concentrate on the exchange of ideas and artifacts between the two sides of the ocean, while Valerio (Chapter 20), Farnsworth (Sidebar 3), and Wolanin (Chapter 5) elaborate on the presence of Italian elements and emotions "transplanted" to Philadelphia by painters and artisans.

The book is inspired in many ways by Ciao Philadelphia and by the events that took place. One of the first conferences that was hosted as part of Ciao Philadelphia was organized with the Pennsylvania Academy of the Fine Arts (PAFA) president and CEO David Brigham by Jody Pinto, an Italian American artist and a lecturer at PAFA, the first art museum and school in the United States. She spoke about her family's history on the evening of Columbus Day 2014 at PAFA. Pinto's family (including her father) had come to Philadelphia at the turn of the twentieth century, were processed at Pier 53 on the Delaware River in Philadelphia (which she discovered only after being selected for the design of the Pier 53 Memorial), and were invited to art classes by Dr. Albert C. Barnes. Pinto's father, Angelo, taught at the Barnes Foundation, and five of his paintings are contained there today side by side with those of Henri Matisse.[16] Jody Pinto was selected as the designer of a modern monument, *Land Buoy*, inaugurated in 2014, to celebrate the one million immigrants who had landed and were processed in Philadelphia at Pier 53—the lesser-known alternative to

Ellis Island (Chapter 21). Pinto's conference contained several of the elements that would craft the future of Ciao Philadelphia. This involved diverse groups listening to the surprising history of poor immigrants from Italy during the mass migration and the influence that their descendants would have on the Philadelphian social fabric.

Another significant and symbolic event of the first Ciao Philadelphia celebration was the 140th anniversary of Guglielmo Marconi. The event was organized by PI-Philly, Professionisti Italiani a Philadelphia, an association of young Italian professionals in the city that included researchers, doctors, lawyers, and businessmen.[17] They challenged companies such as Comcast and universities such as Drexel to create an innovative, one-day-long event that blended history (Marconi's connections with Philadelphia and the Benjamin Franklin Museum), the present (the presence of Italians and Italian Americans in important high-tech institutions), and the future (high-level research opportunities in Philadelphia and in Italy).[18]

In the gallery of pictures that complements this essay, the reader can see some of the events that took place in 2014, 2015, and 2016 in the framework of Ciao Philadelphia. Other pictures of Ciao Philadelphia events can be found in specific chapters to show how the Italian legacy is the common element that connects all parts of this book. These pictures include a concert in Verizon Hall at the Kimmel Center (Prologue), the City Hall Mayor Reception Room (Prologue), the Union League flying the Italian flag (Chapter 8), current students painting at PAFA during a Ciao Philadelphia Italian tour (Chapter 9), a concert at Rowan University (Sidebar 2), a presentation at Conversation Hall, City Hall (Chapter 19), Eddie Lang's mural inauguration (Chapter 22), the Exhibition of Temple University Rome Faculty (Chapter 27), American University of Rome's conference at the Italian Consulate General (Sidebar 7), and Italian-designed sports cars (Chapter 28). I think it is impressive to see the variety of organizations, leaders, themes, and places involved. In addition to the love for Italy, I believe that another driving force was the awareness and the desire to create international opportunities for Philadelphia and Italy together.[19]

Ciao Philadelphia attracted the support of recognized leaders in the region who were also Italian Americans, people such as Joe Jacovini, senior partner and former Chairman of Dilworth, Paxson, LLP, and Nick DeBenedictis, Chairman Emeritus of Aqua America and Chairman of the Board of Directors of Philadelphia Convention and Visitors Bureau (Chapter 19), who over the years cochaired the Consul General Advisory Board, helping me identify areas of potential cooperation between Italy and the Philadelphia region. The goals of the advisory board were to promote pride in the accomplishments of Italian Americans in the Philadelphia region, develop opportunities to reconnect future Philadelphia with future Italy, and attract the next generation of young Italian American millennials to participate in learning activities about their heritage to continue its legacy. Other members of the advisory board were Joseph F. Coradino, Chairman of the Board of Trustees of PREIT;

PI-Philly (Italian Young Professionals in Philadelphia) celebrated the Nobel Prize winner and Italian electrical engineer Gugliemo Marconi, his connection to Philadelphia, and his contributions to wireless telegraphy at "The Masters of Wireless" event at the Bossone Research Center's Atrium at Drexel University, a Ciao Philadelphia event on October 8, 2014.
(Photo: Gary Horn)

Photo of "Forever in Fashion: Costumed Portraiture from the Italian Renaissance to the Present." Artists from Studio Incamminati, School for Contemporary Realist Art, conducted the event on October 27, 2016, as part of Ciao Philadelphia. It was a painting demonstration with costumed models in the presence of Chairman of the Board Frank Giordano. Founded by Nelson and Leona Shanks, the school is modeled on the traditional Italian academia. Even the school's name is filled with symbolism. In Italian, *incamminati* means "moving forward" and invokes the spirit of its namesake studio founded by the Renaissance artist Annibale Carracci.
(Photo: Richard Barnes)

Patrick O'Connor, Chairman of the Board of Trustees, and Richard Englert, President of Temple University, presenting on July 11, 2017. Consul General Canepari is pictured with a proclamation from the Board of Trustees of Temple University highlighting the cooperation established with Italy and the several events created in the framework of the cultural events of Ciao Philadelphia. Among the participants were Provost JoAnne Epps, Vice President Hai Lung Dai, and Vice President Michele Masucci.
(Courtesy Temple University)

Chairman of Dilworth Paxson LLP Joseph Jacovini; CG Andrea Canepari with Roberta, Bianca, and Matteo Canepari; President of the Jefferson University Steve Klasko; and City Representative Sheila Heiss during the event "Celebration of the promotion of the Honorable Andrea Canepari, Consul General of Italy in Philadelphia to Ambassador to the Dominican Republic" where the cooperation with Italy was highlighted, starting from the events organized in the framework of Ciao Philadelphia to the innovative strategic partnership created with the Italian Universita' Cattolica in the educational and medical field. Organized by Jefferson University on June 29, 2017.
(© Thomas Jefferson University Photography Services)

Daniel M. DiLella, principal of Equus Capital Partners; Frank Giordano, President and CEO of the Philly POPS; Joseph Gonnella, Dean Emeritus of Jefferson Medical College; Philip Rinaldi, founding partner, chairman, and chief executive officer of Philadelphia Energy Solutions; Anthony M. Santomero, ninth President of the Federal Reserve Bank of Philadelphia and Professor Emeritus of Finance at the Wharton School of the University of Pennsylvania; Frederick Simeone, Director of the Simeone Automotive Foundation and Museum, former Professor of Neurosurgery at the University of Pennsylvania School of Medicine, and Chairman of Neurosurgery at Pennsylvania Hospital; Stephen M. Sweeney, New Jersey Senate President (2010–present); Pat (Pasquale) Deon, board chairman of SEPTA (the fifth-largest transit system in the United States); Joseph V. Del Raso, partner in the Commercial Department of Pepper Hamilton and Chair of the firm's Italian Desk; Dominic J. Caruso, Executive Vice President and Chief Financial Officer of Johnson and Johnson; Frank Mattei, KPMG Managing Partner in Philadelphia; Bob Schena, Rajant cofounder and CEO; Skip Di Massa, Duane Morris partner; and Paul Tufano, Chairman and Chief Executive Officer of AmeriHealth Caritas.

Ciao Philadelphia also attracted forces and motivated leaders not ethnically linked to Italy. Particularly supportive was the academic world, including leaders such as Steve Klasko, President of Thomas Jefferson University and CEO of Jeffer-

On June 2, 2015, celebration of Festa della Repubblica, Italian National Day, at Drexel University in Philadelphia. Attendees gathered at Drexel University's Gerri C. Lebow Hall, along with Drexel University's President, John Fry, who announced Drexel's engagement in the Italian cultural month, Ciao Philadelphia. In the picture, President of Drexel University, John Fry; CBS 3 anchor, Pat Ciarrocchi; and Italian Consul General. (Photo: Gary Horn)

son Health; John Fry, President of Drexel University; Dick Englert, President of Temple University; and Ali Houshmand, President of Rowan University. They all supported Ciao Philadelphia from its beginning by participating in the events and catalyzing energies that contributed to its success. They immediately understood the inclusive nature of Ciao Philadelphia and supported it as a means of creating opportunities at the international level, as I wrote about more extensively in the Prologue. One of the partners, for example, was Temple University, which has a long history with Italy, symbolized by its more than fifty-year-old Rome program (Chapter 27) and its many Italian American alumni. Temple decided to enthusiastically support Ciao Philadelphia, as demonstrated by the personal involvement of scholars such as Temple Vice President for International Affairs Hai-Lung Dai and Provost JoAnne Epps.

Another partner was Drexel University, which saw in Ciao Philadelphia an opportunity to increase its role as "an important player in Global Philadelphia."[20] Julie Mostov in her essay entitled "Drexel's Global Reach," which is part of the book *Building Drexel: The University and Its City, 1891–2016*, published by Temple University Press in 2017, talks about two among the several events organized by Drexel University in partnership with the Italian Consulate General within the framework of Ciao Philadelphia. The first event she mentions was on "climate proof cities and Italy's cutting-edge approach to urban sustainability."[21] The second one highlighted "key Italian industries and Drexel's growing culinary programs (including a related study abroad program in Rome)."[22]

Rowan University historically offered opportunities to the important Italian American community in South Jersey. Recognizing that history, Rowan University saw the events organized in the framework of Ciao Philadelphia as an opportunity to leverage the Italian heritage present in Gloucester County—and generally in South Jersey—to develop research and economic opportunities with Italy, as also acknowledged by Joe DiStefano in the *Philadelphia Inquirer*.[23]

Ciao Philadelphia was also embraced by leaders from outside the city. It is customary for Philadelphia to

Ciao Philadelphia ceremony at Rowan University, Glassboro, New Jersey. Photo taken of State Senate President Steve Sweeney, Rowan President Dr. Ali Houshmand, and C.G. of Italy in Philadelphia, Andrea Canepari, held at Hollybush Mansion of Rowan University, May 23, 2016. Gloucester County hosts a great percentage of Italian Americans, among them Senator Sweeney. (Courtesy Rowan University)

embrace leaders from outside the city, state, or country, the so-called "Auslander," to quote E. Digby Baltzell.[24] Some of these "outsiders" were great supporters of Ciao Philadelphia because of its inclusive nature. One of them was the North Jersey businessman Philip Rinaldi (here in the picture with Governor Ed Rendell), then CEO of Philadelphia Energy Solutions (PES) and partner of Carlyle group, who had come to assume a leadership role in Philadelphia because of his philanthropic activities in support of the city and its international development.

The Italian American influence can be felt in several sectors at the core of the city, as mentioned by Salvatore Mangione in his essay on the history of Doctor Joe Gonnella (Chapter 26). In a city made famous by eds and meds (Goode, Introduction to Part 4), the links with Italy in the medical field are very important because of Italian Americans who rose to leadership positions, such as Antonio Giordano, Chairman of the Sbarro Health Research Organization (SHRO), Fred Simeone (author of Chapter 28), and Alex Vaccaro, President of the Rothman Orthopedic Institute.

While contemporary Philadelphia is a place where so many Italian Americans reached success, the city was not always easy for immigrants from Italy (as gently remembered in this book by Gilda Battaglia Rorro Baldassari in Sidebar 2). I thought that through the Ciao Philadelphia celebrations, it was also important to remember the stories and the sacrifices of the many Italian immigrants, literate and illiterate, who came to the United States with their traditions to make a new life for themselves and their families. Some of these traditions might appear at odds with the sophisticated Italy portrayed in the museums and in academia, but they are all part of that Italianity that is at the heart of Ciao Philadelphia. The core idea of Ciao Philadelphia was that all aspects of Italian culture needed to be included to have a 360-degree view of what Italianity means, to show unity, and to create a platform to showcase different aspects of the same whole.

The vision that I had for Ciao Philadelphia was to use it as a means to awaken the Italianity of the region and its interest in Italy, as recognized in an article by

Former Philadelphia Mayor and Pennsylvania Governor Ed Rendell, Philadelphia Energy Solutions CEO and Philadelphia energy hub advocate Philip Rinaldi, Italian Consul General, and more than one hundred businesspeople gathered on October 5 to celebrate the kickoff of Ciao Philadelphia 2015 on an Italian boat on the Delaware River.
(Photo: Gary Horn)

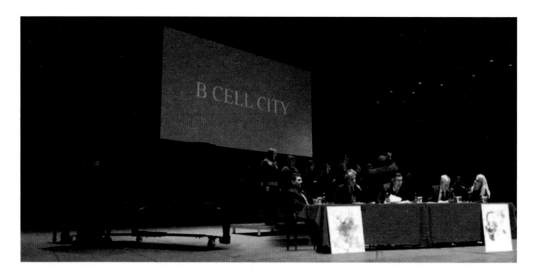

"B Cell City"—an innovative dialogue of biology, medical research, art, and music—organized by Temple University Provost Hai-Lung Dai and Sbarro Foundation President and Temple Professor Antonio Giordano in the frame of the cultural month Ciao Philadelphia. At Temple University Performing Arts Center, October 24, 2015. (Photo: Gary Horn)

Italian cultural month, Ciao Philadelphia, celebrated at Thomas Jefferson Methodist Hospital in Philadelphia in October 2015. (Photo: Gary Horn)

Jeff Blumenthal entitled "Italy Says Ciao Philadelphia" in the *Philadelphia Business Journal* on October 17, 2014. After hosting the international fair to celebrate the sesquicentennial anniversary of U.S. independence (as described in Chapter 16), Italian Americans in Philadelphia today are getting ready to host the celebrations for the 250th anniversary of U.S. independence. Since time and circumstances have changed, I think it is informative to look at the level of participation of Italian Americans in Philadelphia one hundred years later. In 2016, as Consul General of Italy, I was asked by the promoter of the incoming celebrations, Andrew Hohns, to be the honorary founding member of USA250, the organization whose aim is to create momentum and interest throughout the United States for the semiquincentennial celebrations. Hohns, a Wharton graduate, adjunct professor of finance at NYU, and a respected member of the finance community, was appointed in 2018 as a member of the bipartisan U.S. Semiquincentennial Commission chaired by Dan DiLella and directed by Frank Giordano. Hohns, who speaks Italian and teaches the language to his son, believed that Italy could bring an important addition to the celebration as it had done in 1926.

Sometimes the Italian American community is perceived as fractured by cultural, economic, and even geographical divides due to the multiple backgrounds of immigrants coming from various regions of Italy, especially before the unification or in the decades immediately after. One of the goals of Ciao Philadelphia was to reconnect the components of that perceived fracture through a vision. I am particularly impressed by the life of Mariano DiVito, whose story was shared for us in Chapter 25 by Penn law professor Sanchirico, where he cites a study by Dr. Edmund J. Forte about how solid the University of Pennsylvania scholarly connection was with Italy. I had the pleasure to meet Dr. Forte and his wife, Anna, see their commitment to the teaching of the Italian language in the region, and listen to the story of Mariano DiVito. Landing in Philadelphia with no formal education in 1929, Mariano DiVito started his career as a newsboy at what was one of Philadelphia's most prominent hotels, the Bellevue Stratford. Despite not having any connections with any Ivy League institutions such as Penn, and after a lifetime of wisely investing his earnings, upon his death he gave all his savings (1.25 million USD) to endow the first chair in Italian studies at the university founded by Benjamin Franklin. Even without a formal education, he understood the importance of having Italian cultural studies at one of the most respected institutions in Philadelphia and in the United States.

A ranger in Independence National Historical Park during a Ciao Philadelphia tour called "Ciao 18th Century Philadelphia: A Stroll through the Park with Glimpses of 18th Century Italy and 18th Century Philadelphia," October 2015. (Photo: Gary Horn)

New Italian immigrants and old Italian immigrants often are not aware of and do not fully value the connection that they share with each other. Michael Matza, a journalist for the *Philadelphia Inquirer*, who investigates ethnic groups in greater Philadelphia, conducted an investigation about the new Italians in the city. He published the results of his investigation in an article titled "Rich Mixture."[25] The article correctly portrayed the new immigrants as different from the ones who came during the years of mass migrations. However, based on the answers provided by the people interviewed, it was clear that the interviewees did not understand what they had in common with immigrants of the past, and they did not exhibit a particular desire to become living bridges with Italy. When I was interviewed for the article, I suggested that rather than distinguishing among the different waves of immigration, we should see the Italian immigration to the region as a centuries-long thread "with different components"—such as the masons who created stone houses, the factory workers of the Industrial Revolution, and the doctors staffing hospitals now. Blue or white collar, Italian immigrants "are hardworking people, whose contributions are woven into the fabric of the region."[26] Talking with him for the article, I told him that I was proud of the historic ties existing between the region and Italy. In his article, Mazza then remembered that Italians have been part of the Philadelphian social fabric since the colonial times, as shown by Richard N. Juliani in his publication *Building Little Italy: Philadelphia's Italians before Mass Migration*, discussed in Chapter 18. In this book, Ewald (Chapter 2), Valsania (Chapter 3), and Croce (Chapter 4) all talk about the influence of Italian ideas in the legal system, in the relations with the founding fathers, and in the religion of colonial America. Italians and Italian ideas were also felt in Philadelphia during the revolutionary period, in the signing of the Declaration of Independence, and in developing the Constitution. Through the very powerful tours named "Ciao 18th Century Philadelphia: A Stroll through the Park with Glimpses of 18th Century Italy and 18th Century Philadelphia," created in partnership with the Independence National Historical Park and its superintendent, Cynthia MacLeod, these influences, not always obvious, were rediscovered and put into context.

During the Ciao Philadelphia years, one of the slogans that people would hear me say most often was "Everybody loves Italy. So let's give everybody a chance to be Italian in Philadelphia." I owe that slogan to the businessman Vernon Hill, founder of Metro Bank in the United Kingdom and of Commerce Bancorp and Republic Bank in the United States, who gave that idea to me one day when we were discussing how to connect Italy and Philadelphia. I believe that the slogan truly captures the amount of Italy and Italianity there is in Philadelphia. It is that Italianity that represents the natural bridge to contemporary Italy.

The Ciao Philadelphia project finds its natural continuity in this book, which aims to put together under one roof all the Italianity woven into the social fabric of the Philadelphia region, even if it is still sometimes difficult to see that unity. I hope that this book on the Italian legacy in Philadelphia can help raise awareness and become the basis for creating even stronger bridges between the region of Philadelphia and contemporary Italy.

TOP: Ciao Philadelphia has events outside Philadelphia in Maryland, South Jersey, Delaware, and the entire state of Pennsylvania. On October 25, 2016, in Pittsburgh, the "Round Table—Italy and Pennsylvania: An Economic Dialogue on Energy, Research, and the Transatlantic Trade Investment Partnership" was held. It was organized by Duquesne University School of Law and University of Pittsburgh School of Law and its Center for International Legal Education. In the picture are former Governor Tom Corbett, as moderator, with Chancellor Ronald A. Brand, C.G. Andrea Canepari, Dean Emeritus Nicholas P. Cafardi, Antonio Lordi (Siemens USA), and Philip Rinaldi (founding partner, Chairman, and CEO of Philadelphia Energy Solutions), whose vision saved Philadelphia's refineries and strengthened a role for Pennsylvania as an energy hub. (Courtesy University of Pittsburgh)

MIDDLE: In the framework of Ciao Philadelphia 2016, "Made in Italy," a debate on the Italian fashion from unification to the 1950s at Saint Joseph's University. Created by Gabriella Romani, Ph.D., and organized by Paola Giuli, Ph.D., and by Kristen Grimes, Ph.D., Italian studies program, October 6, 2016. (Photo: Richard Barnes)

BOTTOM: "Photos of Pavia from the 19th to the 21st century" at Villanova University's President Lounge. Kickoff ceremony on October 29, 2014, in the presence of Peter M. Donohue, Villanova's President, among the Ciao Philadelphia events organized by Luca Cottini, Ph.D., Italian studies at Villanova. (Photo: Gary Horn)

Top: As an example of the economic dimension of Ciao Philadelphia, an interactive event with Drexel University's Charles D. Close School of Entrepreneurship and Saxbys Coffee. On October 18, 2016, it featured espresso tasting, a discussion of coffee and entrepreneurship, and guest speakers who talked about entrepreneurship in the coffee industry in the United States and Italy. Among the speakers were Dean Donna De Carolis; CEO and founder of Saxbys, Nick Bayer; and the General Manager for Rosito Bisani, Greg Listino. Rosito Bisani is the manufacturer of specialty Italian equipment, including the espresso machines in all Saxbys' cafés. (Photo: Richard Barnes)

Middle: "Ciao Philadelphia, a Night of Italian Wine and Cheese: Tasting and Talk," on October 30, 2015, at the Hospitality and Management Center of Drexel University. (Photo: Gary Horn)

Bottom: On October 3, 2015, "Ciao Philadelphia at Rowan University"— several events such as "Da Vinci's Inventions," organized by the Henry M. Rowan College of Engineering, which brought to life the modern innovations of the first great innovator, artist, and engineer; the lecture "Still Eating Spaghetti, Not Yet Americanized: Italian Immigrants and Their Food"; concerts; solar observations focusing on Italian Galileo Galilei by the Department of Physics and Astronomy; "Galileo's Sky," a planetarium show; and "Italian Opera Aria Lecture and Recital." (Photo: Gary Horn)

Top: Ciao Philadelphia advertising on a SEPTA bus, October 2016. (Photo: Richard Barnes)

Middle: "Aza'io: The Italian Children's Opera," at the International Opera Theater for all the children, directed by Karen Saillant, a Ciao Philadelphia event on October 24, 2015. (Photo: Gary Horn)

Bottom: "Passyunk Passeggiata," on October 5, 2016, organized by the East Passyunk Avenue Business Improvement District in front of the History of Italian Immigration Museum. (Photo: Richard Barnes)

Top: Ciao Philadelphia was always envisioned not as an exclusive Italian ethnic event but as an effort open to friends of Italy and Italian culture, as well as Italians and Italian Americans. In partnership with organizations such as the American Jewish Committee Philadelphia, several initiatives were organized. Among these was "A Tour of Historic Italian and Jewish South Philly" on October 22, 2017. The National Museum of American Jewish History, a Smithsonian Affiliate, organized in October 2016 a Ciao Philadelphia tour (in the picture) called "Becoming American: History of Immigration, 1880s–1920s." (Photo: Richard Barnes)

Middle: As part of Ciao Philadelphia and the Temple's Provost Lectures series, Rome's Mayor and MD, Ignazio Marino, presented "Transplantation: From Surgery to Reviving the Eternal City," on September 24, 2015, at Temple Performing Arts Center, Temple University. (Photo: Ignazio Marino)

Bottom: "We the Italians: Two Flags, One Heart, One Hundred Interviews!" at the History of Italian Immigration Museum, Philadelphia, organized by Filitalia, October 22, 2016, an event of Ciao Philadelphia. In attendance were founder Pasquale F. Nestico, M.D., Paula DeSanctis-Bonavitacola, and Rosetta Miriello. (Photo: Richard Barnes)

NOTES

1. S. Luconi, "Italians and Italy," in *The Encyclopedia of Greater Philadelphia* (New Brunswick, NJ: Rutgers University, 2017).

2. This is not an uncommon theme in diasporas generally and Italian communities abroad are no exception. For a study on the Italian diaspora to the Dominican Republic, see A. Canepari, "Introduction," and Mu-Kien Adriana Sang Ben and A. Canepari, "Diplomatic Relations between Italy and the Dominican Republic," in *The Italian Legacy in the Dominican Republic: History, Architecture, Economy and Society*, ed. A. Canepari (Philadelphia: Saint Joseph's University Press, 2021).

3. J. A. Gambadello, "How Philly Came to Call Its Downtown 'Center City,'" *Philadelphia Inquirer*, May 21, 2019.

4. For a reflection on how the Italian spirit can be communicated and lived in many different contexts, see P. Janni and G. McLean, *The Essence of Italian Culture and the Challenge of a Global Age*, Cultural Heritage and Contemporary Change, series 4, *West Europe*, vol. 5 (Washington, DC: Council for Research in Values and Philosophy, 2003).

5. As written in J. Melissen, *The New Public Diplomacy: Soft Power in International Relations* (London: Palgrave Macmillan UK, 2005). Public diplomacy (i.e., the interactions between diplomats and the foreign public with whom they work) is now not only an instrument of soft power in international relations but also an effect of part of a broader process of change in diplomatic practice calling for transnational collaboration.

6. "Petition to Remove Penn's Landing's Christopher Columbus Monuments," www .change.org/p/mayor-jim-kenney-and-america-500-remove-penn-s-landing-s-christopher -columbus-monuments.

7. In this essay, I am using the two different concepts of Italicity and Italianity. I will not use Italianicity, as described in the fifties by Roland Barthes. According to Barthes, "Italianicity is not Italy, it is the condensed essence of everything that could be Italian, from spaghetti to painting." Elaborating on his analysis of the Panzani pasta and its ad, he wrote that with the word *Italianicity* he was referring to signs associated with Italy outside Italy and therefore not even always perceived as Italian by Italians themselves: "It is a specifically 'French' knowledge (an Italian would barely perceive the connotation of the name [Panzani], no more probably than he would the Italianicity of tomato and pepper), based on a familiarity with certain tourist stereotypes." R. Barthes, *Rhetoric of the Image* (New York: Hill and Wang, 1977), 33–48.

8. C. Mires, "Columbus Day," in *The Encyclopedia of Greater Philadelphia* (New Brunswick, NJ: Rutgers University, 2014), philadelphiaencyclopedia.org/archive/columbus-day/.

9. With different style and motivation than in other U.S. cities, however, there has been serious discussion of Philadelphia's historic monuments and the need to reconsider their purpose. This included a three-day program, culminating with a panel discussion at the Museum of the American Revolution on Columbus Day 2017, as reported by Jeff Gammage in his article "Should Philadelphia Say 'Goodbye, Columbus?" published in the *Philadelphia Inquirer* on October 5, 2017. In the article, Gammage observed that a negative portrayal of Columbus "can hit hard—and meet resistance—in Philadelphia, a place of rich Italian culture and cuisine where the annual Columbus Day parade, scheduled for Sunday, draws thousands." The work of the Monument Lab should also be noted. It began its public phase in 2015 as an independent public art and history studio based in Philadelphia that works with artists, students, activists, municipal agencies, and cultural institutions on exploratory approaches to public

engagement and collective memory. One result of this was the commissioning of a monument to the early African American civil rights leader Octavius Catto, unveiled in 2017.

10. As written in "Christopher Columbus Monument," Venturi, Scott Brown and Associates, http://venturiscottbrown.org/pdfs/ChristopherColumbusMonument01.pdf, on the VSBA website collecting the project writings of Venturi and Scott Brown.

11. Ciao Philadelphia started in 2014 and, in 2021, is in its 8th edition.

12. As an example, the American Jewish Committee (AJC) of Philadelphia/Southern Jersey chapter participated at Ciao Philadelphia in 2015, creating "From Falafel to Fettuccini." The event was attended by the AJC's National Board of Governors, Richard Berkman, and Frederick D. Strober, chairman of the Philadelphia/Southern Jersey chapter of the AJC.

13. Several institutional and economic shareholders embraced Ciao Philadelphia as a way to help the region articulate a more coherent identity, attract foreign investments, and promote trade and tourism. For an academic overview on country or territorial marketing, see M. Aronczyk, *Branding the Nation: The Global Business of National Identity* (New York: Oxford University Press, 2013).

14. In the interview, DeBenedictis stressed the synergy between the promotion of Italian activities and Philadelphia economic and touristic promotion: "The Consul's arrival in August 2013 brought a wave of fresh air to the City and in the entire region, which boasts a GDP of 405 billion dollars, almost that of Switzerland, and the fourth largest Italian-American community in the States (1,418,465 residents, after New York, New Jersey and California)."

15. Published in L. Molinari and A. Canepari, *The Italian Legacy in Washington, D.C.: Architecture, Design, Art and Culture* (Milano: Skira, 2008).

16. From a conversation with Jody Pinto: "When Giuseppi was drafted as a photographer during the war, my father said they told him that if he was in France, he should go to Nice and see Matisse. Joe said he walked around Nice several times before arriving at Matisse's studio. The door opened, Joe introduced (he was in uniform) himself, and Matisse hugged him saying, 'Oh, you are the little Pinto!' and invited him to dinner!"

17. The organizers were Damiano Patron, from Hardware Engineering at Google; Alessia Angelin, research scientist at the Children's Hospital of Philadelphia; Francesco Sgrazzutti, senior architectural designer at Atrium Design Group; Carlo Siracusa, associate professor of Clinical Behavior Medicine at the University of Pennsylvania School of Veterinary Medicine; and Eugenio Boldrini, deputy at the Italian Consulate General.

18. The event could count on the participation of famous scholars such as COSI Chief Executive Officer Frederic Bertley; the CEO of Blonder Tongue Labs, Ted Grauch; the author of *Marconi, Father of Wireless, Grandfather of Radio, Great-Grandfather of the Cell Phone: The Race to Control Long-Distance Wireless*, Calvin D. Trowbridge; a member of the technical staff at Lion Cave Capital LLC, Emiliano Miluzzo; project manager/IEEE R2 treasurer Philip Gonski; and the associate dean for enrollment management and graduate education at Drexel University, Kapil R. Dandekar.

19. About the importance of capitalizing on cultural heritage, or creating a better narrative about a place in order to develop markets and foster economic development, see N. Bandelj and F. Wherry, *The Cultural Wealth of Nations* (Stanford: Stanford University, 2011).

20. J. Mostov, "Drexel's Global Reach," in *Building Drexel: The University and Its City, 1891–2016* (Philadelphia: Temple University Press, 2017), 352.

21. Ibid., 353. The author refers to the event "Climate Proof Cities, Counteracting Climate Change: Urban Resilience Planning," which took place on October 13, 2015.

22. Ibid. The author refers to the event "Ciao Philadelphia, a Night of Italian Wine and Cheese: Tasting and Talk," which took place on October 30, 2015.

23. J. N. DiStefano, "Italy's Man in Philly Promoted to Caribbean," *Philadelphia Inquirer*, May 28, 2017, https://www.inquirer.com/philly/business/italys-man-in-philly-was-match -com-for-deals-20170525.html.

24. E. Digby Baltzell, *Puritan Boston and Quaker Philadelphia* (New Brunswick, NJ: Transaction, 2007), 30.

25. M. Matza, "Rich Mixture," *Philadelphia Inquirer*, November 9, 2016.

26. Ibid.

CONTRIBUTORS

Cav. Dr. Gilda Battaglia Rorro Baldassari, Ed.D., is a former model/actress in Mexico and an award-winning television teacher, author, and educational administrator. She served in New Jersey as Assistant Superintendent for the Trenton Board of Education and both as Chair of the Governor's New Jersey Italian Heritage Commission and as Chair of its Curriculum Project: The Universality of Italian Heritage. For twenty years she was Honorary Vice Consul for Italy in Trenton. She has also published her memoir, *Gilda, Promise Me.*

Ann Blair Brownlee is Associate Curator in the Mediterranean Section at the University of Pennsylvania Museum. A specialist in ancient Greek pottery, she has published widely on Athenian and Corinthian pottery of the sixth century B.C.E. She has also written on the history of collecting classical antiquities in nineteenth- and early twentieth-century Philadelphia.

Andrea Canepari, H.E., is Ambassador of Italy to the Dominican Republic since 2017 when he reopened the embassy. A career diplomat, he was previously Consul General of Italy in Philadelphia, serving as a key mover in the internationalization of the region. He served before in the Italian embassies in Ankara, Turkey, and in Washington, DC. A passionate promoter of the creation of renewed synergies between the Italian communities in his constituencies and Italy, he promoted several public diplomacy initiatives. He served on numerous committees and boards (among them Thomas Jefferson University Presidential Advisory Board, the American Liver Foundation Mid-Atlantic Regional Board, and Philadelphia's Papal Event Committee), and his initiatives received extensive media coverage. He was awarded the biannual 2016 Global Philadelphia Award from Temple University for his activity creating connections between Italy and Pennsylvania. He is coeditor of the book *The Italian Legacy in Washington, D.C.: Architecture, Design, Art and Culture*, published by Skira in 2007, and editor of *The Italian Legacy in the Dominican Republic: History, Architecture, Economics and Society*, published in 2021 by Saint Joseph's University Press and by Umberto Allemandi for the Italian and Spanish editions.

Joseph F. Chorpenning, O.S.F.S., is Editorial Director of Saint Joseph's University Press in Philadelphia. His publications include articles on the medieval and early modern practice of a spiritual or mental pilgrimage to the crèche in the *Newsletter* *of the International Commission for Salesian Studies and Spiritual Life: A Carmelite Journal of Contemporary Spirituality.*

Jeffrey A. Cohen is an architectural historian teaching in the Growth and Structure of Cities Department at Bryn Mawr College. He has written on American architects Benjamin Latrobe and Frank Furness, on early architectural drawings, on urban vernacular housing, and most recently, on nineteenth-century street views aligned with early cadastral atlases—including a series recording key streetscapes crossing Rome and Philadelphia.

Lisa Colletta is Full Professor of English at the American University of Rome. She has published several books related to travel and expatriate literature, among them *The Legacy of the Grand Tour* (Farleigh Dickinson University Press, 2015) and *Voluntary Exiles: British Novelists in Hollywood* (Macmillan, 2013). Her essays have also appeared in numerous journals and books.

Steven Conn is W. E. Smith Professor of History at Miami University in Oxford, Ohio. A Philadelphia kid, Conn has written extensively about the city, including the book *Metropolitan Philadelphia: Living with the Presence of the Past* (University of Pennsylvania Press, 2006).

Carmen R. Croce is Director of Saint Joseph's Press and Curator of University Collections. He has written and curated exhibits on the history of the Jesuits in Philadelphia and their accomplishments at Old St. Joseph's Church, St. Joseph's Prep, and Saint Joseph's University in Philadelphia.

Joseph V. Del Raso, Esq., is a Senior Partner in the law firm Pepper Hamilton LLP. He is Chair Emeritus of both the American University of Rome and the National Italian American Foundation. Del Raso is also a frequent lecturer in the United States and Italy on matters of Italy-America relations and geopolitical affairs. He contributed the article "Reflections of an American of Italian Ancestry" to *Italy @ 150: Italy and the United States Look to the Future*, published by the Embassy of Italy, Washington, DC.

William B. Ewald, Professor of Law and Philosophy at University of Pennsylvania Law School, is an internationally recognized scholar in legal philosophy and comparative law. He is the author of an often-cited article in the *University of Pennsylvania Law Review* on the philosophical foundations of comparative law, "What Was It Like to Try a Rat?" and is currently at work on a book, *The Style of American Law,* that examines the distinctive character of American law from a comparative perspective. This work has led him to write on the legal philosophy of James Wilson, the first professor of law at the University of Pennsylvania. He also works in the philosophy of mathematics and is the editor of a standard sourcebook in the philosophy of mathematics, *From Kant to Hilbert* (Oxford, 1996). He received an award from the John Templeton Foundation to pursue research in the foundations of mathematics.

Jean M. Farnsworth is an independent stained-glass historian. She was an editor of and contributor to the critically acclaimed book *Stained Glass in Catholic Philadelphia* (Saint Joseph's University Press, 2002).

Pietro Frassica is Professor of Italian Literature at Princeton University, and he is Associate Chair and has held the position of director of the interdisciplinary Program in Italian Studies. Author of six books and over one hundred scholarly articles, his scholarship has been in the early Renaissance, the eighteenth century, and contemporary literature (Marinetti, Primo Levi, and Pirandello). In 2010 he was awarded the title of Knight of the Order of Merit of the Italian Republic by the Italian government. In the wider Princeton community, he serves as a trustee at the Dorothea van Dyke McLane Association.

Raffaella Fabiani Giannetto is a landscape historian and critic. Her scholarly research explores both the world of contemporary landscape architecture and that of early modern gardens and landscapes. She is the author of *Medici Gardens: From Making to Design* (2008), for which she received the 2010 Society of Architectural Historians' Elisabeth Blair MacDougall Book Award, and the editor of *Foreign Trends in American Gardens: A History of Exchange, Adaptation, and Reception* (2017).

Jeremy Goode is a journalism graduate of the Klein School of Communication at Temple University who specializes in sports. He currently works for the Ed Snider Youth Hockey Foundation, where he has contributed articles highlighting hockey programming offered through the foundation. He has also written for USTA Southern California, featuring communities that advocated for tennis programming in Southern California.

Judith Goode is Professor Emerita of Anthropology and Urban Studies at Temple University. She has served as Chair of the Anthropology Department and Director of the Urban Studies program. She has published six books, including *The Anthropology of the City, Reshaping Ethnic and Racial Relations in Philadelphia: Immigrants in a Divided City*, and *The New Poverty Studies: The Ethnography of Power, Politics, and Impoverished People in the United States*. These volumes and many journal articles, book chapters, and reviews in academic publications are based on forty years of grant-funded research in Philadelphia about race, immigration, class, and neighborhoods. For the public, she has been a regular contributor of op-ed pieces, radio and TV interviews, and public lectures for local, national, and international audiences. In 2000, she received the Prize for Achievement in the Critical Study of North America from the Society for the Anthropology of North America for her lifetime of work.

Alan Greenberger, Fellow of the American Institute of Architects (FAIA), is Head of the Department of Architecture, Design, and Urbanism at Drexel University. Before that, he practiced with Mitchell/Giurgola Architects and its successor, MGA Partners, for thirty-four years and then became Deputy Mayor for Planning and Economic Development in the City of Philadelphia under then-mayor Michael Nutter.

Cam Grey is Associate Professor of Roman History in the Department of Classical Studies at the University of Pennsylvania. He recently offered the keynote address at a conference cosponsored by the White House Historical Association and the Italian embassy, entitled "Italy in the White House: A Conversation on Historical Perspectives," and has also offered considerations on the reception of Rome in early modern America, published in the *Journal of the Early Republic.*

Albert Gury is an educator, writer, and artist. He is Chair of the Painting Department at the Pennsylvania Academy of the Fine Arts in Philadelphia. Deeply committed to art education, he teaches many college courses on painting, drawing, and art history, as well as teaching art education methods to undergraduate and graduate students. National and international workshops are also a regular part of his engagement in education. He is a lecturer at the Barnes Foundation in Philadelphia. Gury has written three books for Random House on art and art history. In addition, he has authored dozens of articles for museums and art publications such as the Victoria and Albert Museum, *Artists and Craftsman Magazine,* and numerous other venues. Gury is a practicing painter with regular one-person exhibitions at the F.A.N. Gallery in Philadelphia, as well as numerous galleries and museums in other states.

Scott Gabriel Knowles is Professor and Head of the Department of History, Drexel University. He is the author of *The Disaster Experts: Mastering Risk in Modern America* (2011), editor of *Imagining Philadelphia: Edmund Bacon and the Future of the City* (2009), and coeditor (with Richardson Dilworth) of *Building Drexel: The University and Its City, 1891–2016* (2016) and (with Art Molella) *World's Fairs in the Cold War: Science, Technology, and the Culture of Progress.*

David Serkin Ludwig is an award-winning composer who has collaborated with some of the top performing artists, choreographers, writers, and filmmakers of our time. He is the Gie and Lisa Liem Artistic Advisor to the President and Chair of Composition at the Curtis Institute of Music in Philadelphia.

Salvatore Mangione, MD, is Associate Professor of Medicine at the SKMC of Thomas Jefferson University in Philadelphia, where he also directs the Humanities and History of Medicine courses. He is a clinician-educator with a long interest in physical diagnosis, medical history, community service, and the role of the humanities in medicine. His innovative programs and engaging teaching style have been recognized by multiple teaching awards, and his work has been featured in the *New York Times*, the *Los Angeles Times*, the *Wall Street Journal*, the BBC, CNN, NPR, and *Forbes*. Dr. Mangione has been an invited speaker at many national and international meetings, especially in regard to using visual arts to teach bedside observation. He is the author of *Secrets in Physical Diagnosis*.

Dr. Barbara J. Mitnick is an art historian and independent curator who has focused several exhibitions and publications on American history painting. She is the chief contributor and general editor of *The Union League of Philadelphia: The First 150 Years* (2012).

Luca Molinari is Full Professor of Theory of Design at Università "Luigi Vanvitelli," Italy. He is the author of *The House That We Are* (Nottetempo, Milan, 2016) and *Continuità, a Response to Identity Crises: Ernesto Nathan Rogers and Italian Architectural Culture after 1945* (TU Delft, 2008).

Jody Pinto is a public artist, former student and professor of art at PAFA, and founder of Women Organized Against Rape, Philadelphia. Located across the United States, Japan, and Israel, her projects include bridges, waterfronts, and land and water conservation. Her drawings and prints are in museums and private collections.

Inga Saffron is the architecture critic for the *Philadelphia Inquirer*. She is the recipient of the 2014 Pulitzer Prize in Criticism. Her latest book is a collection of her columns, *Becoming Philadelphia: How an Old American City Made Itself New Again*, published by Rutgers University Press.

Chris William Sanchirico is Samuel A. Blank Professor of Law, Business and Public Policy at the University of Pennsylvania, where he has taught since 2003. He has published numerous articles on topics relating to law and economics and is regarded as a leading expert on tax policy. He is also a founding member of the Open Air Jazz Ensemble.

Dr. Fred Simeone is retired Professor of Neurosurgery at the University of Pennsylvania School of Medicine, author of 150 scientific papers, and editor of 11 books. He now serves as Director of the Simeone Automotive Foundation and Museum. Dr. Simeone is coeditor of *The Spine*, currently in its seventh edition, the longest-running continually revised textbook on the subject. He also wrote *The Stewardship of Historically Important Automobiles*, which set the standards for automotive preservation.

Jennifer A. Thompson is Gloria and Jack Drosdick Curator of European Painting and Sculpture and Curator of the John G. Johnson Collection at the Philadelphia Museum of Art. Since joining the museum's Department of European Painting in 1999, she has curated exhibitions on Pierre-Auguste Renoir, Auguste Rodin, and Vincent Van Gogh and has written on medieval manuscript illumination, the French art dealer Paul Durand-Ruel, and collecting in Philadelphia.

Paolo Valentino is a columnist and foreign policy senior correspondent for *Corriere della Sera*, the leading Italian daily. He has been bureau chief in Brussels, Moscow, Berlin, and Washington, covering the biggest events of the last thirty years: the fall of the USSR, the end of Helmut Kohl and the red-green governments in Germany, and the election of Barack Obama to the White House. He has interviewed Helmut Kohl, Gerhard Schroeder, Angela Merkel, Barack Obama, Vladimir Putin, Hassan Rohani, and Hillary Clinton, among others.

Dr. William R. Valerio serves as Patricia Van Burgh Allison Director and CEO of Woodmere Art Museum, a museum dedicated to the artists of Philadelphia. As a result of Dr. Valerio's leadership, Woodmere has become an increasingly vital presence in the cultural life of the region. He has written for *Art in America* and *Architectural Digest*, as well as for countless museum and gallery publications, including Woodmere's own exhibition catalogues, and in recent years those of the Palmer Museum of Penn State University, the La Salle University Art Museum, Hollis Taggart Gallery, and Bridgette Mayer Gallery. Dr. Valerio also produces the podcast *Diving Board*, which offers dialogues with artists about the social issues they explore. By organizing almost one hundred exhibitions and enlarging and digitizing Woodmere's collection, Dr. Valerio has elevated the visibility of Philadelphia's artists and has contributed to a shared appreciation of Philadelphia's unique art and history.

Maurizio Valsania is Professor of American History at the University of Turin, Italy. He is the author of *The Limits of Optimism: Thomas Jefferson's Dualistic Enlightenment* (UVA Press, 2011), *Nature's Man: Thomas Jefferson's Philosophical Anthropology* (UVA Press, 2013), and *Jefferson's Body: A Corporeal Biography* (UVA Press, 2017). He is currently working on a new project on George Washington.

Stephen A. Willier is Associate Professor of Music History at Temple University. He is the author of *Vincenzo Bellini: A Guide to Research* (in its second edition), and his work has also appeared in the *Journal of the American Musicological Society*, *Studi musicali*, and other journals.

Dr. Barbara A. Wolanin is Curator Emerita after serving as Curator for the Architect of the Capitol for thirty years. Part of her job was managing the conservation of murals by Constantino Brumidi and of other art in the U.S. Capitol. Her book *Constantino Brumidi: Artist of the Capitol* was published in 1998.

INDEX

Page number in italics refer to an illustration.

Abreu, Alice, 303
academia, 76, 80–85
Academy of Music, 151, *152–153*
"Acres of Diamonds" (Conwell), 296
Adagio for Strings (Barber), 165
Adams, John, 41–42
Adams, Louisa Catherine, 91–92
Adoration of the Magi (Brumidi), 65
African Americans, 59, 211, 226, 239
Age of Dante, The (Vittorini), 279
Aldrovandi, Luigi, 4
Alessandroni, Eugene, 173–174
Alessi, 131
Alfa Romeo, 308–309, 311, *312*, 352
Alice Pizzeria and Restaurant, 324
Amahl and the Night Visitors (Menotti),
    164–165
Amarotico, Joseph, 222
America-Italy Society of Philadelphia,
    130
America Mourning Her Fallen Brave
    (Haseltine), 102–103
American Academy in Rome, 258
American Conservatorio, 150
American Institute of Architects, 136
American Jewish Committee of
    Philadelphia and Southern New
    Jersey, 10
Amerita Chamber Players, 162
Amerita Orchestra, 130, 159
Angelina's, 323
L'Anima, 323
Antelo, Anthony J., 99
anti-immigrant sentiments, 21, 79, 172,
    180, 190, 195, 197, 279
Antonelli, Severo, 224
Antonelli Institute, 224
Apotheosis of Washington, The (Brumidi),
    62, 65, 68, *69*
archeology, 9, 76, 116–121, *117–118*,
    275–276, 367
architecture: Academy of Music, 151,
    152–153; American Institute of

Architects, 136; Banca D'Italia,
329–331; Bridge of Sighs
(Philadelphia), 334–335; Christopher
Columbus monument, 257, 357, *360*,
361, 383n9; Church of the Gesù
(Philadelphia) and, 56–57; classical
Roman influences and, 21, 327; in
colonial Philadelphia, 21, 28; Drexel
and Co. headquarters (former),
336–338; expansion of Philadelphia
and, 75; Romaldo Giurgola, 183,
249–256; International Style, 345;
Jacob Reed's Sons, 343–345; Jesuit
churches and, 54–55; Longwood
gardens and, 142; Mannerism, 258,
260; Order of the Sons of Italy Lodge,
346–348; Our Lady of Loreto church,
331–332, *333*; Palladio's treatise on,
28; Penn Museum and, 136–137;
Philadelphia and Italian, 31–32;
Philadelphia buildings with Italian
influence, 31–32, 270; Philadelphia
Pantheon, 341–343; public building
and, 76; Richards Medical Research
Laboratories, 345–346; Rodeph
Shalom synagogue, 338–340; Saint
Mary Magdalen de Pazzi Roman
Catholic Church, 328–329; Union
League and, 100; Robert Venturi,
183, 249, 258–262; Washington DC
and, 367. *See also* landscape design;
Palladian architecture
Ardia, Joseph M., 57, 59–60, *60*
Armstrong, Maitland, 92
art: Athenaeum of Philadelphia, 68, 87,
90; Brumidi and, 29, 62, 64–65; cast
collections and, 110–112; Centennial
Exposition of 1876 and, 169–170;
Church of the Gesù (Philadelphia)
and, 57; collection of Italian
material culture and, 76–78; Filippo
Costaggini, 29, 60, 62, 65, *66–69*, 68;
decoration with Italian American,

20; in early Republic, 22; Italian
collection of Philadelphia Museum
of Art, 122, 124–126; Mannerism,
258, 260; multicultural Philadelphia
and, 20; Neapolitan *presepio* and,
144–147; philanthropy and, 76; Pinto
family and, 182–183, 226, 234–237,
370–371; public education and, 221;
stained glass, 223, 232; Union League
of Philadelphia and, 77, 101–102;
Robert Venturi, 183; Wurts collection
and, 93–94. *See also* Pennsylvania
Academy of the Fine Arts (PAFA);
Philadelphia Museum of art
Art of Garden Design in Italy, The
    (Triggs), 140
Assumption of the Virgin (Brumidi), 65
Athenaeum of Philadelphia, 68, 87, 90
Auriemma, Sal, 197
Avalon, Frankie, 245

Badura, Bernard "Ben," 224
Baldi, Charles C. A., Jr., 208–210
Baldino, Joey, 321–322
Baltzell, Digby, 88
Balzani, Ugo, 81–84
Banca Calabrese, 331
Banca D'Italia, 329–331
Banks, Nathan, 100
Barber, Samuel, 164–165
Barnes, Albert, 226, 236
Barnes, Richard, 240
Barnes Foundation, 226, 236, 370
Barthes, Roland, 383n7
Bates, William Nickerson, 121
Battista, Gabriel, 307
Beccaria, Cesare, 28–29, 41–43
Bellevue, 37
Benjamin Franklin Parkway, 223,
    255, 342
Bentham, Jeremy, 42
Berenson, Bernard, 128
Bertoia, Harry, 227–228

Bianchi Company, 310
Black, Jeremy, 96
Blavat, Jerry, 245
Bok, Mary Louise Curtis, 163
Book of Architecture, A (Gibbs, 1728), 34
Borie, Charles Louis, 140
Boston City Hall, 251–252
Botticelli, Sandro, 129
Boyle, Richard (Lord Burlington), 34
Bozzelli, Lorenzo, 331
Brady, Bob, 363
Bridge of Sighs (Philadelphia), 334–335
Briglia-Giannini, Antonietta, 154
Brown, Mather, 44
Brumidi, Constantino, 29, 62, 64–65, 367
Bruno, Jimmy, 241
Building Little Italy (Juliani), 191, 378
Burlington, Lord (Richard Boyle), 34
Burt, Nathaniel, 88
Bush Hill, 37

Camac, William, 89
Campanari, Leandro, 159
Campanella, Roy, 247–248
Canberra Parliament House, 255–256
Canepari, Andrea: awards for, 104–105; Ciao Philadelphia and, 7–9, 349, 357, 360–364, 367, 370–371, 373–378; on Columbus Day, 360–361, 363; on diplomacy, 2–4; on Philadelphia, 364, 367; role as Consul General, 362; on this volume, 367, 370, 377; University of Pennsylvania and, 104; USA250 and, 105, 376
Caproni, Gianni, 299
Caproni/Giust Gallery, 112
Carabinieri Orchestra, 306
Carnell, Laura, 297
Carpenter-Dickinson house, 36
Carpenters' Hall, 36, 37
Carroll, Grisdale and Van Alen, 347
Carter, Joan, 105
Cassils, 114
Castellani, Alessandro, 170
Castiglioni, Luigi, 47
Cathedral Basilica of Saints Peter and Paul, 62, 63–64
Catholic Church: Americanization policies and, 196; food and, 203;

formation of American, 53; immigrant artists and, 223–224; internal tensions in, 193, 196–197; in South Philadelphia, 193; standardization of American devotional practice and, 55. *See also individual churches*; religion
Catto, Octavius, 361
Centennial Exposition of 1876, 79, 167–171
Ceracchi, Giuseppe, 46
Cerisano, Francesco, 364
Chalkley Hall, 37
chamber music, 162
Charles III of Bourbon, King of Naples, 145
Checchia, Anthony, 162, 166
Chestnut Hill, 75
Chestnut Street Theatre (formerly New Theatre), 149
Chianese, C. Thomas, 278
Christ Disputing with the Doctors in the Temple (Salviati), 127
Christopher Columbus monument, 257, 357, 360, 361, 383n9
Church of St. John the Evangelist, 51
Church of St. Mary Magdalen de Pazzi, 57–58
Church of St. Peter Claver, 59
Church of the Gesù (Philadelphia), 56–57, 60
Church of the Gesù (Rome), 55
Church of the Madonna Della Salute, Venice (Rico y Ortega), 102
Ciambella, Anthony, 225–226
Ciao Philadelphia: advisory board and supporters, 14n3, 16n28, 371, 373–375; Canepari and, 7–9, 349, 357, 360–364, 367, 370–371, 373–378; *Corriere della Sera* and, 270, 350–351, 352, 363, 364; extension of to consular area, 8, 363, 379; highlighting of Italian Americans and, 7–9; Jewish community and, 10–11, 382; media coverage of, 8–9, 270, 350–351, 352, 363, 364, 377; slogan for, 378; Union League of Philadelphia and, 7, 9, 365
Cicala, Joe, 322
Cicaterri, Charles, 56–58
Ciongoli, A. Kenneth, 307
Circolo Italiano (Temple), 297–298
Circolo Italiano (UPenn), 277–280, 297

Cities and Cemeteries of Etruria in 1848 (Dennis), 275
City Beautiful movement, 77, 223, 254
civil rights, 181
Civil War (American), 50, 99–100, 167
Claghorn, James, L., 101
Claiborne, Craig, 317
Classic Car Trust, 314
Clifford, Henry, 130
Cliveden house, 37, 38
College of Physicians, 90
Colombo, Joe, 131
Columbus Day, 4, 173–174, 357, 360–361, 363
"Columbus Day" (Mires), 360–361
Complexity and Contradiction in Architecture (Venturi), 260–261
concrete, 340–341
Congregation Mikveh Israel, 11
Conn, Steven, 360
Constitutional Convention, 42–43
Consul, The (Menotti), 164–165
Contucci, Corrado Orlandi, 4, 6
Conwell, Russell, 296
Cope, Walter, 136
Corriere della Sera, 270, 350–351, 363, 364
Corson, Leon William, 124
Cosenza, Arthur, 154
Costaggini, Filippo, 29, 60, 62, 65, 66–69, 68
Costaggini, Louis, 68
Costanza, Frank, 159–160
Costello, Stephen, 155–156
Cozza, Lorenzo, 275–276
crèhe scenes, 78, 144–147
criminal organizations, 195
Croly, Herbert, 135
Crucifixion (Brumidi), 64
Crybaby Pasta, 324
Curtis, Karen, 190
Curtis Institute of Music, 79, 155, 163–166, 165–166

Dal Verme, Francesco, 47
Dante, 279
Da Ponte, Lorenzo, 149–150, 272–273
Da Ponte, Lorenzo L., 273–274
Darren, James, 245
D'Ascenzo, Nicola, 223, 232, 340
D'Ascenzo Studio, 223, 232
David (Michelangelo), cast of, 110–114

Da Vinci Art Alliance, 182, 224, 303
Day, Frank Miles, 136–137
Day, Larry (Lorenzo del Giorno), 225
Day and Klauder, 336
Day before Yesterday, The (Armstrong), 92
DeBenedictis, Nicholas, 218–219, 364, 371, 384n13
Declaration of Love (Ricci), 102
De Costa, Arthur, 225
DeFrancesco, Joey, 241–242
De Furia, Guy Gretano, 278
Dei delitti e delle pene (Beccaria), 42
deindustrialization, 21, 23, 181, 267
DeLancey, William Heathcote, 271, 273–274
Dellaripa, Filomena, 227
Della Valle, S. Andrea, 65
Del Raso, Joseph V., 307, 363
De Martino, Giacomo, 174
Demotis, Gianluca, 302
Department of Parks and Recreation, 215
De Pasquale, Francis, 159
De Pasquale, Gloria, 160
De Pasquale, Joseph, 159–160
De Pasquale, Robert, 159–160
De Pasquale, William, 159–160
Desiderio, Vincent, 226
De Vico, Francesco, 54
Diaz, Armando, 4
DiBerardinis, Michael, 215–216, 353, 363
Di Bruno Bros., 201, 323
Di Collobiano, Augusto Avogadro, 2
Di Genova, Gennara, 331
Di Giuseppe, Enrico, 154–155
DiLella, Daniel L., 106, *107*, 108
Dilworth Paxson LLP, 214
DiMaggio, Joe, 294–295
Di Maria, Francis Xavier, 57, 59
DiSandro, Anthony, 307
Di Stefani family, 322
DiVito, Mariano, 280–281, 377
Donato, Giuseppe, 221, 223
Drama of Pirandello (Vittorini), 279
Dreer, Ferdinand J., 101
Drexel, Anthony, 7, 297, 336
Drexel, Francis A., 59
Drexel, Katherine, 59
Drexel and Co., 336–338, 7
Drexel University, 352, 374, *380*

Dubin, Murray, 189
Du Bois, W.E.B., 189
Du Pont, Pierre, 140–141, 143
Durang, Edward Forest, 328
Dwyer, Gertrude, 234

economics, 99, 167, 197, 211–212, 267
Education of a University President, The (Wachman), 298
Edwards, Parke Emerson, 124
Elkins, William L., 127
Elkins Park, 75
Enlightenment, 20, 22, 27–28, 34, 41
Equestrian Portrait of George Washington (Sully), 101
Esherick House (Kahn), 260
Esposit, Louis, 202
Esposito, Louis, 303
Esposito, Mariella, 202
Esposito's Meats, 199, 202
Etruscan League, 274
Evans, Elizabeth Ann, 144
Evans, Marcia, 144
Exaltation of St. Joseph into Heaven (Costaggini), 60
Eyre, Wilson, 136–140

Fables (Persichetti), 162
Fachechi, Grazia Maria, 94
Fante's Kitchen Shop, 202
Farrand, Beatrix, 137
fascism, 4, 172, 279–280
Ferrari, 309, 310, *313*, 352
FHA mortgage loans, 21, 181
Fidelity Bank, 217–218
Filangieri, Gaetano, 41
finance sector, 267
Finelli, Nunzio (Annunziato), 100–101
Fingerspan (Jody Pinto), 226, *235*
Finotti, Fabio, 352
Fiore, 324
First Reading of the Declaration of Independence (Rothermel), 101
Fish, Hamilton, 168
Fitler, Josephine, 276
Florence synagogue, 338–339
Foglietta, Thomas M., 212–213, 215
Folchi, Peter M., 57–58
folk art, 20
food: collective cooking, 204–205; as cultural marker, 315–316; food cosmopolitanism and, 317; food

traditions, 202–205; fusion cuisine and, 325; gentrification and, 315, 319–320; globalization and, 315–316; marriage and, 204–205; meal planning, 203–204; Ninth Street curbside Market and, 197–202; parish celebrations and, 203; Philadelphia as global city and, 315, 317; shopping and, 203; Union League and culinary history and, 100. *See also* Italian food
Forni, Giacomo Fara, 3
Forte, Fabian, 245
Foulc, Edmond, 126
founding fathers, 41–43. *See also individual names*
1492 Society, 357
Fra Angelico, 129
Francis of Assisi, 144
Frank Leslie's Historical Register, 169–170
Franklin, Benjamin, 41–42, 88, 149, 268
Franklin Institute Science Museum, 341–343
Fraser, James Earle, 342
Fraser, John, 100, 103
Free Interpretation of Plant Forms (Knoll), 228–229
Free Library of Philadelphia, 215
Free Museum of Science and Art, 136–137
Frieze of American History (Brumidi and Costaggini), 62, *69*
Froissart, Jean, 82
Fromboluti, Sideo, 229
From Paesani to White Ethnics (Luconi), 194
Frothingham, Arthur L., 117–118, 275–276
Fry, William Henry, 151
Furness, Frank, 339

Galli, Goffredo, 104
García, Manuel, 150
Garden and Forest (Farrand), 137
Garibaldi, Angelo, 28, 50–51
Garibaldi, Giuseppe, 28, 50, 173
Gasparro, Frank, 221–222
gastronomy. *See* food; Italian food
Genoa, Republic of, 1, 28
gentrification, 190, 268, 315, 319–320
Georgetown University, 53

Giannini, Dusolina, 154
Giannini, Ferruccio, 154, 161
Giannini, Francesco, 161
Giannini, Vittorio, 154, 161
Giannini-Gregory, Eufemia, 154,
    157, 161
GI Bill, 21, 181
Gigliotti, Anthony, 160
Gigliotti, Mark, 160
Giordano, Antonio, 303, 307, 352,
    375, 376
Giordano, Frank, 106–108, 307, 364
Giordano, Nicholas, 306
Giurgola, Romaldo, 183, 249–256
Giust Gallery (formerly Caproni), 112
Glencairn Museum, 144–147
globalization, 23, 181, 267
Gonnella, Giuseppe (Joseph), 269,
    288–295, 375
Goode, Judith, 190; on community food
    systems, 203–205
Goode, W. Wilson, 211
Gracie, Charlie, 246
Grandi, Dino, 4, 5
GrandPré, Mary, 287
grand tours, 20, 22, 32, 75–77, 81,
    87–96
Grassi, John (Giovanni Antonio), 53–54
Great Depression, 21, 22, 180, 198,
    331, 338
Great Migration, 180, 189
Greco, Rosemarie, 217–218
Green, Rose Basile, 306
Griffin, Walter Burley, 254
Grisi, Giulia, 150
Group 55, 229–230
Gualdo, Giovanni, 149
Guarrera, Frank, 155
Guastavino, Rafael, 343
Guida Moseley Brown, 256
Gyllenhaal, Ed, 146–147

Hagia Sophia, 338–339
Hamann, Martin, 100
Hamilton, Alexander, 44–45
Hancock, Walker, 221
Havana Opera Troupe, 150
Haviland, John, 253
health care sector, 21–23, 267. See also
    medicine
Hemings, James, 47
Henrietta Tower Wurts Foundation, 94

higher education, 181, 267, 268, 352. See
    also individual institutions
History of Italian Immigration Museum,
    382
Hofmann, Josef, 163
Hohns, Andrew, 376–377
Holy Cross University, 53
Horticultural Society, 89
housing, 184–188
housing policy, 181, 187–188,
    200–201, 213

Ignatius of Loyola, 52
Il Duce (Antonelli), 224, 225
immigration: after World War II, 5; anti-
    immigrant nativism and, 21, 79; art
    and, 125, 222–231; Consulate General
    of Italy and, 3–4; craftsmen and,
    222–223; due to the Risorgimento,
    99; fascism and, 4; geography
    of different waves of, 179–180;
    largest waves of, 20, 22, 185–187;
    from Liguria, 191; opera and,
    149; Palumbo's and, 210; popular
    associations of, 19; post-World
    War II, 267; regionalism and, 195;
    Sesquicentennial Exposition of 1926
    and, 172
Independence Hall, 2, 9, 36, 43, 212
Independence National Historical Park,
    378
industry: Centennial Exposition
    of 1876 and, 169–170;
    deindustrialization and, 21, 23, 181,
    267; globalization and, 23, 181, 267
International Holocaust Remembrance
    Day, 11
International Opera Theater, 381
Isgro Pasticceria, 199–200, 322–323
Isoleri, Antonio, 193
Italia Oggi, 364
Italian Consulate General: dual degree
    medical program, 10; fascism and,
    4; Galli and, 104; immigration
    and, 3; influence on Philadelphia
    communities and, 3, 5; interaction
    with Italy and, 12; international
    politics and, 4; issue of assimilation
    and, 3–4; Italian courses for
    Philadelphia students and, 10; list of
    consuls, 12–13; mission of, 11–12,
    14n19; office of, 6; preservation of

Italian heritage and, 6–7; threats to
    close, 349, 352; Union League of
    Philadelphia and, 104; World War II
    and, 4, 6
Italian Consul in the United States,
    first, 1
Italian food: contemporary food scene
    in Philadelphia and, 320–324; era
    of mass production and, 316–317; as
    ethnic food, 316; hoagies, 318–319; as
    part of Philadelphia brand, 317–319;
    Philly cheesesteak, 317–318; positive
    associations with, 317; Queen Village
    food scene and, 324–325; Marc Vetri,
    320–322
Italian Legacy in Washington, D.C.,
    The, 105
Italian Market, 171, 197–200
Italian Opera Company, 150
"Italians and Italy" (Luconi), 357
Italy: assassination of Umberto I,
    84; conquest of Libya (1912), 4;
    diplomatic ties to United States, 1–2;
    grand tour circuit and, 20, 22, 32,
    75–76, 75–77, 77, 81, 87–96; Henry
    Charles Lea and, 80–85; immigration
    under fascism and, 4; Mussolini
    and, 279–280; presepio tradition
    and, 144; racing cars and, 309–314;
    Risorgimento and, 99; unification
    of, 1, 3, 13n1, 272; United States
    Centennial Exposition and, 168–171;
    United States Sesquicentennial
    Exposition and, 171–172, 360; Robert
    Venturi and, 258–262

Jacob Reed's Sons, 343–345
Jacovini, Joseph, 8, 214–215, 371, 373
jazz, 183, 239–242
J. Chiurazzi & Fils (Naples), 117–120
Jefferson, Thomas: Beccaria's influence
    and, 43; Enlightenment ideas and,
    28; friendship with Mazzei and, 41;
    friendship with Mussi and, 28–29,
    45–48; Hamilton and, 44–45; interest
    in Italy of, 29, 46–47; knowledge of
    Italian and, 41, 47; Mather Brown's
    portrait of, 44, 45; Palladian
    architecture and, 34, 47; Roman
    Pantheon and, 341; time in Monticello
    and, 48
Jefferson Medical College, 289

Jesuit Order: adaptability of, 52, 60; African Americans and, 59; American West and, 61; Church of St. Mary Magdalen de Pazzi, 57–58; Church of St. Peter Claver, 59; founding fathers and, 29; founding of Jesuit colleges, 53–54; Grassi and, 53; institutions of learning and, 29; Italian Catholic community and, 28; Italian influence of American, 54–55; Literary Society, 57–58; Maryland Province and, 53–54; Native Americans and, 61; Philomelian Society, 58; presepio tradition and, 145; *Ratio Studiorum*, 55; relations with Vatican and, 29; Saint Joseph's University and, 53, 56–60; St. Joseph's Church and, 52–53; standardizing of Catholic devotional life and, 55

Jewish Exponent, 11

Johnson, John G., 127–128

Judy's, 324

Juliani, Richard N., 3–4, 6, 12, 185, 191, 193, 378

Justinian Society, 29

Kahn, Louis, 249, 259–260, 345, 346

Keller, Joseph, 55

Kendrick, Freeland, 174

Kenrick, Francis, 55

Kimball, Fiske, 125–126

Kimmel Center for the Performing Arts, 151

King of Jazz, The, 240

Klasko, Steve, 10

Knoll, Florence, 228–229

Kuhn, Charles, 91–92

Kuhn, Hartman, 92, 93

Kuhn, Peter, 90–91

Kuhn family, 90–92

Ku Klux Klan, 172

LaBan, Craig, 323–325

Land Buoy (Pinto), 370

landscape design: Borie garden, 140; expansion of Philadelphia and, 75; Fairacres, 139–140; gardens and, 21, 78; Italian influences on, 135–139, 141, 143; Longwood gardens and, 136, 140, *141*; Penn Museum and, 136–138, *142*; Villa Gamberaia, 140

Lang, Eddie (Salvatore Massaro), 238, 239–241

Lanza, Joseph, 160

Lanza, Louis, 160

Lanza, Mario, 156–157, 211

Large Space Dream (Amarotico), 222

Latrobe, Benjamin, 39

Laundry Project, Panni Stesi, The (Brancaccio), 365

Laurel Hill, 39

La Viola (East and West), 323

Lea, Henry Charles, 77, 80–85

Lea, Isaac, 126–127

Lea, Matthew Carey, 127

LeBrun, Napoleon, 62, 151

Lecca, Giulio M., 104

Lecky, Arthur, 82

LeClair, Charles, 299

legislation: anti-immigrant sentiment and, 180, 279; Baldi and, 210; Beccaria on law and, 41–42; Jim Crow laws, 180; Anna Verna and, 213

Levenstein, Harvey, 202

Liacouras, Peter, 298

Liberty Bell Pavilion, 253–254

Library Company of Philadelphia, 90

Lincoln, Abraham, 50, 99

Lloyd, Mark Frazier, 277

Locke, Octavia Capuzzi, 227

Longwood Gardens, 136, 140, *141*, 142, *142*

Loyola University, 53

Lucedia (Vittorio Giannini), 161

Luconi, Stefano, 185, 194–196, 203, 357

Lynch, David, 114

Maclay, William, 44

MacLeod, Cynthia, 378

Madison, James, 41–42, 48, 150

Maggio's, 199, 201

Main Line area, 75

Majoni, Giulio Cesare, 4, 104

Malibran, Maria, 150

Mancinelli-Scotti, Francesco, 275–276

Maneval, Philip, 162

Mannerism, 258, 260

Marconi, Guglielmo, 371

Marcus, Millicent, 281

Maretzek, Max, 151

Marino, Ignazio, 303, 382

Mario (opera singer), 150

Marra's, 199

Marsh, George Perkins, 93

Martino, Al, 244–245

Martino, Antonio, 226

Martino, Babette, 227

Martino, Eva, 227

Martino, Giovanni, 226

Martino, Nina, 227

Martino, Pat, 240–241

Martino Commercial Art Studios, 226–227

Maserati 300 S, 311, *312*

Masi, Ernesto, 84

Massaro, Salvatore (Eddie Lang), 238, 239–241

Matisse, Henri, 236

Matza, Michael, 377–378

Mazzanti, Signora (opera singer), 149

Mazzei, Philip, 41, 46

McHarg, Ian, 249

McIlhenny, Henry, 130

McIlhenny, John, 127

McKevitt, Gerald, 54

medicine, 9–10, 269, 288–295

Medium, The (Menotti), 164

Melograno, 302, 323

Menotti, Gian Carlo, 162, 164–165

Meucci, Antonio, 50, 51n1

M/G Associates, 250–254

Miceli, Tony, 242

middle class, 21

Mille Miglia, 311

Mills, Robert, 39

Milson, Toby, 42

Mires, Charlene, 360–361

Mitchell, Ehrman, 250

Mitchell-Furness Coterie, 274

Mitchell/Giurgola Associates, 250–254

"Modern Art" (Eyre), 136

Moffo, Anna, 157–158

Monachesi, Nicola, 68

Monroe, James, 150

Montanaro, Gregory, 106, *107*, 108

Monteverdi, Antonio, 364

Montresor, Giacomo, 150

Moore, Clement Clarke, 273

Moravian Pottery and Tile Works, 344

Morgan, J. Pierpont, 129, 336

Morris, John T., 127

Mt. Pleasant, 35, 36

Museo Nazionale delle Arti del XXI
	Secolo (MAXXI), 132
Museo Nazionale Romano (Rome),
	139
Museum of Archaeology and
	Anthropology. *See* Penn Museum
music: chamber music, 162; composers
	and, 161–162; Curtis Institute of
	Music, 79, 155, 163–166; instruments
	and, 160; jazz, 183, 239–242; opera,
	28, 79, 149–151, 154–158; orchestral,
	149–151, 154–156; Philadelphia
	Orchestra, 79, 91, 151, 158–161;
	Quakers and, 149; "South Philly
	Musicians Remix" mural, 244–246
Mussi, Joseph (Giuseppe), 28, 45–48
Mussolini, Benito, 93–94, 224,
	279–280
Muti, Riccardo, 161, 165
mutual aid associations, 191–192

Naples Archaeological Museum, 116
Napoleon, 90–91
National Italian American Foundation
	(NIAF), 306–307
National Museum of American Jewish
	History, 10
Native Americans, Jesuit Order and, 61
nativism, 21, 79, 172, 180, 190, 195,
	197, 279
*Nativity, The (Adoration of the
	Shepherds)*, 67
Neapolitan *Presepio*, 144–147
Neumann, John, 169, 328
Newall, Mike, 364
New Jersey, 197–198, 201, 203, 207
New Theatre (later Chestnut Street
	Theatre), 149
Norris, Charles, 35–36
Nulty, Eugenius, 81
Nutter, Michael, 9, 349, 352

Olin, Laurie, 139
Olin Partnership, 139
O'Malley, John, 61
opera: Academy of Music, 151, *152–153*;
	Da Pontes and, 28; Italian influence
	on, 79, 149–151, 154–158; Muti's
	Philadelphia Orchestra and, 161;
	Opera Company of Philadelphia, 158;
	Opera Philadelphia, 165; Philadelphia
	Opera House, 151

Opera Company of Philadelphia, 158
Opera Philadelphia, 165
orchestral music: Amerita Orchestra,
	130, 159; composers and, 161–162;
	De Pasquale family and, 159–160;
	instruments and, 160; opera and,
	149–151, 154–156; Philadelphia
	All City Orchestra, 8; Philadelphia
	Orchestra, 79, 91, 130, 151, 158–161;
	Sisters of Mercy Symphony Orchestra,
	159
Order of the Sons of Italy, 4, 5, 195, 368
Order of the Sons of Italy Lodge,
	346–348
Ormandy, Eugene, 159, 161
Our Lady of Loreto church, 331–332,
	333
Our Mother of Consolation (Costaggini),
	68

padrone system, 3, 191
Page, George Nelson, 93
Palazzo Strozzi (Florence), 337
Palladian architecture: American
	exposure to through Britain,
	32–33; British enthusiasm for,
	33–34; classical pediments and,
	39; Enlightenment ideas and, 34;
	examples of, *32–33*, 34, *35–39*;
	fall from favor of, 39; locations in
	Philadelphia for, 34–37; materials and,
	34; period of American fascination
	with, 31–33; in Philadelphia, 352;
	Quattro Libri dell'Architettura
	(Palladio, 1570), 33; triple window
	and, 39; Villa Rotunda and, 37
Palladio, Andrea, 28, 32
Palma, John, 149
Palumbo, Frank, 192–193, 210–211
Palumbo's, 210
Pantheon (Rome), 341–342
Paoli, Pasquale, 41
Paone, Peter, 224–225
Papale, Alex, 224
Papale, Vince, 248
Pappas, Thomas, 105
Paradox of Plenty, The (Levenstein), 202
Paresce, Angelo, 54
Pascuccio, Michael, 160
pasta, 316, 321
Patti, Adelina, 150
Paul, Comegys, 89–90

Paul, James "the Marquis," 90
Paul, John Marshall, 89
Paul, John Rodman, 89–90
Pavarotti, Luciano, 158
Pellegrino, Edmund, 293
Penn, John, 35
Penn Museum: Ciao Philadelphia and, 9,
	367; Estruscan tombs and, 274–276;
	landscape design and, 136–138, *142*;
	Wanamaker Bronzes and, 78, 116–121
Penn Mutual Insurance Company on
	Independence Square, 253–254
Pennoni, C. R. "Chuck," 216–217
Pennsylvania Academy of the Fine Arts
	(PAFA): architecture of, *115*; Camac
	and, 89; cast collection of, 110–114;
	Cast Hall of, 110, *110–112*; Ciao
	Philadelphia and, 9, 367; *David* and,
	78, 112–114; educational curricula of,
	110; Italian American artists and, 182
*Pennsylvania Railroad World War II
	Memorial* (Hancock), 221
Pennsylvania State House, 2, 36
Pepper, John Worrell, 139
Pepper, William, 116, 274–276
Percy, Ann, 131
*Perennial Philadelphians: The Anatomy of
	an American Aristocracy* (Burt), 88
Persichetti, Vincent, 161–162
Pesce, Gaetano, 131
Peters, Edward, 80
Peters, Richard, 34–35
Petit, Adrien, 46–47
Petrillo, Frank L., 331–332
Philadelphia: annexation of Philadelphia
	County and, 75; branding of to
	attract creative workers and tourists,
	268, 315; British trade circuit and,
	27; Broad and Market area, 77;
	buildings with Italian influence in,
	270; centennial celebration and, 76; as
	colonial city, 21–22, 27; contemporary
	food scene in, 320–324; food
	renaissance in, 319–320; Francis
	Kenrick and, 55; globalization and, 23,
	267; Italian architectural styles and,
	28, 31–32, 40; Italian journey through
	in *Corriere della Sera*, 350–351; Italian
	Market, 171; Jewish community in, 10,
	338–339; medical history and, 288;
	move of Capitol to Washington DC
	and, 75; period of mass immigration

and, 21–22, 191–192; population loss and, 267; public-private partnerships and, 268; Quaker roots of, 87–88, 149; Queen Village food scene and, 324–325; Rocky Balboa and, 354–355; socioeconomic equality in colonial times, 27; yellow fever and, 46. *See also* South Philadelphia

Philadelphia All City Orchestra, *8*

Philadelphia Business Journal, 9, 376

Philadelphia Chamber Music Society, 162

Philadelphia Conservatory of Music, 160, 161

Philadelphia Gas Works (PGW), 213

Philadelphia Horticultural Society, 203

Philadelphia Inquirer, 8, 10, 11, 208, 364–365

Philadelphia Magazine, 324

Philadelphia Museum College of Art, 225

Philadelphia Museum of Art: Ciao Philadelphia and, 9, 352, 367; donations from Philadelphians touring Italy, 126–128; early Italian donations, 124; exhibition of immigrant artists, 125; founding of, 122, 124; genesis of in Centennial Exhibition, 78, 122; grand tours and, 78; Italian alcove of, 124–125; Italian American artists and, 182; Johnson Collection and, 127–130; Kimball's Italian acquisitions, 125–126; loan exhibitions devoted to Italian art, 130–131; modern exhibitions, 131–133; Palazzo Soranzo, 125–126; pictured, *123*; Rocky sculpture and, 349, 363; *Splendor of Eighteenth-Century Rome* exhibition, 131–132; travel scholarships to Italy and, 124

Philadelphia Naval Shipyard, 213

Philadelphia Negro, The (Du Bois), 189

Philadelphia Opera House, 151, *368*

Philadelphia Orchestra, 79, 91, 130, 151, 158–161

Philadelphia Pantheon, 341–343

Philadelphia Police Department, 211, 213

Philadelphia University of the Arts, 160

Philadelphia Zoo, 89, 210

Phillips, John S., 127

Philly POPS, 107, 369

Philosophical Society of Philadelphia, 47

Piccirillo, Carlo, 57

Piedmont-Sardinia, Kingdom of, 1–2, 28

Pier 53, 352, 370

Pinto, Angelo, 226, 234, *235*, 236–237, 370

Pinto, Biagio, 226, 234, 236–237

Pinto, Jody, 226, 352, 370–371

Pinto, Josephine, 234, 237

Pinto, Luigi, 234, 237

Pinto, Salvatore, 226, 234, 236–237

PI-Philly, 371, *372*

Pirandello, Luigi, 279, 286–287

Pistoletto, Michelangelo, 132, *133*

Pitcairn, Kathleen Glenn, 147

pizza, 316, 321

Platt, Charles A., 135, 137

Poccardi, Gaetano Emilio, 4, 104

Pohlig, Karl, 159

political philosophy, 19, 27–28, 76

Polk, James K., 54

Portrait of Archbishop Filippo Archinto (Titian), 128, *129*

Port Royal, 37, *39*

poverty, 181

presepi, 78, 144–147

Price, William L., 344

Priests, Parishes and People (Juliani), 193

Primavera, Joseph, 159

Progressive Architecture, 249

prominenti, 182, 191, 194, 208. *See also individual people*

Pron, John, 303

Quattro Libri dell'Architettura (Palladio, 1570), 33

Queen Village, 322, 324–325

race, 180–181, 187–188

railroads, 75

Ralph's Restaurant, 199

Ravara, Joseph (Giuseppe), 1, 28

religion: Americanization policies and, 196; in early Republic, 22; food and, 203; higher education's ties to, 268; Ninth Street Curbside Market and, 197–198; Quaker, 87–88, 149; religious music and, 149; religious tolerance and, 52; South Philadelphia and, 191

Renaissance, 20, 22, 110–111

Rendell, Ed, 212, 218, *219*, 375

Renzi, Matteo, 352

Repplier, Agnes, 53

Res Ipsa, 324

Restaurant School in West Philadelphia, 322

Riboni, Giacinto, 222

Richards Medical Research Laboratories, 345–346

Rinaldi, Lynn, 322

Rinaldi, Philip, 307

Rishel, Joseph J., 131

Risorgimento, 3, 54

Rizzo, Frank (Francis), 211–212

Rocky, 270, 354–355, 363

Rocky Balboa sculpture, 270, 349, 354–355, 363

Rocky (re)Runs exhibit (Da Vinci Art Alliance), 303

Rodeph Shalom synagogue, 338–340

Rogers, James Grafton, 4

Roma Interrotta, 261

Roman College (Rome), 55

Rondinella, Pasquale, 58

Roosevelt, Eleanor, 120

Roosevelt, Theodore, 120

Rosati, Tony, 226

Rota, Giovanni "Nino," 164–165

Rovaris, Corrado, 165

Rowan, Jan, 249–250

Rowan University, 374, *380*

Runge, Gustavus, 151

Ruskin, John, 335

Rydell, Bobby, 246

Ryder, James, 54

Sabatini, Raphael, 227

Sabbione, Luigi Provana del, 4

Saint Joseph's University, 53, 56–60, *379*

Saint Mary Magdalen de Pazzi Roman Catholic Church, 328–329

Saint Rita in Ecstasy (Visco), 224

Samuel S. Fleisher Art Memorial, 144, 182, 234

Salvatori, Henry, 277–278, 280

Samuel Powel house, 36–37

San Gimignano, 345–346

Santore, Charles, 230–231

Sarcone's Bakery, 199, 201–202

Sardinia, Kingdom of, 1, 50

Sbarro, Mario, 303

Scalero, Rosario, 164–165

Scannicchio's, 323

Scarnati, Joseph, 7
Scheel, Fritz, 159
Schiaparelli, Elsa, 131
schools, 196–197, 201
Schuman, William, 161–162
Schweizer, Jacob Otto, 103
sculpture: of Benjamin Franklin
    in Franklin Hall, 342; Cast Hall
    at PAFA, 110–114; Centennial
    Exposition of 1876 and, 170;
    Philadelphia Museum of Art and, 126;
    of Rocky Balboa, 270, 349, 354–355,
    363
segregation, 181
Serkin, Rudolf, 166
Sesquicentennial Exposition of 1926, 79,
    171–174, 360
Sestini, Benedict, 57
Sidney Kimmel Medical College, dual
    degree program, 9–10
Silverman, Ellie, 202
Simeone, Fred, 308, 352, 375
Simeone Foundation Automotive
    Museum, 270, 308–314, 352
Simon and Simon, 339
Sinnock, John Ray, 124
Sisters of Mercy Symphony Orchestra,
    159
slavery, 27, 50
social clubs, 192
Societa di Unione e Fratellanza, 169
Society of Jesus. *See* Jesuit Order
Solaro, Clemente, della Margherita,
    2–3
Somerset Knitting Mills Company, 212
Sommaruga, Giuseppe, 120
Sorgato, Antonio, 128
South Philadelphia: Americanization
    policies and, 196–197; anti-immigrant
    sentiment and, 190, 197; area of,
    185; bankers' row of, 329, 331; banks
    and, 191; before mass migration,
    191; building patterns of, 184–188;
    Catholic church in, 193, 196–197; as
    center of Italian immigration, 179,
    181; cultural markers and, 205–206;
    education and, 197; ethnicity and,
    187–188; food traditions and,
    202–205; gentrification and, 190;
    immigration into, 185–187; interwar
    period, 196–197; Italian priests and,
    191; maps of, *185, 188*; mass migration
    period and, 191–192; mutual aid

associations and, 191–192; Ninth
    Street Curbside Market, 197–202; in
    post-Civil War era, 189; in post-war
    period, 200–202; press and, 191, 194;
    press in, 191, 194; public institutions
    and, 182; regionalism and, 196;
    Rocky Balboa and, 354–356; social
    clubs, 192; social institutions in,
    192–195, 201
South Philadelphia (Dubin), 189, 197
Speno, Frank, 278
sports, 247–248
Squilla, Mark, 9, 363
Squitti, Nicola, 3
St. Augustine Catholic Church
    (Philadelphia), *66–68*
St. Augustine in Glory (Costaggini),
    68
Stearns and Castor, 334–335
Stedman, Charles, 36–37
Stevenson, Sara Yorke, 116, 120–121,
    274–276
Stewardson, John, 136
St. Joseph Patron of the Augustinians
    (Costaggini), 68
St. Joseph's Church (Jesuit), 52–53
St. Louis World's Fair, 116, 119–120
St. Mary Magdalen de Pazzi, 169, 193
Stokowski, Leopold, 159, 163
Stones of Venice, The (Ruskin), 335
Stotesbury, Edward T., 336
Strada Novissima project, 262
Strand, Paul, 352
Stratton, Howard Fremont, 124
Strickland, William, 39
Studio Incamminati, 372
Study for Sans Fin (Donato), *223*

Targa Florio, 312
Tecce, Frederick D., 306
Temple University: Circolo Italiano of,
    297–298; Conwell and, 296–297;
    Louis Esposito and, 202; founding
    of, 296; role in Italian American
    upward mobility of, 269; Roman
    campus and (TUR), 269, 298–304;
    Sbarro Institute for Cancer Research
    and Molecular Medicine, 352; state
    affiliation and, 298; Tyler School of
    Art, 225; as university for immigrants,
    297; Vittorini and, 297–298
Temple University (Hilty), 296
Termini Bros. Bakery, 199–200, 202

Theophano, Janet, 190
Thomas Jefferson Methodist Hospital,
    376
Thomas Jefferson University, 9–11
Thomas Mifflin house, 39
Threads of Life, The (*Old Italian Tales for
    Children*, Vittorini), 287
Toscanini, Arturo, 155, 159, 165
tourism, 268, 384n13
Tower, Henrietta, 93–94, *95*, 127
Trajetta, Philip, 150
Tran, Rosemarie, 302
Translation of St. Augustine to Heaven
    (Costaggini), *68*
Trattoria Carina, 324
Travaline, Frank, 278–279
Trumbauer, Horace, 103, 129
Turin Internationale Esposizione
    (1884), 128
TV Guide, 230–231
*Twentieth-Century Harmony: Creative
    Aspects and Practice* (Persichetti),
    162
Tyler School of Arts, 298–299

Union League of Philadelphia, The:
    architecture and, 102; art and, 77,
    101–102; Broad Street League House,
    103; Carmac and, 89; Ciao Philadelphia
    and, 7, 9, *365*; Fifteenth Street League
    House, *102*, 103; founding of, 99;
    Italian immigrants and, 99–101,
    105–106; League House fire (1866),
    100; Lincoln and, 99, 102–103; Lincoln
    Memorial Room, 103; National Italian
    American Foundation (NIAF) and,
    306; pictured, *98*; women and, 105
unions, 181, 212
United States: Centennial Exposition
    of 1876, 79, 167–171; Civil War of,
    50, 99–100, 167; consuls of, 90–91;
    Giuseppe Garibaldi's connection
    with, 50; Italian architecture and,
    28, 31–32, 40, 270; Jesuits and,
    55, 61; Jewish communities in,
    338–339; landscape design and,
    135–136; religious tolerance and, 52;
    Semiquincentennial Commission,
    106; Sesquicentennial Exposition of
    1926, 79, 171–174, 360
United Way Building, 252–253
Università Cattolica del Sacro Cuore
    (UCSC), 9–10

University of Pennsylvania: in 1830, 271–272; Andrea Canepari and, 104; Center for Italian Studies, 352; Circolo Italiano of, 276–280; classical Italian culture and, 268–269; Da Pontes and, 28, 269, 272–274; Dean Holmes Perkins of the School of Fine Arts, 249; Mariano DiVito and, 280–281; globalization and, 268; international population of, 269; Italian language classes and, 273; John Rodman Paul and, 90; Kislak Center for Special Collections, 80, 82; as model for American higher education, 88; Penn Archives, 277; role in Italian American upward mobility of, 269; Wannamaker and, 297. *See also* Penn Museum

University of the Arts, 225

urban policy, 21

Vaccaro, Alex, 375

Valente, Benita, 166

Valentino, Paolo, 270, 364

Vanna House (Venturi), 260, *261*

Varbero, Richard, 190, 196–197

Varricchio, Armando, 7

Venice Biennale (2009), 132

Venturi, Robert, 183, 249, 258–262, 361

Venturi, Scott Brown and Associates, Inc., 257

Venuti, Joe (Giuseppe), 239–240

Venuti, Lawrence, 302–303

Verna, Anna, 213

Vernon house, 37

Vetri, Marc, 320–322

Victor Café, 322

Villa di Roma, 323

Villanova University, 352, *379*

Villehardouin, 82

Villiger, Burchard, 56–57, 60

Virgin and Child (da Settignano), 126, *127*

Visco, Anthony, 223–224

Vitale, Ferruccio, 142

Vitiello, Justin, 302

Vitruvius Britannicus (1715–1725), 34

Vittorini, Domenico, 278–280, 286–287

Voltaire, 42

Wachman, Marvin, 298–299

Walker, Dean, 131

Walking Sculpture (Scultura da passeggio) (Pistoletto), 132, *133*

Walnut Grove, 37, 38

Walter, Thomas Ustick, 68

Wanamaker, John, 78, 81, 116–120, 275–276, 297

Wanamaker Bronzes, 78, 116–121

Washington, George, 1, 41, 44–45

Watson and Huckel, 330

Wharton, Edith, 135, 137

Widener, P.A.B., 127–128

Wills Eye Hospital, 90

Wil-o-Wisp (Rose), 133

Wilson, James, 42

Windrim, John T., 341

Wolanin, Barbara, 367

women, 105, 190, 227

Wood, James Frederic, 58, 62

Woodmere Art Museum, 222, 231

Woodstock College (MD), 55

World War I, Consulate General and, 4

World War II, 4, 22, 180

Wright Brothers Memorial (NC), 250–251

Wurts, George Washington, 93–94, 95, 127

Wurts, Henrietta Tower, 93–94, 95, 127

Yale Perspecta, 250

yellow fever, 46

Young Woman Looking in a Mirror (Riboni), 222

Zigrosser, Carl, 130

Zodiac magazine, 262